Labour Market Economics

Theory, Evidence and Policy in Canada

Labour Market Economics

Theory, Evidence and Policy in Canada

Morley Gunderson
Professor of Economics
University of Toronto: Centre for Industrial Relations;
Faculty of Management Studies; Scarborough College

McGraw-Hill Ryerson Limited

Toronto	Montreal	New York	St. Louis	San Francisco
Auckland	Bogota	Guatemala	Hamburg	Johannesburg
Lisbon	London	Madrid	Mexico	New Delhi	Panama
Paris	San Juan	São Paulo	Singapore	Sydney	Tokyo

LABOUR MARKET ECONOMICS:
Theory, Evidence and Policy in Canada

ISBN 0-07-082989-6

2 3 4 5 6 7 8 9 0   D   9 8 7 6 5 4 3 2 1

Printed and bound in Canada

Canadian Cataloguing in Publication Data

Gunderson, Morley, 1945
  Labour market economics

Includes bibliographies and index.
ISBN 0-07-082989-6

1. Labor economics.   2. Labor supply — Canada.
I. Title.

HD5728.G85   331'.0971   C79-094562-2

Care has been taken to trace ownership of copyright
material contained in this text. The publishers will gladly
take any information that will enable them to rectify any
reference or credit in subsequent editions. For permission to
use copyrighted materials, grateful acknowledgement is
made to the copyright holders listed on pages xvi–xvii,
which are hereby made a part of this copyright page.

To my parents,
Ann and Magnus

Contents

Preface

As the subtitle indicates, the emphasis of the book is on a *balance* between economic *theory*, factual empirical *evidence*, and *policy* relevance. The intention is to integrate labour economics with the mainstream, and some of the newer developments, of economics. All too often labour courses and their textbooks have been regarded as outside the mainstream of economics. Students took courses in economic theory (often because they were required to) and some took courses in labour (often to get a relief from economic theory). The two seldom interrelated, hence reinforcing the impression that, in labour economics, theory was irrelevant and description and institutional analysis all important. This book tries to bridge the gap between economic theory and labour market analysis by indicating that the field of labour economics is fertile ground for the application of economic theory and of econometric analysis to interesting and relevant policy issues. As a result, each chapter is organized around the following questions: Why are we interested in this problem? What does economic theory imply about the issue? What is the empirical evidence; that is, what are the facts? What are the policy implications and trade-offs — specifically, what can we expect to happen from alternative policy scenarios?

As the title itself indicates, the emphasis of this book is on the *economic* aspects of the *market* for labour. For some persons, such an emphasis may appear misguided, given various peculiar characteristics of the labour market — a variety of factors with goals that often conflict; an abundance of sociological, legislative and institutional constraints; and a complex price (wage) structure with moral overtones because of the human element and because wages are often called upon both to allocate labour efficiently and to curb poverty. Because of these and other peculiarities, some have argued that the labour market is fundamentally different from other markets and that, therefore, economics is largely irrelevant — or at most can play only a minor role — in analysing labour market phenomenon.

Although there are important differences between labour markets and many other markets — and they are what makes labour economics so interesting — a basic theme of this book is that these differences are ones of degree and not of kind. Rather than making economics irrelevant to the analysis of the labour market, these characteristics make economics even more relevant in understanding some of the basic underlying forces and in analysing the impact, and the reasons for the emergence, of a variety of sociological, legislative, and institutional constraints. In essence, the complexity of the labour market makes a basic theoretical framework even more necessary in order to understand the basic underlying forces, and not miss the forest for the trees.

The book is meant to provide a consistent theoretical framework that not only can be applied to current policy issues but also to new policy issues as they change and emerge over time. Policies that are relevant today may not be relevant tomorrow, but a good theoretical foundation will always be relevant in analysing changing issues.

Although the emphasis is on Canadian examples, illustrations, and problems, they will be discussed within the context of a more general theoretical framework that is applicable to the labour problems of most developed economies. Often empirical evidence is cited pertaining to other countries, especially the United States, because this is where the bulk of empirical studies have been conducted. Empirical studies in Canada tend to be numerous in some areas and scant in others. For example, we have reasonably good evidence in such areas as labour force participation, occupational wage structures, unemployment insurance, and the wage-price-unemployment relationship, and evidence is mounting in the areas of discrimination and public sector wage determination. However, we have few empirical studies of the retirement decision, or the impact of unions, minimum wage laws, and income maintenance programs. Hopefully we will, in time, have a larger stock of cumulative empirical knowledge pertaining to the Canadian labour market.

The basic format of the text involves an analysis of the essential elements of a labour market — the various dimensions of labour supply and demand and their interaction in alternative market structures to determine wages, employment and unemployment. Within this format many of the newer issues of labour economics are dealt with, including fertility and family formation, the retirement decision, the work incentive effects of alternative income maintenance schemes, flexible working hours, human capital theory, sex discrimination, and public sector wage determination.

The important issues of poverty and personal income distribution are raised throughout the text. Of particular relevance are Chapters 3 on the work incentive effects of alternative income maintenance schemes (e.g., negative income taxes, welfare, wage subsidies and unemployment insurance), Chapter 7 on human capital, Chapter 12 on the dual and radical critiques, and Chapter 14 on occupational wage structures.

By trying to integrate labour market analysis with the mainstream of economic theory, the text reflects the prevailing neoclassical paradigm with its emphasis on microeconomic foundations involving optimization subject to constraints. However, alternative perspectives and paradigms are discussed — some would say not enough, given their potential, and others would say too much, given their actual impact.

Each chapter ends with a series of questions designed to recapitulate some of the material of the chapter, to integrate material across chapters, to suggest possible criticisms of the analyses, and to extend the analyses to some issues that have not been dealt with specifically. In some instances, the questions are ones that currently have not been answered satisfactorily by labour economists, and it may even be that they are unanswerable, given our current state of knowledge.

In addition, each chapter ends with a set of references and further readings, mostly from the economics and labour journals that are listed in the key at the beginning of the text. The references are mainly Canadian, American and, to a lesser extent, British. Obviously, these references will soon become dated; hence, there is no substitute for a judicious reading of the appropriate current journals to keep abreast of current developments in the field.

The text was written for students who have had an introductory course in economics and preferably — but not necessarily — a course in microeconomics. Calculus and econometrics are sometimes utilized, usually in appendices or self-contained mathematical sections that can be omitted by those without the requisite training. The text is also suitable as a basis for graduate labour courses in business schools as well as economics departments. In fact the manuscript was used by the author to teach labour courses at both graduate and undergraduate levels to both economics and M.B.A. students.

Various persons have aided in the preparation of this book. For encouragement, helpful discussions, and for having read portions of the manuscript, I am indebted to many of my colleagues at the University of Toronto, in particular Jon Cohen, Sheila Eastman, John Ham, Gregg Jump, Frank Mathewson, Noah Meltz, Jim Pesando, Sam Rea, Frank Reid and Dave Stager. Members of the International Labour Organization and the International Institute for Labour Studies, where I spent a sabbatical year, provided a helpful input: I am particularly grateful to Alan Gladstone, Gerald Starr and Martin Tracy. The influence of many of my former teachers — in particular Glen Cain, W. Lee Hansen and the late Gerald Somers — is evident throughout the text. I am also indebted to the numerous students at the University of Toronto who, by utilizing earlier drafts of the material, detected errors and provided suggestions for clarification. Staff and students at the Centre for Industrial Relations provided invaluable assistance: I am particularly indebted to Cam Christie, Marcelle Elhadad, Wanda Filiszewski, Dorothy and Jean Newman, Elizabeth Perry, Gary Rabbior, Wray Roulston, Marian Stanley and Fay Sulley. Deborah Campbell provided her usual friendly efficiency in typing, correcting, editing and proofreading the entire manuscript: any remaining errors, of course, are hers. To all these people I am deeply indebted, not only for their assistance and encouragement, but also for their friendliness and sense of humour — all of which was so important to me while writing the text.

It is conventional to thank one's spouse and children for tolerating neglect and abuse while the manuscript was in progress. For better or worse, mine tolerated none: had they done so, this book would have been finished much earlier! However, because of them, I did enjoy writing the book. I am especially grateful to Melanie for helping me maintain a proper perspective.

REFERENCES AND FURTHER READINGS

Doeringer, P.   Determinants of the structure of industrial type labor markets. *ILRR* 19 (January 1967) 206–220.

Dunlop, J.   Policy decisions and research in economic and industrial relations. *ILRR* 30 (April 1977) 275–282.

Gunderson, M.   Labor relations in Canada. *The Canadian Economy*. Toronto: Gage, 1977.

Kerr, C.   Labor markets: their character and consequences. *AER* 40 (May 1950) 278-291.

McNulty, P.   Labor market analysis and the development of labor economics. *ILRR* 19 (July 1966) 538–548.

Ostry, S.   The Canadian labour market. *Canadian Labour in Transition*, R. Miller and F. Isbester (eds.). Scarborough: Prentice-Hall, 1971.

Pentland, H.   The development of a capitalistic labour market in Canada. *Canadian Journal of Economics and Political Science* 25 (November 1959) 450-461.

Rottenberg, S.   On choice in labour markets. *ILRR* 9 (January 1956) 183-199. Comments by R. Lampman and reply 9 (July 1956) 629-641.

ACKNOWLEDGEMENTS

F. Weiskoff, "Women's Place in the Labor Market," *American Economic Review* 62 (May 1972), page 164, and H. Zellner, "Discrimination Against Women, Occupational Segregation, and the Relative Wage," *American Economic Review Proceedings* 62 (May 1972), page 157.

D. Brady, "Equal Pay for Women Workers," *Annals of the American Academy of Political and Social Science* (May 1947), pages 53 and 57.

J. Addison and J. Burton, "Wage Adjustment Processes: A Synthetic Treatment," *British Journal of Industrial Relations* 16 (July 1978), page 221.

To Butterworths for Institute for Research on Public Policy, for permission to reproduce material from Morley Gunderson, "Public-Private Wage and Non-Wage Differentials in Canada: Some Calculations From Published Tabulations," pages 128-66, and Richard M. Bird, "The Growth of the Public Service in Canada," pages 19-44, in David K. Foot, ed., *Public Employment and Compensation in Canada: Myths and Realities*, Toronto: Butterworths for Institute for Research on Public Policy, 1978.

P. Doeringer and M. Piore, *Internal Labour Markets and Manpower Analysis*, Lexington, Mass.: D.C. Heath, 1971, pages 85 and 165; D. Gordon, *Theories of Poverty and Underemployment*, Lexington, Mass.: D.C. Heath, 1972, pages 53 and 65.

To Journal of Economics and Business, for permission to reproduce material from C. Lin and J. Landon, "Market Structure, Nonpecuniary Factors and Professional Salaries: Registered Nurses," *Journal of Economics and Business* 28 (Winter 1976), page 151.

To Macmillan Company of Canada, for permission to use material from S. Ostry and M. Zaida, *Labour Economics in Canada* 3rd ed., Toronto: Macmillan of Canada, 1979, pages 17, 80, 81, 202-3.

T. Riblich, "Negative Income Taxes and Education," in T. Orr and others (eds.), *Income Maintenace*, Chicago: Markham, 1971, page 309.

To the Minister of Supply and Services Canada, for permission to reproduce material from D. Maki, *Search Behaviour in Canadian Job Markets*, Ottawa: Economic Council of Canada, 1971, page 24; N. Meltz and D. Stager, *The Occupational Structure of Earnings in Canada, 1931-1975*, Anti-Inflation Board Report, Ottawa: Supply and Services, 1979, page 4; B. Wilkinson, *Studies in the Economics of Education*, Economics and Research Branch, Ottawa: Canada Department of Labour, 1965, page 556; M. Gunderson, "Work Patterns," in *Opportunity for Choice: A Goal for Women in Canada*, edited by G. Cook, Ottawa: Statistics Canada, 1976, page 97. Reproduced by permission of the Minister of Supply and Services Canada.

To Queen's University Industrial Relations Centre, for permission to reproduce material from David Smith, *The Dual Labour Market Theory: A Canadian Perspective*, Kingston: Queen's University Industrial Relations Centre, 1976, page 3, and from P. Kumar, *Relative Wage Differentials in Canadian Industries*, Kingston: Queen's University Industrial Relations Centre, 1975, page 33.

H.G. Lewis, *Unionism and Relative Wages in the United States*, Chicago: University of Chicago Press, 1963, page 194.

To University of Toronto Press, for permission to use material from Morley Gunderson, "Earnings Differentials Between the Public and Private Sectors," *Canadian Journal of Economics*, XII, 2, University of Toronto Press, May 1979, pages 228-242.

L. Reynolds and C. Taft, *The Evolution of Wage Structure*, New Haven: Yale University Press, 1956, page 357.

KEY TO JOURNAL ABBREVIATIONS USED IN REFERENCES AND FURTHER READINGS

AER	American Economic Review
BJIR	British Journal of Industrial Relations
BPEA	Brookings Papers on Economic Activity
CJE	Canadian Journal of Economics
CPP	Canadian Public Policy
EI	Economic Inquiry (formerly Western Economic Journal)
EJ	Economic Journal
IER	International Economic Review
ILRR	Industrial and Labor Relations Review
ILR	International Labour Review
IR	Industrial Relations
IRJ	Industrial Relations Journal
IRRA	Industrial Relations Research Association Proceedings
JHR	Journal of Human Resources
JPE	Journal of Political Economy
MLR	Monthly Labor Review
QJE	Quarterly Journal of Economics
R. E. Stats.	Review of Economics and Statistics
R. E. Studies	Review of Economic Studies
RI/IR	Relations Industrielles/Industrial Relations
SEJ	Southern Economic Journal
WEJ	Western Economic Journal (now Economic Inquiry)

Part 1

Labour Supply

Chapter 1

Population, Fertility and Family Formation

Labour supply has a dimension of quality, and of quantity. The *quality* of labour supply encompasses elements of human capital such as education, training, mobility, and health, and of human relations such as job enrichment, morale, and alienation. Although obviously important in the analysis of labour markets, the human relations aspects are more appropriately covered in texts on organization behaviour. The human capital elements are discussed in the concluding section of Part I on Labour Supply.

The *quantity* dimension of labour supply involves determining the size of various quantity elements, including our domestic population, that portion of our population that participates in labour force activity, and the hours of work of those who are in the labour force. The size of our domestic population in turn depends on fertility and deaths, as well as immigration and emigration. The dimensions of immigration and emigration are dealt with in Chapter 16 on regional wage structures and geographic mobility. Fertility behaviour is the focus of this section.

The importance of understanding fertility behaviour is highlighted by the many problems that have arisen recently because, in part, of a basic failure to predict demographic changes in the size and composition of our population. Heavy demands were placed on our educational institutions and housing markets as the post World War II baby-boom population passed through various phases of education and began to purchase housing. The massive entry of this generation into the labour market during the late 1960s created labour market adjustment problems, not the least of which was teenage unemployment. Potential labour shortages have been predicted for the 1980s in Canada, in part because of low birth rates in the 1960s. When the post World War II baby-boom population hits retirement age in the early 2000s, there could be a dependency problem if there are insufficient persons in the labour force at that time to sustain a large retired population.

An understanding of fertility behaviour and family formation would also be useful for other current policy issues such as the impact on family formation of income maintenance schemes, and the effect of child raising activities on related household decisions such as labour force participation and hours of work outside the home. Of crucial concern in a discussion of labour supply is our ability to predict future changes in our birth rate.

Until recent years, predicting fertility patterns was largely the purview of demographers, whose predictions were based largely on extrapolation from past trends. Such predictions usually assumed that the underlying structural relationships that determine fertility remain constant. Because of dramatic changes in these underlying factors, however, recent changes in fertility have departed from historical patterns. Lacking a theoretical explanation for the determinants of fertility, demographers were often at a loss to explain current patterns.

Partly out of dissatisfaction with predictions based on demographic extrapolation, economists have recently applied some of the basic concepts of economics to the question of fertility and family formation. Some have heralded the application as a bold and innovative step; others have treated it as simply another absurd encroachment of economics into questions that are fundamentally noneconomic in nature. The application of economics, it would appear, has provided some new insights into fertility and family formation, even though the process of family formation is one in which noneconomic factors play an extremely important role.

ECONOMIC THEORY OF FERTILITY

Consumer Demand Theory

The economic theory of fertility is basically an application of standard microeconomic consumer demand theory to household decision making. Consumer demand theory gives us the fundamental law of demand — the quantity purchased of a commodity is negatively related to its price; that is, as prices rise, the quantity demanded drops. This occurs because a price change has both income and substitution effects. The substitution effect of a price increase occurs as we substitute cheaper goods for the more expensive commodity, hence demanding less of the good whose price has risen. The income effect of a price increase occurs because the price increase is akin to a reduction in our wealth, and consequently we have less to spend on all normal goods, including the commodity whose price has risen. Normal goods are defined as ones that we spend less on when our income declines.

Other factors, of course, can shift this demand curve relationship between prices and quantity demanded. Specifically, an increase in our income or wealth would shift the demand schedule outwards (upwards and to the right) as we would be able to buy more of all normal goods. An increase in the price of substitute commodities would similarly shift it outwards, while an increase in the demand for complementary commodities would shift it inwards. Tastes and preferences — largely regarded by economists as exogenous or predetermined in some unknown fashion — could shift the demand schedule in an undetermined fashion.

Largely based on the pioneering work of Becker (1960) and Mincer (1963), economists have applied the basic framework of consumer demand theory to the decision to have children. Although many find it obnoxious to think of children, even analogously, as if they are "consumer durables", few would deny that at least some families alter their child-bearing decisions because they cannot yet afford to have children (perhaps until they have at least saved for the down payment on a house or have finished paying for their education) or because it is too costly to have a child (perhaps because it would mean an interruption in a wife's career in the labour market). Cain (1971, p.412), for example, estimates the total cost of having a child to be approximately $31,000—obviously not an inconsequential figure. As long as these and other economic factors affect the decision to have children for some families, then economic factors will have some predictive power in explaining variations in birth rates.

Analogous to consumer demand theory, the basic variables affecting the fertility decision are income, the price or cost of a child, the price of related goods, tastes and preferences, and technology. As we will see, however, non-economic factors also play a strong role.

Variables Affecting Fertility

Income
Economic theory predicts that, *other things being equal*, there will be a positive relationship between income and the desired number of children. This goes against casual empiricism, since we tend to think of poor families or poor countries as having more children per family. The problem, of course, is that in the real world other things are not equal. Specifically, factors such as contraceptive knowledge and the cost of having children tend to be related to the income variable, so that it becomes difficult to separate the pure effect of income alone. Poor families, for example, may have more children because they lack knowledge of family planning techniques. If we could hold these and other factors influencing the number of children constant, economic theory predicts a positive relationship between income and number of children.

As Easterlin (1971) points out, however, the relationship between income and number of children is not as simple as that postulated by conventional economic theory. Specifically, new generations with higher incomes get exposed to whole new sets of wants that may serve as substitutes for the gratification previously obtained from raising a family. Some activities now affordable with a higher income—such as travel and entertainment outside the home—may actually conflict with raising a family. In other circumstances, the higher income may simply allow people to buy the new technology (contraceptive devices, abortion, family planning information) that enables them to have fewer children. In such circumstances, we may expect a negative relationship between income and family size, and this may offset the positive relationship predicted from conventional economic theory.

Price or Cost of Children
Although the value of time spent on raising a child in the home is an

important cost associated with children, the main element in the cost of having a child is the income forgone by the spouse (in our society this tends to be the wife) who takes time away from labour market activity to bear and raise the child. Cain (1971, p.412), for example, estimates the additional housework associated with raising a first child to have a present value of approximately $6,100, and the forgone income of the wife to be approximately $11,500. The forgone income of the wife tends to be positively related to such things as her education, training, labour market skills, and job opportunities. In addition to the immediate income forgone while not working, the effect can be longer run, involving the deterioration of work skills and the interruption of careers for women who take time out for child raising.

An increase in the potential earnings of wives can have both income and substitution effects on the decision to have children. The substitution effect says that wives with high potential earnings will have fewer children because their higher opportunity cost (forgone income) of having a child induces them to substitute away from the expensive alternative of having children and to engage in less expensive activities that do not impinge as much on their earnings capacity. The income effect, on the other hand, says that wives with a high earnings capacity can contribute more to family income and this may enable the family to spend more on all normal commodities, including greater expenditures on children. Thus the income and substitution effects of a change in the wife's earnings capacity have opposing effects on desired family size.

Price of Related Goods
Having children entails the purchase of a variety of related commodities that are usually complementary to the raising of children. Medical expenses must be incurred as well as food, shelter, clothing, education, and day-care expenses. A rise in the price of such complementary goods, in theory at least, would tend to reduce our desired number of children. Conversely, a fall in their price — perhaps from state subsidies to medical care, education or day care — could encourage larger family sizes. In most cases, the cost of any one of these related commodities is probably not large enough, nor does it vary sufficiently, to have any appreciable effect on family size. However, dramatic changes in the private cost of some of these items — such as free university tuition or universally free day care — could have an impact, as could any trend in the overall extent of state subsidies for medical care, education, or day care.

Tastes and Preferences
Economists tend to regard tastes and preferences as exogenously given from outside the economic system. In the area of family formation, our tastes and preferences have been dramatically changed, related to our ideas on religion, family planning (including abortion), and the women's liberation movement in general. These factors have all changed over time in a fashion that would

encourage smaller family sizes.

Some would argue that these changes were not really exogenous to the economic system, but rather were a result of some of the more fundamental economic changes. For example, such factors as improved job opportunities for females may have made women's liberation more necessary to ensure more equal employment opportunities. Cause and effect works both ways: tastes and preferences both shape, and are shaped, by the economic system.

Education also has an important bearing on tastes and preferences. Not only does it raise the forgone income from raising children, but increased education may also widen our horizon for other goods (travel, entertainment outside the home), enable family planning, and encourage self-fulfilment through means other than having children.

Technology

Technology is often used as a general rubric to describe the general technological and environmental factors that influence our economic decisions. In the area of fertility and family formation, birth control knowledge and contraceptive devices—especially "the pill"—have had an important impact on the number of children, primarily by equilibrating the actual with the desired number of children. Medical advances with vascetomies and tubiligation can be expected to have a similar impact. The reduction in infant mortality that has occurred over time should also reduce the number of births since, in times of high infant mortality, it was often necessary to have large families simply to have a few children survive to adult age.

A medical advance that could have a dramatic impact on the number of children born would be the discovery of how to influence the sex of a child. If this were possible, then it would not be necessary for some couples to continue having children until they got at least one boy or girl, or whatever sex combination they desired in the family.

Most of the technological advances discussed so far are ones that would encourage or enable smaller families. Some, such as reduced danger and discomforts during pregnancy, and advances in fertility drugs and operations, could work in the opposite direction to encourage or enable more child bearing.

ADDITIONAL ASPECTS OF THE ECONOMICS OF FERTILITY

Before examining the data on fertility to see if the economic theory is empirically verified, it is first necessary to state some refinements of the theory. These additional aspects are especially important to help define the exact form of the variables to be used in the empirical work, and in interpreting the results.

Investment Aspects

In the previous analysis, children were treated as though they were analogous to consumer durables, with expenditures being made on children because of the direct pleasures that they bring. In less-developed economies and perhaps in rural societies, children may also have an investment component. Not only are their services valued on the farm, but also they can serve as a form of pension in that, with the extended family, children can take care of parents upon their retirement. This could be important in societies where minimal care of the aged is not provided through public pensions, medical care or homes for the aged. To the extent that children have this additional investment component in less-developed economies and in rural societies, we may expect larger families in those circumstances. In addition, as Neher (1971) points out, alternative pension arrangements could serve as a population control device by reducing the investment need for children.

Quality vs. Quantity

In conventional consumer demand theory, we tend to think in terms of price and quantity — the way we label the axis on a demand curve diagram. It is possible, of course, that more of something can be purchased either through an increase in the quantity purchased, or an increase in its quality, or both. An increase in our income, for example, may enable us to buy a second car or a better first car. Similarly an increase in our income may enable us to afford to have more children, or it may be used for higher expenditures (education, travel) on the same number of children. This has obvious implications for empirical work since it is possible that high income families may have fewer children (rather than more, as economic theory would predict when we hold other factors constant) because they incur higher expenditures per child — they substitute quality for quantity.

Spacing and Timing of Children

Economic analysis not only has implications for the desired family size, but also for the spacing and timing of children. In fact, in response to a higher (opportunity) cost of having children, families may try to have their children closer together in time. Having two children born a year apart, for example, is less costly in terms of income forgone than having two children born three years apart, since the latter usually implies more time out of the labour market. For this reason, we would expect women who have high potential earnings to have not only fewer children but also to have them over a shorter time period.

Desired vs. Actual

Consumer demand theory deals with factors influencing the desired family size. Obviously in this area of family formation, there may be a considerable gap between the desired and the actual family size. Unwanted pregnancies are a common phenomenon, as is the inability to have children and, possibly, even to adopt. The gap between desired and actual fertility is a natural result in an area where rational planning does not always prevail and where social mores are strong. In some instances, however, it results from time lags, imperfect information, and insufficient technology (especially medical technology), and many of these factors can be influenced by economic forces.

Short Run vs. Long Run

Family planning is obviously a long-run decision-making process. Consequently, the variables we examine should be cast in long-run terms. It is our long-run permanent wealth, for example, that will influence our family size decisions. Short-run or temporary changes in that wealth would at best have a small impact, perhaps by interjecting an element of uncertainty into the decision-making process. Thus, for example, young couples who have a low temporary income because they are engaged in higher education may have large families because their permanent income is high. A temporary bout of unemployment for a wife would probably reduce family size by only a small amount given that her long-run income could be high, although now perhaps subject to a slight degree of uncertainty.

Simultaneous Decision Process

The decision to have children is intricately related to a variety of other household decisions, such as the decision to get married, to participate in the labour force, to engage in geographic mobility, and even to become separated or divorced. From a theoretical point of view, this means that the simultaneous decision-making process should be considered in specifying the underlying structural determinants of fertility behaviour. From a policy point of view, the simultaneity implies that policies influencing any of these other factors will also influence the fertility decision.

EMPIRICAL RESULTS

The empirical evidence on fertility behaviour is confusing to interpret because of the difficulty of holding other factors constant when observing empirical behaviour. For example, it is difficult to isolate the effect of family income, independent of the effect of the wife's education, because highly educated wives tend to marry high income husbands. If we observe fewer children in high income families, is this because of their high income (recall that economic theory predicts the opposite), or is it because wives in such families tend to be highly educated and hence their forgone income or cost of having children is high?

Statistical techniques such as multiple regression analysis have been used by econometricians to isolate the effect of a single variable, while holding the impact of all other factors constant. This can also be achieved by cross-tabulations of the data or restricting the analysis to families of the same characteristics except for the one characteristic whose impact is under examination. Figure 1.1 summarizes the general nature of the empirical results as found in such studies as Becker (1960), Cain and Weininger (1973), and Mincer (1963).

As Figure 1.1(a) illustrates, there exists a negative gross relationship

Figure 1.1 Gross and Partial Relationships Between Fertility and Incomes

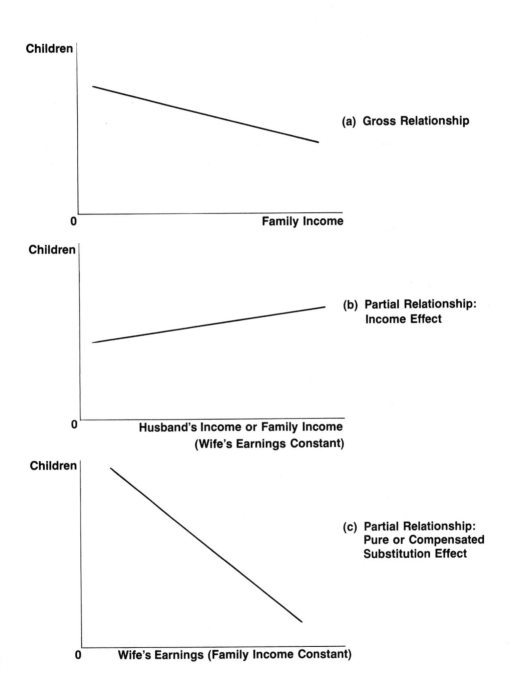

between number of children per family and the income of the family when other things (specifically the education of the wife) are *not* held constant. This casual empiricism has led to the conclusion that people in poverty (or poor countries) have larger families and this tends to exacerbate their poverty. While this conclusion may be true at face value, it tends to mask the real reasons for the larger family size, that reason being the lower education of wives and hence lower forgone income or opportunity cost of children for poorer families. This is illustrated in Figures 1.1(b) and 1.1(c).

Figure 1.1(b) illustrates that when we hold other things equal — specifically such factors as the wife's education or income as well as contraceptive knowledge — then we do observe the positive relationship between the number of children and income. The predictions of economic theory are empirically verified in that, other things equal, we have more children as our income or wealth increases: children are like "normal goods" rather than "inferior goods"! Cain and Weininger (1973), for example, estimate that a $100 increase in the income of husbands is associated with an increase of approximately 10 children per 1000 women in an area. Their estimated income elasticity of demand for children is approximately .20, indicating that a 1 per cent increase in income is associated with a one-fifth of one per cent increase in the demand for children.

Figure 1.1(c) illustrates this actual relationship between the number of children and their opportunity cost as represented by the wife's potential labour market earnings. Other things equal, families with wives who have high potential earnings have fewer children because the opportunity cost of having children is high. Cain and Weininger (1973), for example, estimate that a $100 increase in the wife's potential annual earnings is associated with a reduction of 20 children per 1000 women in an area. Since the wife's annual earnings has both an income and a substitution effect, and since their estimate of the income effect (from the husband's income) was an increase of 10 children per $100 of income, then we could subtract this income effect to get the pure or compensated substitution effect from an increase in the wife's earnings; that is, the income compensated pure substitution effect would be $-20 - 10 = -30$ children per 1000 women for every $100 increase in the wife's earnings, holding constant the family income. This decomposition of a given price effect into its component income and substitution effects is formally given in Appendix 1-1.

Clearly the cost of children, as represented by the forgone income of the wife, plays an important role in our desire to have children. In fact this substitution effect appears more important than the income effect, so that the gross relationship between the number of children and the potential income of the wife is still negative. It is this fact that gives rise to the negative relationship between the number of children and family income as depicted in Figure 1.1(a). High income families have fewer children because of their high opportunity cost (depicted in Figure 1.1(c)): because of the higher income itself they would have more children (depicted in Figure 1.1(b)). Conversely, low-income families have more children because of their low opportunity cost, not because of their low-income *per se*.

POLICY IMPLICATIONS

Perhaps one of the most interesting policy implications to emerge from the economic analysis of fertility is that a viable population control policy, for less-developed economies especially, is to open up job opportunities for women to work. This will raise the (opportunity) cost of having children and, if the empirical estimates are applicable, this should outweigh any tendency to have more children from the additional income generated by their employment. Usually when we think of population control policies, we tend to focus attention on family planning and the dissemination of contraceptive technology. While these factors are obviously important, we should not omit consideration of the operation of economic forces as children become relatively more expensive to people with viable job opportunities.

The economics of family formation also suggests that more than Malthusian checks may be at work to prevent overpopulation. According to Malthus, the only check on population growth would be starvation, malnutrition, and wars resulting from overpopulation, thus earning economics the title of "the dismal science". The economics of fertility suggests that an alternative natural check on family size will occur because labour market alternatives simply make children an extremely expensive alternative. Thus improved opportunities can be as viable a natural check as starvation and malnutrition, perhaps leading to relabelling of economics as the optimistic science.

The economics of fertility also indicates that any transfer payment or subsidized service that is based on the number of children will have income and substitution effects that work in the same direction to encourage larger family sizes. Increases in the family allowance, for example, will in theory encourage larger families because the additional income enables people to afford to have more children (the income effect) and because the cost of raising a child is reduced by the amount of the allowance (the substitution effect). These effects could also be at work for subsidies to day care and education as well as welfare payments and tax exemptions based on the number of dependents. While such payments would theoretically at least work in the direction of increasing family size, the magnitude of the effect would probably be very small since these transfers usually do not amount to much.

Appendix 1-1

Separating Income and Substitution Effects in Fertility Equations

From a linear regression of fertility, C, on husband's income Y_H and wife's income Y_W, we estimate the regression coefficients b_y and b_p. Equation (1) illustrates the relationship, omitting the constant term and other variables.

$$C = b_y Y_H + b_p Y_W \tag{1}$$

The effect, on fertility, of a unit change in the husband's income is $\partial C / \partial Y_H = b_y$. The effect on fertility of a unit change in the wife's income is $\partial C / \partial Y_W = b_p$: this has both income and substitution effects, however, since increases in the wife's earnings both raise the opportunity cost of having children and increase family income. We are assuming that increases in the husband's income has only an income effect, since they tend not to be responsible for child care. In order to separate the income and substitution effects and derive the pure or compensated substitution effect, add and subtract $b_y Y_W$ to the right-hand side of equation (1).

$$C = b_y(Y_H + Y_W) + (b_p - b_y)Y_W \tag{2}$$

Define $Y_H + Y_W = Y_F$ as family income and $b_p - b_y = b_s$ as the pure or compensated substitution effect. Thus

$$C = b_y Y_F + b_s Y_W \tag{3}$$

Here the effect of an increase in the earnings of the wife, holding family income constant so that we are calculating a pure substitution effect, is $\partial C / \partial Y_W = b_s$. Thus to get the pure substitution effect it is necessary to subtract the income effect from the gross price effect; that is, $b_s = b_p - b_y$.

Summarizing the Cain and Weininger (1973) data would give an approximation of equation (1) as $C = 10 Y_H - 20 Y_W$. The gross or uncompensated price effect is -20, the income effect $+10$, and the pure or compensated substitution effect is calculated as $-20 - 10 = -30$.

Similarly, Mincer (1963) uses 1950 data on 400 families and estimates the following relationship via multiple regression analysis. The dependent variable C is the number of children per family and Y_H and Y_W are the earnings of the husband and wife in units of a thousand dollars.

$$C = .10 Y_H - .09 Y_W + \text{other variables.}$$

An additional $1000 of husband's income is associated with an addition of 1/10th of a child per family; that is, $\partial C / \partial Y_H = .10$. An additional $1000 of the wife's income is associated with a reduction of .09 children; that is, $\partial C/\partial Y_W = -.09$. For the wife, the negative substitution effect dominates the positive income effect, so that their combined effect leads to fewer children when her earnings increase. Her pure or compensated substitution effect is calculated as the gross price effect minus the income effect $(-.09 -.10 = -.19)$.

QUESTIONS

1. Based on your knowledge of the economic theory of fertility and family formation, indicate the expected impact on the birth rate of increases in each of the following: women's wages, family allowances, the basic income tax exemption for each dependent, and the education of women.
2. Why has there been a long-run decline in fertility over time, even though income has risen?
3. What does the economic theory of fertility tell us about a viable population policy for less-developed economies experiencing a population explosion?
4. What does the economic theory of fertility tell us about the expected population problem in the year 2000?
5. What does the economics of fertility tell us about family size and urban versus rural location?
6. Cain (1971, p.412) has stated that "there are a number of prices included in the overall price of a child, and each component price is potentially changeable by means of a wide variety of policy actions". Discuss this statement and indicate the policies that can have an impact on the decision to have children.
7. In the regression equation, $C = .10 \, Y_H - .20 \, E_W$, relating births per family, C, to the husband's income Y_H, and the wife's education E_W, evaluate the income elasticity of demand for children for the average family. Assume that the average husband's income is 9 when Y_H is measured in units of $1000, and that the average number of children per family is 3. Evaluate the income elasticity of demand for children for poorer families whose husband's average income is 5 when Y_H is measured in units of $1000 and whose average number of children is 2. From the information given in the regression equation, can you calculate the pure or compensated substitution effect for changes in the wife's income?

REFERENCES AND FURTHER READINGS

Adelman, J. An econometric analysis of population growth. *AER* 52 (June 1963) 314-339.

Becker, G. An economic analysis of fertility. *Demographic and Economic Change in Developed Countries*. Princeton: Princeton University Press, 1960, 209-231.

Becker, G. and N. Tomes. Child endorsements and the quantity and quality of children. *JPE* 84 (August 1976) S143-S162.

Behrman, S., L. Corsa and R. Freedman (eds.) *Fertility and Family Planning.* Ann Arbor: University of Michigan Press, 1969.

Ben-Porath, Y. Fertility responses to child mortality. *JPE* 84 (August 1976) S163-S178.

Ben-Porath, Y. First generation effects on second generation fertility. *Demography* 12 (August 1975) 397-405.

Ben-Porath, Y. Notes on the micro-economics of fertility. *International Social Science Journal* 26 (No. 2, 1974) 227-234.

Blake, J. Are babies consumer durables? *Population Studies* (March 1968) 5-25.

Blandy, R. The welfare analysis of fertility reduction. *EJ* (March 1974) 109-129.

Boyd, M. Eichler M. and Hofley J. Family: functions, formation, and fertility. *Opportunity for Choice: A Goal for Women in Canada*, G. Cook (ed.). Ottawa: Information Canada, 1976, 13-52.

Branson, W. Social legislation and the birth rate in nineteenth century Britain. *WEJ* (March 1968) 134-149.

Butz, W. and M. Ward. The emergence of countercyclical U. S. fertility. *AER* 69 (June 1979) 318-328.

Cain, G. The effect of income maintenance laws on fertility in the U.S. *Aspects of Population Growth Policy*, R. Parke and C. Westoff (eds.). Washington: Government Printing Office, 1973.

Cain, G. Issues in the economics of a population policy for the United States. *AER* 61 (May 1971) 408-417.

Cain, G. and M. Dooley. Estimation of a model of labor supply, fertility, and wages of married women. *JPE* 84 (August 1976) S179-S200.

Cain, G. and A. Weininger. Economic determinants of fertility: results from cross-sectional aggregate data. *Demography* 10 (May 1973) 205-223.

Charles, E. Differential fertility in Canada, 1931. *Canadian Journal of Economics and Political Science* 9 (1943).

Concepcion, M. Female labor force participation and fertility. *ILR* 109 (May-June 1974) 503-517.

Conger, D. and J. Campbell, Simultaneity in the birth rate equation: the effects of education, labour force participation, income and health. *Econometrica* 46 (May 1978) 631-641.

Easterlin, R. Towards a socioeconomic theory of fertility: survey of recent research on economic factors in American fertility. *Fertility and Family Planning: A World View*, S. Behrman and others (eds.). Ann Arbor: University of Michigan Press, 1969, 127-156.

Easterlin, R. Economic-demographic interactions and long swings in economic growth. *AER* 56 (December 1966) 1063-1105.

Enke, S. Population growth and economic growth. *Public Interest* 32 (Summer 1973).

Enke, S. The economic aspects of slow population growth. *EJ* (March 1966).

Fishen, P. and W. Quinn. A cross-sectional analysis of fertility. *American Economist* 19 (Fall 1975) 64-68.

Fleisher, B. Mother's home time and the production of child quality. *Demography* 14 (May 1977) 197-212.

Fleisher, B. and G. Rhodes. Fertility, women's wage rates, and labor supply. *AER* 69 (March 1979) 14-24.

Freedman, D. The relation of economic status to fertility. *AER* 53 (June 1963) 414-426.

Freedman, R. and L. Coombs. Economic considerations in family growth decisions. *Population Studies* (November 1966) 197-222.

Freedman, R. and L. Coombs. Childspacing and family economic position. *American Sociological Review* (October 1966) 631-648.

Friedlander, S. and M. Silver. A quantitative study of the determinants of fertility behavior. *Demography* 4 (Issues 1, 1967).

Gardner, B. Economic aspects of the fertility of rural-farm and urban women. *SEJ* 38 (April 1972) 518-524.

Gregory, P. and J. Campbell. Fertility interaction and modernization turning points. *JPE* 84 (August 1976) 835-848.

Gregory, P., J. Campbell and B. Cheng. A simultaneous equation model of birth rates in the United States. *R. E. Stats.* 54 (November 1972) 374-380.

Gregory, P., J. Campbell and B. Cheng. A cost-inclusive simultaneous equation model of birth rates. *Econometrica* 40 (July 1972) 41-47.

Harman, A. *Fertility and Economic Behavior of Families in the Philippines.* Santa Monica, California: Rand Corporation, 1970.

Hashimoto, M. Economics of postwar fertility in Japan. *JPE* 82 Part 2 (March/April 1974) S170-S194.

Heckman, J. and R. Willis. Estimation of a stochastic model of reproduction. *Household Production and Consumption*, N. Terleckyj (ed.). New York: Columbia University Press, 1975.

Henripin, J. *Trends and Factors of Fertility in Canada.* Ottawa: Information Canada, 1972.

Hurd, W. The decline of the Canadian birth rate. *Canadian Journal of Economics and Political Science* 3 (1937) 40-57.

Illing, W. and others. *Population, Family, Household and Labour Force.* Staff Study No. 19. Ottawa: Economic Council, 1967.

Journal of Political Economy. New economic approaches to fertility, T. Paul Schultz (ed.) 81 Part 2 (March/April 1973).

Keeley, M. The economics of family formation. *Economic Enquiry* 15 (April 1977) 238-250.

Leibenstein, H. An interpretation of the economic theory of fertility. *Journal of Economic Literature* 12 (June 1974) 457-487. Comment by Kelly and reply (June 1974) 461-11.

Leibenstein, H. An economic theory of fertility decline. *QJE* 89 (February 1975) 1-31. Comment by W. Cullison and reply 91 (May 1977) 345-350.

Leibenstein, H. Socio-economic fertility theories and their relevance to population policies. *ILR* 109 (May-June 1974) 443-459.

Leibowitz, A. Home investments in children. *JPE* 82 Part 2 (March/April 1974) S111-S131.

Lindert, P. *Fertility and Scarcity in America.* Princeton: Princeton University Press, 1977.

Meeker, E. Freedom, economic opportunity, .nd fertility: black Americans, 1860-1910. *EI* (July 1977) 397-412.

Mincer, J. Market prices, opportunity costs, and income effects. *Measurement in Economics.* Stanford University Press, 1963, 67-82.

Namboodiri, N. Some observations on the economic framework for fertility analysis. *Population Studies* 26 (July 1972) 185-206.

Neher, P. Peasants, procreation and pensions. *AER* 61 (June 1971) 380-389. Comment by M. Ferber and reply 62 (June 1972) 451-452, and comment by W. Robinson and reply 62 (December 1972) 977-979.

Nerlov, M. Household and economy: toward a new theory of population and economic growth. *JPE* 82 (March/April 1974) S200-S218.

Nerlov, M. and P. Schultz. *Love and Life Between the Census: A Model of Family Decision Making in Puerto Rico, 1950-1960.* Santa Monica, California: Rand Corporation, 1970.

Olnek, M. and B. Wolf. A note on some evidence on the Easterlin hypothesis. *JPE* 86 (October 1978) 953-958.

Phelps, E. Population increase. *CJE* 1 (August 1968) 497-518. Comment by J. Isbister and reply 2 (August 1969) 455-461.

Phillips, L., H. Votey and D. Maxwell. A synthesis of the economic and demographic models of fertility. *R. E. Stats.* 51 (August 1969) 298-308.

Rosenberg, W. A note on the relationship of family size and income in New Zealand. *Economic Record* 47 (September 1971).

Rozenweig, M. The demand for children in farm households. *JPE* 85 (February 1977) 123-146.

Schorr, A. The family cycle and income development. *Social Security Bulletin* 29 (February 1966) 14-25.

Schultz, T. P. An economic model of family planning and fertility. *JPE* 77 (March/April 1969) 153-180.

Schultz, T. P. The Influence of fertility on labour supply of married women: simultaneous equation estimates. *Research in Labour Economics,* vol. 2, R. Ehrenberg (ed.). Greenwich, Conn.: JAI Press, 1978.

Silver, M. Births, marriages and business cycle in the United States. *JPE* 73 (June 1965) 237-255.

Simon, J. *The Effects of Income on Fertility.* Chapel Hill: University of North Carolina Press, 1974.

Simon, J. The effect of income on fertility. *Population Studies* 23 (November 1969).

Statistics Canada. *Fertility in Canada.* 1971 Census Profile Study No. 99-706. Ottawa: Information Canada, 1976.

Stolnitz, G. The demographic transition: from high to low birth rates and death rates. *Population: The Vital Revolution,* R. Freedman (ed.). New York: Anchor Books, 1964.

Suits, D. et. al. Birth control econometric simulation. *IER* 16 (February 1975) 92-111.

Sweets, T. Differentials in the rate of fertility decline 1960-1970. *Family Planning Perspectives* 6 (Spring 1974) 103-107.

Sweezy, A. The economic explanation of fertility changes in the United States. *Population Studies* 26 (July 1971).

Venieris, Y., F. Sebold and R. Harper. The impact of economic, technological and demographic factors on aggregate births. *R. E. Stats.* 55 (November 1973) 493-497.

Votey, H. The optimum population and growth: a new look. *Journal of Economic Theory* 1 (October 1969) 273-290.

Wachter, M. A time series fertility equation: the potential for a baby-boom in the 1980's. *IER* 16 (October 1975) 609-624.

Weintraub, R. The birthrate and economic development, an empirical study. *Econometrica* 40 (October 1962).

Winegarden, C. The fertility of AFDC women: an econometric analysis. *Journal of Economics and Business* 13 (Spring 1974) 159-166.

Chapter 2

Work-Leisure Choice Theory

Once the magnitude of the domestic population is determined, the next step is to analyse the various dimensions of labour supply for that population. Quantity dimensions of labour supply involve labour force participation, retirement, and the hours of work decision.

The basic theoretical framework underlying all of these dimensions of labour supply is the work-leisure choice model. This chapter develops the work-leisure choice model and uses it to decompose the income and substitution effects of a wage change, and to derive the individual's supply curve of labour. In addition, the basic model is criticized and expanded. In subsequent chapters the model is applied to analyse the work incentive effects of alternative income maintenance schemes, the labour force participation and retirement decisions, and the various dimensions of hours of work.

BASIC WORK-LEISURE MODEL

The work-leisure choice theory is simply an application of standard microeconomic theory (indifference curve analysis) to the household's choice between income and leisure, where leisure is broadly interpreted as non-labour market activities including household work and education, as well as pure leisure activities. The individual is indifferent (has the same welfare) between the various combinations of income and leisure as given by the indifference curve U_0 in Figure 2-1(a). The slope of the indifference curve exhibits a diminishing marginal rate of substitution between income and leisure. For example, at point A, the individual has an abundance of income and hence is willing to give up considerable income to obtain more leisure; hence the steeply sloped indifference curve at point A. At point B, the individual has an abundance of leisure and hence is willing to give up considerable leisure (i.e. work more) to obtain more labour income; hence, the relatively flat indifference curve at point B. At intermediate points such as C, income and leisure are better substitutes because the individual is not saturated with either. Higher indifference curves such as U_1 represent higher levels of utility or welfare since they involve more of both income and leisure.

The individual will try to move to the highest indifference curve possible, constrained by the potential income constraint as given in Figure 2-1(b). This is a "potential" income constraint because it indicates varying potential amounts of income that can be obtained by giving up leisure and working at the market wage rate. The actual amount of income will depend

18

Figure 2.1 Income-Leisure Indifference Curves, Wage Constraint, and Equilibrium

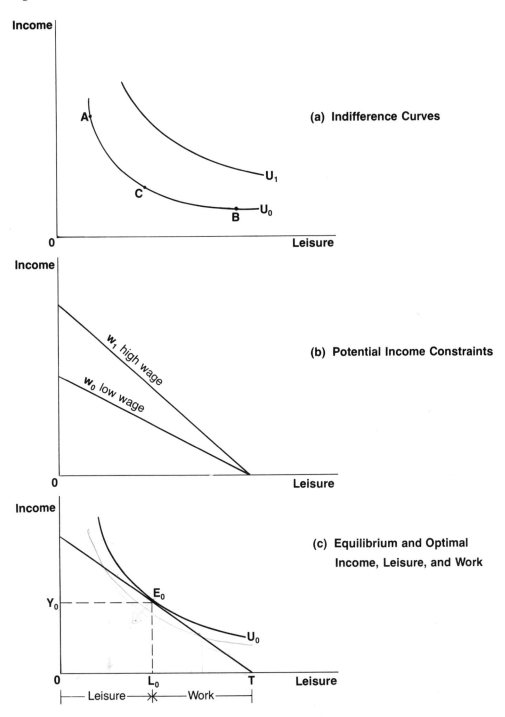

on the chosen amount of work. Alternative phrases for the potential income constraint include wage, budget, wealth, income and full-income constraint.

The slope of the potential income constraint line depends on the individual's labour market wage rate. Persons with a high market wage rate, such as w_1 where $w_1 > w_0$, will be able to earn more income by giving up leisure and working more; hence the slope of w_1 is steeper than the slope of w_0. Note that work is measured from right to left; for analytical purposes it is regarded as the residual between the maximum amount of leisure available and the optimal amount of leisure chosen.

Perhaps the simplest way to understand how wage changes (as well as other factors such as taxes and transfers which will be examined later) affect the potential income constraint is to first mark the end point on the leisure axis. This end point is the maximum amount of leisure available; depending on the units in which leisure is measured, it could be 24 hours per day, 7 days per week, 52 weeks per year, or some combination such as 8760 hours per year. The potential income constraint is then derived by plotting the person's income as he gives up leisure and works additional units; that is, as he moves leftward from the maximum leisure end point. For a constant wage rate, this income constraint would be a straight line, since a unit of work would yield the same additional income throughout the range of work time. The end point on the income axis would be the maximum income the individual could attain by working all of the time; that is, by having zero leisure. As we will see later, the work-incentive effects of alternative income maintenance schemes can be analysed by simply indicating what happens to the individual's potential income constraint as a result of the income transfer.

By putting the individual's potential income constraint and indifference curve together (Figure 2-1 (c)), we can obtain the individual's optimal amount of income and leisure (and hence we can obtain the optimal work or labour supply). The utility maximizing individual will move to the highest indifference curve possible, constrained by the labour market earnings as given by the potential income constraint w_0. The highest feasible indifference curve in Figure 2-1(c) involves the point of tangency E_0 with optimal income Y_0, leisure L_0, and labour supply or work $T - L_0$. One can easily verify that E_0 is the utility maximizing equilibrium by seeing what would happen if the individual were at any point other than E_0.

INCOME AND SUBSTITUTION EFFECTS OF A WAGE CHANGE

What will happen to the equilibrium amount of work effort if wages are increased? On the one hand, the individual may work more because the returns for work are greater; that is, the opportunity cost of leisure or the income forgone by not working is higher and hence the person may substitute away from leisure. This is termed the substitution effect and, in the case of a wage increase, it leads to increased work. On the other hand, the higher wage rate means that the person now has more potential lifetime wealth from which to buy more of all normal goods including leisure. Alternatively stated, with the higher wage rate, individuals can reach their target level of income sooner and hence they can afford not to have to work as much. This is termed the income effect, and in the case of a wage increase it leads to reduced work. This assumes that leisure is a normal good, defined in economics as a good that we spend more on when income increases. In the case of a wage change, the income and substitution effects work in the opposite direction; hence, it is ultimately an empirical proposition as to whether a wage increase would increase or decrease the supply of work effort.

The income and substitution effects are illustrated more rigorously in Figure 2-2. After the wage increase from w_0 to w_1, the new equilibrium is E_2. Like all price changes, this increase in the price of leisure can be decomposed into both an income and substitution effect. The income effect can be illustrated by drawing a line parallel to the potential income constraint w_0 but tangent to the new indifference curve U_1. Since the lines are parallel, the

Figure 2.2 Income and Substitution Effects of a Wage Increase

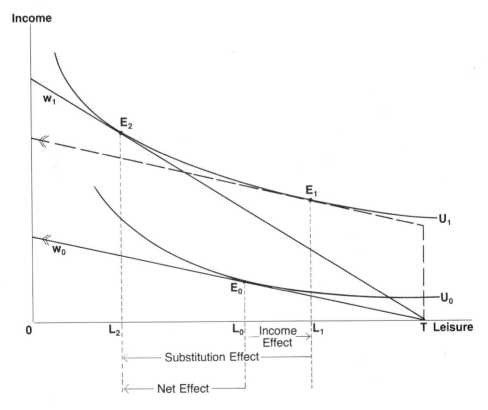

relative price of leisure is the same at E_o and E_1. Consequently the difference between E_o and E_1 is purely a matter of having more wealth (higher potential income constraint) from which to buy more of all normal goods including leisure. Hence E_1 lies above and to the right of E_o and consequently involves less work effort and more leisure. The difference between E_1 and E_2 is now a pure (or income compensated) substitution effect, since relative incomes are held constant (as evidenced by their constant evaluation on the same indifference curve U_1) and only the relative price of leisure is different. The relative price of leisure is higher on the steeper wage constraint w_1 as evidenced by the fact that giving up a unit of leisure (i.e. working more) yields more income. Consequently, the individual will substitute away from the more expensive leisure and work more: the pure (compensated) substitution effect of a wage increase will unambiguously increase work effort. In Figure 2-2, the substitution effect dominates the income effect; hence, on net, the wage increase resulted in increased work effort.

DERIVING THE INDIVIDUAL SUPPLY CURVE OF LABOUR

As the early writings of Robbins (1930) indicate, the work-leisure choice framework can be used to derive the individual's labour supply schedule, which indicates the amount of labour that will be offered at various wage rates. As Figure 2-2 indicates, we already have two points on that supply schedule: at wage rate w_o the amount of labour supply (work) is $T - L_o$, and at wage rate w_1 the amount of labour supply is $T - L_2$. In this particular case, labour supply increased as wages increased because the substitution effect outweighed the income effect. By varying the wage rate, we can obtain a schedule of corresponding equilibrium amounts of work and hence trace out the individual's labour supply curve.

Derivation of an individual's labour supply schedule is further illustrated by the specific example of Figure 2-3 where leisure and work are measured in units of hours per day and wages in units of wages per hour. Income is the hourly wage multiplied by the hours of work. Figure 2-3(a) illustrates the equilibrium hours of work (measured from right to left) of 8 hours per day for a wage rate of $3/hr. The corresponding daily income is $24 per day. This gives us one point on the individual's labour supply schedule of Figure 2-3(c): at $3/hr the labour supply would be 8 hours. In Figure 2-3(b), wages are then raised to $5/hr and the individual is observed to increase work effort to 12 hours per day. This yields a second point on the labour supply schedule of Figure 2-3(c). In this particular case, the substitution effect of the wage increase outweighs the income effect so that hours of work have increased. In Figure 2-3(b), wages are next raised to $7/hr and the individual is observed to decrease work effort to 10 hours per day. This yields a third point on the labour supply schedule of Figure 2-3(c). At the higher wage rate, the income effect of the wage increase begins to dominate the substitution effect and the labour supply schedule becomes backward bending. In fact,

Figure 2.3 Deriving the Individual Supply Curve of Labour

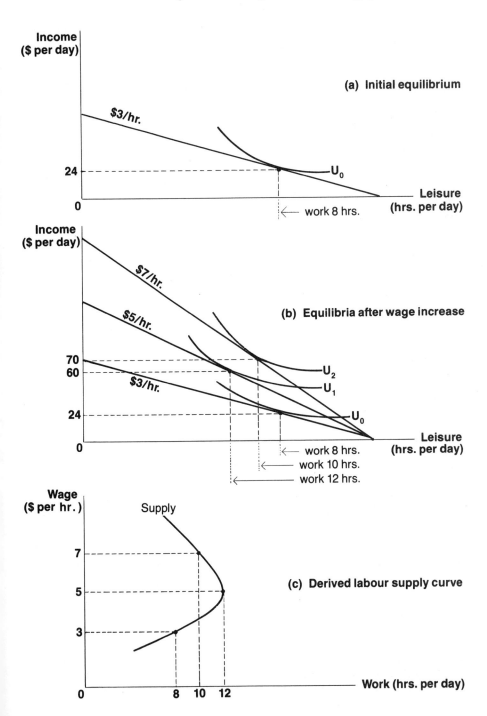

this may be a reasonable approximation for many individuals: at low wage rates they have an abundance of unmet needs, so that higher wages will induce them to work more in order to fulfill these needs; at higher wages many of their needs are fulfilled, so that additional wage increases will be used to purchase leisure.

CRITICISMS OF THE WORK-LEISURE FRAMEWORK

The work-leisure choice framework has been criticized in a variety of areas. Many of these criticisms, however, are not really criticisms of the basic framework. Rather they are extensions of the model and reminders of its limitations.

There is the belief that many individuals do not really have a choice between work and leisure. This may especially be the case for poor persons at a subsistence level of income, or people who are permanently attached to the labour force or who are required to work a fixed period of time if they are to work. These criticisms should not negate the viability of the work-leisure framework; in fact, they can easily be incorporated into the basic model. Poor persons existing at a subsistence income have a wage constraint close to origin and an indifference curve between income and leisure that is flat to the right of the existing equilibrium—since they are at subsistence, they are unable to give up any income even for large increases in leisure. To the left of the existing equilibrium, their indifference curve could have a low slope indicating that they are willing to give up considerable leisure to attain the higher income and consumption patterns of middle class status.

People who are required to work a fixed period of time would not face a continuous wage constraint, but rather would be relegated to a specific point on that wage constraint, or to not working at all. This can be depicted in the work-leisure choice framework and, as we will see later, gives rise to interesting implications with respect to overtime and moonlighting. The point is simply that rather than negating the viability of the work-leisure model, these observations highlight its usefulness in analysing the impact of the different preferences and of the objective constraints facing individuals.

The work-leisure choice framework has also been criticized on the grounds that leisure is not a "normal" good. For low-income people, leisure may be an inferior good because they don't have the income to really enjoy the leisure. An increase in their income, other things being equal, may actually encourage work incentives since, for example, the more expensive vacation or the chance to send one of the children to a university now becomes a reality. Again, this does not negate the theory, since it does not deny the possibility that leisure is an inferior good. In fact, the basic theory of consumer demand merely states that an increase in income will lead to increased expenditure on all normal goods: this increased expenditure on leisure could well mean a lesser quantity of leisure and more quality leisure, in which case work incentives are increased.

Perhaps the most substantial modification of the basic work-leisure model is that offered by exponents of the "household production" view, sometimes termed the "new home economics", as evidenced in the writings of Gary Becker (1965). According to this view, households are producers as well as consumers. They combine inputs of time and market goods in the household production function to produce commodities which ultimately yield satisfaction. Such commodities could include meals, sleeping, or viewing a play. In this framework, a wage increase would not only affect our work-leisure decision but also induce a substitution away from time-intensive activities and into more goods-intensive activities. In addition, this view emphasizes the multifaceted nature of leisure activities, ranging from pure leisure which we may consume for its own sake, to productive leisure which could enhance our future earning power.

QUESTIONS

1. In Figure 2-1(c), why is E_0 a stable equilibrium? In other words, why would the individual not move along the potential income constraint line W_0 to some other feasible combination of income and leisure? Why would he not move to a feasible point below the wage constraint line? Why would he not move to a point above the indifference curve U_0?
2. What would happen to an individual's labour supply schedule if leisure is an inferior good?
3. Use the basic work-leisure choice framework to analyse the possible labour supply response of various groups to changes in their wage rate. The different groups could include the following: poor who are at minimum subsistence and who aspire to middle class consumption patterns; wealthy who have acquired an abundance of material goods and who now aspire to be members of the idle rich; primary workers who have a fairly strong attachment to the labour force and who are reluctant to change their hours of work; and secondary workers who have a weak attachment to the labour force and who have viable alternatives to labour market work.
4. Illustrate the case where an individual responds differently to a wage increase and a wage decrease of the same magnitude. Specifically, have the person become "locked in" to a certain consumption pattern associated with the higher wage.
5. Depict the following situations in the basic work-leisure choice diagram: when an individual works beyond his normal working hours, he becomes less productive and hence is paid less per hour; when an individual works beyond his normal working hours, an overtime premium is paid; the person takes a training program and increases his labour market productivity and wage; the government subsidizes the individual's wage by fifty percent; the government imposes a tax of twenty percent on labour market earnings; the government imposes a progressive income

tax; the government gives everyone a basic demogrant of 1000 dollars per year.
6. Suppose an individual is on the backward bending portion of his labour supply curve. Is there a sufficiently high wage such that his hours of work will go to zero?

REFERENCES AND FURTHER READINGS

Abbott, M. and O. Ashenfelter. Labor supply, commodity demand, and the allocation of time. *R. E. Studies* 42 (October 1977) 389-411.

Aigner, D. An appropriate econometric framework for estimating a labor supply function from the SEO file. *IER* 15 (February 1974) 59-68.

Ashenfelter, O. and J. Heckman. The estimation of income and substitution effects in a model of family labor supply. *Econometrica* 42 (January 1974) 73-85.

Barzel, Y. The determination of daily hours and wages. *QJE* 87 (May 1973) 220-238.

Barzel, Y. and R. McDonald. Assets, subsistence and the supply curve for labor. *AER* 63 (September 1973) 621-633.

Becker, G. A theory of the allocation of time. *EJ* 75 (September 1965) 493-517.

Berg, E. Backward sloping labor supply functions in dual economies—the African case. *QJE* 75 (August 1961).

Conlisk, J. Simple dynamic effects in work-leisure choice: a skeptical comment on the static theory. *JHR* 3 (Summer 1968) 324-326.

Darrough, M. A model of consumption and leisure in an intertemporal framework: a systematic treatment using Japanese data. *IER* 18 (October 1977) 677-696.

Deserpa, A. On the comparative statics of time allocation theory. *CJE* 8 (February 1975) 101-111.

Fan, L. Leisure and time elements in consumer behavior. *SEJ* 38 (April 1972) 478-484.

Feldstein, M. Estimating the supply curve of working hours. *Oxford Economic Papers* 20 (August 1968) 74-80.

Finegan, T. Hours of work in the United States: a cross-sectional analysis. *JPE* 70 (October 1962) 452-470.

Fishelson, G. Simple dynamic effects in work-leisure choice: a rejoinder to the skeptical comment on the static theory. *JHR* 6 (Spring 1971) 248-249.

Ghez, G. and G. Becker. *The Allocation of Goods and Time Over the Life Cycle.* New York: National Bureau of Economic Research, 1975.

Gilbert, F. and R. Pfouts. A theory of the responsiveness of hours of work to changes in money rates. *R. E. Stats.* (May 1958) 116-121.

Gronau, R. The intrafamily allocation of time: the value of housewive's time. *AER* 63 (September 1973) 634-651.

Hanock, G. The backward-bending supply of labor. *JPE* 73 (December 1965) 636-642.

Heckman, J. Shadow prices, market wages and labor supply. *Econometrica* 42 (July 1974) 679-694.

Heckman, J. Life cycle consumption and labor supply. *AER* 64 (March 1974) 188-194.

Kagel, J., R. Battalio, R. Winkler and E. Fisher. Job choice and total labor supply: an experimental analysis. *SEJ* 44 (July 1977) 13-24.

Kaun, D. A comment on the work-leisure myth. *Review of Radical Political Economy* I (May 1969) 85-88.

Kosters, M. Income and substitution effects in a family labor supply model. P-3339. Santa Monica, California: Rand Corporation, 1965.

Lampman, R. (ed.). Income redistribution and the labor supply: a symposium. *JHR* 3 (Summer 1968).

Lancaster, K. A new approach to consumer theory. *JPE* 74 (April 1976) 132-157.

Landsberger, M. Children's age as a factor affecting the simultaneous determination of consumption and labor supply. *SEJ* 40 (October 1973) 279-288.

Lewis, H. G. Economics of time and labor supply. *AER* 65 (May 1975) 29-36.

Lewis, H. G. Hours of work and hours of leisure. *IRRA* (December 1956) 196-206.

Mabry, B. Income-leisure analysis and the salaried professional. *IR* 8 (February 1969) 162-173.

Miracle, M. and B. Fetter. Backward-sloping labor-supply functions and African economic behavior. *Economic Development and Cultural Change* 18 (January 1970) 240-251.

Moses, L. Income, leisure and wage pressure. *EJ* 72 (June 1962) 320-334.

O'Conner, J. Smith and Marshall on the individual's supply of labor. *ILRR* 14 (January 1961).

Owen, J. The demand for leisure. *JPE* 79 (January/February 1971) 56-76.

Owen, J. *The Price of Leisure*. Montreal: McGill-Queen's University Press, 1970.

Parsons, D. Health, family structure and labor supply. *AER* 67 (September 1977) 703-712.

Pollak, R. and M. Wachter. The relevance of the household production function and its implications for the allocation of time. *JPE* 83 (April 1975) 255-278. Comment by W. Barnett and reply 85 (October 1977) 1073-1086.

Robbins, L. On the elasticity of demand for income in terms of effort. *Economica* (June 1930) 123-129.

Ryder, H., F. Stafford and P. Stephan. Labor, leisure and training over the life cycle. *IER* 17 (October 1976) 651-674.

Sharir, S. The income leisure model: a diagrammatic extension. *Economic Record* (March 1975) 93-98.

Sharir, S. and Y. Weiss. The role of absolute and relative wage differentials in the choice of work activity. *JPE* 82 (November/December 1974) 1269-1275.

Sheshinski, E. On the individual's lifetime allocation between education and work. *Metroeconomica* 20 (April/June 1968) 42-49.

Smith, J. Assets, savings and labor supply. *EI* (October 1977) 551-573.

Terleckyj, N. *Household Production and Consumption.* New York: National Bureau of Economic Research, 1975.

Vatter. On the folklore of the backward sloping supply curve. *ILRR* 14 (July 1961). Comment by Finegan (January 1962).

Wales, T. Estimation of a labor supply curve for self-employed business proprietors. *IER* 14 (February 1973) 69-80.

Wales, T. and A. Woodland. Estimation of household utility functions and labor supply response. *IER* 17 (June 1976) 397-410.

Weiss, Y. On the optimal pattern of labor supply. *EJ* 82 (December 1972) 1293-1311.

Winston, G. Income and the aggregate allocation of effort. *AER* 55 (May 1965).

Chapter 3

Work Incentive Effects of Alternative Income Maintenance Schemes

In large part as a response to the problem of poverty, various income maintenance schemes have been proposed to raise the income of the poor and to supplement low wages. One concern with many of these proposals is that they may reduce work incentives and hence exacerbate poverty in the long run. If an income maintenance program provides little incentive to work, this would raise the cost of the program to taxpayers and hence make the program politically less acceptable. In addition, it could prevent the poor from acquiring the on-the-job training and labour market experience that may raise their income in the long run. Clearly, it is important to understand the exact way in which income maintenance schemes could alter work incentives. The income maintenance programs examined here are demogrants, negative income taxes, welfare, wage subsidies, and unemployment insurance.

STATIC PARTIAL EQUILIBRIUM EFFECTS IN THEORY

The basic work-leisure choice framework provides a convenient starting point to analyse the work incentive effects of alternative income maintenance schemes. At this point, the analysis is restricted to the static, partial-equilibrium effects of alternative income maintenance programs. Later, the analysis is extended to dynamic changes that can occur over time and to general equilibrium effects that can occur as the impact of the program works its way through the whole economic system.

Income maintenance alters the individual's potential income constraint in a specific fashion. In order to analyse the effect of these programs on the income constraint (and ultimately on work incentives or labour supply), first ask what happens to the income constraint at the intersection on the leisure axes, and second, what happens to the income constraint as the individual gives up leisure and works more? Throughout this analysis, Y is defined as income after taxes and transfer payments, and E as labour market earnings, equal to wages times hours worked. $E = W \times \text{HOURS WORKED}$

Demogrant
Perhaps the simplest income maintenance program to analyse is the demogrant. As the name implies, a demogrant means an income grant to a specific

29

demographic group, such as female headed families with children, or all persons aged 60 and over, or all family units irrespective of their wealth. Guaranteed annual income proposals, for example, usually involve giving all individuals or families a specific grant.

As illustrated by the dashed line in Figure 3-1(a), the demogrant would shift the potential income constraint vertically upwards by the amount of the grant. The slope of the new income constraint would be equal to the slope of the original constraint since the relative price of leisure has not changed. Thus there is no substitution effect involved with the demogrant. Assuming leisure is a normal good, the new equilibrium under the demogrant, E_d, would be above and to the right of the original equilibrium; that is, work incentives would unambiguously be reduced. This occurs because the demogrant involves only a leisure-inducing pure income effect. The increase in actual take-home income, however, is less than the amount of the demogrant because some of the demogrant was used to buy leisure, hence reducing earned income. This can readily be shown in Figure 3-1(a).

Negative Income Tax

Negative-income-tax plans involve an income guarantee, and a positive tax rate applied to labour market earnings. Income after taxes and transfers would be $Y = G + (1 - t)E$, where G is the basic guarantee, t is the tax rate, and Y and E as defined earlier are take-home pay and labour market earnings respectively. Most negative-income-tax plans differ in so far as they involve different values of the basic guarantee and the tax rate. The term *negative* income tax is used because recipients will receive more from the guarantee than they will pay out in taxes, even though they do face a positive tax rate.

A negative-income-tax plan with a constant tax rate is illustrated by the dashed line in Figure 3-1(b). As with the demogrant, at the point of maximum leisure the basic income guarantee shifts the potential income constraint upwards by the amount of the guarantee: even if the individual does not work, he has positive income equal to the amount of the guarantee. As the individual works, however, his labour market earnings are subject to a positive tax rate. His take-home pay does not rise as fast as his labour market earnings; hence, his income constraint under the negative-income-tax plan is less steeply sloped than his original labour market income constraint.

Assuming leisure is a normal good, the new equilibrium for recipients of the negative-income-tax plan will unambiguously lie to the right of the original equilibrium: work incentives are unambiguously reduced in this static, partial equilibrium framework. This occurs because both the income and substitution effects work in the same direction to reduce work effort. The tax increase on earned income reduces the relative price of leisure, inducing a substitution into leisure and hence reducing work effort. The tax increase also has an income effect (working in the opposite direction); however, for *recipients* this is outweighed by the guarantee, so that on net their new potential income constraint is always above the original constraint

Figure 3.1 Work Incentive Effects of Income Maintenance Plans

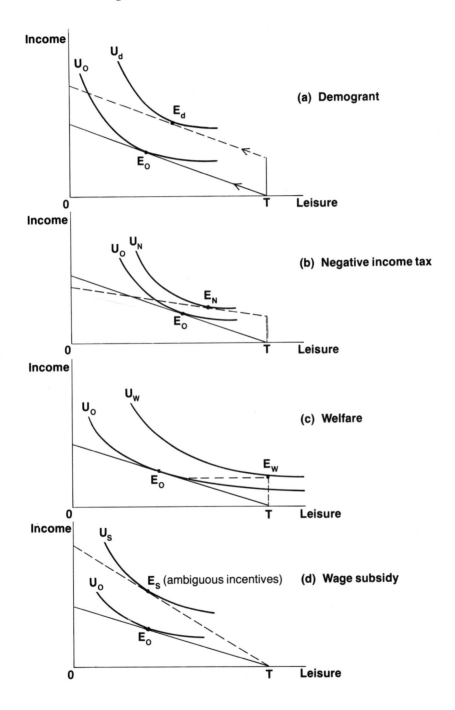

—that is why they are defined as recipients. Because the potential income of recipients is increased, they will buy more of all normal goods including leisure. Thus the income effect works in the same direction as the substitution effect to reduce work effort.

Although the static, partial equilibrium, work-leisure choice framework predicts that work incentives will be unambiguously reduced as a result of a negative-income-tax plan, this does not negate the viability of such a program. The adverse work incentive effects may be small, or the increased "leisure" may be used productively as in job search, mobility, education or increased household activities. In addition, the reduction in labour supply may have other desirable side effects, such as raising the wages of low wage labour since it is now a relatively scarcer factor of production. Also the adverse incentive effects were predicted when a negative income tax was imposed in a world without other taxes and transfers. In the real world, a negative income tax may replace some welfare programs which have even larger adverse incentive effects and in this sense work incentives may increase relative to incentives under welfare. Many of these dynamic, general equilibrium effects will be discussed in more detail in subsequent sections. Suffice it to say at this point that the basic conclusions from the work-leisure model must be kept in proper perspective. This is not to say that the static, partial equilibrium conclusions should be ignored. Rather, it suggests that empirical information is needed on the magnitude of any adverse work incentive effects and information is needed on the form in which "leisure" is taken.

Welfare

For those who are eligible for welfare, their new potential income constraint is given by the dashed line in Figure 3-1(c). Even if they do not work, they are given the welfare payment. Hence, at the point of maximum leisure (zero work), their income constraint shifts vertically upwards by the amount of the welfare payment. Under *many* welfare programs, as individuals work and receive labour market earnings, they are required to forgo welfare payments by the exact amount of their labour market earnings. In this sense, there is a 100 percent tax on earnings. Their potential income constraint is thus horizontal at the amount of the welfare payment: as they work and earn income, they forgo a comparable amount in welfare and hence their income does not increase. Every dollar earned results in a dollar reduction in welfare. Of course, once they reach their original labour market wage constraint, then their take-home pay will be indicated by their original wage constraint: at this point their welfare payments have been reduced to zero so they cannot be "taxed" any further by being required to give up welfare.

If the welfare payment is sufficiently high, the individual would have a strong incentive to move to the corner solution at E_w where he would not work at all. There is no incentive to work more (more to the left of E_w), because of the 100 percent implicit tax on work incentives that arises because the individual has to give up an equivalent amount of welfare for every dollar earned. Even though the person's take-home pay, Y, is lower at E_w than E_o, he chooses E_w because it involves considerably more leisure. Clearly welfare has extreme potential adverse effects on work incentives. Of course, for many people on welfare, work is not a viable alternative if they are perhaps disabled or unemployable. Yet for others, work would be a viable alternative if there would not be this 100 percent implicit tax on earned income.

This analysis suggests a variety of ways of reducing the number of people on welfare. Traditionally we think of making eligibility requirements more stringent or reducing the magnitude of welfare for those who are eligible. These changes would, of course, work. In Figure 3-1(c), for example, if the welfare payment were lowered to an amount lower than the height of U_o at the point of maximum leisure, then there would be no incentive to go on welfare since the individual would be maximizing utility at E_o. Although successful in reducing the number of people on welfare, these changes may have undesirable side effects, not the least of which is denying welfare to those in need.

One alternative to these policies would be to increase the market wage rate of those on welfare and thereby encourage them to voluntarily leave welfare and earn income. In Figure 3-1(c), an increase in the market wage rate would pivot the wage constraint upwards from T. At some higher wage rate, the individual clearly could be induced to move to a higher indifference curve that would involve more work effort than under welfare (i.e. a new equilibrium to the left of E_w). The increased market wage could come about through training, job information, mobility, a government wage subsidy, or institutional pressures such as minimum wages or unionization. Obviously these policies may be costly, or in the case of minimum wages and unionization, may involve a loss of jobs. However, they could have the benefit of voluntarily reducing the number of people on welfare and hence increasing work incentives.

Another way of improving work incentives would be to reduce the 100 percent implicit tax on welfare. In some welfare programs, this is accomplished by requiring welfare recipients to give up only a portion of their welfare if they earn income by working. For example, if recipients are required to give up 50 cents in welfare for every dollar earned in the labour market, they would have some incentive to work because the implicit tax rate would be 50 percent. In Figure 3-1(c), this could be shown by a wage constraint starting at E_w, with a negative slope of 50 percent of the slope of the labour market wage constraint, reflecting the fact that the recipient takes home 50 percent of every dollar earned by working.

An alternative solution to reducing the number of welfare recipients would be to alter the preferences of welfare recipients away from being on welfare and towards labour market activity. In Figure 3-1(c), this would imply changing the shape of the indifference curves. If, for example, at all points to the right of E_o, the indifference curve U_o were flat, then the individual would not have opted for the welfare equilibrium E_w. The flat indifference curve would indicate a reluctance to accept any cut in income even to get substantial increases in leisure. Traditionally, preferences have been altered by attaching a social stigma to being on welfare. Alternatively, preferences could be altered towards income earning activities, perhaps by making potential recipients feel more a part of the non-welfare society or perhaps by attempting to break the inter-generational cycle of welfare.

Wage Subsidy

Since one of the problems with the negative income tax and welfare is that the tax on earnings may discourage work effort, some have suggested that rather than tax additional earnings, the government should subsidize wages in an attempt to encourage work. Although there are a variety of forms of a wage subsidy — most often associated with the proposals of Kesselman (1969, 1971, 1973) — the simplest wage subsidy schemes have the common result that the recipient's per hour wage rate is supplemented by a government subsidy. This could be accomplished, for example, by having the government guarantee a minimum wage w_G, and then applying a tax rate t_w, to the market wage rate w, in which case the person's wage rate after the subsidy w_s, would be $w_s = w_G + (1 - t_w)$ w. If, for example, the government guaranteed a minimum wage of $1.50 per hour, and applied a wage tax of 50 percent, then a person whose market wage is $2.00 per hour would now receive a post-subsidy wage of $1.50 + (1 - .5) 2 = \$2.50$, or a per hour wage subsidy of $.50. Alternatively, as Haveman (1973, p.59) suggests, the subsidy could be an earnings subsidy which would involve a subsidy that is a given proportion of earnings and hence wages for low income recipients. For example, the government could agree to subsidize low income workers by supplementing their earnings by a fixed percentage, say 50 percent, of their earnings. Although this would change the potential income constraint the same as the wage subsidy, as we will see later it may involve different dynamic incentive effects because it doesn't involve a guaranteed wage or a tax on wages.

The static, partial equilibrium effect of the wage subsidy is illustrated by the dashed line in Figure 3-1(d). For the recipients, it is exactly like a wage increase, hence the potential income constraint rotates upwards from the point of maximum leisure T. If the person does not work (i.e. is at T), his income is still zero even though his wage is subsidized. However, as the person works more, his take-home pay rises more under the wage subsidy than would be the case if he were only receiving his market wage.

Just as an increase in wages has both an income and a substitution effect working in opposite directions in so far as they affect work incentives, so will the wage subsidy have an ambiguous effect on work incentives. The higher wage means higher potential income from which to buy more of all normal goods including leisure; hence, work incentives are reduced via the income effect. This income effect would be at work even though the individual has to work to receive the income: the increased leisure could come in the form of reduced hours or longer vacations or periodic withdrawals from the labour force or reduced work from another family member. The higher wage also means that the price (opportunity cost) of leisure has now increased; hence, work incentives are increased via this substitution effect. On net, theory does not indicate which effect dominates; hence the work incentive effects of a wage subsidy are ultimately an empirical proposition.

Although the work incentive effects of a wage subsidy are theoretically indeterminant, Garfinkel (1973) and Kesselman (1969) show that, other things equal (the recipients' welfare, their post-transfer income, or the size of the subsidy), the adverse work incentive effects of the wage subsidy are not as great as those of the negative income tax. This is illustrated in Figure 3-2 for the case where the recipients' welfare is held constant at U_o so that they are indifferent between the two plans. The equilibrium E_s under the wage subsidy *must* lie to the left of the equilibrium E_N under the negative tax. This is so because the potential income constraint under the wage subsidy is

Figure 3.2   Work Incentive Effects of Wage Subsidy vs. Negative Income Tax

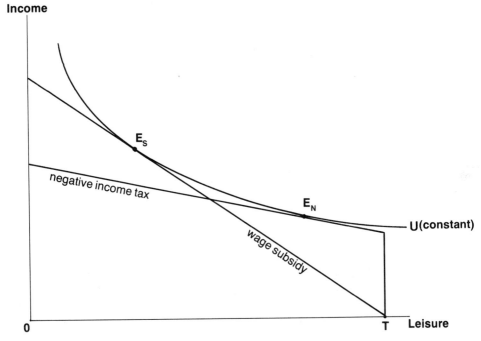

steeper than the negative income tax constraint since it involves a net subsidy to the wage of recipients. Since the wage subsidy constraint must be tangent to U_0 in order for the recipients to be indifferent between the two plans, this tangency must be to the left of E_N because only to the left of E_N is the indifference curve more steeply sloped than at E_N (when we have less leisure, more income is required to give up a unit of leisure and remain indifferent).

Although the work incentive effects are greater under a wage subsidy than a negative income tax, this does not necessarily make the wage subsidy a better plan. One distinct disadvantage of the wage subsidy is that it does nothing to maintain the income of those who are unable to work. Although it may help the working poor, it does nothing to help those who legitimately cannot work. For the latter group, a negative-income-tax plan would at least provide a guaranteed minimum income. Zeckhauser and Schuck (1970) have suggested having both plans and allowing an individual to choose between them.

Unemployment Insurance

In 1971 Canada's unemployment insurance legislation was changed to allow easier eligibility, extended coverage, larger benefits, and a larger duration of benefits. In part because of the high unemployment rate that prevailed during the 1970s, there has been considerable criticism of the changes. Specifically the concern was that the changes reduced the incentive to work and hence increased unemployment.

The work-leisure choice framework can be used to analyse the static, partial equilibrium effect that unemployment insurance will have on work incentives. Although the exact details of the Canadian legislation are extremely complicated, their theoretical impact can be captured by a stylized example of an unemployment insurance scheme which gives recipients two-thirds of their weekly pay for a maximum period of one-half of a year (26 weeks).

This hypothetical scheme is illustrated in Figure 3-3, using a one year time horizon. If the individual is eligible for unemployment insurance, then if he doesn't work during the year (52 weeks leisure), his potential income is equal to two-thirds of his weekly earnings times the twenty-six weeks he is eligible to receive unemployment insurance (i.e. $Y = (2/3)26E$ where E is his weekly earnings). This means that at 52 weeks of leisure his potential income constraint is shifted vertically upwards by an amount equal to one-third of the height of his maximum yearly income where the income constraint crosses the income axis at zero leisure. The one-third height represents the fact that without working the person can collect up to two-thirds of his earnings for one-half of a year. As the person works (moves from right to left from the maximum 52 weeks of leisure), he can earn his weekly earnings as well as his unemployment insurance for a maximum period of 26 weeks.

Figure 3.3   Income Constraint For a Simplified Unemployment Insurance Scheme

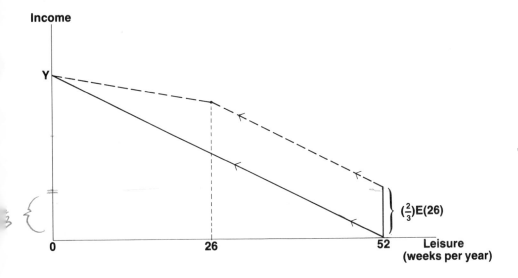

Thus his unemployment insurance constraint line is parallel to his original wage constraint between 52 and 26 weeks of leisure. If he works beyond 26 weeks in the year he takes home his weekly earnings, but forgoes the chance to collect the two-thirds of his weekly earnings through unemployment insurance. This occurs because he cannot legally work and collect unemployment insurance at the same time. Thus between 26 and 0 weeks of leisure, the unemployment insurance constraint has a negative slope, in this particular case, of one-third, reflecting the fact that work beyond 26 weeks only increases potential income by one-third since one forgoes the unemployment insurance of two-thirds of the weekly wage.

Clearly, for some individuals there may be an incentive to become unemployed and collect unemployment insurance. In fact the potential income constraint under unemployment insurance is similar to the constraint under a negative income tax (Figure 3-1(b)). Hence unemployment insurance will have income and substitution effects working in the same direction to *potentially* decrease work incentives. The adverse work incentive effects are potential because the vast majority of people will not collect unemployment insurance. Many are not eligible, and most of those who are eligible would not leave their job because they may not be able to return once they have exhausted unemployment insurance. However, for many with a guaranteed job — be it seasonal, or with family friends, or in household activity, or perhaps one of many low-paid dead end jobs that can't attract other workers

—there may be an incentive to collect unemployment insurance. In addition, the incentive would certainly be there for those who have lost their job, perhaps because of a recessionary phase in the business cycle, and hence who have no labour market alternatives. Unemployment that is induced by unemployment insurance is discussed further in Chapter 18 on Unemployment.

LONG-RUN DYNAMIC EFFECTS OF INCOME MAINTENANCE

The previous analysis dealt with the short-run, static effects of income maintenance programs on the incentive to work. It was found, not surprisingly, that most forms of income maintenance would probably reduce work incentives in the short run. Some, such as the demogrant and welfare, would reduce effort more than others. The wage subsidy was the only program analysed that raised the possibility (but not necessity) of increasing work incentives.

In a dynamic context, over a longer period of time, other factors may be affected by the particular income maintenance program, and these in turn may affect work incentives. Some of these dynamic factors are discussed in Boskin (1967), Conlisk (1968), Garfinkel (1973), Kesselman (1969, 1974), Rea (1973, 1974), and Ribbich (1971). The most important factors that could change over time are motivation and human capital formation, the latter involving investments in education, training, health, mobility or job search. Obviously, income maintenance programs could affect these factors, and they in turn could affect work incentives, leading to a modification of the original conclusions concerning the adverse incentive effects of most income maintenance schemes.

Conlisk (1968), for example, criticized the static, work-leisure model for ignoring the effects of income maintenance schemes on motivation to work. In a formal, dynamic model, he illustrated the common-sense conclusion that an income maintenance program that supplemented low incomes may increase the motivation of low income people to work and that, in the long run, this may offset the static, adverse incentive effects. Their increased motivation to work could occur as their increased income expands their aspirations and preferences for additional income as they "get hooked" on a new set of wants or incur debts and mortgages associated with middle income consumption patterns.

In his criticism of the work-leisure "myth", Kaun (1969) emphasizes that leisure may be an inferior good for low-income people, mainly because they do not have the income to enjoy the leisure. Rather than purchase an additional "quantity" of leisure with their supplemented income, they may choose to work more and purchase higher "quality" leisure, in the form of shorter but perhaps more expensive leisure.

Perhaps the most important long-run adjustments that result from income maintenance programs occur in the area of changes in the *quality* of labour. This process—termed human capital formation—involves incurring costs in the present to increase earnings capacity in the future. Economic theory predicts that human capital formation occurs until the extra benefits are no longer worth the extra costs. If income maintenance schemes increase the benefits from human capital formation, then human capital formation would increase; if income maintenance increases the costs (where costs include the forgone income or opportunity cost of not working), then human capital formation would decrease. Therefore, to analyse the effect of income maintenance on the quality of labour, we must know how it affects the benefits and costs of human capital formation via such processes as education, training, mobility, health or job search.

Since most of the income maintenance schemes result in a reduction of work incentives, then there would be a reduction in the benefit period from which to recoup the investment costs of human capital formation. In addition, if work incentives are reduced, experience and informal on-the-job training (learning by doing) are reduced and skill obsolescence becomes more likely. This is especially the case if the reduced work incentives involve leaving the labour force for an extended period of time. These factors would tend to reduce human capital formation. Since the wage subsidy involves the possibility (but not necessity) of increased work incentives, it has the potential of increasing human capital formation. On the other hand, a reduction in labour supply may provide the time necessary for productive activities like job search or education. An example may clarify these forces. Consider the case when an income supplement program encourages a family to reduce its labour supply by having one of its members withdraw from the labour force. This person will not only lose the experience and informal training associated with the labour market, but will have little incentive to acquire formal training or job search that would improve labour market productivity. On the other hand, the withdrawal from the labour force may enable this person to have the time to engage in such activities as formal education or job search that could improve labour market productivity in the future.

Income maintenance programs may also affect human capital formation through their impact on the tax rate of recipients. If they involve a tax on labour earnings, as with the negative income tax and welfare, then there is less incentive to acquire human capital since the *benefits* in the form of higher earnings will be taxed. On the other hand, since after-tax earnings are reduced, the income forgone during the human capital formation period is reduced; hence the opportunity *cost* of human capital formation decreases and this may encourage improvements in labour quality. The net effect of the tax increase depends on the relative strength of the above two forces which, in turn, depends on the length of time of the human capital formation period and the degree of permanency of the income maintenance scheme. If the human capital formation takes a long time or if the income maintenance program is temporary, so that the opportunity cost is reduced during the human capital formation period but earnings are not reduced afterwards, then investment in human capital will increase. However, in the more usual case that would involve a short human capital formation period and a more permanent income maintenance program, then investment in labour quality would decrease.

The dynamic work incentive effects from the tax in a wage subsidy scheme are more complicated and depend on the particular form of the wage subsidy. If, as outlined earlier, the wage subsidy involves a guaranteed minimum wage and a tax on market wages, then there would be less incentive to engage in human capital formation to raise wages because of the tax on wages. And, if the guaranteed minimum wage were independent of the market wage, then there would be no incentive to raise one's market wage so as to get a higher guaranteed wage. On the other hand, if the subsidy were an earnings subsidy (e.g. Haveman, 1973, p.59) that was a certain percentage of earnings and hence wages, then there would be an incentive to increase wages through human capital formation to get a larger subsidy. This is illustrated in Rea (1973, 1974, pp. 42-44).

Since income maintenance programs by definition increase the potential wealth of the recipients, this wealth effect may encourage human capital formation in a variety of ways. The extra income could be used to finance the investment, which for low income families may be important, especially if they were previously unable to borrow to finance their investment in human capital. In addition, the increased wealth may alter preferences towards income earning activities, and hence encourage human capital formation that would improve future income. Finally, the increased wealth may encourage the consumption of such things as education and, to the extent that the consumption and investment components of such activities are inseparable, human capital formation would increase.

Income maintenance schemes may also increase human capital formation through what may be termed an eligibility effect. Individuals may engage in human capital investments in order to be eligible for income maintenance schemes, either because their income would be sufficiently reduced while in the human capital process, or because human capital formation may be a sufficient condition for receipt of the income support. This would lower the opportunity cost of human capital formation, since the loss of labour market earnings would be lessened by the income support. In the case of those eligible for a negative income tax, for example, the opportunity cost of human capital formation would be their potential earnings less the guarantee. Hence human capital formation would increase. This process is described in Ribich's (1971, p.309) discussion of the effect of a negative income tax on the decision to acquire further education: "An individual who is currently spending a good part of his time earning income will find that if he chooses to spend some of that time in pursuit of education, the forgone earnings portion of his educational investment will be at least partially covered out of public funds.

For some individuals the subsidy will of course not apply, since their incomes during an education program will not drop below the levels required for payment eligibility, but for many others the negative income tax will figure in decisions about undertaking full-time education or training."

Clearly the long-run, dynamic incentive effects that income maintenance programs will have on human capital formation are extremely complicated. They differ depending upon the particular income maintenance scheme, and even for a given scheme the effects are often theoretically ambiguous. This highlights the importance of obtaining empirical evidence not only on the short-run work incentive effects on the *quantity* of labour supplied, but also on the long-run incentives on the *quality* of labour. Only with this evidence will we know whether the long run effects exacerbate or mitigate the short-run effects which usually predict a reduction in work effect.

GENERAL EQUILIBRIUM EFFECTS OF INCOME MAINTENANCE

Income maintenance programs will also have general equilibrium effects as their initial impact is spread through the economy as a whole and has feedbacks on the behaviour of recipients. Of particular interest is the general equilibrium effect on the (before-tax) market wages of both recipients and taxpayers.

Browning (1973) discusses the general equilibrium effect for a negative income tax and a wage subsidy: the former will be illustrated here. Since a negative income tax unambiguously reduces work incentives, then the reduction in labour supply will raise the market wages of transfer recipients. This is illustrated in Figure 3-4 where S_0 is the supply of transfer recipient labour without the negative income tax and S_N represents the new reduced supply after the program. S_N lies to the left of S_0 by an amount equal to the sum of the labour supply reductions of all recipients. Clearly their wages after the negative income tax will rise to w_N. If the supply of labour is upward sloping to the right, then this increase in their market wage will induce an increase in labour supply (along S_N), thereby offsetting some of the initial adverse work incentives. In the final equilibrium, the reduction in labour supply will be only $N_0 - N_G$, not $N_0 - N_N$.

This has important policy implications since it suggests not only that the adverse work incentives will be partly offset, but also that the pre-transfer income of recipients is less likely to fall because, although their labour supply is reduced, their market wage increases. In addition, the increased market wage suggests that minimum wage legislation would be less necessary for recipients since market forces will serve to raise their market wage. This conclusion is in marked contrast to the suggestion that minimum wage laws would have to be more strictly enforced to prevent employers from cutting wages, knowing that the government will support the earnings

Figure 3.4   General Equilibrium Effects of a Negative Income Tax

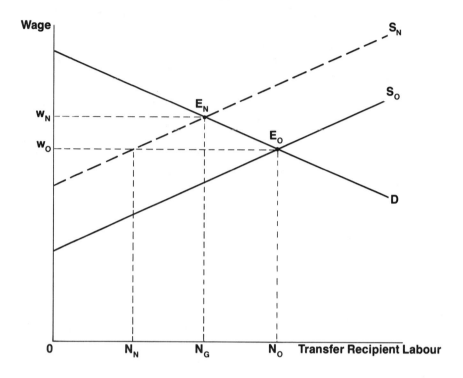

of low wage individuals. This latter conclusion is based on the tenuous assumption that firms pay wages on the basis of the economic needs of their employees and it ignores the basic economic forces that would be at work to raise wages of workers in reduced supply.

A negative income tax will also have an effect on the wages, income and welfare of the rest of society—those who pay for the plan. The pre-tax income of the rest of society (taxpayers) will fall because of their reduced overall productivity that occurs, in turn, because they work with fewer units of transfer recipient labour. It is possible that the income of *some* taxpayers will rise if they are good substitutes for the transfer recipient labour that is in reduced supply. Nevertheless, on net their income as a group must fall because their productivity is reduced as they work with fewer units of transfer recipient labour.

This has important policy implications since it suggests that the cost of the program to the rest of society is not only the transfer cost (the income supplement to the recipients), but also the lower income that taxpayers have because of their reduced productivity. This general equilibrium effect may lead to more resistance on the part of taxpayers to such a program.

EVIDENCE OF INCENTIVE EFFECTS

Since most of the income maintenance schemes discussed here — demogrants, negative income taxes, wage subsidies — are not commonly in existence, we do not have direct evidence on their incentive effects. We can obtain, however, some insight into their probable impact by examining the literature that relates various measures of labour supply to various parameters related to the income maintenance scheme, notably wages and non-labour income. In addition, results from experiments in the U.S. are available on the incentive effects of various negative income tax plans. These results are discussed in more detail in Cain (1974), Peckman and Timpane (1975), and Watts and Rees (1973).

Results from the non-experimental literature are of dubious use in analysing the work incentive effects of low income families, not only because of their wide variation in results, but also because they generally apply to middle and high income families. In spite of their wide variation in results, they generally confirm the static predictions of the work-leisure model. Other things being equal, an increase in non-linear income (such as would come about from a demogrant, a negative income tax guarantee, welfare, or unemployment insurance) reduces labour supply, confirming the existence of a pure income effect. Other things being equal (including family income), a decrease in wages (such as would come about from the tax rate in a negative income tax or welfare) also decreases labour supply, confirming the existence of a net or pure or compensated substitution effect. For most groups in the economy, the income effect appears to dominate the substitution effect, so that wage increases have been associated with a reduction in labour supply. For women, especially married women, the substitution effect appears to dominate the income effect, so that wage increases have been associated with an increase in labour supply.

This suggests that for most income maintenance programs, work incentives will be altered as predicted by the static theory. Demogrants involve only a pure income effect which would reduce incentives similar to increases in non-labour income. Negative income taxes, welfare, and unemployment insurance have income and pure substitution effects working in the same direction to reduce incentives. Wage subsidies with their income and substitution effects working in the opposite direction would probably reduce work incentives for most groups except females, especially married females.

Because of the variety of results from these empirical studies, and because they were not obtained by observing the behaviour of low income individuals, experiments have been conducted using low income families. The available evidence comes mainly from the U.S. negative-income-tax experiment in New Jersey. Different families were given varying amounts of basic guaranteed income and the labour market earnings was subjected to various tax rates. Their work behaviour was then compared to that of a control group of similar families that were not under a negative-income-tax plan. For plans with a basic guarantee near the poverty level of income, and tax rates in the neighbourhood of 30-50 percent, there was an overall 5-10 percent reduction in labour supply, with little variation from the different tax rates and with the largest reduction coming in the form of reduced labour force participation of married women. In the non-labour supply dimension, the results indicated no adverse effects on such aspects of behaviour as fertility, education, and self-esteem, and in fact there was some evidence of slight improvements in such factors as housing services and labour force behaviour.

To the extent that these results can be generalized as the likely response of all low income families to a permanent negative-income-tax plan, they have important policy implications. They do suggest that the adverse work incentive effects are small, even under plans of a fairly high guarantee and low tax rate, especially when compared to the extreme adverse incentive effects of welfare. In addition, the evidence suggests that the reduction in labour supply was used, in part at least, for productive activities, including household work and job search. Although we do not have a complete picture of the dynamic or general equilibrium impact, the limited evidence does not point to any extreme adverse effects. Perhaps the best summary statement of the policy implications for work incentives arising out of the negative-income-tax experiments is given by Rees in his overview of the experimental results (Cain 1973, p.180): ''The burden of proof would now appear to be on those who assert that income maintenance programs for intact families will have very large effects on labour supply''.

QUESTIONS

1. Use the work-leisure choice diagram to illustrate that, under normal circumstances, if an individual is given a demogrant, take-home pay will not increase by as much as the demogrant. Why is this so?
2. Illustrate the work incentive effects of a demogrant on a disabled person who is unable to work.
3. The negative income tax involves a positive guarantee which has a pure income effect reducing work effort. It also involves a tax increase on the earned income of recipients, and this has both an income and substitution effect working in the opposite direction in their effect on work incentives. Consequently, we are unable to predict unambiguously the static, partial-equilibrium effects that a negative income tax plan would have on work incentives. Indicate why this last statement is wrong.
4. Use the work-leisure choice diagram to illustrate the following cases where an individual is: unwilling to go on welfare because the welfare payment is too low; indifferent between welfare and work; induced to move off welfare because of an increase in his wage; induced to move off welfare because of a change in his preferences between income and leisure; induced to move off welfare by a reduction of the 100 percent implicit tax on earnings.

5. What is the break-even wage rate for the wage subsidy scheme outlined in the text? (The break-even wage is the wage rate at which the post-subsidy wage equals the market wage so that the subsidy is zero).
6. Use the work-leisure framework to illustrate that if we hold the post-subsidy income of the recipients constant or the size of the subsidy constant, a negative income tax will involve more adverse work incentives than would a wage subsidy.
7. In an unemployment insurance diagram like Figure 3-3, depict the case where the individual must work eight weeks before becoming eligible to collect unemployment insurance.
8. Compare the effects that a wage subsidy and a negative income tax would have on the decision to acquire more education that is labour market oriented.
9. Indicate the general equilibrium effects of a wage subsidy on the market wages and work incentives of recipients, and on the income of the rest of society. Assume that the labour supply schedule of transfer recipient labour is upward sloping to the right.

REFERENCES AND FURTHER READINGS

Albin, P. and B. Stein. The constrained demand for public assistance. *JHR* 3 (Summer 1968) 300-311.

Barth, M. Market effects of a wage subsidy. *ILRR* 27 (July 1974) 572-585.

Barth, M. and D. Greenberg. Incentive effects of some pure and mixed transfer systems. *JHR* (Spring 1971) 149-170.

Bishop, J. The general equilibrium impact of alternative antipoverty strategies. *ILRR* 32 (January 1979) 205-223.

Boskin, M. The negative income tax and the supply of work effort. *National Tax Journal* 20 (December 1967) 355-357.

Brehm, C. and T. Saving. The demand for general assistance payments. *AER* 54 (December 1964) 1002-1018. Comment by B. Stein and P. Albin, 57 (June 1967) 575-588.

Browning, E. Alternative programs for income redistribution: the NIT and the NWT. *AER* 63 (March 1973) 38-49.

Burke, V. and A. Townsend. Public welfare and work incentive. Joint Economic Committee, *Studies in Public Welfare*, No. 14. Washington: U.S. Government Printing Office, 1974.

Burtless, G. and J. Hausman. The effect of taxation on labor supply: evaluating the Gary negative income tax experiment. *JPE* 86 (December 1978) 1103-1130.

Cain, G. (ed.). Symposium articles — the graduated work incentive experiment. *JHR* 9 (Spring 1974).

Cain, G. amd H. Watts. *Income Maintenance and Labor Supply.* Chicago: Rand McNally, 1973.

Conlisk, J. Simple dynamic effects in work-leisure choice: a skeptical comment on the static theory. *JHR* 3 (Summer 1968) 324-326.

Cook, P., G. Jump, C. Hodgins and C. Szabo. *Economic Impact of Selected Government Programs Directed Toward the Labour Market.* Ottawa: Economic Council of Canada, 1976.

Garfinkel, I. Income transfer programs and work effort: a review. *Studies in Public Welfare*, Joint Economic Committee. Washington: U.S. Government Printing Office, 1974.

Garfinkel, I. A skeptical note on the optimality of wage subsidy programs. *AER* 63 (June 1973) 447-453.

Garfinkel, I. and S. Masters. *Estimating Labor Supply Effects of Income Maintenance Alternatives.* New York: Academic Press, 1978.

Green C. Implementing income supplements: the case for a tax credit approach, *Canadian Tax Journal* 21 (Sept.-Oct. 1973) 426-440.

Green, C. Negative taxes and the monetary incentives to work: the static theory. *JHR* 3 (Summer 1968) 280-288.

Green, C. *Negative Taxes and the Poverty Problem.* Washington: Brookings, 1967.

Hanoch, G. and M. Honig. The labor supply curve under income maintenance programs. *Journal of Public Economics* 9 (February 1978) 1-16.

Haveman, R. Work-conditioned subsidies as an income maintenance strategy. *Studies in Public Welfare*, Joint Economic Committee. Washington: U.S. Government Printing Office, 1973.

Heckman, J. Effects of child-care programs on women's work effort. *JPE* 82 (March/April 1974) S136-S163.

Hoffman, R. and B. Schiller. Work incentives of the poor: a reconsideration. *R. E. Stats.* 52 (November 1970) 447-449.

Kasper, H. Welfare payments and work incentive. *JHR* 3 (Winter 1968) 86-110.

Kaun, D. A comment on the work-leisure myth. *Review of Radical Political Economy* 1 (May 1969) 85-88.

Keeley, M., P. Robbins, R. Spiegelman and R. West. The labor supply effects and costs of alternative income tax programs. *JHR* 13 (Winter 1978) 3-36.

Keeley, M., P. Robbins, R. Spiegelman and R. West. The estimation of labor supply models using experimental data. *AER* 68 (December 1975) 873-887.

Kesselman, J. Tax effects on job search, training and work effort. *Journal of Public Economics* 6 (October 1976) 255-272.

Kesselman, J. Egalitarianism of earnings and income taxes. *Journal of Public Economics* 5 (April/May 1976) 285-302.

Kesselman, J. A comprehensive approach to income maintenance: SWIFT. *Journal of Public Economics* 2 (February 1973) 59-88.

Kesselman, J. Conditional subsidies in income maintenance. *WEJ* 9 (March 1971) 1-20.

Kesselman, J. Labour supply effects of income, income-work, and wage subsidies. *JHR* 4 (Summer 1969) 275-292.

Kesselman, J. Guaranteeing wages: a modest proposal. *Commonwealth* 89 (March 1969) 700-703.

Kesselman, J. and I. Garfinkel. Professor Friedman meet Lady Rhys-Williams: NIT vs. CIT. *Journal of Public Economics* 10 (October 1978) 179-216.

Killingsworth, M. Must a negative income tax reduce labor supply? *JHR* 11 (Summer 1976) 354-365.

Kurtz, M. and R. Spiegelman. The Seattle experiment. *AER Proceedings* 61 (May 1971) 22-29.

Leuthold, J. The effect of taxation on the hours worked by married women. *ILRR* 31 (July 1978) 520-526.

Leuthold, J. An empirical study of formula income transfers and the work decision of the poor. *JHR* 3 (Summer 1968) 312-323.

Levy, F. The labor supply of female household heads, or AFDC work incentives don't work too well. *JHR* 14 (Winter 1979) 76-97.

Lurie, I. *Integrating Income Maintenance Programs.* New York: Academic Press, 1975.

Masters, S. and I. Garfinkel. *Estimating the Labor Supply Effects of Income-Maintenance Alternatives.* New York: Academic Press, 1978.

Meyer, J. The impact of welfare benefit levels and tax rates on the labor supply of poor women. *R. E. Stats.* 17 (May 1975) 236-237.

Muth, R. *The Evaluation of Selected Present and Potential Poverty Programs.* Study S-244. Arlington: Institute of Defense Analyses, 1966.

Peckman, J. and P. Timpane (eds.). *Work Incentives and Income Guarantee: The New Jersey Negative Income Tax Experiment.* Washington: Brookings, 1975.

Perlman, R. A negative income tax plan for maintaining work incentives. *JHR* 3 (Summer 1968) 289-299.

President's Commission in Income Maintenance Programs. *Technical Studies.* Washington: U.S. Government Printing Office, 1970.

Rea, S. Investment in human capital under a negative income tax. *CJE* 10 (November 1977) 607-620.

Rea, S. Trade-offs between alternative income maintenance programs. *Studies in Public Welfare,* Joint Economic Committee. Washington: U.S. Government Printing Office, 1974.

Rea, S. Incentive effects of alternative negative income tax plans. *Journal of Public Economics* 3 (August 1974) 237-249.

Ribich, T. Negative income taxes and education. *Income Maintenance*, L. Orr and others (eds.). Chicago: Markham, 1971, 308-324.

Rosen, H. Tax illusion and the labor supply of married women. *R. E. Stats.* 58 (May 1976) 167-172.

Rosen, H. Taxes in a labor supply model with joint wage-hours determination. *Econometrica* 44 (May 1976) 485-507.

Swan, N. P. MacRae and C. Steinberg. *Income Maintenance Programs: Their Effect on Labour Supply and Aggregate Demand in the Maritimes.* Ottawa: Economic Council of Canada, 1976.

Tella, A., D. Tella and C. Green. *The Hours of Work and Family Income Response to Negative Income Tax Plans.* Washington: W. E. Upjohn Institute, 1972.

Watts, H. and A. Rees (eds.). *The New Jersey Income Maintenance Experiment.* New York: Academic Press, 1978.

Watts, H. and A. Rees (eds.). *The New Jersey Graduated Work Incentive Experiments,* Vols. 1-3. Madison: University of Wisconsin Institute for Research on Poverty, 1973.

Zeckhauser, R. and P. Schuck. An alternative to the Nixon income maintenance plan. *Public Interest* 19 (Spring 1970) 120-130.

Chapter 4

Labour Force Participation

The labour force participation decision is basically a decision to participate in labour market activities as opposed to other activities such as household work, education or retirement. As such it influences the size and composition of our labour force and it has an impact on household activities, education and retirement programs.

The policy implications of these changes can be dramatic. Changes in the size and composition of our labour force affect our growth and unemployment rates, as well as the occupational and sex composition of the labour force. The latter in turn affect such factors as relative wages, demands for unionization, day care, and equal pay and equal employment opportunity legislation. Changes in household activities can involve family formation and mobility. Retirement programs can be affected in so far as new labour force participants will add contributions to pension funds, while those who retire (i.e. do not participate in the labour force) will be a drain on the funds.

Clearly, various public policy decisions are both affected by, and have an impact on, the labour force participation decision. Consequently, it is useful to be able to forecast changes in labour force participation and to predict the impact of policy changes on this decision. This requires an understanding of the determinants of the labour force participation decision. The basic theoretical framework for analysing this decision is the work-leisure choice model, developed formally in Chapter 2. In this chapter, the framework is presented in a less formal and more heuristic fashion, as it is applied to the labour force participation decision. Before presenting the theory and empirical evidence, however, it is necessary to discuss a variety of definitions associated with the labour force concept.

DEFINING THE LABOUR FORCE

The labour force (LF) basically consists of persons who are working or looking for work: it consists of the employed (E) plus unemployed (U). Those who are not in the labour force (NLF) are usually students, retired people, housewives, female heads of families, and some "discouraged workers" who simply gave up searching for work (according to labour force surveys, the latter are usually not considered as unemployed because they are not actively seeking work). In Canada, estimates of these various groups are based on a monthly survey of the non-institutional, civilian population 15 years and over, excluding the Yukon, Northwest Territories and reservations: these constitute the universe or population (POP) from which the survey samples.

49

By way of definition, then, the overall labour force participation rate (LFPR) is simply that portion of the eligible population that participates in labour force activity, either employed or unemployed: that is, $LFPR \equiv LF/POP \equiv (E + U)/POP$. (The $\equiv$ rather than $=$ sign simply illustrates that this is purely a definitional relationship; it is not a behavioural relationship derived from any underlying theory of labour market behaviour.) The unemployment rate (UR) is simply that portion of the labour force that is unemployed, i.e. $UR \equiv U/LF \equiv U/(E + U)$. This does not include "discouraged workers" who have given up searching for work, since they are usually categorized as outside the labour force. Other definitions can be illustrated by algebraic manipulation; that is,

$$POP \equiv LF + NLF \equiv E + U + NLF \text{ and } U \equiv LF - E.$$

The Canadian Labour Force Survey conducted by Statistics Canada is currently based on a monthly sample of approximately 55,000 households and the results are published monthly in *The Labour Force* (Cat. No. 71-001). Between 1945 and 1952, the survey was quarterly, and in 1976 it was revised substantially: a comprehensive description of the old survey is given in D.B.S. *Canadian Labour Force Survey — Methodology* (Cat. No. 71-504), and the new survey is described in Macredie and Petrie (1976), and Ostry and Zaidi (1979 pp. 4-8). The new survey is more comprehensive and detailed, giving more information on part-time workers and persons who are marginally in or out of the labour force (e.g. unemployed who are not really looking for work and discouraged workers who actually would look for work if they thought that some were available). In addition, the survey asks more questions on the reasons for not working, the methods of job search, and the activities of non workers. The new survey also provides a larger sample so as to give a better provincial and regional breakdown.

While the Labour Force Survey provides the most often used estimates for our labour force and unemployment figures, other sources are available. In particular, the Canadian Census is conducted every ten years, the most recent being in 1971 referring to activity during 1970. The census is more comprehensive (not being based on a sample from a larger population), and consequently includes richer details on such factors as unemployment by industry and occupation. However, its use is limited because it is conducted only every decade and its reliability on labour force questions may be questioned because, unlike the Labour Force Survey, it does not focus only on labour force activity.

LABOUR FORCE PARTICIPATION THEORY

The labour force participation decision is simply one element of labour supply, with the underlying theoretical framework of the work-leisure choice model giving us the economic determinants of the labour supply decision.

The work-leisure model indicated that, other things being equal, more leisure (non-labour-market activities) would be demanded the more income that we have (income effect) and the lower the relative price of leisure (substitution effect). As in our discussion of the work-leisure choice model, leisure is simply a short form for non-labour market activities such as household work, education or retirement.

Applying this to the labour force participation decision, leisure should increase (participation decrease) if we have more income, or if the cost of leisure decreases. The cost of leisure is an opportunity cost: that is, the earnings that are forgone by engaging in leisure as opposed to labour market activities. The higher the forgone earnings, the greater the opportunity cost of leisure, the less leisure demanded, and hence the greater the tendency to participate in labour market activities.

Alternatively stated, an increase in one's potential lifetime earnings will have two opposing effects on the decision to participate in labour force activities. Like all prices, this increased price or opportunity cost of leisure has both an income and a substitution effect. The income effect indicates that, because of the increased earnings, we can buy more of all "normal" commodities including leisure, and hence we participate less in labour market activities. The substitution effect indicates that, because of the higher price or opportunity cost of leisure, we buy less leisure and engage in more labour market activities. The two effects work in the opposite direction; [1] consequently we must appeal to the empirical evidence to see which dominates.

EMPIRICAL EVIDENCE, MARRIED FEMALES

The basic theory of labour force participation is usually tested with data on married women since they have considerable flexibility to respond to the determinants of labour force participation. In addition, their responses have been dramatic in recent years, and this has policy implications for such things as sex discrimination, family formation, and the demand for day-care facilities.

Empirical evidence in both Canada and the United States tends to confirm the expectations based on the economic theory of labour force participation. For Canada, some illustrative figures are given in Table 4.1. Labour force participation rates are higher for married women with a high

---

[1] This is contrary to the "basic law of demand" which states that, for normal goods, the income and substitution effects work in the same direction, so that the rise in the price of a commodity unequivocally reduces the demand for that commodity. The substitution effect reduces our demand as we substitute cheaper commodities for the one whose price has risen. The income effect reduces our demand for all commodities, including the one whose price has risen, because the price rise in effect reduces our real disposable income. In the case of a rise in the price of leisure, however, our real income increases, and hence we can buy more of all commodities including the more expensive leisure.

education, [2] reflecting their high opportunity cost of not working, as well as, perhaps, preferences for labour market as opposed to household work. The impact of the income effect is illustrated by the decline in their participation as family income increases. With higher family income, the household can afford to buy more of everything, including the opportunity to have some members not participate in labour market activities. Alternatively stated, low family income, or perhaps poverty, will compel many married women to engage in labour market activities. The presence of children, especially pre-school age children, is a strong deterrent to the labour force participation of married women. In economic terms, the presence of children raises their "home wage" and hence encourages them to engage in household rather than labour market work.

These results are also confirmed when the determinants of the labour force participation of married women are analysed via multiple regression analysis, which enables one to estimate the separate, partial effect of one variable while holding other factors constant (e.g. Allingham and Spencer (1968), Ostry (1968), Spencer and Featherstone (1970), Spencer (1973), Skoulas (1974), and Gunderson (1976)). For example, in Gunderson (1976,

TABLE 4.1
LABOUR FORCE PARTICIPATION RATES OF MARRIED WOMEN AGE 15-64, HUSBAND PRESENT, CANADA 1971

Education	
Incomplete high school	.36
Complete high school	.50
Complete university	.55
Family income less wife's own earnings	
$3,000 or less	.47
$3,000 — 5,999	.44
$6,000 — 8,999	.44
$9,000 — 11,999	.38
$12,000 — 14,999	.33
$15,000 or over	.27
Child status	
No children	.57
Pre-school children only	.30
School children only	.42
Both pre-school and school children	.25

Source: Extracted from M. Gunderson, "Work Patterns", In *Opportunity for Choice: A Goal for Women in Canada* edited by G. Cook, Ottawa: Statistics Canada, 1976, p.100, 101. (Based on special tabulations from the 1971 Canadian Census.)

---

[2] Empirical studies using the individual as the unit of observation tend to use the education of women to reflect their expected labour market earnings, since for those who do not engage in labour market activities their actual earnings are not observed. An alternative is to estimate their expected wages from a wage equation based on the determinants of their wages. When aggregate data is used, then the average wage in the community can also be used as a measure of the expected earnings of labour force participants.

p.7) the probability of participation was 23 percentage points higher for university graduates as opposed to those who did not complete high school; it was 35 percentage points lower for married women who had both pre-school and school aged children as opposed to those who had no children; and it was 24 percentage points lower for those who had family income of over 15,000 dollars as opposed to less than 3,000 dollars per year.

ADDED AND DISCOURAGED WORKER EFFECTS

Labour force participation is also responsive to changes in unemployment in the economy. Specifically, in periods of high unemployment people may become discouraged from looking for work and drop out of the labour force, returning to the household or to school or perhaps even entering early retirement. This is termed the discouraged worker effect. On the other hand, in periods of high unemployment, some may enter the labour force to supplement family income that may have deteriorated during the period of high unemployment. This is termed the added worker effect.

Changes in unemployment are a proxy for transitory changes in expected wages and other income, and thus the discouraged and added worker effects can be interpreted as short-run substitution and income effects respectively. That is, if unemployment is high, then opportunities in the labour market are lowered temporarily: the price of leisure (opportunity cost or forgone income from not working) is reduced temporarily and hence people substitute leisure for labour market activities. On the other hand, the high unemployment means that it is more likely that family income is lowered temporarily, and additional members may have to participate in labour market activities so as to restore that income.

Since the added (income) and discouraged (substitution) worker effects operate in the opposite direction, it is necessary to appeal to the empirical evidence to see which dominates. Again, most of the empirical tests have been based on data of married women since they are likely to respond to changes in unemployment.

In the U.S., the empirical evidence clearly indicates the dominance of the discouraged worker effect for most married women. That is, in periods of high unemployment, women become discouraged from entering the labour force to look for work, and this dominates any tendency to add themselves to the labour force to maintain their family income. In Canada, however, the empirical evidence is mixed. Studies based on time series data — Proulx (1969), Officer and Anderson (1969), Davies (1971), Swidinsky (1973), Donner and Lazar (1974), and Swan (1974)—often find the added worker effect to dominate, although the discouraged worker effect appears to be becoming more predominant over time. Cross-section studies comparing participation rates across census areas or participation probabilities for different married women tend to show mixed results. Based on data from the early 1960s, Ostry (1968) and Spencer and Featherstone (1970) cite evidence of an added worker effect, while Swidinsky (1973) finds evidence of a weak discouraged worker effect, and Skoulas (1974) finds no relationship between participation and unemployment. Based on more current data, Spencer (1973) and Skoulas (1974) find evidence of a weak discouraged worker effect and Gunderson (1977) finds no evidence of any substantial added worker effect, but possible evidence of a discouraged worker effect.

Clearly the Canadian evidence is by no means conclusive. At most, one may say that the discouraged worker effect appears to be becoming more predominant over time, but that it is not as strong as in the U.S.

HIDDEN UNEMPLOYMENT

The discouraged worker effect also gives rise to the problem of hidden unemployment—a topic that we will return to in a later chapter on unemployment. During a recession when the unemployment rate is high, there will also be a large number of discouraged workers who do not look for work because they believe that no work is available. They are considered as outside of the labour force because they are not working or actively looking for work. However, because they would look for work were it not for the high unemployment rate, they are often considered as the hidden unemployed; that is, people who the unemployment figures tend to miss because they are considered as outside of the labour force rather than as unemployed persons in the labour force.

In this sense, in time of high unemployment our unemployment figures may understate the true unemployment by missing those discouraged workers who constitute the hidden unemployed. Recent developments in our Labour Force Survey, in fact, have been designed to ascertain this hidden or disguised unemployment, and to find out why they are not looking for jobs.

The notion of the discouraged worker is especially important as groups like married women and teenagers become a larger portion of our potential labour force. Such persons often have a loose attachment to the labour force, moving in and out in response to changing economic conditions. They often, but not always, have other family income upon which to rely. For these reasons they are often labelled secondary or marginal workers — unfortunate misnomers if they are used to belittle their employment problems or the contribution to the family income of such workers. This is especially the case if they are contrasted with the terms primary workers or breadwinners, terms that are often used to describe the employment position of males.

However, because of their flexibility with respect to labour market activities, married women and teenagers do constitute a large potential of discouraged workers who would enter the labour force and look for work if employment prospects increased. Hence, the recent emphasis in labour force surveys to find out exactly what these people are doing, and why they are not looking for work.

Clearly the decision to include such persons either in the category of unemployed, or as outside of the labour force, is a difficult one. What is more important, however, than labelling them as either unemployed or outside of the labour force, is to know their approximate magnitude and the degree to which they seriously would look for work if employment prospects improved. Only then can we attach meaning to the phrase "hidden unemployed".

MAJOR LONG-RUN TRENDS

The basic theory of labour force participation also helps explain the major long-run trends that have been observed with respect to labour force participation in Canada. The trends, as shown in Table 4.2, include a fairly stable and high participation rate for middle aged males, a drop in the participation rates of older and younger persons, and an increase in the participation rate of females.

The high and fairly stable participation rate of middle aged males indicates their continuous strong attachment to labour market activities. Until the 1960s, 98 to 99 per cent of males 25-34 participated in labour market activities: the corresponding figures for men 35-64 was 95 to 97 per cent. Only during the 1960s did a very slight fall occur, until by 1971 the participation rates were 93 per cent for males 25-34 and 89 per cent for males 35-64. Clearly, these are still high figures — the highest of any age and sex groups — yet they do indicate that in recent years labour force participation is not the sole activity for these persons. Continuing education and early retirement have extended even into the age groups that were once thought to be exclusively involved in labour market activity.

The continuous drop in the participation rate of older males over 65 — from 60 per cent in 1921 to 24 per cent in 1971 — indicates the increasing tendency to retire from labour market activities. To a large extent this may reflect a pure wealth or income effect; that is, as we become wealthier over time we buy more of everything, including leisure in the form of early retirement. It may also reflect increased social insurance benefits and the availability of private and public pension funds. The decrease in self employment, where retirement comes later and where pensions have not always been arranged, may also have contributed to the growth of early retirement. The early retirement decision is particularly remarkable when one considers that health factors and life expectancy increases have enabled people to participate longer in labour force activities. The fact that they do not indicates the strength of the economic factors inducing retirement, namely increased income and pension coverage. Because of their obvious importance, and the growing policy concern in this area of retirement, these factors are examined in more detail in Chapter 5.

The drop in the participation rates of younger persons 14-19, at least until the 1960s, reflects their increased educational activities, as institutionalized in the higher legal school leaving age and the increase in the length of the school year. Whether this resulted from an increased awareness of the value of education, or simply greater "consumption" of educational activities as society becomes wealthier, remains an open question: presumably both the investment and consumption aspects have contributed. The rural to urban shift that has gone on over time also would reduce participation, since in agricultural sectors younger persons tend to work on the farms.

The fact that the continuous drop in participation of younger males seems to have ceased during the 1960s is interesting. Some of this change may be explained by the fact that the youngest age category in 1971 is 15-19, not 14-19, and presumably even in earlier years many 14-year-olds would be in school and hence not participating in the labour force. In essence, the 15-19 age category is simply likely to have more participants than the 14-19 category, since 14-year-olds tend to be in school.

Perhaps the most dramatic change that has occurred is the increased labour force participation of females. The trend has been continuous —from 16 per cent in 1901 to 40 per cent in 1971. However, the most dramatic changes have occurred during the 1950s and especially the 1960s. Although not shown in the data of Table 4.2, the increase has been most dramatic for married women, increasing, for example, from 25 per cent in 1953 to 40 per cent in 1973.

The situation for women, especially married women, seems to be an

TABLE 4.2
LABOUR FORCE PARTICIPATION RATES BY AGE AND SEX, CANADA, CENSUS YEARS 1901-1971

Year	Sex	14-19[a]	20-24	25-34	35-64	65+	All Ages
1901	Male	n.a.	n.a.	n.a.	n.a.	n.a.	88
	Female	n.a.	n.a.	n.a.	n.a.	n.a.	16
1911	Male	n.a.	n.a.	n.a.	n.a.	n.a.	91
	Female	n.a.	n.a.	n.a.	n.a.	n.a.	19
1921	Male	68	94	98	97	60	90
	Female	30	40	20	12	7	20
1931	Male	57	94	99	97	57	87
	Female	27	47	24	13	6	22
1941	Male	55	93	99	96	48	86
	Female	27	47	28	15	6	23
1951	Male	54	94	98	95	40	84
	Female	34	49	25	20	5	24
1961	Male	41	94	98	95	31	81
	Female	32	51	29	30	6	29
1971	Male	47	87	93	89	24	76
	Female	37	63	45	42	8	40

Note: [a] For 1971, the youngest age group is 15-19.

Source: M. Gunderson, "Work Patterns", in *Opportunity for Choice: A Goal for Women in Canada,* edited by G. Cook, Ottawa: Statistics Canada, 1976, p. 97. Reproduced by permission of the Minister of Supply and Services Canada. Figures for 1971 were computed from the 1971 Census of Canada, *Labour Force and Individual Income,* Cat. No. 94-704, Bulletin 3.1-4, October 1974, Table 9. Figures for the other years are from S. Ostry and F. Denton, *Historical Estimates of the Canadian Labour Force,* 1961 Census Monograph, Ottawa: Queen's Printer, 1967.

exception to the general rule whereby, as labour market earnings have increased over time, participation in the labour market has decreased. In essence, for most other groups—men and younger and older workers—the participation supply schedule has been backward bending (upwards to the left); that is, the income effect of the earnings increase has outweighed the substitution effect. Most groups have used their additional earnings power to buy more leisure and this has outweighed any tendency to buy less leisure because its price — opportunity cost or forgone income — is higher. For women, especially married women, however, the participation supply schedule has been forward sloping (upward to the right) over time, indicating the dominance of the substitution over the income effect.

The dramatic increase in the labour force participation of women reflects a variety of factors, many of them a result as much as a cause of their increased participation. Increased female education that is more labour market oriented makes the opportunity cost of not working much higher. Having fewer children, and having them spaced more closely together, reduces the "home wage" and enables labour force participation. Household work has become easier, due to technological changes and substitutes for household production in such things as child care, cleaning, food preparation, and even entertainment, although there still does not appear to be a sharing of household tasks between husband and wife when both engage in labour market activity (Gunderson (1976, p.96)). The decline in the participation of other groups, namely the young and the old, has helped create a vacuum that the large influx of women has filled: in essence, their increased participation has tended to offset the decreased participation of other groups. The rapid growth of white-collar and part-time jobs has also been conducive to the growth of female employment, as has been the increased social acceptance of women working outside the home. The women's liberation movement itself has helped change these attitudes, both on the part of society at large, and on the part of women themselves. Legislative changes— especially equal pay and equal employment opportunity legislation, as well as unemployment insurance—may have helped make labour force participation more attractive for women although, as we will see in later chapters, their impact may be ambiguous.

Clearly these various factors have had an impact by encouraging the labour force participation of women, and this impact has been sufficiently strong to offset the tendency — observed in most other groups —to participate less as we become wealthier over time. What is particularly noticeable concerning these factors that have influenced the labour force participation of women is that they are both a cause and an effect of their increased participation. This also highlights the importance of the simultaneous and interrelated nature of many household decisions, such as the decision to marry, have children, and participate in the labour force, as well as the choice of occupation and region in which people work. The participation decision, like other labour market and household decisions, cannot be viewed in isolation.

Appendix 4.1

Separating Income and Substitution Effects in Participation Equations

From a linear regression of the labour force participation rate of married women, P, on their non-labour income, Y_H, and on their own expected earnings, Y_W, we estimate the regression coefficients b_y and b_p. This is illustrated in equation (1), where the constant term and other variables are omitted for illustrative purposes.

$$P = b_y Y_H + b_p Y_W \tag{1}$$

The effect on the labour force participation of married women of an increase in their non-labour income (e.g. husband's income) is $\partial P/\partial Y_H = b_y$. This is expected to be negative, reflecting the pure income effect of purchasing more leisure (less participation) from additional income.

The effect on participation of an increase in the expected earnings of women themselves is $\partial P/\partial Y_W = b_p$. This has both an income and a substitution effect working in opposite directions. The substitution effect would increase participation by making the opportunity cost of leisure more expensive, hence inducing women to substitute non-leisure activities (participation) for leisure activities. The income effect reduces participation because with the higher expected income, women would buy more of everything, including leisure. To a certain extent the income effect may be blunted by the fact that in order to buy the leisure they would have to participate in the labour force to earn the income. However, in a sufficiently long time-horizon, women may not participate in a given period because their high expected income enables them to achieve a target level of income by participating for a shorter time period.

In order to separate the income and substitution effects and derive the pure or compensated substitution effect, add and subtract $b_y Y_W$ to the right-hand side of equation (1). This yields

$$P = b_y(Y_H + Y_W) + (b_p - b_y)Y_W \tag{2}$$

Define $Y_F = Y_H + Y_W$ as family income and $b_s = b_p - b_y$ as the pure or compensated substitution effect. Thus

$$P = b_y Y_F + b_s Y_W \tag{3}$$

The effect of an increase in the expected earnings of married women, holding family income constant so that we are calculating a pure substitution effect, is $\partial P/\partial Y_W = b\ s$. Thus to get the pure substitution effect it is necessary to subtract the income effect from the gross price effect: that is, $b_s = b_p - b_y$.

QUESTIONS

1. Given the basic determinants of labour force participation, do you feel that the main trends in labour force participation will continue into the future?

2. Indicate the expected impact on the labour force participation of married women of changes in each of the following factors, other things held constant:

   (a) an increase in the education of women;
   (b) a more equal sharing of household responsibilities between husband and wife;
   (c) a reduction in the average number of children;
   (d) an increased tendency to have children spaced more closely together;
   (e) an increase in the earnings of husbands;
   (f) day care paid out of general tax revenues;
   (g) allowing day care expenses to be tax deductible;
   (h) paying housewives a fixed sum out of general tax revenues for household work.

3. In U.S. studies, and in Canadian empirical studies based on cross-section data, evidence of a net discouraged worker effect tends to be found. However, Canadian studies based on time series data often find evidence of a net added worker effect. How might these differences be explained?

4. Assume that the following regression equation has been estimated where P_W is the labour force participation rate of married women (measured in per cent with the average $\bar{P} = 35.0$), Y_H is husband's income (measured in thousands of dollars with average $\bar{Y}_H = 10$), Y_W is wife's expected income (measured in thousands of dollars with average $\bar{Y}_W = 6$) and u_H is the male unemployment rate (measured in per cent with average $\bar{u}_H = 6.0$):

$$P_W = -7.0Y_H + 18Y_W - .5u_H$$

   (a) What is the expected effect of an increase of 1,000 dollars in the income of husbands on the participation rate of their wives?
   (b) What is the expected effect of an increase of 1,000 dollars in the income of the wives themselves?
   (c) Decompose the latter impact into its separate income and substitution effects.
   (d) Given the magnitude of the latter two effects, what would be the impact on female participation of an equal pay policy that increased the expected earnings of females by 1,000 dollars while at the same time decreasing the expected earnings of their husbands by 1,000 dollars?

(e) Calculate the pure income and the gross or uncompensated wage elasticities of participation, evaluated at the means.

(f) Does this equation shed any light on why the labour force participation of married women has increased over time, even though their non-labour income has also increased?

(g) What does the equation tell us about the relative importance of the added and discouraged worker effect?

(h) If the unemployment rate of males were to drop to a "full employment" of 2 per cent, what would have been the participation rate of married women?

(i) What does this tell us about hidden unemployment that may exist when the unemployment rate is above the full employment level?

REFERENCES AND FURTHER READINGS

Abbott, M. and O. Ashenfelter. Labor supply, commodity demand, and the allocation of time. *R. E. Studies* 42 (October 1977) 389-411.

Adams, A. Who's in the labor force? *AER Proceedings* 69 (May 1979) 38-42.

Albani, E., D. Ellante and M. Jackson. Primary workers, secondary workers and aggregate wages. *SEJ* 42 (January 1967) 471-479.

Albani, E. and M. Jackson. The job vacancy unemployment ratio and labour force participation. *ILRR* 29 (April 1976) 412-419.

Allingham, J. *Women Who Work: Part 1, The Relative Importance of Age, Education and Marital Status for Participation in the Labour Force.* Special Labour Force Studies No. 5. Ottawa: Dominion Bureau of Statistics, 1967.

Allingham, J. *The Demographic Background to Change in the Number and Composition of Female Wage Earners in Canada.* Special Labour Force Studies, Series B, No. 1. Ottawa: Dominion Bureau of Statistics, 1967.

Allingham, J. and B. Spencer. *Women Who Work: Part 2, Married Women in the Labour Force: The Influence of Age, Education, Child-bearing Status and Residence.* Special Labour Force Studies, Series B, No. 2. Ottawa: Dominion Bureau of Statistics, 1968.

Barth, P. Unemployment and labor force participation. *SEJ* 34 (January 1968) 375-382.

Bednarzik, R. and D. Klein. Labor force trends: a synthesis and analysis. *MLR* 100 (November 1977) 3-11.

Bell, D. Why participation rates of black and white wives differ. *JHR* 9 (Fall 1974) 465-479.

Ben-Porath, Y. Labor-force participation rates and the supply of labor. *JPE* 81 (May/June 1973) 697-704.

Berkowitz, M. and W. Johnson. Health and labor force participation. *JHR* 9 (Winter 1974) 117-128.

Berg, S. Backward sloping labour supply functions in dual economies: the African case. *QJE* 75 (August 1961) 468-492.

Berg, S. and T. Dalton. Labor force participation in goods and services. *R. E. Stats.* 57 (November 1975) 518-522.

Black, S. and R. Russel. Participation functions and potential labor force. *ILRR* 24 (October 1970) 84-94.

Bonin, J. and W. Davis. Labor force responsiveness to short-run variations in economic opportunity. *SEJ* 28 (October 1971) 161-172.

Bowen, W. and T. Finegan. *The Economics of Labor Force Participation.* Princeton, N.J.: Princeton University Press, 1969.

Bowen, W. and T. Finegan. Labor force participation and unemployment. *Employment Policy and the Labor Market*, A. Ross (ed.). Berkeley: University of California Press, 1965.

Cain, G. Unemployment and the labor force participation rate of secondary workers. *ILRR* 20 (January 1967) 275-297.

Cain, G. *Married Women in the Labor Force.* Chicago: University of Chicago Press, 1966.

Cain G. and H. Watts. *Income Maintenance and Labor Supply: Econometric Studies.* Chicago: Rand McNally, 1973.

Coen, R. Labor force and unemployment in the 1920's and 1930's: a re-examination based on post-war experience. *R. E. Stats.* 55 (February 1973) 46-55.

Cohen, M., R. Lerman and S. Rea. Area employment conditions and labor-force participation: a microstudy. *JPE* 79 (September/October 1971) 1151-1157,

Cohen, M., S. Rea and R. Lerman. *A Micro Model of Labor Supply.* BLS Staff Paper. Washington: U.S. Government Printing Office, 1970.

Cooper, S. and D. Johnson. Comments on the Dernburg, Strand, Duchler approach. *IR* 6 (October 1966).

Cullison, W. An employment pressure index as an alternative measure of labor market condition. *R. E. Stats.* 57 (February 1975) 115-121.

Davis, N. *Cycles and Trends in Labour Force Participation, 1953-1968.* Special Labour Force Studies, Series B, No. 5. Ottawa: Dominion Bureau of Statistics, 1971.

Davis, N. *Some Methods of Analysing Cross-Classified Census Data: The Case of Labour Force Participation Rates.* Special Labour Force Studies, Series B, No. 3. Ottawa: Dominion Bureau of Statistics, 1969.

Denton, F. A simulation model of month-to-month labour force movement in Canada. *IER* 14 (June 1973) 293-311.

Denton, F. and S. Ostry. *Historical Estimates of the Canadian Labour Force.* 1961 Census Monograph. Ottawa: Dominion Bureau of Statistics, 1967.

Dernburg, T. and K. Strand. Hidden unemployment 1953- 1962. *AER* 56 (March 1966) 71-95.

Devens, R. Labor force trends: a bibliography. *MLR* 100 (October 1977) 12-14.

Donner, A. and F. Lazar. Employment expectations and labour force participation in Canada. *RI/IR* 29 (No. 2, 1974) 320-330.

Douglas, P. and E. Schoenberg. Studies in the supply curve of labour. *JPE* (February 1937) 45-79.

Durand, J. *Labor Force in the United States, 1890- 1960*. New York: Social Science Research Council, 1948.

Elizaga, J. The participation of women in the labour force of Latin America: fertility and other factors. *ILR* 109 (May/June 1974) 519-538.

Fair, R. Labor force participation, wage rates, and money illusion. *R. E. Stats.* 53 (May 1971) 164-168.

Feldstein, M. Estimating the supply curve of working hours. *Oxford Economic Papers* 20 (March 1968) 74-80.

Fellegi, J., G. Gray and R. Platek. The new design of the Canadian labour force survey. *Journal of American Statistical Association* (May 1967) 465-481.

Fields, J. A comparison of intercity differences in the labor force participation ratio of married women in 1970, with 1940, 1950 and 1960. *JHR* 11 (Fall 1976) 568-577.

Finegan, T. Improving our information on discouraged workers. *MLR* 101 (September 1978) 15-25.

Fleisher, B. The economics of labor force participation: a review article. *JHR* 6 (Spring 1971) 139-148.

Fleisher, B. and G. Rhodes. Unemployment and the labor force participation of married women: a simultaneous model. *R. E. Stats.* 68 (November 1976) 398-406.

Gendreau, N. Youth participation in the labour force: 1953-1970. *Notes on Labour Statistics*. Statistics Canada #72-207, 1971.

Gilroy, C. Counting the labor force with the current population survey. *AER Proceedings* 69 (May 1979) 48-53.

Goodman, J. Spectral analysis of the dependence of labor force participation on unemployment and wages. *R. E. Stats.* 61 (August 1974) 390-393.

Gramm, W. The labor force decision of married female teachers: a discriminant analysis approach. *R. E. Stats.* 55 (August 1973) 341-348. Comment by A. Baqueiro, J. Breen, D. Mead and D. Wise and reply 58 (May 1976) 241-244.

Gunderson, M. Logit estimates of labour force participation based on census cross tabulations. *CJE* 10 (August 1977) 453-462.

Gunderson, M. Work Patterns. *Opportunity for Choice: A Goal for Women in Canada*, G. Cook (ed.). Ottawa: Statistics Canada, 1976, 94-103.

Hansen, W.L. Cyclical sensitivity of the labor force. *AER* 51 (June 1961) 299-309.

Hartley, M. and N. Revanker. Labour supply under uncertainty and the rate of unemployment. *AER* 64 (March 1974) 170-175. Comments by D. Sjoquist 66 (May 1976) 929-930 and G. Yaniv 69 (March 1979) 203-205.

Heckman, J. A partial survey of recent research on the labor supply of women. *AER Proceedings* 68 (May 1978) 200-207.

Heckman, J. Shadow prices, market wages and labor supply. *Econometrica* 42 (July 1974) 679-694.

Heckman, J. and R. Willis. A beta-logistic model for the analysis of segmented labor force participation of married women. *JPE* 85 (February 1977) 27-58. Comment by J. Mincer and H. Ofek and reply 87 (February 1979) 197-211.

Hughes, B. Direct income and substitution effects in participation decision. *JPE* 80 (July/August 1972) 793-795.

King, A. Industrial structure, the flexibility of working hours, and women's labor force participation. *R. E. Stats.* 60 (August 1978) 399-407.

Korbel, J. Labor force entry and attachment of young people. *Journal of American Statistical Association* (March 1966).

Kraft, A. Preference orderings as determinants of the labor force behaviour of married women. *WEJ* 11 (September 1973) 270-284.

Kreps, J. and R. Clark. *Sex, Age and Work.* Baltimore: Johns Hopkins Press, 1975.

Kuch, P. and S. Sharir. Added and discouraged worker effects in Canada. *CJE* 11 (February 1978) 112-120.

Leigh, D. Labor force participation of male youths being in low-income urban areas. *ILRR* 27 (January 1974) 242-248.

Long, C. *The Labor Force Under Changing Income and Employment.* Princeton, N.J.: Princeton University Press, 1958.

Macredie, I. and B. Petrie. *The Canadian Labour Force Survey.* Ottawa: Labour Force Survey Division, Statistics Canada, 1976.

Mincer, J. Determining the number of hidden unemployed. *MLR* 96 (March 1973) 27-30.

Mincer, J. Labor force participation. *International Encyclopedia of Social Science*, Vol. 8. New York: Macmillan, 1968.

Mincer, J. Labor force participation and unemployment. A review of recent evidence. *Prosperity and Unemployment*, R. and M. Gordon (eds.). New York: John Wiley and Sons, 1966.

Mincer, J. Labor force participation of married women. *Aspects of Labor Economics.* Princeton, N.J.: Princeton University Press, 1962.

Mohoney, T. Factors determining the labor force participation of married women. *ILRR* 14 (July 1961).

Montague, J. and J. Vandercamp. *A Study of Labour Market Adjustment.* Vancouver: University of British Columbia Institute of Industrial Relations, 1966.

Mooney, J. Urban poverty and labor force participation. *AER* 57 (March 1967) 104-119. Comment by G. Cain and J. Mincer and reply 59 (March 1969) 85-96.

Morgenstern, R. and W. Hamovitch. Labour force supply of married women in part-time and full-time employment. *ILRR* 30 (October 1976) 59-67).

Mujahid, G. The measurement of disguised unemployment: a comment. *CJE* 6 (February 1973) 128-129.

Officer, L. and P. Anderson. Labour force participation in Canada. *CJE* 2 (May 1969) 278-287.

Offner, P. Labor force participation in the ghetto. *JHR* 4 (Fall 1972) 460-481.

Okuguchi, K. The labour force participation ratio and the speed of adjustment. *Economica* 35 (November 1969).

Ostry, S. *The Female Worker in Canada*. 1961 Census Monograph. Ottawa: Dominion Bureau of Statistics, 1968.

Ostry, S. *Provincial Differences in Labour Force Participation*. 1961 Census Monograph. Ottawa: Dominion Bureau of Statistics, 1968.

Ostry, S. and M. Zaidi. *Labour Economics in Canada*. 3rd Ed. Toronto: Macmillan, 1979.

Otsuki, T. Short-run behavior of the labor force in response to the fluctuations in aggregate demand. *IRRA* (December 1970) 70-75.

Parker, J. and L. Shaw. Labor force participation within metropolitan areas. *SEJ* 34 (April 1968) 538-547.

Parnes, H. Labor force participation and labor mobility. *A Review of Industrial Relations Research*, W. Ginsburg (ed.). Madison, Wisconsin: Industrial Relations Research Association, 1970.

Pfannestiel, M. Adjustment of the size of the labor force. *AER* 63 (May 1968) 212-226.

Proulx, Pierre-Paul. La variabilité cyclique des taux de participation à la main d'ouvre au Canada. *CJE* 2 (May 1969) 268-277. Comments by L. Officer and P. Anderson, and R. Swidinsky, 3 (February 1970) 145-151.

Rea, S. Unemployment and the supply of labor. *JHR* 9 (Spring 1974) 279-289.

Rosen, R. Working wives: an economic study. *Studies in Household Economic Behavior*. New Haven, Conn.: Yale University Press, 1958.

Rosen, S. and F. Welch. Labor supply and income redistribution. *R. E. Stats.* 53 (August 1971) 278-282.

Rosenblum, M. Discouraged workers and unemployment. *MLR* 97 (September 1974) 28-29.

Ruggeri, G. Hidden unemployment by age and sex in Canada. *RI/IR* 30 (No. 2, 1975) 181-195.

Sandell, S. Attitudes towards market work and the effect of wage rates on the lifetime labor supply of married women. *JHR* 12 (Summer 1977) 379-386.

Sawers, L. Urban poverty and labor force participation. *AER* 62 (June 1972) 414-421.

Schweitzer, S. and R. Smith. The persistence of the discouraged worker effect. *ILRR* 27 (January 1974) 249-260.

Sjedule, T., N. Skoulas, and K. Newton. *The Impact of Economy-Wide Changes on the Labour Force: An Econometric Analysis*. Ottawa: Economic Council of Canada, 1976.

Skoulas, N. *Determinants of the Participation Rate of Married Women in the Canadian Labour Force*. Ottawa: Information Canada, 1974.

Sloan, F. Physician supply behaviour. *ILRR* 28 (July 1974) 549-560.

Sloan, F. and S. Richupan. Short-run supply responses of professional nurses. *JHR* 10 (Spring 1975) 241-257.

Sobol, M. A dynamic analysis of labour force participation of married women of childbearing age. *JHR* (Fall 1973) 497-505.

Spencer, B. Determinants of the labor force participation of married women: a micro-study of Toronto households. *CJE* 6 (May 1973) 222-238.

Spencer, B. and D. Featherstone. *Married Female Labour Force Participation: A Micro Study*. Special Labour Force Studies, Series B, No. 4. Ottawa: Dominion Bureau of Statistics, 1970.

Stern, R. Reasons for non-participation in the labor force. *MLR* 90 (July 1967) 22-27.

Strand, K. and T. Dernberg. Cyclical variation and labor force participation. *R. E. Stats.* 46 (November 1964) 378-391.

Strand, K., T. Dernberg, and J. Strucker. Forecasting labor force participation rates: a parametric approach. *IR* 41 (February 1965) 69-83.

Strober, M. Wives' labour force behaviour and family consumption patterns. *AER Proceedings* 67 (February 1977) 419-427.

Sum, A. Female labor force participation: why projections have been too low. *MLR* 100 (July 1977) 18-24.

Swan, N. The responses of labor supply to demand in Canadian regions. *CJE* 7 (August 1974) 418-433.

Swindinsky, R. Unemployment and labour force participation: the Canadian experience. *RI/IR* 28 (No. 1, 1973) 56-75.

Tella, A. Labor force sensitivity to employment by age and sex. *IR* 4 (February 1965) 69-83.

Tella, A. The relations of labour force to employment. *ILRR* 17 (April 1964) 454-469.

Uhler, R. and R. Kunin. A theory of labor force participation. *IR* 11 (February 1972) 107-115.

Van Til, S. Race, poverty and labour participation. *Social Science Quarterly* 55 (December 1974) 657-669.

Vatter, H. On the folklore of the backward sloping supply curve. *ILRR* 14 (July 1961) 578-586. Comment by R. Finegan and reply 15 (January 1962) 230-236.

Wachter, M. Intermediate swings in labor-force participation. *BPEA* (No. 2, 1977) 545-576.

Wachter, M. A labor supply model for secondary workers. *R. E. Stats.* 54 (May 1972) 141-151.

Wales, T. Estimation of a labor supply curve for self- employed business proprietors. *IER* 14 (February 1973) 69-80.

Walter, J. Labor force participation of deprived urban youth in a developing country. *American Economist* 19 (February 1973) 60-63.

Woytinsky, W. *Additional Workers and the Volume of Unemployment in the Depression.* Washington: Social Science Research Council, 1940.

Chapter 5

Retirement Decision and Pensions

INTRODUCTION

The retirement decision is essentially a decision by older persons not to participate in the labour force. Hence it is amenable to analysis utilizing labour force participation theory, and its underlying work-leisure choice model. The retirement decision is treated separately simply because it is an area of increasing policy concern and, as the references indicate, it has developed its own empirical literature.

The notion of retirement has many meanings, ranging from outright leaving of the labour force, to a reduction of hours worked, to simply moving into a less onerous job. The process itself may also be gradual, beginning with a reduction in time worked (perhaps associated with a job change) and ending in full retirement. Throughout this chapter, we will generally talk of retirement as leaving the labour force; however, the importance of various forms of quasi-retirement and the often gradual nature of the retirement process should be kept in mind.

Policy Importance

The policy importance of the retirement decision stems from the fact that it can have an impact on so many elements of social policy. For the individuals themselves, and their families, the retirement decision has implications ranging from their financial status to their psychological state. For the economy as a whole, the retirement decision also has macroeconomic implications with respect to such factors as private savings, unemployment, and the size of the labour force, all of which have implications for the level of national income.

In addition, there is concern over the solvency of public pension funds if large numbers retire and few are in the labour force to pay into the fund. This problem may be especially acute around the turn of the century, when the post World War II baby boom population reaches potential retirement age and, depending on fertility factors and patterns of female labour force participation,[1] when there may be few other participants in the labour force paying into the funds. The problem will be compounded if high unemploy-

---

[1] The impact on public pension funds of the increase in female labour force participation, documented in Chapter 4, is potentially important but difficult to predict with certainty. Their increased participation implies a contribution to the fund, as they contribute through payroll taxes and employer contributions, and as their working means that they are not eligible for dependency benefits. On the other hand, they will become eligible to withdraw from the fund

ment and low productivity increases result in low labour market earnings and hence a smaller tax base for social insurance pensions.

The policy importance of the retirement decision is further heightened by the fact that it is an area where policy changes can affect the retirement decision. This is especially the case with respect to such "policy parameters"[2] as the mandatory retirement age and the nature and availability of pension funds. However, to know the expected impact of changes in these factors, we must know the theoretical determinants of the retirement decision, and the empirical evidence on the retirement response.

THEORETICAL DETERMINANTS OF RETIREMENT

Mandatory Retirement Age

As indicated by Kittner (1977, p. 60), the term mandatory retirement provisions refers to both compulsory retirement provisions and automatic retirement provisions. Under the latter, people *have* to retire at a specific age and they cannot be retained by the company. Under compulsory retirement provisions, however, the company can compel the worker to retire at a specific age, but it can also retain the services of a worker, usually on a year-to-year basis.

The term mandatory retirement is somewhat of a misnomer, since there is no magic age embodied in *legislation* that says a person *must* retire by a specific age. The mandatory retirement age may be part of an employer's personnel policy, or it may be negotiated in a collective agreement. In addition, there is an age at which public pensions become available, although they do not *prevent* people from continuing to work. As well, aspects of labour legislation may not apply to workers beyond a specific age. Thus the so-called mandatory retirement age—of which age 65 appears to be the magic number in North America — is really a result of personnel policy and is influenced, but not determined, by government programs. It is neither fixed nor immutable.

This is illustrated by the fact that Europe and the United States appear

upon retirement. The net impact of these opposing forces is an empirical proposition, depending on such factors as the size of the payroll tax for their contributions, their expected length of stay in the labour force, their expected retirement age, and their life expectancy after retirement.

Similarly, the impact on public pension funds of the tendency towards reduced labour force participation (i.e. early retirement) on the part of older males is also an empirical proposition. Their early retirement implies a loss to the fund in that they are withdrawing retirement benefits for a longer period and they are not contributing to the fund since they are not working. On the other hand, they are withdrawing at a reduced rate if they retire before the retirement age that gives them the full benefit rate.

[2] The term policy parameters refers to elements of public policy that can be changed, such as a tax rate or an income guarantee, or the age at which a person becomes eligible for income support.

to be moving in the opposite direction with respect to changes in the mandatory retirement age. Presumably to help alleviate problems of youth unemployment, in Europe the tendency is to encourage a lowering of the retirement age. In the U.S., on the other hand, the trend seems to be in the opposite direction. Recent legislation has removed any mandatory retirement age in the federal public service and has forbidden a mandatory retirement age below 70 in most other sectors. Certainly, workers can retire before age 70, and employers may try to induce them to do so. Nevertheless, they cannot be forced to retire against their wishes.

The fact that the raising of the mandatory retirement age in the U.S. came at a time when human rights were receiving emphasis in government policy suggests that one of the motivating factors may have been concern over the human rights of older workers. For many, the psychological implications of abrupt retirement can be extremely harmful, especially in a society where the elderly are seldom afforded any other special position within the community and where the extended family is no longer prominent. The raising of the mandatory retirement age also may have been motivated by concern over the financial solvency of public retirement funds as proportionately more people reach retirement age, and draw on the funds at the same time as there are proportionately fewer persons contributing to the funds.

Whatever the motivation for the raising of the mandatory retirement age, it can obviously have a potential impact on the retirement decision. This impact will probably be greatest in those occupations that provide the greatest satisfaction from work itself, notably the large and growing professional and white-collar sector. For those occupations with less intrinsic work satisfaction, notably blue-collar assembly-line work, the trend will probably remain towards early retirement, in spite of an increase in the mandatory retirement age.[3]

Raising the mandatory retirement age will also alter company personnel policies since companies can expect to have older workers remaining longer in employment. Consequently, companies would probably be more selective in their hiring decision and they may adapt job conditions to older workers. In addition, companies would have to develop policies for redundant older workers who do not want to retire. Such policies could range from dismissal procedures to encouraging retirement through attractive pension or termination schemes to altering job conditions so that the older workers are not redundant. Actuarial adjustments in pensions may also have to be made.

Youth unemployment would also be affected by raising the mandatory

---

[3] Barfield and Morgan (1978) report, for example, that in the U.S. auto industry large numbers of workers retired early in response to negotiated supplementary early retirement benefits and the "30 and out" provisions that enabled workers to retire on a substantial pension after 30 years of service. In addition, their survey results indicated that younger persons were more likely to report plans to retire early, perhaps because of work dissatisfaction or a feeling of security with respect to their expected income and savings.

retirement age. To the extent that older workers postpone retirement, they may reduce the number of jobs available for youth. However, to the extent that companies become reluctant to hire older people if the mandatory retirement age is removed, they may hire more youths. The effect on youth unemployment is therefore ambiguous.

As well as being an exogenous determinant of the retirement decision, the mandatory retirement age is also itself endogenously determined by the retirement decision. As indicated earlier, it is neither fixed nor immutable. It can change in response to other basic forces that affect the retirement decision. In essence, it can be regarded as the institutional embodiments of a collective retirement decision, although concern with the rigidity of a specific mandatory retirement age for all people suggests that this collective decision is certainly not shared by all. What then are these other basic forces that affect the retirement decision, either directly as people are induced to retire, or indirectly as pressure is exerted to change the mandatory retirement age or the age at which various retirement benefits become available?

Wealth and Earnings

Economic theory, in particular the work-leisure choice theory as discussed earlier, indicates that the demand for leisure—as indicated, for example, by the decision to retire early—is positively related to one's wealth, and is related to expected earnings in an indeterminate fashion. The wealth effect is positive, reflecting a pure income effect: with more wealth we buy more of all normal goods, including leisure in the form of retirement. The impact of expected earnings is indeterminate, reflecting the opposing influences of income and substitution effects. An increase in expected earnings increases the income forgone if one retires and therefore raises the (opportunity) cost of retirement: this has a pure substitution effect reducing the demand for retirement leisure. On the other hand, an increase in expected earnings also means an increase in expected wealth and, just like wealth from non-labour sources, this would increase the demand for retirement leisure. Since the income and substitution effects work in opposite directions, then the impact on retirement of an increase in expected earnings is ultimately an empirical proposition. Thus the increase in our earnings that has gone on over time, and that presumably will continue, should have an indeterminate effect on the retirement decision.

Social Insurance Pension

By altering our wealth and net earnings position, social insurance schemes can also affect the retirement decision. Social insurance [4] refers to public

---

[4] The terminology becomes confusing because the social insurance scheme in the U.S. comes under the *Social Security Act*, passed in 1935. However, in addition to retirement, the Act covers disability, medical care for the aged, and more recently Supplementary Security Income which is really a national minimum welfare payment. In spite of these other features of the Act, social insurance in the U.S. is generally referred to as social security. In Europe,

pension schemes that are financed by compulsory employer and employee payroll contributions, and that pay earnings-related pensions to those who qualify by virtue of their age and work experience. As the term "insurance" implies, receipts depend on contributions, and the fund is usually designed to be self-financing without support from general tax revenues.

Other Pension Schemes

Other pensions often can be received at the same time as the social insurance pension. In particular, universal pensions are a flat rate paid out of general tax revenues to persons who reach a specified age. Receipt of the pension is not earnings related in the sense that it does not depend on having worked, nor is receipt of the pension means-tested since it is a flat rate irrespective of income or need. The term demogrant is often applied to this type of program whereby a flat rate is given to a specific demographic group—in this case, all those over the specified age. Popular parlance often uses the term "old-age pension" because receipt is forthcoming at a specific age, or "government pension" because it comes from general tax revenues rather than payroll taxes.

In addition to social insurance and universal pensions, private pensions may also exist. They can be arranged through employment — often termed "company pensions"—or through private financial institutions. They are really a form of private savings, earmarked for retirement. A fourth pension system — social assistance — may also be available to those who qualify through an age and means test, indicating financial need. Such social assistance is really a form of "welfare" payment out of general tax revenues, and is designed to supplement the income of the elderly who are in need.

All of the various pension schemes can have a potential impact on work incentives and hence the retirement decision. Social assistance pensions will have the same potential impact as welfare, and universal pensions will have the same potential impact as a demogrant, both of which have been discussed in Chapter 3. The retirement decision can also be affected by features of private pensions, for example the right to retire on a full company pension at the age of 55, or after 30 years of service.

Features of Social Insurance

Social insurance pensions have received particular attention in recent years because many of their features are ones that can induce early retirement. Social insurance usually involves payment of an earnings-related pension upon retirement; however, if the recipient continues to work and earn income, then the pension gets reduced. This pension reduction — often termed the *retirement test* or work-income test — is really an implicit tax on earnings. It is implicit in that it involves forgoing pension payments as one earns additional income. In addition, there is usually an explicit payroll tax on earnings used to finance the social insurance fund.

---

however, social security generally refers to all income maintenance schemes, including social insurance, but also including family benefit schemes and public assistance or welfare.

As Kirkpatrick (1974) indicates, the retirement test tends to be prevelant in the vast majority of countries with social insurance. Developing economies usually require complete withdrawal from the labour force in order to receive the pension (i.e., implicit 100 per cent tax on earnings) mainly because such countries cannot afford to pay pensions to people who also work. On the other hand, some countries with the longest history of social insurance schemes have no retirement test, allowing the person to retain their full earnings and pension. The motivation for this may be different: in France it appears to be because pension benefits are low and earnings are needed to supplement income; in Germany it appears to be because of a desire to encourage the work ethic.

In the Canada Pension Plan the retirement test was eliminated in 1975. In the U.S., recipients who work are allowed to keep their full pension as long as their earnings do not exceed a specific amount; thereafter, pension benefits are reduced by $.50 for every $1.00 earned (50 per cent implicit tax) up to another specified amount, and after this pensions are reduced by $1.00 for every $1.00 earned (100 per cent implicit tax).

Effect on Retirement

These features of the Canadian and American social insurance schemes can have a substantial impact on the retirement decision. The pension itself, like all fixed benefit payments, has a pure income effect inducing retirement. In addition, for those who work, the implicit tax of the pension reduction associated with the retirement test, and the explicit payroll tax used to finance the scheme, both lower the returns to work and hence make retirement more financially attractive. That is, both taxes involve a substitution effect towards retirement because the opportunity cost of leisure in the form of retirement is lowered by the amount of the tax on forgone earnings. To be sure, the tax on earnings also involves an income effect working in the opposite direction; that is, our reduced after-tax income means we can buy less of everything including leisure in the form of retirement. However, this income effect is outweighed by the income effect of the pension itself, since for all potential recipients their income is *at least* as high when social insurance is available. Thus, as with the negative income tax plans analysed in Chapter 3, both the substitution effect and the (net) income effect of the features of social insurance serve to unambiguously induce retirement.

Modelling Social Insurance in Work-Leisure Framework

These features of social insurance and their impact on retirement can be modelled somewhat more formally, along the lines of the work-leisure framework developed in Chapter 2. With Y defined as income after taxes and transfers, W the wage rate, T the maximum amount of leisure (L) available, B the pension received upon retiring, p the explicit payroll tax used to finance social insurance, and t the implicit tax involved in the pension reduction through the retirement test, the budget constraint with social insurance is:

$$Y = B + (1 - p - t)W(T - L)$$

This can be compared to the constraint without social insurance, which is:

$$Y = W(T - L).$$

The new budget constraint is illustrated in Figure 5.1 for various possible social insurance schemes. Figure 5.1(a) illustrates the case when there is no retirement test; that is, the recipient is given a pension and is allowed to work without forgoing retirement. (For simplicity, the payroll tax for financing the pension has been ignored. With the payroll tax as a fixed percentage of earnings, the budget constraint would have rotated downwards from the point B.) The new budget constraint is $Y = B + W(T - L)$ when $p = 0$ and $t = 0$. Such a pension scheme simply has a pure income effect, encouraging potential recipients to retire. Although not shown in the diagram, the new utility function would be tangent to the new budget constraint, at a point such as E_p above and to the right of the original point E_o. The new point may be at B, in which case the recipient retired completely, or it may be at a point like E_p, signifying partial retirement, or it may be at a point vertically above E_o, in which case the recipient continued to work the same as before and received the full pension.

Figure 5.1(b) illustrates the new budget constraint under a full retirement test whereby the pension recipient is required to give up to $1.00 of pension for every $1.00 earned. This implicit 100% tax rate makes the budget constraint similar to the one for welfare discussed in Chapter 3, and the adverse work incentive effects are similar. In particular, there will be a strong incentive to retire completely (move to point B).

The typical case with a partial retirement test is illustrated in Figure 5.1(c). The first arm of the budget constraint, TB, indicates the pension benefits payable upon complete retirement. (Income is $Y_b = TB$ when leisure is OT.) The second arm, BC, illustrates that up to a specific amount of labour market earnings, $Y_c - Y_b$, for working $T - L_c$, the recipient may keep the full pension benefits of Y_b ($=TB$), so that his total income with pension and labour market earnings could be up to Y_c. The new arm of the budget constraint is parallel to the original constraint of TY_m because the implicit tax is zero; that is, recipients who work keep their full labour market earnings.

The third arm, CD, illustrates the implicit tax that is involved when the recipient is required to give back a portion of the pension for the additional labour market earnings of $Y_d - Y_c$ that results from the additional work of $L_c - L_d$. An implicit tax of 50% results in the slope of CD being one-half of the slope of the original constraint TY_m; that is, for every dollar earned, the recipient forgoes $.50 in pension. When the recipient's labour earnings exceed $Y_d - Y_b$, then the pension is reduced by the same amount of the additional earnings and the fourth arm of the budget constraint is the horizontal portion DE, reflecting the 100% implicit tax rate for any additional work activity of $L_d - L_e$. At the point E, the person would no longer receive any pension, and any additional work activity of $L_e - 0$ would result in additional income as shown by the fifth arm of the budget constraint EY_m.

Figure 5.1   Budget Constraints Under Social Insurance Pensions
(Assuming payroll tax p = 0)

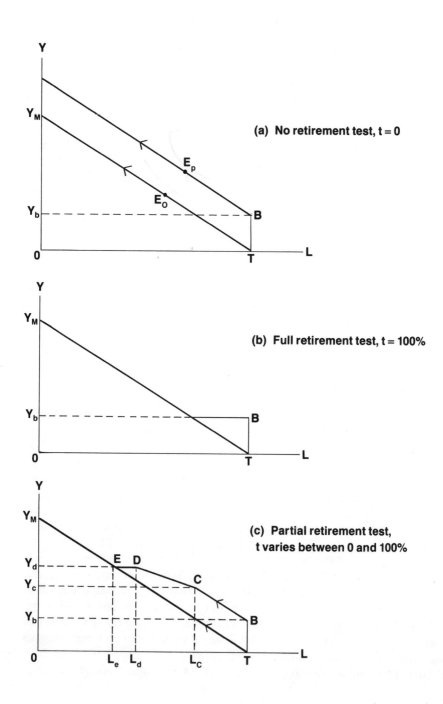

(a) No retirement test, t = 0

(b) Full retirement test, t = 100%

(c) Partial retirement test,
     t varies between 0 and 100%

The work incentive effects of the new budget constraint, $TBCDEY_m$, are such as to unambiguously induce retirement. Basically two things have happened. The budget constraint has shifted outward (upward to the right) from the original constraint of TY_m and this has a wealth or income effect encouraging the purchase of more leisure in the form of retirement. In addition, the slope of the new budget constraint is always equal to or less than the original constraint; that is, the opportunity cost of leisure is reduced and this would encourage the substitution of leisure for other commodities. Both the income and the substitution effect of the partial retirement test work in the same direction to encourage early retirement.

Obviously not all eligible people respond immediately to the incentive effects of the partial retirement test. The analysis is complicated by the existence of private pension plans, early retirement schemes, and by the fact that pension receipts are often a portion of previous earnings.[5] Nevertheless, the fact remains that social insurance pensions as they presently exist in North America theoretically will encourage early retirement on the part of some individuals.

Health and Other Determinants of Retirement

In addition to the mandatory retirement age, wealth and earnings, and the existence of social insurance and other pensions, the retirement decision can be affected by other factors. The changing nature of work towards more white-collar jobs and away from physical tasks may make it feasible for many to work longer. As well, the decline of the extended family may make retirement less attractive. On the other hand, as Long (1958) pointed out, men may be induced into early retirement to the extent that their jobs are competed away by the influx of women into the labour force.

Of prime importance in the retirement decision, however, is the potential impact of health. People approaching the usual retirement age obviously can be subject to health problems that could encourage them to retire. This may be the case, particularly if their accumulated wealth or pension income enables them to retire at a reasonable income. The various determinants of the retirement decision are obviously interrelated.

EMPIRICAL EVIDENCE

The empirical evidence on the determinants of the retirement decision is reviewed in both Campbell and Campbell (1976), and Boskin (1977). Basically, there have been two techniques — survey interviews and labour force participation studies — that have been used to estimate the relative impor-

---

[5] For the pre-retirement years, elements of a wage subsidy may be involved in pension plans whereby receipts are based on earnings, for example, in the last five years of work, or the five years of highest earnings. In such circumstances, the returns to an additional year of work may involve not only the additional earnings but also the additional future pension that results from the higher earnings.

tance of the determinants of the retirement decision, and these two techniques tend to give conflicting answers with respect to the importance of health factors as opposed to social insurance.

Survey interviews asking people why they have retired, or would retire, usually find that ill health is the prime motivating factor — and that social insurance pensions have not induced early retirement. This is the conclusion reached in the study by Steiner and Dorfman (1959) and in numerous studies by the U.S. Social Security Administration as reviewed in Campbell and Campbell (1976, pp. 372-3). The interview technique may yield biased results, however, in that respondents may feel that retiring for reasons of ill health is a more socially acceptable response than retiring because of social insurance pensions. In addition, in retrospective surveys taken after retirement, the respondent's health may have declined since retirement, and this may induce them to respond that ill health was a motivating factor.

In contrast to the interview surveys, econometric studies of the *actual* retirement decision generally find that retirement is strongly affected by the retirement inducing features of social insurance pensions. This is the case in the studies by Peckman, Aaron and Taussig (1968) and Feldstein (1974b) based on international data, and by Boskin (1977) and Quinn (1977) based on U.S. data. In addition, econometric studies of the *planned* retirement decision, based on prospective survey data, also find the economic features of pensions to be retirement inducing. This is the case in Barfield and Morgan (1969), and Hall and Johnson (1978).

Boskin (1977), for example, found that the income effect from expected social security pension benefits was seven times more powerful in inducing retirement than the income effect from other assets. This he attributed to a variety of factors: social security benefits are certain, since they are guaranteed for the remainder of one's life and often indexed against inflation; income from assets can be bequested, and therefore the elderly may not want to use up the income by retiring early; and people may be reluctant to borrow against the imputed income from assets like a house, because they may completely use up their assets. In contrast to the studies based on interview surveys, Boskin finds that ill health is not an important inducement to retire early.

Quinn (1977), on the other hand, finds that reporting a health limitation and being eligible for social security and other pensions were equally important factors in inducing retirement. He also found that persons reporting a health limitation were much more likely than those without a health limitation to retire if they were eligible for pensions. This suggests that eligibility for pensions is a strong factor *enabling* those with ill health to retire early, at the same time as the features of social security also *encourage* the early retirement of others.

Based on prospective survey data of the planned retirement decision, Barfield and Morgan (1969) find expected retirement income to be the most important determinant of the retirement decision, with poor health also encouraging plans for early retirement. Hall and Johnson (1978) also find that both social insurance and ill health are retirement inducing, and that government pensions provide much larger inducements to early retirement than private pensions.

In summary, the econometric studies [6] of the retirement decision are conclusive in finding the features of social security pensions to encourage retirement. The impact of *reported* health limitations is still open to debate, although pensions appear to be a strong factor enabling those with ill health to retire early.

The importance of the economic factors inducing retirement is also supported by statistical tabulations presented in Campbell and Campbell (1976). They cite the dramatic increase in retirement at age 65 when people become eligible for full social security benefits, the large increases in retirement just after amendments that extended the coverage and benefits of social security, the continuous trend towards early retirement at the same time as social security benefits increased over time, and the dramatic increase in early retirement when social security paid partial benefits for early retirement. To be sure, other factors have been at work at the same time to alter the retirement decision. Nevertheless, the evidence from basic statistical tabulations as well as econometric studies both tend to confirm that economic factors—especially the features of social insurance pension schemes—tend to encourage early retirement.

SOME POLICY ISSUES

The fact that social insurance pensions have a substantial impact on the retirement decision has important policy implications. This is especially the case since many features of pension schemes are policy parameters, subject to change by policy makers. This is the case with respect to such features as the retirement test (implicit tax on earnings as pensions are reduced if one continues to work), the explicit payroll tax used to finance social insurance, the replacement ratio (amount of social insurance benefits relative to pre-retirement earnings), coverage and eligibility for social insurance, pensions

---

[6] Evidence from econometric studies of labour force participation as discussed in Chapter 4 would also support the importance of economic factors in inducing retirement. Such studies generally found a positive income elasticity of demand for leisure and a negative (pure, compensated) wage elasticity of demand for leisure. However, one should be cautious in utilizing these results to infer retirement responses, even for those studies based on the labour force participation of the aged. Firstly, if non-labour income included pension income then this would be an endogenous, not exogenous, variable; that is, the retirement response would influence the amount of non-labour income rather than vice versa. Secondly, if Boskin's (1977) finding of a greater income elasticity for pension income as opposed to other non-labour income is correct, then the income elasticities based on participation equations for the elderly could not be used directly to infer retirement responses from pension income.

for early retirement, and the indexing of pensions for inflation. In addition, features of private pensions can be altered through their tax status, portability, and the mandatory retirement age.

As Kirkpatrick (1974, pp. 14-16) indicates, experience outside North America also suggests that features of social insurance can be altered selectively to achieve very specific human resource objectives. Communist countries have often reduced the retirement test for older workers willing to work in specific occupations, industries and geographic areas experiencing labour shortages. Many European countries and Japan have utilized social insurance to encourage early retirement in agricul..re so as to promote efficiency by reducing the number of agricultural workers. Specifically, farmers may be required to sell their land or cease full-time farming in order to receive a pension.

Clearly, retirement policies can and do have a substantial impact on the retirement decision, and this in turn has implications for a variety of factors including the size, composition and deployment of our labour force, the extent of poverty, the magnitude of private savings, company personnel policies, and the solvency of social insurance funds. Because of this importance, the retirement decision merits careful analysis if it is to be altered by various policy instruments. Hopefully labour market analysis can contribute to this area of growing policy concern.

QUESTIONS

1. Outline the main areas of public policy that are affected by the retirement decision. Discuss the impact on these areas of public policy of a policy of making the mandatory retirement age illegal.
2. Outline the main features of pension schemes that can be considered as policy parameters, subject to change by policy makers.
3. Discuss the main factors that affect the solvency of the social insurance pension fund. Indicate how these factors are changing over time and what this implies about the solvency of the fund. What assurances do we have that future generations will accept increased payroll taxes if the solvency of the fund becomes in doubt?
4. Discuss the extent to which the mandatory retirement age is both an exogenous determinant of the retirement decision, and an endogenous result of the retirement decision.
5. Discuss the econometric problems involved with each of the following ways of estimating the retirement response and indicate what you would do to account for these problems:
   (a) estimating a labour force participation equation based on micro data where the unit of observation is the individual who either participates or does not participate in the labour force;
   (b) estimating an hours-of-work equation based on micro data where retired persons would be clustered at zero hours of work;

(c) estimating a labour force participation equation based on micro data
with the individual as the unit of observation and with a non-labour
income variable that includes social insurance benefits.

6. Discuss the expected impact on the retirement decision of an increase in
each of the following factors:
(a) non-labour wealth;
(b) labour market earnings;
(c) earnings of spouse;
(d) replacement ratio in social insurance pensions;
(e) retirement test;
(f) payroll tax to finance social insurance.

7. Based on Figure 5.1(a) draw the indifference curves, before and after
the pension, for persons who:
(a) retire completely;
(b) retire partially;
(c) work the same.
Compare their income in each case.

8. Based on Figure 5.1(b), draw the indifference curves for a person who is
indifferent between retiring completely and continuing to work. Why
would a person ever be indifferent between these two alternatives
assuming that retirement is regarded positively? Based on the various
factors given in the diagram, indicate how people may be induced to
stay in the labour force rather than retire.

9. Based on Figure 5.1(c), draw the indifference curve for a person who:
(a) retires completely;
(b) works part time and only earns income up to the maximum amount
before it becomes retirement tested;
(c) works and earns income up to the maximum amount before it
becomes retirement tested at a 100% implicit tax;
(d) works and earns so much income that no pension is forthcoming.
Compare the pension cost under each alternative.

10. Assume that an individual earned an average of $10,000 during his last 5
years prior to retirement. Depict the budget constraint for a social
insurance pension with a replacement rate of 50%, and a retirement test
allowing one to earn up to $2,000 without having to forgo any pension,
but which requires a pension reduction of $.50 for every dollar for
income between $2,000 and $4,000, and requires one to completely
forgo pension income if earnings exceed $4,000.

11. Indicate why pensions may actually increase poverty as it is
conventionally measured.

12. Discuss the advantage and disadvantage of the full retirement test
versus no retirement test.

13. What would you expect to happen to company personnel policies if a
mandatory retirement age were made illegal?

14. Do you think that the trend towards early retirement will continue into the future?
15. If the retirement test is an implicit tax on earnings and if a tax increase has an ambiguous effect on work incentives, why is it that the features of social insurance pensions can be said to unambiguously encourage retirement?
16. You have been asked to estimate the impact on retirement of a policy of raising the replacement rate from 40% to 60%, and of lowering the implicit tax of the retirement test from 50% to 30%. You have access to comprehensive microeconomic data whe.. the individual is the unit of observation. Specify an appropriate regression equation for estimating the retirement response and indicate how you would simulate the impact of the changes in the two policy parameters.

REFERENCES AND FURTHER READINGS

Barfield, R. and J. Morgan. Trends in planned early retirement. *The Gerontologist* 18 (February 1978) 13-18.

Barfield, R. and J. Morgan. *Early Retirement: The Decision and the Experience and a Second Look.* Ann Arbor, Michigan: University of Michigan Press, 1974.

Bell, D. Prevalence of private retirement plans. *MLR* 98 (October 1975) 17-20.

Boskin, M. Social security and retirement decisions. *EI* 15 (January 1977) 1-25.

Brittain, J. The incidence of social security payroll taxes. *AER* 61 (March 1971). Comment by M. Feldstein and reply 62 (September 1972) 735-742.

Browning, E. Why the social insurance budget is too large in a democracy. *EI* 13 (September 1975) 373-388. Comment by K. Greene and reply 15 (July 1977) 449-457, and comment by B. Bridges and reply 41 (January 1978) 133-142.

Burkhauser, R. The pension acceptance decision of older workers. *JHR* 14 (Winter 1979) 63-75.

Burkhauser, R. and J. Turner. A time series analysis of social security and its effects on the market work of men at younger ages. *JPE* 86 (August 1978) 701-716.

Campbell, C. and R. Campbell. Conflicting views on the effect of old-age and survivors insurance on retirement. *EI* 14 (September 1976) 369-387. Comment by V. Reno, A. Fox and L. Mallan and reply 15 (October 1977) 619-623.

Diamond, P. A framework for social security analysis. *JPE* 8 (December 1977) 275-298.

Ehrenberg, R. Retirement policies, employment and unemployment. *AER Proceedings* 69 (May 1979) 131-136.

Feldstein, M. Social security, induced retirement and aggregate capital accumulation. *JPE* 82 (September 1974) 905-926.

Gustman, A. and M. Segal. Interstate variations in teachers' pensions. *IR* 16 (October 1977) 335-344.

Hall, A. and T. Johnson. *Social security, health and retirement plans.* Menlo Park, California: SRI International, 1978.

Halpern, J. Raising the mandatory retirement age. *New England Economic Review* (May/June 1978) 23-35.

Hemming, R. The effect of state and private pensions on retirement behaviour and personal capital accumulation. *R. E. Studies* 44 (February 1977) 169-172.

Higuchi, T. Old-age pensions and retirement. *ILR* (October 1964).

Hu, S.C. Social security, the supply of labour and capital accumulation. *AER* 69 (June 1979) 274-283.

Kirkpatrick, E. The retirement test: an international study. *Social Security Bulletin* (July 1974) 3-16.

Kittner, D. Forced retirement: how common is it? *MLR* (December 1977) 60-61.

Kreps, J. and J. Spengler. Economics of aging: a survey. *Journal of Economic Literature* 16 (September 1978).

Long, C. *The Labour Force Under Changing Income and Employment.* Princeton, N.J.: Princeton University Press, 1958.

Organization for Economic Cooperation and Development. *Flexibility of Retirement Age.* Paris: OECD, 1971.

Palmore, E. Retirement patterns among aged men. *Social Security Bulletin* 34 (June 1971) 3-17.

Peckman, J., H. Aaron, and N. Taussig. *Social Security: Perspectives for Reform.* Washington: Brookings Institute, 1968.

Pellechio, A. Social security financing and retirement behavior. *AER Proceedings* 69 (May 1979) 284-287.

Pesando, J. and S. Rea. *Public and Private Pensions in Canada.* Ontario Economic Council Study. Toronto: University of Toronto Press, 1977.

Phillips, S. and L. Fletcher. The future of the portable pension concept. *ILRR* 30 (January 1977) 197-204.

Quinn, J. *The early retirement decision: evidence from the 1969 retirement history study.* Washington, D.C.: U.S. Department of Health, Education and Welfare, Social Security Administration, Staff Paper 29, 1978.

Quinn, J. Microeconomic determinants of early retirement: a cross section view of white married men. *JHR* 12 (Summer 1977) 329-346.

Quinn, J. Job characteristics and early retirement. *IR* 17 (October 1978) 315-328.

Reno, V. Why men stop working at or before age 65. *Social Security Bulletin* (June 1971).

Rones, P. Older men—the choice between work and retirement. *MLR* 101 (November 1978) 3-10.

Sheppard, H. The issue of mandatory retirement. *Annals of the American Academy of Political and Social Science* 438 (July 1978) 40-49.

Smirnov, S. The employment of old-age pensioners in the U.S.S.R. *ILR* 116 (July/August) 87-94.

Smith, J. On the labor supply effects of age-related income maintenance programs. *JHR* 10 (Winter 1975) 25-43.

Steiner, P. and R. Dorfman. *The Economic Status of the Aged.* Berkeley: University of California Press, 1959.

Wolfbein, S. and E. Burgess. Employment and retirement. *Aging in Western Societies,* E. Burgess (ed.). Chicago, 1961.

Chapter 6

Hours of Work

The hours-of-work aspect of labour supply has a variety of dimensions including hours-per-day, days-per-week and weeks-per-year. Changes in any or all of these dimensions can alter the hours-of-work aspect of our labour supply decision. Phenomenon such as the eight-hour day, the shorter work week, and increased vacation time are institutional embodiments of a reduction in hours of work. Similarly, moonlighting and overtime are institutional arrangements that alter the typical pattern of hours of work.

In the short run, hours of work appear to be relatively fixed with little scope for individual variation. The eight-hour day, five-day work week and fixed vacation period are fairly standard for most wage and salary earners. However, as we will analyse later in this chapter, the increased importance of flexible working hours is altering these arrangements. In addition, occupational choice provides an element of flexibility as people choose jobs partly on the basis of the hours of work required.

Greater flexibility is possible in the long run when firms and workers have sufficient time to adjust to new preferences and constraints they may face. The adjustment process may be subtle, as for example when workers choose jobs partly on the basis of the hours of work required. Or it may be overt, as for example when workers bargain through their unions for longer vacations or a reduced work week or workday.

The policy importance of the hours-of-work decision is illustrated in a variety of ways. Changes in the hours-of-work decision can affect not only the quantity but also the quality of our overall labour supply (and hence national output), as well as absenteeism, turnover, employment opportunities, and the demand for related activities, notably those involving leisure time and flexible working hours. Changes in hours of work, in turn, can be affected by changes in the age and sex structure of the labour force, as well as government policies and laws and, of course, the basic economic determinants—wealth and expected earnings. Only by analysing these determinants can we forecast the future time pattern of hours of work and predict the impact of alternative policies and institutional arrangements.

THEORETICAL DETERMINANTS OF HOURS OF WORK

Institutional Factors

At first glance it appears that hours of work are largely influenced by institutional factors. Unions have fought long and successfully for reduced working hours in a variety of forms. Labour standards legislation has specified maximum hours that can be worked and has required overtime premiums in certain circumstances. In addition, as we will analyse later, legislation can affect the number of hours for which it is optimal to employ certain types of labour. The age and sex structure of the work-force can also affect hours worked because of the varying preferences for leisure and work activities amongst various elements of the work-force.

However, rather than exerting independent influences on the choice of hours of work, many of these factors can be thought of as being the institutional embodiments through which the preferences of the work-force are registered. Presumably unions have pushed for reduced hours because this is what the rank and file wanted, given their changing circumstances. Similarly, legislation governing hours of work would change in response to the pressures of the parties influencing the legislative process. What then are the basic forces that, in part at least, have worked through these institutional channels to alter the hours-of-work decision?

Economic Factors

As with the labour force participation decision, the basic economic determinants of the hours-of-work decision are one's wealth and expected wage — the respective income and price variables of economic theory. The work-leisure choice framework predicts that an increase in our non-labour wealth will have a pure income effect increasing our demand for leisure and hence reducing our hours of work. An increase in our expected wage will have both an income and a substitution effect, each working in the opposite direction. On the one hand, the increased expected wage means that the price (opportunity cost, forgone income) of leisure has gone up, and hence we would "buy" less leisure and work more hours. On the other hand, the increased expected wage means that our potential wealth is higher, and as with non-labour wealth, this means an increased demand for leisure and a reduction in our hours of work. To ascertain the net impact of these respective substitution and income effects of a wage change, we must appeal to the empirical evidence.

EMPIRICAL EVIDENCE

Trend Data

The analysis of trends in the work week is complicated by the various measures of hours of work. As discussed in Hameed and Cullen (undated, p.3), the most common measures used in Canada include standard hours, actual hours worked, and hours paid for. All measures, however, suggest the same trend: a pronounced and continuous decline over time in hours of work.

This is illustrated in Table 6.1, which traces the standard work week in

TABLE 6.1
**HOURS WORKED IN NON-OFFICE MANUFACTURING, CANADA
1931-71.**

Year	Standard Weekly Hours[a]	Hours Net of Vacations & Holidays
1901	58.6	n.a.
1911	56.5	n.a.
1921	50.3	n.a.
1931	49.6	n.a.
1941	49.0	n.a.
1951	43.6	40.7
1961	41.5	38.1
1971	40.6	36.7

Note: [a] Standard hours are usually determined by collective agreements or company policies, and they are the hours beyond which overtime rates are paid.

Source: Figures for 1901-1971 for standard weekly hours are from S. Ostry and M. Zaidi, *Labour Economics in Canada,* 3rd ed. Toronto: Macmillan, 1979 pp. 80, 81. Figures for 1951-1971 for hours net of vacations and holidays are from Labour Canada (1974, p.6). Both sources used as their primary data the Survey of Working Conditions conducted annually by the Canada Department of Labour and published as *Wage Rates, Salaries and Hours of Labour.*

Canadian manufacturing. Between 1901 and 1971 the standard work week declined from almost 60 hours to approximately 40 hours. The decline slowed down in the depression years of the 1930s, and the war years of the 1940s, and it appears to be slower in the 1950s and 1960s. However, as the last column illustrates, when vacations and holidays are considered the decline in average working hours is more noticeable. In essence, in recent years the work-force has reduced its working hours more in the form of increased vacations and holidays rather than a reduction in hours worked per week.

This long-run decline in hours of work suggests the dominance of the income effect over the substitution effect with respect to the hours-of-work decision. That is, as our wages have increased over time, the resulting increased income has been used to buy more leisure in the form of reduced hours of work, and this has dominated any tendency to buy less leisure because it is more expensive as wages increase. The income effect of the wage increase appears to have dominated the substitution effect, with the result that hours of work have similarly decreased over time as wages have increased.

Econometric Studies

More precise estimates of these income and substitution effects can be gleaned from econometric studies of the determinants of hours of work.

Finegan (1962) used multiple regression analysis to estimate an hours of work (per week) equation for males based on U.S. occupational data. The independent or explanatory variables included hourly wages (cents per hour), as well as a variety of control variables designed to control for other factors that influence hours of work, such as marital status, education, age and race. The estimated regression coefficient for the hourly wage variable was a statistically significant $-.085$, indicating that a one cent per hour increase in the wage rate is associated with a .085 reduction in hours worked per week. Alternatively stated, an 11.5 cent increase in the hourly wage is associated with approximately a one hour decrease in hours worked per week. Clearly, the income effect of the wage increase dominates its substitution effect, so that wage increases tend to be associated with reductions in hours worked. Thus the historical decline in hours of work would be expected from the increase in wages that has gone on over time. If one were to add the income effect resulting from increases in non-labour income (e.g. income of spouse), the decline in hours worked is even more predictable.

The elasticity of supply of hours with respect to wages (i.e. percentage change in hours that results from a one per cent change in wages) is calculated as $\varepsilon_{HW} = (\partial H/\partial W)\,(W/H)$. Assuming an average wage W of 150 cents per hour and an average work week H of 40 hours per week in 1962, and based on the estimated regression coefficient, $\partial H/\partial W$, of $-.085$, the calculated elasticity is $\varepsilon_{HW} = -.085\,(150/40) = -.32$ approximately. Thus a one per cent increase in wages is associated with approximately a one-third of one per cent reduction in hours worked.

MOONLIGHTING, OVERTIME AND FLEXIBLE WORKING HOURS

Any analysis of the hours-of-work decision must confront the following basic question: why is it that some people moonlight at a second job at a wage less than their market wage or their first job, while others require an overtime premium to work more? This apparent anomaly occurs because people who moonlight are underemployed at the going wage on their main job while people who require an overtime premium are already overemployed at the going wage on their main job. Underemployment and overemployment, in turn, occur because different workers have different preferences and they tend to be confronted with an institutionally fixed work schedule. The fixed hours of work, in turn, can arise because of such factors as legislation, union pressure, or company personnel policy. Again, economic theory will enable us to analyse the labour market impact of these important institutional constraints.

The fixed hours-of-work phenomenon is illustrated in Figure 6.1(a). In this case, the worker is faced with two constraints. The first is the usual budget constraint L_tY_t as determined by the person's hourly wage. This restricts the worker's maximum choice set to the triangular area L_tY_tO. The second constraint of the fixed workday of L_tL_c hours (recall work is

Figure 6.1   Fixed Hours Constraint, Underemployment, and Moonlighting

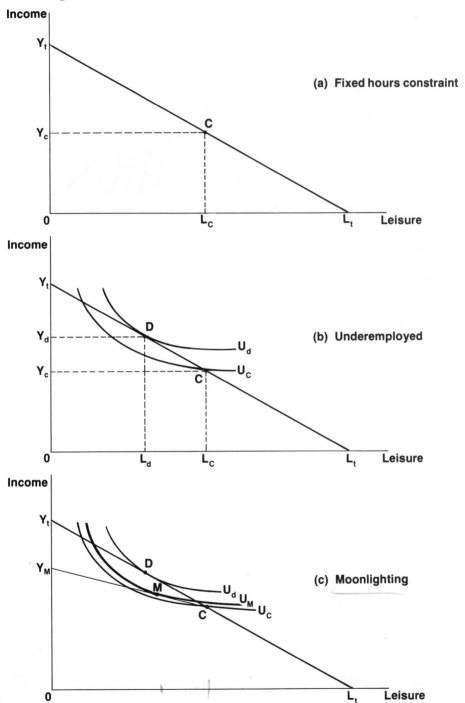

measured from right to left) restricts the worker's maximum choice set to the area L_cCY_cO: the worker can take no more leisure than OL_c (work no more than L_tL_c), and no more income than OY_c even if he worked more than L_tL_c. In effect, this reduces the worker's realistic choice set to the point C since C will always be preferred to other points within L_cCY_cO.

Moonlighting and Underemployment

Some individuals, however, may have preferences such that they would prefer to work more hours at the going wage rate. Figure 6.1(b) illustrates the case for an individual whose preferences (indifference curve U_d) are such that he would prefer to be at D, working L_tL_d hours at the going wage and and taking home an income of Y_d. However, because of the hours of work constraint, the worker must be at C, obviously being less well off since $U_c <$ U_d. In fact, the difference between U_d and U_c is a measure of how much the worker would be willing to give up in order to have the fixed hours constraint relaxed.

A variety of implications follow from this analysis. The worker is *underemployed* because he would like to work more at the going wage rate. Because of the additional constraint of the fixed working hours, the worker is also less well off ($U_c < U_d$) and may be seeking a different job that would enable him to achieve his desired equilibrium at D. In addition, the worker may be willing to *moonlight* and do additional work at a wage rate that is lower than the wage rate of the first job.

This moonlighting rate is illustrated in Figure 6.1(c) by the budget constraint CY_m. (To simplify the diagram the details of Figure 6.1(b) have been omitted.) This new budget constraint rotates downward from CY_t because the moonlighting wage, which is less than the regular wage as given by CY_t, applies only to hours of work beyond L_tL_c. In spite of the lower moonlighting wage, the worker is willing to work more hours (move from c to m) because of the greater utility associated with the move ($U_m > U_c$). That is, workers who are underemployed at the going wage rate would be willing to moonlight at a lower wage rate on their secondary job.

Overtime and Overemployment

Other individuals, however, may have preferences such that they would prefer to work fewer hours at the going wage rate. Figure 6.2(a) illustrates the situation where the worker would prefer (maximize utility) to be at D, working L_tL_d hours for an income of Y_d. However, because of the institution-ally fixed workday, he is compelled to be at C, being less well off ($U_c < U_d$) even though he takes home more income ($Y_c > Y_d$).

Such a worker is *overemployed* at the going wage rate and consequently would support policies to reduce the institutionally fixed work week. In addition, he also may be seeking a different job that would enable him to

Figure 6.2   Overemployment and Overtime

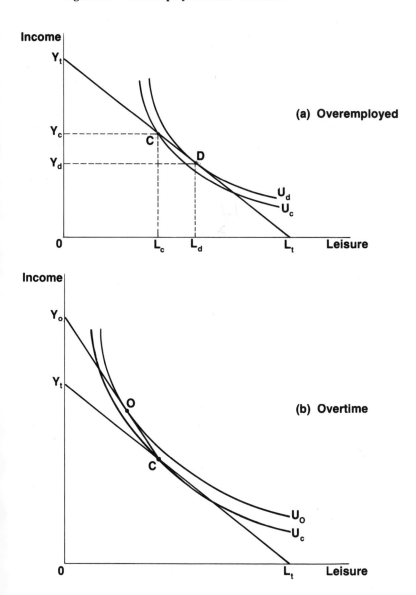

work fewer hours at the going wage rate, and he may even exhibit absentee-ism and tardiness as ways of moving towards his desired work week. Because such a worker is already overemployed at the going wage rate, he would not willingly work more hours at the wage rate; however, he may be induced to do so by an *overtime* premium.

This overtime premium is illustrated in Figure 6.2(b) by the budget constraint CY_0 that rotates upwards from CY_t because the overtime premium, which is greater than the normal wage L_tY_t, applies only to overtime hours of work beyond L_tL_c. If, for example, the overtime premium is time-and-one-half, then the overtime budget constraint has a fifty per cent greater slope than the regular straight-time budget constraint. As long as the worker is willing to give up some leisure for additional income, then there is an overtime premium that will induce him to work more, for example, to move to point O on Figure 6.2(b) (on the indifference curve U_0). Because the worker is overemployed at the going wage rate, the overtime premium is necessary to get him to work more hours.

The person works longer hours even though he was overemployed at the going wage rate because the overtime premium basically is a pure substitution effect, making the price (opportunity cost, income forgone) of leisure higher only for the overtime hours. That is, the budget constraint rotates upwards *only* for the overtime hours; consequently, it does not have an income effect for the normal straight-time hours. Recall that the substitution effect was illustrated by a changed *slope* in the budget constraint, while the income effect was illustrated by a *parallel shift* of the constraint. Since the overtime premium changes the slope for the overtime hours, it is essentially a work-inducing substitution effect, with no leisure-inducing income effect.

Overtime Premium Versus Straight-time Equivalent

The importance of the absence of the income effect in the overtime premium can be illustrated by a comparison of the overtime premium with the straight-time equivalent. One might logically ask the question: if workers are constantly working overtime, why not institutionalize that into a longer workday and pay them the straight-time equivalent of their normal wage plus their overtime wage?

This alternative is illustrated in Figure 6.3. The overtime situation is illustrated by the budget constraint L_tCY_0 with L_tC being the normal wage paid during the regular workday and CY_0 being the overtime premium paid for overtime hours. The regular workday would be L_tL_c hours and overtime hours would be L_cL_0. (To simplify the diagram, these points are not shown; however, as in Figure 6.2(a), they are simply the points on the horizontal leisure axis vertically below their corresponding equilibrium points.) The straight-time hourly equivalent for L_tL_0 hours of work is given by the budget constraint L_tO, the slope of which is a weighted average of the slopes of the regular wage L_tC and the overtime premium CO. The straight-time hourly equivalent is derived by simply taking the earnings associated with the overtime plus regular time hours of work, L_tL_0, and determining the straight-time wage, L_tO, that would yield the same earnings.

A worker who is paid the straight-time equivalent, however, would not voluntarily remain at O, but rather would move to the point S which

Figure 6.3 Overtime Premium Versus Straight-time Equivalent

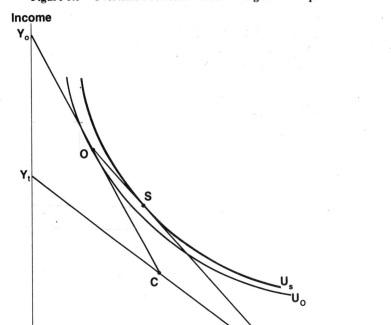

involves less work. This is so because the wage line L_tSO has a leisure inducing income effect, whereas the overtime premium COY_0 is dominated by the work inducing substitution effect (rotation of the budget constraint). In essence, since the overtime premium is paid only for hours *beyond* the regular workday, the person has to work more to get the additional income.

Overtime premiums, therefore, may be a rational way for employers to get their existing work-force voluntarily to work more hours, even if they are overemployed at their regular workday. Employers, in turn, may want to work their existing work-force longer hours, rather than hiring additional workers, so as to spread their fixed hiring costs over longer hours. The importance of these fixed hiring costs will be analysed in more detail when labour demand is discussed.

Workers need not be overemployed at their going wage rate for the overtime premium to work. One can easily portray the situation for a worker in equilibrium at the regular wage rate who would unambiguously work more when offered an overtime wage premium, but who may work less if offered a straight-time hourly wage increase. Firms that want to work their existing work-force longer hours may prefer a wage package that involves a low regular wage and a high overtime premium, to a package that costs them the same but that involves a straight-time wage increase.

Again, what at first glance appears to be costly and irrational actions on the part of firms—in this case the coexistence of overtime and moonlighting rates and a preference for overtime premiums over straight-time equivalent earnings — may well be rational actions when viewed in the larger picture where the parties are optimizing with respect to legal-institutional constraints and when the varying preferences of individual workers are considered. Rather than rendering economic theory irrelevant in the force of such constraints, they highlight the usefulness of economics in analysing the impact of the constraints and in explaining why, in fact, they may rise as an endogenous institutional response to the peculiarities of the labour market.

Flexible Working Hours

The basic work-leisure choice framework is also useful in understanding the phenomenon of flexible working hours (often termed flexitime) that has increased dramatically in recent years. Specifically, economic theory indicates that there are gains to be had by following flexitime to meet the divergent tastes and preferences of different workers. Of course , these gains must be weighed against the additional costs that flexitime may impose. Such costs could include costs of monitoring, supervision, communication and co-ordination that are involved as workers have greater flexibility in choosing their working hours. Recent increases in the use of flexitime, however, suggest the benefits are outweighing the costs in many circumstances.

The benefits of flexitime are illustrated in Figure 6.4. The point C illustrates where workers are constrained to operate given the all-or-nothing choice of working L_tL_c hours (points on the leisure axis are not marked, to simplify the diagram) at the going wage L_tY_t. However, many workers have different preferences. Some, for example, may prefer to be at point D. Because they are overemployed at the going wage rate, their discontent ($U_c < U_d$) may be exhibited in the form of costly absenteeism, high turnover, and perhaps reduced morale and productivity.

Obviously firms that allowed such workers to work their desired hours of work could save on these costs. Alternatively, such firms could lower their wage rates and still retain their work-force. This is illustrated by the wage line L_tY_f, which could be lowered until the point of tangency, F, with the original utility curve U_c. Workers are equally well off at C and F (same level of utility U_c) even though F implies a lower wage rate, simply because they are at an equilibrium with respect to their hours of work. In essence, they are

Figure 6.4   Gains From Flexitime

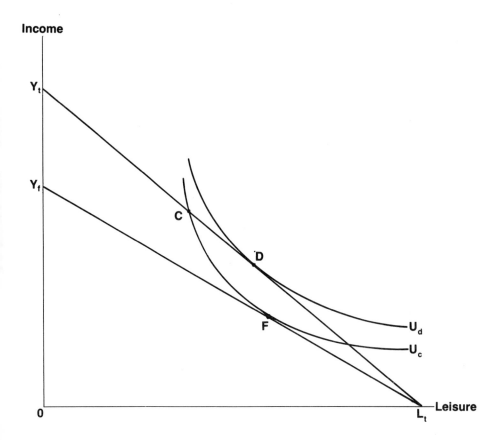

willing to give up wages in return for a work schedule that meets their preferences.

Competition for such jobs would ensure that firms could offer lower wages in return for more flexible work schedules. In this sense, the gains from flexitime could be recouped by the firm to cover the other costs that may be associated with flexitime. Firms that offer more flexible hours need not lower wages, but may take the benefits in the form of reduced absenteeism, lower turnover and improved worker morale. Various combinations of reduced wages (downward rotated wage line) and improved worker morale (higher indifference curve), of course, are possible.

The realities of flexitime are such that, subject to certain limitations, firms usually allow workers to work a fixed number of hours, but to work them at times of their own choosing. Whatever the form of flexitime, the basic point remains: there are gains to be had by following flexitime to meet the divergent tastes and preferences of workers.

QUESTIONS

1. Indicate the various ways in which workers may alter their hours-of-work decision and discuss the factors that may influence why a particular way is chosen. Discuss, for example, why increased vacation time may be chosen over a shorter workday.
2. Indicate the ways in which some of the recent decline in average hours worked may be explained by changes in the age and sex structure of our work-force.
3. What factors may influence our decision to alter labour supply through changes in hours of work rather than labour force participation? Is it possible that some groups may choose to increase one dimension of labour supply while simultaneously decreasing another?
4. Utilize economic theory to suggest the relevant variables and their functional form that are appropriate for estimating the determinants of hours of work.
5. Discuss the econometric problems involved in estimating an hours-of-work equation based on microeconomic data where the individual is the unit of observation. If the full sample were to include those who worked and those who did not work, how might you construct a variable to reflect the expected wage for those who did not work?
6. Based on the diagrams of Figure 6.1, illustrate how an underemployed worker would respond to:
   (a) an offer to work as many more hours as the worker would like at the going wage;
   (b) payment of an overtime premium for hours of work beyond C;
   (c) an offer to work an additional fixed number of hours, as determined by the employee at the going wage.
7. Based on the diagrams of Figure 6.2, illustrate how an overemployed worker would respond to:
   (a) an offer to work as many more hours as the worker would like at the going wage;
   (b) payment of a moonlighting rate for hours of work beyond C.
8. Based on Figure 6.2(b), precisely illustrate the following overtime rates for hours worked beyond L_tL_c:
   (a) time-and-one-half,
   (b) double-time,
   (c) time-and-one-half for the first two hours of overtime, and double-time thereafter.
9. Why might a company constantly pay an overtime premium rather than pay the straight-time hourly equivalent? For example, if a company was paying its workers five dollars an hour for the first eight hours and 7.50

dollars for the next two hours (for a total of 55 dollars per 10 hour day), why might the company not be willing to offer its workers the straight-time hourly equivalent of 5.50 dollars per hour since that is in fact what they are earning?

10. Based on Figure 6.3, why wouldn't the company simply offer the all-or-nothing choice of working L_tO_t hours for the straight-time hourly equivalent wage of L_tSO? Why might unions bargain for the straight-time equivalent?

11. Utilize your knowledge of the income-leisure choice framework to illustrate formally the proposition that there are gains to be had by allowing flexitime to meet the divergent tastes and preferences of different workers. Who would ultimately receive these gains?

12. Specifically, what are some of the costs that might be involved in various forms of flexitime and how might these costs be minimized?

REFERENCES AND FURTHER READINGS

Ashenfelter, O. and J. Heckman. Estimating labor-supply functions. *Income Maintenance and Labor Supply*, G. Cain and H. Watts (eds.). Chicago: Rand McNally, 1973.

AFL-CIO. Shorter hours: tool to combat unemployment. *Labour and the National Economy*, W. Bowen (ed.). New York: Norton, 1965.

Bardham, P. Labor supply functions in a poor agrarian economy. *AER* 69 (March 1979) 73-83.

Barzel, Y. The determination of daily hours and wages. *QJE* 87 (May 1973) 220-238.

Becker, G. A theory of the allocation of time. *EJ* 75 (September 1965) 493-517.

Berg, E. Backward sloping labor supply functions in dual economies: the African case. *QJE* 75 (August 1961).

Best, F. Preferences in worklife scheduling and work- leisure tradeoffs. *MLR* 101 (June 1978) 31-37.

Brandmein, S. Recent progress toward reducing work hours. *MLR* 79 (November 1956).

Bronfenbrenner, M. and J. Mossin. The shorter work week and the labor supply. *SEJ* 33 (January 1967) 322-331.

Dankert, C. Hours of work. *Labour and the National Economy*, W. Bowen (ed.). New York: Norton, 1965.

Dankert, C. Shorter hours in theory and practice. *ILRR* 15 (April 1962) 307-322.

Dankert, C., F. Mann and H. Northrup (eds.). *Hours of Work*. Industrial Relations Research Association. New York: Harper and Row, 1965.

Da Vanzo, J., D. De Tray and D. Greenberg. The sensitivity of male labor supply estimates to choice of assumption. *R. E. Stats.* 68 (August 1976) 313-325.

Devans, R. The average work week: two surveys compared. *MLR* 101 (July 1978) 3-8.

Ehrenberg, R. *Fringe Benefits and Overtime Behavior: Theoretical and Economic Analysis*. Lexington, Mass.: D.C. Heath, 1972.

Ehrenberg, R. The impact of the overtime premium on employment and hours in U.S. industry. *WEJ* 9 (June 1971) 199-207.

Ehrenberg, R. Absenteeism and the overtime decision. *AER* 60 (June 1970) 352-357.

Evans, A. *Hours of Work*. Geneva: International Labour Organization, 1975.

Fan, L. Leisure and time elements in consumer behavior. *SEJ* 38 (April 1972) 478-484.

Feldstein, M. Estimating the supply curve of working hours. *Oxford Economic Papers* 20 (August 1968).

Finegan, T. Hours of work in the United States: a cross- sectional analysis. *JPE* 70 (October 1962) 452-470.

Fishelson, G. Simple dynamic effects in work-leisure choice: a rejoinder to the skeptical comment on the static theory. *JHR* 6 (Spring 1971) 248-249.

Garbarino, J. Fringe benefits and overtime as barriers to expanding employment. *ILRR* 17 (April 1964) 426-442.

Ghez, G. and G. Becker. *The Allocation of Time and Goods over the Life Cycle*. New York: Columbia University Press, 1975.

Gilbert, F. and R. Pfouts. A theory of the responsiveness of hours of work to changes in money rates. *R. E. Stats.* (May 1958) 116-121.

Hall, R. Wages, income and hours of work in the U.S. labor force. *Income Maintenance and Labor Supply*, G. Cain and H. Watts (eds.). Chicago: Rand McNally, 1973.

Hameed, S. and D. Cullen. *Work and Leisure in Canada*. Edmonton: University of Alberta, 1971.

Hameed, S. and G. Paul. *3 or 4 Day Work Week*. Edmonton: University of Alberta, 1974.

Hanock, G. The backward-bending supply of labor. *JPE* 73 (December 1965)

Johnson, T. Zealots and malingerers: results of firm specific human capital investments. *SEJ* 41 (April 1975) 613- 626.

Jones, E. State legislation and hours of work in manufacturing. *SEJ* 41 (April 1975) 602-612.

Kalachek, E., W. Mellow and F. Raines. The male labor supply function reconsidered. *ILRR* 31 (April 1978) 356-367.

Kerr, C. Economic growth: shortcomings of the work week—discussion. *AER Proceedings* 46 (May 1956) 220-221.

Kniesner, T. The full-time workweek in the United States, 1900-1970. *ILRR* 30 (October 1976) 3-15.

Kraps, J. Lifetime tradeoffs between work and play. *IRRA* (December 1968) 307-316.

Labour Canada. *Trends in Working Time*. Ottawa: Wages Research Division, Economics and Research Branch, 1974.

Leon, G. and R. Bednarzik. A profile of women on part- time schedules. *MLR* 10 (October 1978) 3-12.

Leslie, D. Hours and overtime in British and United States manufacturing industries. *BJIR* 14 (July 1976) 194-201.

Lewis, H. Hours of work and hours of leisure. *IRRA* (December 1956) 196-206.

Mabry, B. Income-leisure analysis and the salaried professional. *IR* 8 (February 1969) 162-173.

Mauziri, A. Empirical evidence on labor supply: the case of dentists. *IRRA* (December 1966) 354-364.

McCormick, B. Hours of work in British industry. *ILRR* 12 (April 1959) 423-433.

Meissner, M. The long arm of the job: a study of work and leisure. *IR* 10 (October 1971) 239-260.

Miracle, M. and B. Fetter. Backward-sloping labor-supply functions and African economic behavior. *Economic Development and Cultural Change* 18 (January 1970) 240-251.

Moses, L. Income, leisure and wage pressure. *EJ* 72 (June 1962) 320-334.

Newton, K., and N. Leckie. Determinants of weekly work hours in Canada. *RI/IR* 34 (No. 2, 1979) 257-271.

Northrup, H., J. Wilson and K. Rose. The twelve hour shift in the petroleum and chemical industries. *ILRR* 32 (April 1979) 312-326.

Olsen, E.O. The effort level, work time and profit maximization. *SEJ* 42 (April 1976) 644-652.

Owen, J. Flexitime: some problems and solutions. *ILRR* 30 (January 1977) 152-160.

Owen, J. Workweek and leisure: an analysis of trends, 1945-1975. *MLR* 99 (August 1976) 3-8.

Owen, J. *The Price of Leisure*. Montreal: McGill-Queen's University Press, 1975.

Perlman, R. Observations on overtime and moonlighting. *SEJ* 33 (October 1966) 237-244.

Reder, M. The cost of the shorter work week. *IRRA* (December 1956) 207-221.

Reza, A. Labour supply and demand, absenteeism, and union behaviour. *R. E. Studies* 42 (April 1975) 237-248.

Rosen, S. On the interindustry wage and hours structure. *JPE* 78 (March/April 1969) 249-273.

Ross, D. A new view of leisure. *RI/IR* 27 (No. 4, 1972) 746-756.

Sherman, R. and T. Witlet. Notes on overtime, moonlighting and the shorter work week. *SEJ* 35 (July 1968) 78-81.

Sloan, F. and S. Richupan. Short-run supply responses of professional nurses: a micro analysis. *JHR* 10 (Spring 1975) 241-257.

Sloan, P. Economic aspects of shift and night work. *ILR* 117 (March/April 1978) 129-142.

Sowell, T. The shorter work week controversy. *ILRR* 8 (January 1965).

Stein, H. An economist looks at the shorter work week. *Personnel* 35 (September/October 1958) 60-65.

Tandan, N. *Workers with Long Hours.* Special Labour Force Studies, Series A, No. 9. Ottawa: Information Canada, 1972.

Ulman, L. Union wage policy and the supply of labour. *QJE* 65 (May 1951) 237-251.

Vahovich, S. Physicians' supply decisions by specialty. *IR* 16 (February 1977) 51-60.

Vatter, H. On the folklore of the backward sloping supply curve. *ILRR* 14 (July 1961) 578-586. Comment by T. A. Finegan and reply 15 (January 1962) 230-236.

Weeks, W. Collective bargaining and part-time work in Ontario. *RI/IR* 33 (No. 1, 1978) 80-90.

Wilensky, H. The moonlighter: a product of relative deprivation. *IR* 3 (October 1963).

Winston, G. An international comparison of income and hours of work. *R. E. Stats.* 48 (February 1966) 28-39.

Winston, G. Income and the aggregate allocation of effort. *AER Proceedings* 55 (May 1965) 375-385.

Chapter 7

Human Capital Theory: Applications to Training and Job Search

Throughout this section on labour supply we have emphasized the *quantity* aspects of labour supply, ranging from family formation to labour force participation to hours of work. Labour supply also has a *quality* dimension encompassing human capital elements such as education, training, labour market information, mobility and health. While the economics of education and health economics are often the subject matter of separate courses and textbooks, they have a common theoretical thread — that of human capital theory — along with training, job search, and mobility. This chapter presents the basic human capital theory and applies it mainly to the areas of training and the acquisition of labour market information in connection with the job search process.

HUMAN CAPITAL THEORY

The essence of human capital theory is that investments are made in human resources so as to improve their productivity. Costs are incurred in the expectation of future benefits: hence, the term "investment in human resources." Like all investments, the key question becomes: is it economically worthwhile? The answer to this question depends on whether or not benefits exceed costs by a sufficient amount. Before dealing with the investment criteria whereby this is established, it is worthwhile to expand on the concepts of costs and benefits as utilized in human capital theory. In this chapter, only the basics are touched upon. A wealth of refinements and precise methodological techniques is contained in the extensive literature on human capital theory and its application.

Costs and Benefits

In calculating the costs of human capital, it is important to recognize not only direct costs, such as books or tuition fees in acquiring university education, but also the opportunity cost or income forgone while people acquire the human capital. For students in university or workers in lengthy training programs, such costs can be the largest component of the total cost. Its evaluation can prove difficult because it requires an estimation of what they would have earned had they not engaged in human capital formation.

99

In addition, it is important to try to distinguish between the consumption and the investment components of human capital formation, since it is only the investment costs that are relevant for the investment decision. In reality this separation may be difficult or impossible—how does one separate the consumption from the investment costs of acquiring a university degree? Nevertheless, the distinction must be made qualitatively, if not quantitatively, especially in comparing programs where the consumption and investment components may differ considerably.

A distinction must also be made between private and social costs and benefits. Private costs and benefits are those that accrue to the parties doing the investment and as such will be considered in their own calculations. Social costs and benefits are all those that are accrued by society, including not only private costs and benefits but also any third-party effects or externalities that accrue to parties who are not directly involved in the investment decision. Training disadvantaged workers, for example, may yield an external benefit in the form of reduced crime, and this benefit should be considered by society at large even though it may not enter the calculations of individuals doing the investment.

A further distinction can be made between real costs and benefits as opposed to pecuniary or distributional or transfer costs and benefits. Real costs involve the use of real resources, and should be considered whether those resources have a monetary value or not. Pecuniary or transfer costs and benefits do not involve the use of real resources, but rather involve a transfer from one group to another: some gain while others lose. While it may be important to note the existence of such transfers for specific groups, it is inappropriate to include them in the calculation of social costs and benefits since, by definition, gains by one party involve losses by another. For example, the savings in unemployment insurance payments that may result from a retraining program are worthy of noting, and for the unemployment insurance fund they may be a private saving, yet from the point of view of society they represent a reduction in a transfer payment, not a newly created real benefit. Similarly, the installation of a retraining facility in a community may raise local prices for construction facilities, and this may be an additional cost for local residents: yet it is a pecuniary cost since it involves a transfer from local residents to those who raised the prices. While such a transfer may involve a loss to local residents, it is not a real resource cost to society as a whole, since it represents a gain for other parties.

From the point of view of the efficient allocation of resources, only real resource costs and benefits matter. Transfers represent offsetting gains and losses. However, from the point of view of distributive equity or fairness, society may choose to value those gains and losses differently. In addition, costs and benefits to different groups may be valued differently in the economic calculus.

Thus, in the calculation of the benefits from a training program, it is conceivable to weigh the benefits more for a poor disadvantaged worker than an advantaged worker. The appropriate weighting scheme obviously poses a problem, but it could be based on the implicit weights involved in other government programs or perhaps in the progressive income tax structure, or it could simply be based on explicit weights that reflect a pure value judgement.

Care must also be exercised in imputing a macroeconomic impact from investment programs. It is often tempting, for example, to multiply the benefits of some program to capture the multiplier effect as the investment sets up further rounds of spending throughout the economy. Or it is tempting to document the employment expansion that may accompany a particular investment program. The error in this reasoning occurs because it ignores the fact that the opportunities forgone, as resources were devoted to this particular investment rather than to some other one, also have a multiplier and employment creation effect. It is true that the multiplier effects may be different in magnitude (for example, if they involve different leakages into imports), and they may occur in different regions. While these factors may be worthy of note, they do not justify the imputation of a multiplier effect for all human capital investments. This is especially the case since, in general, fiscal policy is available with its multiplier effects to alter the levels of aggregate demand in the economy.

Investment Criteria

Once costs and benefits are appropriately calculated, it is necessary to compare them to see if the human capital investment is economically worthwhile. Since the costs and benefits usually occur over a different time period, comparison of the two requires discounting at some appropriate rate of interest so as to obtain the present value of costs and benefits. In the Canadian Treasury Board document, *Benefit-Cost Analysis Guide* (1976), alternative discount rates are discussed including the private sector rate of return on investments, and the return on government loans. After discussing the different alternatives, they suggest performing a sensitivity analysis by calculating the present value of costs and benefits for a range of real discount rates of, for example, five, ten, and fifteen per cent.

Once the present value of costs and benefits are appropriately calculated, there remains the problem of comparing them to see if the investment is economically worthwhile. The usual investment criteria is to undertake the investment if the net present value of benefits is positive, which is the same as a discounted benefit/cost ratio of greater than one. Alternatively one could estimate the rate of return that equates the present value of benefits with the present value of costs, and this implied rate of return could be compared with the opportunity cost of capital (e.g., market rate of interest or yield on government bonds). If the implied rate of return exceeds the opportunity cost of capital then the investment should be undertaken.

The *Benefit-Cost Analysis Guide* (1976) discusses the conditions under which some of these investment criteria are inappropriate for choosing amongst projects. In general, the conclusion that is reached is that the appropriate efficiency criteria is to maximize the net present value of benefits minus costs because, by definition, this contributes most to the welfare of society.

The problems of evaluation are illustrated further when we examine two human resource or manpower policies — training and labour market information associated with job search. A third manpower policy area — mobility and migration— that is often evaluated with human capital theory is examined in a later chapter on regional wage differentials. In addition, the human capital approach will be utilized when we examine the determination of individual wages, and the job search methodology will be discussed further when we analyse the microeconomic foundations of the Phillips curve relationship between aggregate wages and unemployment.

TRAINING

As Dymond (1972, p.72) points out, in international terms Canada tends to rank second only to Sweden regarding resources devoted to training. Obviously a human resource program of this importance merits scrutiny to ensure the efficient and equitable investment of public resources.

In this section, we focus on some *economic* aspects of training rather than on an institutional description of training in Canada: the latter is given in various readings referred to at the end of the chapter, for example, Dymond (1972), Gunderson (1974), Jain and Hines (1973), Meltz (1969), and Somers (1971). The main focus of our analysis is to shed light on the following questions: Who pays for training? Is a government subsidy warranted? How should training be evaluated?

Who Pays?

In his classic work on the subject, Becker (1964, pp. 11-28) illustrates that the trainee will pay for *general* training and the sponsoring company will pay for *specific* training. General training is training that can be used in various firms, not just in firms that provide the training. Consequently, in a competitive market, firms will bid for this training by offering a higher wage equal to the value of the training. Since competition ensures that the trainee reaps the benefits of general training in the form of higher earnings, then the trainee would be willing to bear the cost of training as long as benefits exceed costs. If a company were to bear the cost of such training they would still have to bid against other companies for the services of the trainee.

With specific training, however, the training is useful only in the company that provides the training. Consequently, other companies have no incentive to pay higher earnings for such training and the trainee would not bear the cost because of an inability to reap the benefits in the form of higher earnings. The sponsoring company, however, would bear the cost providing they exceed the benefits. In addition, the sponsoring company would not have to pay a higher wage for those persons with specific training since other firms are not competing for such trainees. At most, the sponsoring company may pay such trainees a wage premium to reduce their turnover and hence to increase the benefit period for the company to recoup its investment costs.

In competitive markets, then, sponsoring companies will pay for specific training and trainees will pay for general training. The form of payment may be subtle, as, for example, when trainees in an apprenticeship program forgo earnings by accepting a lower wage rate during the training period, or when companies forgo some output from workers when they provide them with on-the-job training.

In practice the distinction between general and specific training can be difficult to make. Training often contains elements of both. Even training that is geared to the specific production processes of a particular firm often contains elements that are transferable and the completion of such training can serve as a *signal* to firms that the trainee is capable of learning new skills even if the particular skills themselves are not transferable. On the other hand, general training that is provided in a particular firm may be somewhat more useful in the sponsoring company simply because the trainee is more familiar with that company. In such circumstances the costs and benefits are often shared between the trainee and the sponsoring company, with the trainee receiving benefits in the form of higher earnings and the sponsoring company receiving benefits in the form of higher worker productivity for which it does not have to pay a higher wage.

Appropriate Role of Government

If trainees will pay for general training and sponsoring companies will pay for specific training, and if they will share the costs and benefits of training that has elements of both, why should governments be involved in the training process? In other words, are there situations when the private unregulated market does not provide a socially optimal amount of training?

This possibility may exist for trainees who cannot afford to purchase training (perhaps by accepting a lower wage during the training period) and who cannot borrow because of an inability to use their human capital (future earnings) as collateral for a loan. Subsidies to training the disadvantaged may be particularly appealing to taxpayers who prefer to support transfer programs that are associated with work activity. Recent concern with the working poor who work full time but at a wage that is too low to yield a level of income above the poverty line also suggests the possibility of supporting training programs for disadvantaged workers.

The private market may also yield a less than socially optimal amount of training to the extent that training generates external (spillover, third-party) benefits that are not paid for in the market. In such circumstances firms and individuals would have no incentive to consider such benefits in their investment calculations and consequently may under-invest in training. As Judy (1970, p. 47) points out, externalities may exist in the form of vacuum effects when trainees move up the occupation ladder and vacate a job that is filled by a member of the unemployed, or they may exist in the form of complimentary multiplier effects as trainees reduce structural bottlenecks that previously resulted in the unemployment of related workers.

A sub-optimal amount of general training may also be provided by companies where on-the-job training is a natural by-product of their production process. Workers simply acquire training in their every day work tasks. However, because it is difficult to know how much training they are acquiring and at what cost, they may be reluctant to pay for such training. In such circumstances, training may have public-good characteristics in that the training is available to all workers and yet it is difficult to exclude those who don't pay for the training. To be sure, only those who are willing to work for lower wages could be hired (and in this way non-payers are excluded). However, the indirect nature of the training makes it difficult for the purchasers to know how much training they are acquiring.

At the macroeconomic level, training may also yield benefits to the general public in the sense of helping the economy achieve such goals as growth, full employment, price stability, a viable balance of payments, and a more equitable distribution of income. As an anti-cyclical device to reduce the inflation-unemployment trade-off, training may be particularly effective in absorbing some of the unemployed during a recession and in providing supplies of skilled workers when structural bottlenecks may otherwise lead to inflation.

While these arguments justifying government support for training may be *theoretically plausible*, we have very little evidence of their *practical applicability*. On the distributional impact, the evidence appears conflicting. Internal evaluations reported in *Manpower Training* (1975) suggest that training has been effective in raising graduates out of poverty. However, Dymond (1973, pp. 70, 71) concludes that training ''was of most benefit to persons in least need of training in order to compete in the labour market''. Gunderson (1974, p. 11) found that ''larger government subsidies were found to go to companies that provide on-the-job training to advantaged rather than disadvantaged workers''; and in a review of a variety of studies from Manitoba, MacMillan and Tullock (1973) conclude that training the disadvantaged may not be efficient and would have to be justified on broader social principles of equity. Conflicting evidence on the distributional impact of training is also reported for the U.S. in Goldstein (1972).

Evidence on the importance of external benefits from training is also difficult to document. In theory, there is also the possibility that vacuum and complimentary multiplier effects may be offset by displacement effects, as trained workers simply take the job of another worker (possibly many workers) and displace that person into the ranks of the unemployed.

At the macroeconomic level there is also little evidence on the usefulness of training in achieving our macroeconomic objectives. More important, there are *theoretical* reasons for questioning the appropriateness of the use of training as a policy instrument to achieve macroeconomic goals. Of what social value is training if it simply reduces our *measured* unemployment rate by enrolling the unemployed in training programs where they become classified as outside of the labour force rather than as unemployed? If government subsidization leads employers and employees to engage in training activities that they otherwise would not find profitable, could this not lead to a misallocation of resources which in turn could lead to an inflationary cost increase and a worsening of the inflation-unemployment trade-off? How exactly would government support of training lead to improved growth, and why is the growth rate under government subsidized training any more desirable than the growth rate that results from the amount of training that would occur in the free market without government support? Surely, these basic questions have to be answered — or at least dealt with — before one accepts a major role for the government in the training process.

Evaluation

One possible role for the government is in the provision of *information* on training programs: Where are they? What makes them successful? What complimentary and alternative policies are effective? To a certain extent the private market may not provide sufficient information because of its public goods characteristics—once provided, the information is available to all, and it is difficult to exclude those who don't pay for the information. Because the private market may not provide sufficient information in such circumstances, there may be a role for the government.

Evaluations of training programs can provide useful information, especially in ascertaining their success or failure. Cost-benefit evaluations based on Canadian data are discussed, for example, in MacMillan and Tullock (1973), Manpower and Immigration (1975), and Strang and Whittingham (1970). Most studies find that benefits exceed costs by a substantial margin, with benefit/cost ratios of 6/1 and 3/1 not being uncommon.

Given the difficulty of appropriately ascertaining costs and benefits, the absolute magnitude of the ratio itself may be subject to question. Consequently, in human resource programs at least, benefit-cost analysts often rely on cruder comparisons, coupled with subjective evaluations. For example, different programs may be ranked on the bases of benefit/cost ratios, or ratios may be calculated for different individuals within programs. Alternative measures of success may also be employed. In evaluating the success of Canadian training programs, for example, Gunderson (1973, 1974) utilized such factors as graduation from the program, retention by the sponsoring company, productivity improvements, and wage gains.

LABOUR MARKET INFORMATION AND JOB SEARCH

The acquisition of labour market information in the process of job search provides another example of the application of human capital analysis. While the process is discussed in more detail in subsequent chapters when mobility and migration are dealt with in the context of wage determination, the basic human capital aspects are discussed in this section. To illustrate the human capital framework, we focus on the job search process of employees. Employer search is discussed in Maki (1971, Chapter 3) and Lippman and McCall (June 1976).

Theoretical Framework

The human capital aspects of the job search process can be illustrated in the simple diagram of Figure 7.1. For low levels of search, the marginal costs of search are fairly low because low-cost, usually informal, search processes can be used. For example, friends and relatives can be contacted, want ads examined, and perhaps a few telephone calls made. As the search continues, however, more costly processes are often necessary to acquire additional labour market information. For example, it may be necessary to apply directly to a company or to sign up with an employment service. In some cases it may even be necessary to change locations or to quit working if one

Figure 7.1   Optimal Job Search

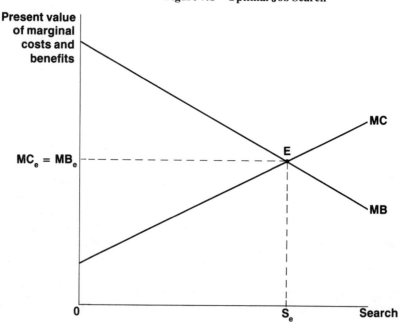

already has a job. For these reasons the marginal cost of search probably rises with the amount of job search undertaken. In Figure 7.1 the marginal cost of search is depicted as a linear (straight line) function of search. This need not be the case, for example, if costs increased exponentially as one moved into more intensive and/or longer search activities.

The marginal benefits of search, on the other hand, probably are a declining function of the amount of search undertaken. As with costs, in Figure 7.1 the benefits are depicted as a linear function of search only for illustrative purposes. One starts out the search process with an examination of the most promising alternatives and then continues examining further activities in the hope of finding an even better one. Obviously, a better alternative may occur; however, one may encounter diminishing returns with respect to the additional information. As search continues it becomes less likely—but still possible—that a better offer will be received simply because there are fewer options left to examine.

Given the costs and benefits of additional search, the rational investor will acquire labour market information and engage in search until the point E, where the marginal benefits exactly equal the marginal cost. To the left of E, the benefits of additional search exceed the cost and hence additional search is worthwhile; to the right of E, the benefits of additional search are not worth the costs. In this sense E will be a stable equilibrium with S_e being the optimal amount of search activity.

Factors Determining Optimal Search

This simple human capital framework is useful to illustrate how the optimal amount of search depends on the various factors underlying the shapes of the marginal cost and benefit schedules. For example, young workers probably have a low marginal cost of search schedule because they have fewer psychic ties to their existing jobs and they are less locked in to pensions and seniority ties. In addition, they may rely on family income in order to cushion the costly search process and wait for the right job. Their marginal benefit schedule may be high because of a long expected benefit period from which to recoup the investment costs. Given their low marginal cost schedule and high marginal benefit schedule, their optimal length of search will be longer. In essence they are less likely to take the first job that comes along.

Aggregate economic conditions can also affect the schedules and hence the optimal duration of search. In periods of high unemployment the marginal cost of search is increased because it is more likely that an offer may be taken up by someone else who is unemployed. In essence, searching longer may be costly because of the potential loss of earlier offers.

Institutional factors can also change the cost and benefit schedules and hence the optimal search activity. Unemployment insurance and portable pensions would reduce the cost of search and hence increase the amount of search. Demographic factors can also play a role. For example, an increase in the proportion of young people in the labour force could lead to more frictional unemployment because of the greater amount of optimal search activity.

Types of Search Activity

Workers can engage in a variety of search activities ranging from informal discussions with friends and relatives to more formal activities such as contacting private or public employment agencies. In addition, varying degrees of success can be associated with each of these activities.

Table 7.1 utilizes data presented in Maki (1972) to indicate the most common search activities used by employees in Canada. As column one indicates, the most popular measure was to contact a Canada Manpower Centre. For most of the unemployed, however, this would be automatic as they register to collect unemployment insurance benefits. Informal techniques, such as contacting friends and relatives and local employers, were also popular.

Using an activity, however, does not mean that it will be successful. Column two indicates the effectiveness of the search activity: the activities

TABLE 7.1
SEARCH ACTIVITY OF UNEMPLOYED, [a] CANADA, 1968

Search Activity[b]	Per cent Using the Activity	Effectiveness of Activity[c]
Local employers	.6738	.1007
Friends and relatives	.5781	.0281
Outside employers and newspapers	.3576	.0057
Other [d]	.1253	.0013
Letters of application	.2843	−.0063
Local newspapers	.2948	−.0283
Private agencies	.1768	−.0507
Canada manpower centre	.7604	−.0885

Notes: [a]The data is based on a special questionnaire added to the January 1969 Labour Force Survey. All persons who had been unemployed for a cumulative total of five or more weeks during the calendar year of 1968 were requested to complete the special questionnaire.

[b]Ranked in descending order of their effectiveness in finding a job.

[c]Effectiveness is defined as the change in the probability of finding a job when the particular search activity was used relative to the average success of all the search activities. The entries are the adjusted coefficients that result from a regression equation using a binary coded dependent variable, coded one if the respondent found a job, zero otherwise. Other explanatory variables such as age, sex, education, marital status, region, occupation and industry were also included in the regression.

[d]As, for example, specified by the respondent.

Source: D. Maki, *Search Behaviour in Canadian Job Markets,* Ottawa: Economic Council of Canada, 1971, page 24. Reproduced by permission of the Minister of Supply and Services Canada.

themselves are ranked in the descending order of their effectiveness. Clearly the informal search activities, such as friends and relatives and local employers, are more successful than formal activities, such as using a private or public employment agency. In their study based on U.S. data, Sheppard and Belitsky (1966, p. 94) also rank the informal job seeking technique of contacting friends and relatives to be most effective for all skill levels.

The effectiveness of a technique in finding a job does not necessarily mean that the technique is best from an investment point of view. For example, the technique may be effective but costly (especially if it involved *intensive* search activity) or it may be effective in helping one to find a job, but not a permanent job at a high wage. As human capital theory reminds us, a complete evaluation of the success of various search activities would require a cost benefit analysis. While the data of Table 7.1 does not provide us with sufficient information to do a cost benefit analysis, it does provide useful information that can be employed as an *input* into the policy making process.

QUESTIONS

1. Discuss the analogy between physical and human capital.
2. How would you evaluate the extent to which your acquiring a university education is a sound investment economically? Be precise in the information you would require and exactly what you would do with it.
3. You have been asked to evaluate an on-the-job training program in a particular company. Specify exactly what sort of information you require and what you would do with it.
4. The federal government supports a variety of human resource programs including education, training, mobility, labour market information and health. Could you suggest any techniques that may be useful to suggest how resources should be allocated to the various functions?
5. Should governments subsidize human resource programs? If so, why? Be precise in your answer by indicating where, if anywhere, the private market may fail to yield a socially optimal amount of human resource development.
6. Assume that you are deciding whether or not to acquire a four year university degree. Your only consideration at this moment is the degree as an investment for yourself. Costs per year are tuition fees $600, and books $100. The government also pays to the university an equivalent amount to your tuition fees to cover the real cost. If you didn't go to university, you would have earned $6,000 per year as an acrobat. With a university degree, however, you know that you can earn $10,000 per year as an acrobat. Because of the nature of your chosen occupation, your time horizon for the investment decision is exactly 10 years after university; that is, if the investment is to be worthwhile, it must be so within a 10 year period after graduation. The market rate of interest is 5%. Would you make the investment in a degree?

7. Compare the virtues of on-the-job versus institutional training.
8. Give an example of each of the following as errors in a cost-benefit calculation: ignoring opportunity cost; failing to discount benefits; double counting; considering sunk cost with no alternative value; ignoring a real externality; considering a pecuniary externality; and ignoring consumption benefits.

REFERENCES AND FURTHER READINGS

A. Human Capital Theory and Cost Benefit Evaluations

[Additional readings in this area can be found in the bibliographies in the following entries.]

Becker, G. *Human Capital and the Personal Distribution of Income*. Ann Arbor, Michigan: Institute of Public Administration and Department of Economics, 1967.

Becker, G. *Human Capital*. New York: National Bureau of Economic Research, 1964.

Blaug, M. The empirical status of human capital theory. *Journal of Economic Literature* 14 (September 1976) 827-856.

Blaug, M. *Economics of Education: A Selected Annotated Bibliography*. Oxford: Pergamon Press, 1966.

Commission on Post-Secondary Education in Ontario. *Cost and Benefit Study of Post-Secondary Education in Ontario*. Toronto: Queen's Printer, 1972.

Hansen, W.L. (ed.). *Education, Income and Human Capital*. New York: National Bureau of Economic Research, 1970.

Journal of Political Economy, Supplement, 70, Part 2 (October 1962).

Mehmet, O. *Who Benefits from the Ontario University System: A Benefit-Cost Analysis by Income Groups*. Toronto: Ontario Economic Council, 1978.

Mincer, J. Investment in human capital and personal income distribution. *JPE* 66 (August 1958) 281-302.

Rosen, S. Human capital: a survey of empirical research, *Research in Labor Economics*, R. Ehrenberg (ed.). Greenwich, Conn.: JAI Press, 1977.

Schultz, T. *Investment in Human Capital*. New York: Free Press, 1971.

Schultz, T. Investment in human capital. *AER* 51 68 (March 1961) 1-17.

Schultz, T. Capital formation by education. *JPE* (December 1960) 571-584.

Schultz, T. Investment in man: an economist's view. *Social Science Review* (June 1959) 109-117.

Somers, G. and W.D. Wood (eds.). *Cost-Benefit Analysis of Manpower Policies*. Kingston: Queen's University Industrial Relations Centre, 1965.

Thurow, L. *Investment in Human Capital*. Belmont, California: Wadsworth, 1970.

Treasury Board. *Benefit-Cost Analysis Guide*. Ottawa: Supply and Services, 1976.

Walsh, J. Capital concept applied to man. *QJE* (February 1935) 255-285.

Weisbrod, B. The valuation of human capital. *JPE* 69 (October 1961)
    425-437.

Wilkinson, B. *Studies in the Economics of Education.* Ottawa: Department of
    Labour, 1965.

Wood, W.D. and H.F. Campbell. *Cost-Benefit Analysis and the Economics of
    Investment in Human Resources.* Kingston: Queen's University
    Industrial Relations Centre, 1970.

B. Training

Adams, A. The stock of human capital and differences in post-school formal
    occupational training for middle-aged men. *SEJ* 44 (April 1978)
    929-936.

Bartel, A. and G. Borjas. Specific training and its effects on the human
    capital investment profile. *SEJ* 44 (October 1977) 333-341.

Bateman, W. An application of cost-benefit analysis to the work-experience
    program. *AER Proceedings* 57 (May 1967) 80-90.

Block, F. (ed.). Evaluating manower training programs, *Research in Labor
    Economics,* Supplement 1. Greenwich, Conn.: JAI Press, 1976.

Borus, M. *The Economic Benefits and Costs of Retraining.* Lexington, Mass.:
    D. C. Heath, 1971.

Borus, M. A benefit-cost analysis of the economic effectiveness of
    retraining the unemployed. *Yale Economic Essays* 4 (Fall 1964)
    371-427.

Commission on Post Secondary Education in Ontario. *Manpower Retraining
    Programs in Ontario.* Toronto: Queen's Printer, 1972.

Conley, R. A benefit cost analysis of the vocational rehabilitation program.
    JHR 4 (Spring 1969) 226-252.

Dodge, D. *Returns to Investment in University Training: The Case of Canadian
    Accountants, Engineers and Scientists.* Kingston: Queen's University
    Industrial Relations Centre, 1972.

Donaldson, D. and B. Eaton. Firm-specific human capital: a shared
    investment or optimal entrapment? *CJE* 9 (August 1976) 462-472.
    Comment by S. Eastman and reply 10 (August 1977) 472-475.

Drouet, P. Economic criteria governing the choice of vocational training
    systems. *ILR* 98 (September 1968) 193-223.

Dymond, W. Canadian manpower policy: a policy in search of a problem.
    IRRA (December 1972) 69-78.

Dymond, W. (Chairman). *Training for Ontario's Future: Report of the Task
    Force on Industrial Training.* Toronto: Ontario Ministry of Colleges
    and Universities, 1973.

Eckaus, R. Economic criteria for education and training. *R. E. Stats.* 46
    (May 1964) 181-190.

Goldstein, J. *The Effectiveness of Manpower Training Programs: A Review of
    Research on the Impact on the Poor.* Washington: U.S. Government
    Printing Office, 1972.

Goodman, R. Hiring, training and retraining the hard-core. *IR* 9 (October 1969) 54-66.

Gunderson, M. Training in Canada: progress and problems. *International Journal of Social Economics* 4 (No. 1, 1974) 1-24.

Gunderson, M. The case for government supported training. *RI/IR* 29 (December 1974) 709-726.

Gunderson, M. Training subsidies and disadvantaged workers: regression with a limited dependent variable. *CJE* 7 (November 1974) 69-82.

Gunderson, M. Retention of trainees: a study with dichotomous dependent variables. *Journal of Econometrics* 2 (May 1974) 79-93.

Gunderson, M. Determinants of individual success in on-the-job training. *JHR* 8 (Fall 1973) 472-484.

Holtman, A. On-the-job training, obsolescence, options and retraining. *SEJ* 38 (January 1972) 414-417.

Holtman, A. Joint products and on-the-job training. *JPE* 79 (July-August 1971) 929-931.

Holtman, A. and V.K. Smith. Uncertainty and the durability of on-the-job training. *SEJ* 44 (July 1977) 36-42. Also, an extension, 45 (January 1979) 855-857.

Hughes, J. The role of manpower retraining programs: a critical look at retraining in the United Kingdom. *BJIR* 10 (July 1972) 206-223.

Jain, H. and R. Hines. Current objectives of Canadian federal manpower programs. *RI/IR* 28 (No. 1, 1973) 125-148.

Judy, R. *Conceptual Problems and a Theoretical Framework for Analysing the Distribution of Benefits from Government Assisted Training-in-Industry.* Toronto: Systems Research Group, 1970.

Legace, M. *Industry-Sponsored Training Programs in Ontario.* Toronto: Ontario Ministry of Labour, 1973.

MacMillan, J., P. Nickel and L. Clark. *A New Approach for Evaluating Northern Training Programs.* Winnipeg: Centre for Settlement Studies, University of Manitoba, 1975.

MacMillan, J. and J. Tullock. *Guidelines for Manpower Planning.* Winnipeg, Man.: Department of Agricultural Economics, University of Manitoba, 1973.

Main, E. A nationwide evaluation of MDTA institutional training. *JHR* 3 (Spring 1968) 159-170.

Maki, D. The direct effect of the occupational training of adults program on Canadian unemployment rates. *CJE* 5 (February 1972) 125-130.

Manpower and Immigration. *Manpower Training: Summary Highlights.* Ottawa, 1975.

Mehmet, O. A critical appraisal of the economic rationale of government subsidized manpower training. *RI/IR* 25 (No. 3, 1970) 568-580.

Mehmet, O. Evaluation of institutional and on-the-job manpower training in Ontario. *CJE* 4 (August 1971) 362-373.

Meltz, N. Identifying sources of imbalance in individual labour markets. *RI/IR* 31 (No. 2, 1976) 224-246.

Meltz, N. Implications of manpower and immigration policy. *Issues in Canadian Economics,* L. Officer and L. Smith (eds). Toronto: McGraw-Hill Ryerson, 1974.

Meltz, N. Manpower policy: nature, objectives, perspectives. *RI/IR* 24 (January 1969) 38-43.

Metcalf, D. Pay dispersion, information and returns to search in a professional labour market. *R. E. Studies* 40 (October 1973) 491-506.

Mincer, J. On-the-job training: costs, returns and some implications. *JPE* Supplement, 70, Part 2 (October 1962) 50-79.

Moore, L. *Manpower Planning for Canadians: An Anthology.* Vancouver, B.C.: University of British Columbia Institute of Industrial Relations, 1975.

Newton, K. The rationale for government involvement in manpower training in Canada: theory and evidence. *RI/IR* 32 (No. 3, 1977) 399-414.

Newton, K. A countercyclical training program for Canada. *RI/IR* 26 (No. 4, 1971) 865-889.

Oatey, M. The economics of training. *BJIR* 8 (March 1970) 1-21.

Piore, M. On-the-job training and adjustment to technological change. *JHR* 3 (Fall 1968) 435-449.

Sewel, D. *Training the Poor.* Kingston: Queen's University Industrial Relations Centre, 1971.

Sewel, D. A critique of cost-benefit analysis of training. *MLR* 90 (September 1967) 45-51.

Scott, L. The economic effectiveness of on-the-job training. *ILRR* 23 (January 1970) 220-236.

Solie, R. Employment effects of retraining the unemployed. *ILRR* 21 (January 1968) 210-225.

Somers, G. Federal manpower policies. *Canadian Labour in Transition,* R. Miller and F. Isbester (eds.). Toronto: Prentice Hall, 1971.

Somers, G. *Retraining the Unemployed.* Madison: University of Wisconsin Press, 1968.

Somers, G. Retraining: an evaluation of gains and costs. *Employment Policy and the Labor Market,* A. Ross (ed.). Berkeley: University of California Press, 1965.

Strang, A. and F. Whittingham. *A Proposed Methodology for Cost-Benefit Analysis of Government Supported Training-in-Industry.* Toronto: Ontario Department of Labour, 1970.

Stromsdorfer, E. Determinants of economic success in retraining the unemployed: the West Virginia experience. *JHR* 3 (Spring 1968) 139-158.

Tabbush, V. Investment in training: a broader approach. *JHR* 12 (Spring 1977) 252-257.

Thirwell, J. Government manpower policies in Great Britain: their rationale and benefits. *BJIR* 10 (July 1972) 165-179.

Thomas, B., J. Moxham, and J. Jones. A cost benefit analysis of industrial training. *BJIR* 7 (July 1969) 231-264.

Truesdell, L. Determinants of the demand for manpower training. *RI/IR* 30 (No. 3, 1975) 424-434.

Weber, A., F. Cassell, and W. Ginsburg (eds.). *Public-Private Manpower Policies.* Madison, Wisconsin: Industrial Relations Research Association, 1969.

Weisbrod, B. Conceptual issues in evaluating training programs. *MLR* 89 (October 1966) 1091-1097.

Woodhall, M. Investment in industrial training. *BJIR* 12 (March 1974) 71-90.

Ziderman, A. Costs and benefits of manpower training programmes in Great Britain. *BJIR* 13 (July 1975) 223-244.

C. Labour Market Information and Job Search

[This section usually does not include readings on the macroeconomics of job search and its implications for unemployment and the Phillips curve, nor does it usually include related readings on job search and its implications for quits, turnover and mobility. The latter material is contained in references in part D, following this section.]

Barnes, W. Job search models, the duration of unemployment and the asking wage. *JHR* 10 (Spring 1975) 230-240.

Barron, J. and S. McCafferty. Job search, labour supply and the quit decision. *AER* 67 (September 1977) 683-691.

Bradshaw, T. Job seeking methods used by unemployed workers. *MLR* 96 (February 1973) 35-42.

Burdett, K. A theory of employee job search and quit rates. *AER* 68 (March 1978) 212-220.

Eaton, B. and P. Neher. Unemployment, underemployment and optimal job search. *JPE* 83 (April 1975) 355-376.

Economic Council of Canada. *People and Jobs: A Study of the Canadian Labour Market.* Ottawa: Information Canada, 1976, Ch. 7.

Economic Council of Canada. *Eighth Annual Review.* September 1971, Ch. 8.

Feinberg, R. The forerunners of the job search theory. *EI* 41 (January 1978) 126-132.

Freeman, R. *The Market for College-Trained Manpower: A Study in the Economics of Career Choice.* Cambridge, Mass.: Harvard University Press, 1971.

Gronau, R. Wage comparisons—a selectivity bias. *JPE* 82 (November/December 1974) 1119-1145. Comment by H. G. Lewis, 1145-1156.

Gower, D. *Job Search Patterns in Canada.* Special Labour Force Survey, No. 71-525. Ottawa: Statistics Canada, 1971.

Holt, C. and others. *The Unemployment-Inflation Dilemma: A Manpower Solution.* Washington: Urban Institute, 1971.

Johnson, W. A theory of job shopping. *QJE* 92 (May 1978) 261-278.

Keiffer, N. and G. Neumann. An empirical job search model, with a test of a constant reservation-wage hypothesis. *JPE* 87 (February 1979) 89-108.

Lippman, S. and J. McCall (eds.). *Studies in the Economics of Search.* Amsterdam: North-Holland, 1979.

Lippman, S. and J. McCall. Job search in a dynamic economy. *Journal of Economic Theory* 12 (1976).

Lippman, S. and J. McCall. The economics of job search: a survey. *Economic Enquiry* (June 1976) 155-189 and (September 1976) 347-368. Comment by G. Borjas and M. Goldberg 41 (January 1978) 119-125.

Maki, D. *Search Behaviour in Canadian Job Markets.* Special Study No. 15. Ottawa: Economic Council, 1971.

McCafferty, S. A theory of semi-permanent wage search. *SEJ* 45 (July 1978) 46-62.

McCall, J. Economics of information and job search. *QJE* (February 1970) 113-126. Comment by Peterson and reply (February 1972) 127-134.

Melnik, A. Search strategy in semicompetitive labor markets: the case of MBA graduates. *Quarterly Review of Economics and Business* 11 (Winter 1971) 47-53.

Meltz, *Study of Labour Market Information Systems.* Ottawa: Department of Manpower and Immigration, 1968.

Meltz, N. Labour market information and analysis in Canada. *The Canadian Labour Market,* A. Kruger and N. Meltz (eds.). Toronto: University of Toronto Centre for Industrial Relations, 1968.

Metcalf, D. Pay dispersion, information and returns to search in a professional labour market. *R. E. Studies* 40 (October 1973) 491-506.

Parsons, D. Quit rates over time: a search and information approach. *AER* 63 (June 1973) 390-401.

Peterson, R. Economics of information and job search: another view. *QJE* 86 (February 1972) 127-131.

Pissarides, C. Risk, job search and income distribution. *JPE* 82 (November/December 1974) 1255-1269.

Rees, A. Information networks in labor markets. *AER* 56 (May 1966) 559-566.

Rees, A. and G. Shultz. *Workers and Wages in an Urban Labor Market.* Chicago: University of Chicago Press, 1962.

Reid, G. Job search and the effectiveness of job-finding methods. *ILRR* 25 (July 1972) 479-495.

Sheppard, H. and A. Beltsky. *The Job Hunt.* Baltimore: Johns Hopkins Press, 1966.

Spence, M. Job market signalling. *QJE* 87 (August 1973) 355-374.

Stevens, D. Job search techniques: a new index of effectiveness. *Quarterly Review of Economics and Business* 12 (Summer 1972) 99-104.

Stephenson, S. The economics of youth job search behaviour. *R. E. Stats.* 58 (February 1976) 104-111.

Stigler, G. Information in the labor market. *JPE* Supplement 70 (October 1962) 94-105.

Toikka, R. The economics of information: labour market aspects. *Swedish Journal of Economics* 76 (March 1974) 62-72.

Ulman, J. Interfirm differences in the cost search for clerical workers. *Journal of Business* (April 1968) 153-165.

Ullman, J. and G. Huber. Are job banks improving the labor market information system? *ILRR* 27 (January 1974) 171-185.

Whipple, D. A generalized theory of job search. *JPE* 81 (November/December 1973) 1170-1189.

D. Turnover, Quits and Layoffs

Barron, J. and S. McCafferty. Job search, labor supply and the quit decision. *AER* 63 (September 1977) 683-691.

Barth, P. A time series analysis of layoff rates. *JHR* 6 (Fall 1971).

Block, R. The impact of seniority provisions on the manufacturing quit rate. *ILRR* 31 (July 1978) 474-488.

Burton, J. and J. Parker. Interindustry variations in voluntary labor mobility. *ILRR* 22 (January 1969) 199-216.

Feldstein, M. The importance of temporary layoffs. *BPEA* (No. 3, 1975) 725-745.

Gannon, M. and U. Braineu. Employee tenure in the temporary help industry. *IR* 10 (May 1971) 168-175.

Hall, R. Turnover in the labor force. *BPEA* (No. 3 1972) 709-756.

Inskeep, G. Statistically guided employee selection: an approach to the labor turnover problem. *Personnel Journal* 49 (January 1970) 15-24.

Mattila, J. Job quitting and frictional unemployment. *AER* 64 (March 1974) 235-239.

Mortensen, D. Specific capital and labor turnover. *Bell Journal of Economics* 9 (Autumn 1978) 572-586.

Nickell, S. Wage structures and quit rates. *IER* 17 (February 1976) 191-203.

Parsons, D. Models of labor market turnover, *Research in Labor Economics,* R. Ehrenberg (ed.). Greenwich, Conn.: JAI Press, 1979.

Parsons, D. Quit rates over time. *AER* 63 (June 1973) 390-401.

Parsons, D. Specific human capital: an application to quit rates and layoff rates. *JPE* 80 (November/December 1972) 1120-1143.

Pencavel, J. Wages, specific training, and labor turnover in U.S. manufacturing. *IER* 13 (February 1972) 53-64.

Robertson, G. Absenteeism and labour turnover in selected Ontario industries. *RI/IR* 34 (No. 1, 1979) 86-107.

Salop, S. Wage differentials in a dynamic theory of the firm. *Journal of Economic Theory* 6 (December 1973) 321-344.

Smith, R. and C. Holt. A job search—turnover analysis of the black-white unemployment rate. *IRRA* (December 1970) 76-86.

Stoikov, V. and R. Raimon. Differences in quit rate among industries. *AER* 63 (December 1968) 1283-1298.

Uyar, K. Markov chain forecasts of employee replacement needs. *IR* 11 (February 1972) 96-106.

Wales, T. Quit rates in manufacturing industries in the United States. *CJE* 3 (February 1970) 123-139.

Wickens, M. An econometric model of labour turnover in the U.K. manufacturing industries 1956-1973. *R. E. Studies* 45 (October 1978) 469-478.

Part II

Labour Demand

Chapter 8

Demand For Labour in Competitive Markets[1]

DERIVING DEMAND FOR LABOUR

The marginal productivity theory of labour demand asserts that the demand for labour is a derived demand, derived from the demand for the output produced by firms. The firm's demand curve for labour is simply a schedule showing the profit maximizing amounts of labour employed by a firm at various possible wage rates. Analytically, it is obtained by varying the wage rate that a firm faces for a given homogeneous type of labour, and tracing out the profit maximizing quantity of labour that will be employed by the firm.

Isoquants, Isocosts and Equilibrium

This is depicted geometrically in Figure 8.1. The top part of the diagram, Figure 8.1(a), gives the firm's isoquant Q_o, which shows the various combinations of labour N and all other inputs, represented by capital K, that can produce a given level of output Q_o, via the firm's production function that can be written in general form as $Q = Q(K,N)$. The slope of the isoquant exhibits a diminishing marginal rate of substitution between the inputs. That is, in the upper left segment when an abundance of capital is used, a considerable increase in the use of capital is required for a small reduction in the use of labour, if output is to be maintained. In the lower right segment when an abundance of labour is used, labour is a poor substitute for capital, and considerable labour savings are possible for small increases in the use of capital. In the middle segment of the isoquant, labour and capital are both good substitutes. Successively higher isoquants or levels of output, such as Q_1, can be produced by successively larger amounts of inputs.

Figure 8.1(b) illustrates the firm's budget constraint or isocost line K_mN_m, depicting the various maximum combinations of capital and labour the firm can employ, given their market prices and the expenditures of the firm. Algebraically, the isocost line is $C = rK + wN$ where r is the price of capital and w the price of labour, or wage rate. The position and shape of

---

[1] This chapter does not deal directly with the extensive macroeconomic literature on how the demand for labour varies over the business cycle in response to changes in output, real wages, and the price of other inputs. This literature has been useful in understanding productivity and employment and hours-of work changes over the business cycle. Hamermesh (1976) refers to much of this literature and uses it to provide estimates of the elasticity of demand for labour based on time series data.

Figure 8.1   Isoquants, Isocost, and Equilibrium

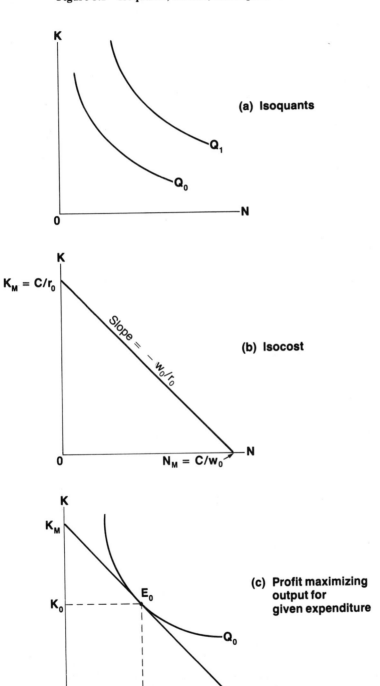

(a) Isoquants

(b) Isocost

(c) Profit maximizing
output for
given expenditure

the isocost line can be determined by solving for the two intercepts or end points and the slope of the line between them. From the isocost equation, for fixed prices r_o and w_o, these end points are $N_m = C/w_o$ when $K = 0$, and $K_m = C/r_o$ when $N = 0$. The slope is simply minus the rise divided by the run or $-[C/r_o \div C/w_o] = -w_o/r_o$, that is, the price of labour relative to the price of capital. This is a straight line as long as w and r are constant for these given types of labour and capital.

A profit maximizing firm will maximize the output that can be produced for a given level of cost, or alternatively it will minimize the cost for a given level of output. Figure 8.1(c) combines the isoquants and isocost to illustrate the maximum output (isoquant) that the firm can attain given its resource expenditure constraint (isocost). This is clearly E_o where the isocost is tangent to the isoquant.

At E_o, the profit maximizing amounts of labour and capital, respectively used to produce Q_o units of output, are N_o and K_o. This gives us one point on the demand curve for labour, as depicted later in Figure 8.3. That is, at the wage rate w_o the firm employs N_o units of labour.

Deriving the Firm's Labour Demand Schedule

The complete labour demand schedule, for the long run when the firm can vary both capital and labour, can be obtained simply by varying the wage rate and tracing out the new, equilibrium, profit-maximizing amounts of labour that would be employed. This is illustrated in Figure 8.2. For example, an increase in the wage rate from w_o to w_1 would rotate the isocost line downwards as in Figure 8.2(a). This is so because if the firm spent all of its expenditures on capital it would be at the same maximum point $K_m = C/r_o$. However, if it spent all of its budget on the higher priced labour then the maximum amount of labour it could employ would be reduced to a point like $N = C/w_1$ corresponding to the higher price of labour. Since $w_1 > w_o$ then $N_n < N_m$. Also, the slope of the new budget constraint would be greater than the original; that is, $w_1/r_o > w_o/r_o$.

As depicted in Figure 8.2(b), given the new isocost corresponding to the higher wage rate w_1, the firm will maximize output for a given level of cost by moving to a lower level of output Q_1, operating at E_1 and employing N_1 units of labour. This yields a second point on the firm's demand curve for labour depicted in Figure 8.2(c). That is, a lower level of employment N_1 corresponds to the higher wage rate w_1.

Clearly one could trace out the full demand schedule by varying the wage rate and observing the profit maximizing amounts of labour that would be employed. In normal circumstances, the demand schedule would be downward sloping (that is, higher wages associated with a reduced demand for labour) both because the firm would substitute cheaper inputs for the more expensive labour (substitution effect), and because it would reduce its scale of operations because of the wage and hence cost increase (scale effect).

Figure 8.2 Deriving the Labour Demand Schedule

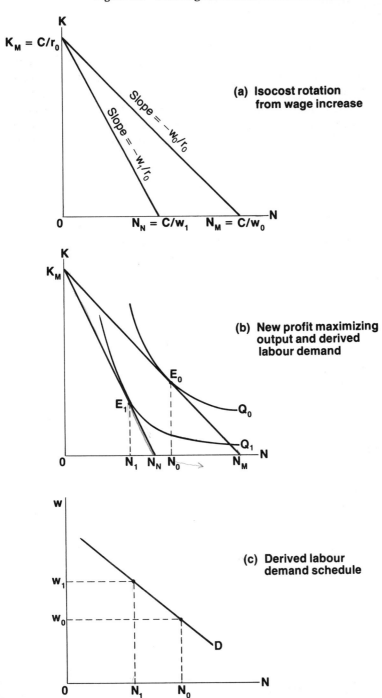

(a) Isocost rotation from wage increase

(b) New profit maximizing output and derived labour demand

(c) Derived labour demand schedule

Separating Scale and Substitution Effects of a Wage Change

Figure 8.3 illustrates how the wage increase from w_0 to w_1 can be separated into its component parts — a substitution effect and a scale or expansion effect. The negative substitution effect occurs as the firm substitutes cheaper capital for the more expensive labour, therefore reducing the quantity of labour demanded. Under normal circumstances, the negative scale effect occurs as a wage increase leads to a higher marginal cost of production which, in turn, reduces the firm's optimal output and hence derived demand

Figure 8.3   Substitution and Scale Effects of a Wage Change

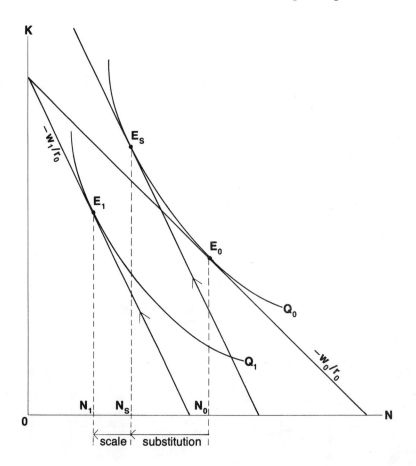

for labour. Thus the scale and substitution effects reinforce each other to lead to an unambiguously inverse relationship between wages and the firm's demand for labour.[2]

The scale effect can be isolated by hypothetically compensating the firm for its lost output so that it would operate on the original isoquant Q_0. This is illustrated by the hypothetical isocost line that is parallel to the new isocost w_1/r_0, but tangent to the original isoquant Q_0 at E_s. The only difference between E_s and E_1 is the scale of operation of the firm (Q_0 as opposed to Q_1), since the relative price of labour and capital are the same; that is, both are w_1/r_0. Therefore, $N_s - N_1$ can be thought of as the scale effect — the reduction in employment that comes about to the extent that the firm reduces its scale of operations in response to the wage increase. Under normal circumstances, the scale effect can be thought of as working through the following scenario: wage increases imply cost increases, which lead to a reduced optimal scale of output, which in turn leads to a reduced demand for labour.

The difference between E_0 and E_s, on the other hand, is simply due to the different slopes of the isocost lines. They both represent the same scale of output, Q_0. Consequently, the difference between E_0 and E_s reflects the pure substitution of capital for labour to produce the same scale of output, Q_0. Therefore, $N_0 - N_s$ can be thought of as a pure or compensated substitution effect, representing the substitution of cheaper inputs for the inputs whose price has risen. Both scale and substitution effects work in the same direction to yield an unambiguously downward sloping demand schedule for labour.

---

[2] Nagatani (1978) proves that this is true even when labour is an inferior factor of production; that is, when the firm's production function is such that less labour is employed when the firm expands output. When labour is an inferior factor of production and wages increase, the firm's marginal cost of production actually decreases. This occurs because, after the wage increase, in order to expand production the firm uses less of the more expensive labour and more of the relatively cheaper capital. The decreased marginal cost of production then leads to an increased optimal output which, in the case of the inferior factor, means less labour employed. In essence, the reverse effect from output to employment in the case of inferior factors is negated by the reverse effect on the firm's marginal cost schedule.

This can be illustrated more rigorously by examining what happens to the firm's costs as wages increase. The firm's total cost function can be written as $TC_Q = wN + rK$ and marginal cost is $MC_Q = \partial TC/\partial Q = w\partial N/\partial Q + r\partial K/\partial Q$. The change in marginal cost that results from a wage change is therefore $\partial MC_Q/\partial w = \partial N/\partial Q$. If N is a normal factor of production, then by definition $\partial N/\partial Q > 0$ and therefore $\partial MC_Q/\partial w > 0$. That is, the usual scale effect is in operation: a wage increase leads to higher marginal cost, which results in reduced output and hence a lower derived demand for labour.

However, if N is an inferior factor, then $\partial N/\partial Q < 0$ and therefore $\partial MC_Q/\partial w < 0$ because $\partial N/\partial Q = \partial MC_Q/\partial w$. The scale effect then operates as follows: a wage increase reduces marginal cost, which results in increased output and, because of the inferiority of the factor, a lower derived demand for labour. Thus, the change in the derived demand for labour that results from the firm's changing its scale of output in response to the wage increase is unambiguously negative.

At this point, it may be worth highlighting a common misconception concerning the reason for the downward sloping demand for labour. The demand is for a given homogeneous type of labour; consequently, it does *not* slope downwards because, as the firm uses more labour, it uses poorer quality labour and hence pays a lower wage. It may well be true that when firms expand their work-force they often have to use poorer quality labour. Nevertheless for analytical purposes it is useful to assume a given, homogeneous type of labour so that the impact, on labour demand, of changes in the wage rate for that type of labour can be analysed. Any change in the productivity of labour that occurs does so because of the changes in the mix of inputs, not because the firm is delving more into the reserve of less qualified labour.

For example, at the original equilibrium E_0 in Figure 8.3, less capital is employed per unit of labour than at E_1. Consequently, the marginal productivity of N_0 units of labour associated with the lower rate, w_0, is lower than the marginal productivity of N_1 units of labour associated with the higher wage of w_1. That is, the wage increase induces a substitution of capital for labour which in turn results in an increase in the marginal productivity of labour relative to capital in the firm. The lower wage is associated with a lower marginal productivity of labour not because the firm utilized a poorer quality of labour (embodying less human capital), but rather because the firm used less capital per unit of labour when wages were lower. The downward sloping demand for labour occurs because of the substitution and scale effects for a given homogeneous type of labour (which in turn leads to a change in the marginal productivity of this given type of labour), not because of the use of a different quality of labour.

Wages and Marginal Productivity of Labour

The relationship between wages and the marginal productivity of labour can be understood more clearly by illustrating that the firm's demand schedule for labour is the locus of points for which wages just equal the value of the marginal product of labour, VMP_n, which in turn equals the marginal physical product of labour, MPP_n, times the price, p, at which that product is sold. The firm maximizes profits by employing an extra unit of labour until its marginal cost, MC_n, just equals the marginal revenue, MR_n, generated by that extra unit of labour. Assuming that the firm can sell all of its output at the going market price, p^*, then the marginal revenue generated by an extra unit of labour equals the value of the marginal product of labour, that is $MR_n \equiv VMP_n \equiv MPP_n \cdot p^*$. Assuming that the firm can buy all of the labour it wants in competitive labour markets at the going wage rate, w^*, then the marginal cost of an additional unit of labour is simply that wage rate: that is, $MC_n = w^*$. Therefore, the profit maximizing rule that $MC_n = MR_n$ implies that the firm will demand labour until $w^* = VMP_n = MPP_n \cdot p^*$. The profit maximizing firm's demand schedule for labour is therefore the locus of points for which wages just equal the value of the marginal product of labour. Alternatively stated, it is the locus of points for which the real wage rate, w^*/p^*, equals the marginal physical product of labour.

Mathematical Exposition

The firm's demand schedule for labour can also be derived using calculus. Profits to the firm are revenues minus cost. That is, $\pi = pQ(N,K) - wN - rK$. Firms are assumed to be competitive in the product and input markets and hence p, w and r are fixed. The profit maximizing firm maximizes profits by employing labour until there are no additional profits from employing an extra unit of labour: that is, until $\partial\pi/\partial N = 0$. This, in turn, implies $p\partial Q/\partial N - w = 0$. Profits are being *maximized* here since $\partial^2\pi/\partial N^2 = \partial^2 Q/\partial N^2 < 0$ by the assumption of diminishing marginal productivity. Since $\partial Q/\partial N \equiv MPP_n$ then the firm's profit maximizing demand schedule for labour is the locus of points for which $w = MPP_n p = VMP_n$; that is, for which the money wage rate equals the value of the marginal product of labour, or alternatively stated, for which the real wage rate equals the marginal physical product of labour.

The same results can be obtained using the more general technique of Lagrangian multipliers. Profits are defined as

$$\pi = pQ - wN - rK \tag{1}$$

and the production function can be written as

$$Q = Q(N,K) \tag{2}$$

The Lagrangian expression which incorporates the profit function to be maximized and the constraint of the production function is written as:

$$L = pQ - w \cdot N - r \cdot K - \lambda[Q - Q(N,K)] \tag{3}$$

Setting all partial derivations equal to zero so as to obtain an optimum yields:

$$\partial L/\partial N = -w + \lambda\partial Q/\partial N = 0 \tag{4}$$
$$\partial L/\partial K = -r + \lambda\partial Q/\partial K = 0 \tag{5}$$
$$\partial L/\partial Q = p - \lambda = 0 \tag{6}$$
$$\partial L/\partial\lambda = -Q + Q(N,K) = 0 \tag{7}$$

Equation (7) simply ensures that the constraint is being satisfied when profits are being maximized. Substituting (6) into (4) yields

$$w = p\,\partial Q/\partial N \tag{4'}$$

That is, the profit maximizing demand for labour is the locus of points for which wages are equal to the value of the marginal product of labour (i.e. the price of the product times the marginal physical product of labour).

Industry Demand for Labour

The previous analysis dealt with the demand for labour at the level of aggregation of the individual firm. The industry demand for labour would be the aggregate of the quantities demanded by the various firms composing the industry. At the industry level, however, an additional factor must be considered and this can have feedback effects on the firms comprising the industry.

At the industry level, the price of the output produced by the various firms in the industry may change in response to changes in the industry supply of that output. For example, in response to a wage decrease, the supply of output in the industry would increase because of the lower labour cost of production. This increase in industry supply would lead to a drop in the industry price level, assuming that the demand for output is not perfectly price elastic. This drop in the price of the product leads to a reduction in industry output relative to the output that would have been produced had it not been necessary to lower prices to sell the output. This in turn leads to a choking off of the increase in the demand for labour in the firms comprising the industry. In essence, the expansion of employment occasioned by the wage decrease is not as large as it would have been had the industry not had to lower product prices to sell the additional output.

At the level of the individual firm, when this general equilibrium effect is considered, the increased demand for labour, occasioned by a wage decrease, may be reduced somewhat because of the feedback effect of higher product prices. Consequently the demand for labour in each individual firm is more inelastic when this feedback effect is considered, and therefore the aggregate demand for labour in the industry is more inelastic than simply the sums of the individual demand schedules from the firms comprising the industry.

ELASTICITY OF DEMAND FOR LABOUR

The previous analysis indicated that the demand for labour is a negative function of the wage rate. Consequently, in this static, partial-equilibrium framework, an exogenous increase in wages, other things held constant, would lead to a reduction in the quantity of labour demanded. The exogenous increase in wages, for example, could emanate from a union wage demand, a wage parity scheme, or wage fixing legislation, such as minimum wages, equal pay, fair wage legislation or extension legislation. Although there may be offsetting factors (to be discussed later), it is important to realize that economic theory predicts that there will be an adverse employment effect from these wage increases. The magnitude of the adverse employment effect depends on the elasticity of the derived demand for labour. As illustrated in Figure 8.4, if the demand for labour is inelastic (Figure 8.4(a)), then the adverse employment effect is small: if the demand is elastic (Figure 8.4(b)), then the adverse employment effect is large.

From a policy perspective it is important to know the expected magnitude of these adverse employment effects because they may offset other possible benefits of the exogenous wage increase. Consequently, it is important to know the determinants of the elasticity of demand for labour. As

Figure 8.4   Inelastic and Elastic Demand For Labour

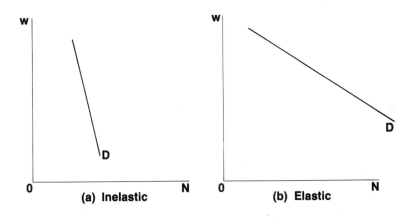

(a) Inelastic   (b) Elastic

originally outlined by Marshall and formalized by Hicks (1963, pp. 241-46 and 374-84), the basic determinants of the elasticity of demand for labour are the availability of substitute inputs, the elasticity of supply of substitute inputs, the elasticity of demand for output, and the ratio of labour cost to total cost. Each of these factors will be discussed in turn, in the context of an inelastic demand for labour (Figure 8.4(a)) which implies a wage increase being associated with a small adverse employment effect.

Availability of Substitute Inputs

The derived demand for labour will be inelastic, and hence the adverse employment effect of an exogenous wage increase will be small, if alternative inputs cannot be substituted easily for the higher priced labour. This would be depicted by an isoquant that is more L-shaped as opposed to a negatively sloped straight line; that is, the marginal rate of technical substitution between other inputs and labour is small.

The inability to substitute alternative inputs could be technologically determined, as for example if the particular type of labour is essential to the production process, or it could be institutionally determined, as for example if the union prevents such substitution as contracting-out or the use of non-union labour or the introduction of new technology. Time also is a factor, since in the long run the possibility of substituting cheaper inputs is more feasible.

Examples of workers for whom substitute inputs may not *readily* be available could include construction craftsmen, teachers, and professionals with specialized skills. Even in these cases, however, substitutions are technically possible in the long run, especially when one considers alternative production processes and delivery systems (e.g. prefabricated construction, larger class size with more audio-visual aids, and the use of paraprofessionals).

Elasticity of Supply of Substitute Inputs

The substitution of alternative inputs can also be affected by changes in the price of these inputs. If the substitutes are relatively *inelastic* in supply, so that an increase in the demand for the inputs will lead to an increase in their price, then this price increase may choke off some of the increased usage of these substitutes. In general, this is probably not an important factor, however, because it is unlikely that the firm or industry where the wage increase occurs is such a large purchaser of alternative inputs that it affects their price. Certainly in the long run, the supply of substitute inputs is likely to be more elastic.

Elasticity of Demand for Output

Since the demand for labour is derived from the output produced by the firm, then the elasticity of the demand for labour will depend on the price elasticity of the demand for the output or services produced by the firm. If the demand for the output produced by the firm is inelastic, so that a price increase (engendered by a wage increase) will not lead to a large reduction in the quantity demanded, then the derived demand for labour will also be inelastic. In such circumstances, the wage increase can be passed on to consumers in the form of higher product prices without there being much of a reduction in the demand for those products and hence in the derived demand for labour.

   This could be the case, for example, in construction, especially non-residential construction where there are few alternatives to building in a particular location. It could also be the case in tariff-protected industries, or in public services where few alternatives are available, or in most sectors in the short run. On the other hand, in fiercely competitive sectors, such as the garment trades or coal mining, where alternative products are available, then the demand for the product is probably quite price elastic. In these circumstances, the derived demand for labour would be elastic and a wage increase would lead to a large reduction in the quantity of labour demanded.

Ratio of Labour Cost to Total Cost

The extent to which labour cost is an important component of total cost can also affect the responsiveness of employment to wage changes. Specifically, the demand for labour will be inelastic, and hence the adverse employment effect of a wage increase small, if labour cost is a small portion of total cost.[3] In such circumstances the scale effect would be small; that is, the firm would not have to reduce its output much because the cost increase emanating from the wage increase would be small. In addition, there is the possibility that if wage costs are a small portion of total cost then any wage increase more easily could be absorbed by the firm or passed on to consumers.

Examples of wage cost for a particular group of workers being a small portion of total cost could include construction craftworkers, airline pilots and employed professionals (e.g. engineers and architects) on many projects. In such circumstances their wage increases simply may not matter much to the employer, and consequently their wage demands may not be tempered much by the threat of reduced employment. On the other hand, the wages of government workers and miners may constitute a large portion of the total cost in their respective trades. The resultant elastic demand for labour may thereby temper their wage demands.

Summary of Examples

The previous discussion of the determinants of the elasticity of demand for labour suggested that in some cases the various determinants worked in the same direction to give rise to an inelastic demand. Such could be the case, for example, for many skilled construction trades or airline pilots, where there are few good substitute inputs, the demand for the output is relatively price inelastic, and labour cost is a small portion of total cost. Consequently, wage demands would be less tempered by the threat of reduced employment.

On the other hand, in other sectors like the garment trades or mining, the determinants of the elasticity of demand for labour give rise to an elastic demand. Especially in the long run, substitute inputs are readily available, the demand for the output is relatively price elastic, and labour cost is a significant portion of total cost. In such circumstances wage demands may be tempered by the possibility of reduced employment associated with the elastic demand for labour. Alternatively, as we will discuss in a later section on unionism, wage demands may be accompanied by complementary policies designed to reduce the adverse employment effect or, as in the case of some workers, the adverse employment effect may simply be accepted as a necessary by-product of wage increases.

Clearly, knowledge of the elasticity of demand for particular types of labour is important for policy purposes so as to predict the adverse employment effect that may emanate from such factors as minimum wage and equal

---

[3] Hicks (1963, pp. 245-6) proves formally that this is true as long as the elasticity of demand for the final product is greater than the elasticity of substitution between the inputs. This illustrates the "importance of being unimportant" as long as consumers can substitute away from the higher priced product more easily than producers can substitute away from higher priced labour.

pay laws, or wage increases associated with unionization, occupational licensing or arbitrated wage settlements. Estimates of the elasticity of the demand for the particular type of labour being affected would be useful, to predict the employment effect of an exogenous wage increase. However, even without precise numerical estimates,[4] judicious statements still can be made based on the importance of the various factors that determine the elasticity of the demand for labour.

MINIMUM WAGE LEGISLATION

Minimum wage laws provide a useful illustration of the practical relevance of our theoretical knowledge of the determinants of the derived demand for labour. In Canada, labour matters usually are under provincial jurisdiction; hence, each province has its own minimum wage law. Federal labour laws cover slightly under 10 per cent of Canadian workers. Industries of an inter-provincial or international nature—for example, inter-provincial transportation and telephone communication, air transport, broadcasting, shipping and banks—are under federal jurisdiction. The influence of federal laws may be larger to the extent that they serve as a model for comparable provincial legislation.

The rationale behind minimum wage laws has not always been clear and explicit. Curbing poverty among the working poor, preventing "exploitation" of the unorganized non-union sector, preventing "unfair" low-wage competition, have all been suggested as possible rationales. In the early days of union organizing, it is alleged, minimum wage laws were also instituted to curb unionization — in that, if the wages of unorganized labour could be raised through government legislation, there would be less need for unions. As is so often the case with legislation, its actual impact may be different from its intended impact, or at least it may have unintended side effects. Economic theory may be of some help in shedding light on this issue.

Expected Impact

Competitive economic theory predicts that in the long-run, minimum wage laws will have an adverse employment effect; that is, employment will be reduced relative to what it would have been in the absence of the minimum wage. This is illustrated in Figure 8.5 where w_c and N_c are the competitive

---

[4] Hamermesh, D. (1976) reviewed an extensive empirical literature in the U.S. that can be used to calculate estimates of the elasticity of demand for labour. He concluded that, based largely on private sector data in the U.S., this elasticity ranged from a low of $-.09$ to a high of $-.62$, with a medium estimate of $-.32$, over a time period of one year. That is, a one percent increase in wages would lead to approximately a one-third of one percent reduction in employment after a one year time period. This adverse employment effect was roughly equally divided between the substitution and scale effect; that is, the substitution and scale elasticities were approximately equal.

Figure 8.5 Minimum Wage

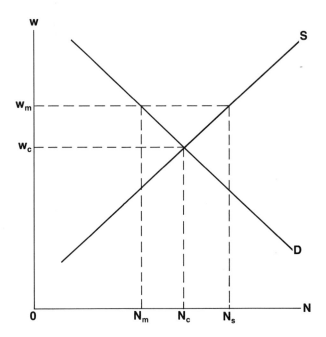

wage and competitive level of employment, respectively, in a particular labour market. After the imposition of the minimum wage, w_m, employers will reduce their demand for labour to N_m. Thus $(N_c - N_m)$ is the adverse employment effect associated with the minimum wage. In addition to the $(N_c - N_m)$ workers who would not be employed because of the minimum wage, an additional $(N_s - N_c)$ workers would be vying for these jobs because the minimum wage is higher than the competitive wage. Thus the queue of applicants for the reduced number of jobs is $(N_s - N_m)$, with $(N_c - N_m)$ representing workers laid-off because of the minimum wage and $(N_s - N_c)$ representing new potential recruits who are attracted to the minimum wage jobs.

The adverse employment effect $(N_c - N_m)$ occurs as firms substitute other relatively cheaper inputs for the higher priced labour, and as they reduce output in response to the higher costs. These are the familiar substitution and scale effects, respectively, that give rise to the downward-sloping demand schedule for labour. The adverse employment effect need not mean an increase in measured unemployment: some who lose jobs in the covered sector may go to the uncovered sector or drop out of the labour force.

The magnitude of this adverse employment effect depends on the elasticity of the derived demand for labour. If the demand for labour were relatively inelastic then the adverse employment effect would be small. Unfortunately, in those sectors most affected by minimum wage legislation— low wage industries like textiles, sales, service and tourism—the demand for labour is likely to be fairly elastic, especially in the long run, reflecting the availability of substitute inputs and products as well as the fact that labour costs are often a substantial proportion of the total cost. In addition, since many of these sectors are often thought of as "fiercely competitive", it is unlikely that the minimum wage cost increases could be absorbed by the industry through a reduction in monopoly profits.

Possible Offsetting Factors

In a dynamic context, other things are changing at the same time as the minimum wage, and these changes may offset, in part at least, the adverse employment effect. For example, the demand for labour could increase perhaps because of an exogenous increase in the demand for output or because of an increase in the price of substitute inputs. While this may mitigate some, or perhaps even all, of the unemployment associated with the minimum wage, it is still true that employment would be even higher were it not for the minimum wage. Hence there is still an adverse employment effect relative to the situation with no minimum wage. This can easily be illustrated in Figure 8.5 by shifting the demand schedule upwards and to the right and tracing out the new level of employment with and without the minimum wage.

It is possible that some of the adverse employment effect may be offset by what could be labelled a "shock effect". Because of the cost pressure associated with the higher minimum wage, employers may be induced into utilizing other cost-saving devices that they should have introduced even without the minimum wage. The minimum wage simply served as the catalyst for the introduction of cost-saving efficiencies. Similarly labour itself may be induced into becoming more productive, perhaps because of the higher wage or perhaps because of the queue of applicants vying for their jobs. The existence of these shock effects, however, requires that there be some slack in the system; that is, that firms were not maximizing profits in the first place, because otherwise they would have instituted these possibilities even without the minimum wage.

There are possible situations when employers may be able to absorb the wage cost increases without reducing employment. If the firm were an oligopolist and would lose a substantial share of the market by raising its product price, it may try to absorb the wage cost increase. (This situation of oligopoly with a kinked demand curve is developed more formally in Chapter 10.) However, it is likely that the low wage industries that are most affected by the minimum wage are likely to be extremely competitive rather than oligopolistic.

Similarly, employers who dominate the local labour market may not have to pay a competitive wage rate. In such circumstances the minimum wage may simply compel the employer to pay what would be a competitive wage. (This situation of monopsony and its implications for minimum wage legislation is developed more formally in Chapter 11.) Once again, however, it is unlikely that the industries that are most affected by minimum wages are those dominated by one or a few employers. Rather, the employers most affected tend to be small in size and competing in a labour market that has large pools of unskilled labour.

Thus while there is the theoretical possibility of these factors offsetting, in part at least, the adverse employment effect of minimum wage laws, their practical relevance is in question. It is unlikely that they could be of great importance in the long run, especially in those low wage sectors most affected by minimum wages. This leaves us with the inescapable conclusion that, in all probability, minimum wage laws reduce employment opportunities. In addition, the impact will fall disproportionately on unskilled workers who are often most in need of work experience. This is the case, for example, with respect to younger workers and women who could utilize employment, even at low wages, as a means to acquire the on-the-job training and labour market experience necessary to move on to higher paying jobs. For this reason, some would argue that minimum wage laws actually harm the very people they are allegedly designed to help.

This does not necessarily mean that minimum wage laws are undesirable, although that probably is the conclusion of most economists. The benefits of the wage increases to some have to be weighed against the costs of reduced employment opportunities to others. In addition, some would argue that even if minimum wages do reduce employment opportunities, it is in jobs that should not exist in the first place. It may be better to have these jobs eradicated and the unemployed workers trained for higher-wage jobs.

Empirical Evidence on Actual Impact

As may be expected, it is difficult to ascertain the actual impact of minimum wage legislation, largely because so many other factors are also changing over time, and it may take a long time for all of the adjustments to occur. In addition, the adjustment processes may be subtle and difficult to document empirically. For example, a clothing manufacturer, when faced with a minimum wage increase, may contract-out to households to do specific tasks, such as sewing on buttons or collars, or a restaurant may increase its usage of pre-packaged foods. How does one accurately compare the employment reduction in the clothing establishment or restaurant with the employment creation in the household or the food processing sector, to arrive at a net employment effect of the minimum wage?

In spite of the obvious difficulties, there have been numerous attempts to measure the employment impact of minimum wage laws, mainly in the

United States. After a thorough survey of the empirical evidence up until the late 1960s, Kaufman and Foran (1968) conclude that the overwhelming bulk of evidence supports the predictions of economic theory. Additional empirical evidence since that time seems to continue to support that contention. This is especially the case with the large number of recent studies — for example Moore (1971), Kosters and Welch (1972), Adie (1973), Katz (1973), Welch (1974, 1976), Mincer (1976) and Ragan (1977) — that have documented a substantial adverse employment effect on teenagers.

QUESTIONS

1. The marginal productivity theory of labour demand has been criticized for being unrealistic in its assumptions, and for ignoring a wealth of information available to us from other sources. Evaluate.
2. Why is the point E_0 in Figure 8.1(c) a stable equilibrium? Depict the firm's expansion path. Depict the isoquant for a firm whose technology is such that it must utilize labour and capital in fixed proportions to produce its output. Depict the scale and substitution effect of a wage decrease in such a circumstance. Depict the firm's expansion path.
3. What is meant by an inferior factor of production? How would the firm's demand for labour be altered if labour were an inferior factor of production?
4. "The firm's demand for labour is a negative function of the wage because, as the firm uses more labour, it has to utilize poorer quality labour, and hence pays a lower wage." Discuss.
5. Discuss the firm's short-run demand for labour when its capital is fixed.
6. Derive the firm's demand schedule for labour if it were a monopolist that could influence the price at which it sells its output. That is, relax the assumption that product prices are fixed and trace through the implications.
7. Why is the firm's demand for labour more inelastic when one considers the general equilibrium feedback from changes in the product price at the industry level?
8. Utilize Figure 8.5 to depict the situation where the demand schedule for labour exogenously shifts upward to the right at the same time as the minimum wage is set at w_m.
   (a) Could the minimum wage be redundant?
   (b) Could employment increase relative to its earlier level of N_c?
   (c) If employment increased, is it correct to say that minimum wage legislation has an adverse employment effect?
   (d) If so, what is its magnitude?
9. Why might unions support minimum wage legislation?
10. If minimum wage laws actually harm the people they are designed to assist, can you explain their seeming political popularity?

11. Discuss various problems associated with measuring the employment impact of minimum wage legislation.
12. Some jurisdictions in Canada have different minimum wages for different groups such as construction workers, learners and probationary workers, and students. Would you support such policies?
13. What alternative policies may be feasible to achieve the objectives of minimum wage laws?
14. What complementary policies may be desirable to accompany minimum wage legislation?
15. Evaluate minimum wage legislation as an anti-poverty device.
16. In terms of personal characteristics, *who* would you expect to be most affected by minimum wage laws?
17. Evaluate the practical importance of the various possible offsetting factors that could mitigate the adverse employment effect of a minimum wage increase.
18. Would you support a 20 per cent increase in the minimum wage in all jurisdictions in Canada? Why or why not?
19. Based on your knowledge of labour market theory, outline the expected impact of a minimum wage increase on each of the following:
    (a) employment and unemployment of workers in the sector covered by the minimum wage;
    (b) employment and unemployment of workers in the non-covered sector;
    (c) occupational wage structure;
    (d) union wages;
    (e) labour force participation rates of women and youths.

REFERENCES AND FURTHER READINGS

A. Labour Demand

Archibald, G.C. Testing marginal productivity theory. *R. E. Stats.* 27 (June 1960) 210-213.

Ashenfelter, O. and R. Ehrenberg. The demand for labor in the public sector. *Labour in the Public and Nonprofit Sectors*, D. Hamermesh (ed.). Princeton: Princeton University Press, 1975.

Bassett, L. and T. Borcherding. The firm, the industry, and the long-run demand for factors of production. *CJE* 3 (February 1970) 140-144.

Berry, R.A. Price of capital, income, and the demand for labor in developing countries. *SEJ* 44 (January 1978) 457-469.

Bishop, R. A firm's short-run and long-run demands for a factor. *WEJ* (March 1967).

Brent, W. The wages fund controversy revisited. *CJE* 33 (November 1967) 509-528.

Cotterill, P. The elasticity of demand for low wage labour. *SEJ* 41 (January 1975) 520-526.

Diewert, E. A note on the elasticity of derived demand in the n-factor case. *Economica* 38 (1971) 192-198.

Ehrenberg, R. The demand for state and local government employees. *AER* 63 (June 1973) 366-379.

Ehrenberg, R. *The Demand for State and Local Government Employees: An Econometric Analysis.* Lexington, Mass.: D. C. Heath, 1972.

Freeman, R. Demand for labor in a nonprofit market: university faculty. *Labor in the Public and Nonprofit Sectors,* D. Hamermesh (ed.). Princeton: Princeton University Press, 1975.

Gottschalk, P. A comparison of marginal productivity and earnings by occupation. *ILRR* 31 (April 1978) 368-378.

Hamermesh, D. Econometric studies of labour demand and their application to policy analysis. *JHR* 11 (Fall 1976) 507-525.

Hicks, J. *Theory of Wages*, 2nd ed. London: Macmillan, 1963, 241-246, 374.

Johnson, G. The demand for labor by educational category. *SEJ* 37 (October 1970) 190-204.

Kotowitz, Y. Capital-labor substitutions in Canadian manufacturing 1926-1939 and 1946-1961. *CJE* 1 (August 1968) 619-632.

Laudadio, L. A note on the elasticity of demand. *CJE* 1 (November 1968) 825-827.

Lester, R. Shortcomings of marginal analysis for wage-employment problems. *AER* 37 (March 1946) 63-82.

Machlup, F. Marginal analysis and empirical research. *AER* 36 (September 1946) 519-528.

Maurice, S. Long run factor demanded in a perfectly competitive industry. *JPE* 80 (November/December 1972) 1271-1279.

McInnis, M. Long-run changes in the industrial structure of the Canadian work force. *CJE* 4 (August 1971) 353-361.

Meltz, N. *Changes in the Occupational Composition of the Canadian Labour Force, 1931-1961.* Ottawa: Queen's Printer, 1965.

Meltz, N. The female worker: occupational trends in Canada. *Changing Pattern in Women's Employment.* Ottawa: Women's Bureau, Canada Department of Labour, 1966, 32-52.

Minasian, J. Elasticity of substitution and constant output demand curves for labor. *JPE* 69 (June 1961) 261-270.

Mishan, E. The demand for labor in a classical and Keynesian framework. *JPE* 72 (December 1964).

Nagatani, K. Substitution and scale effects in factor demands. *CJE* 11 (August 1978) 521-526.

Ostry, S. *The occupational composition of the Canadian Labour Force, 1961 Census Monograph.* Ottawa: Dominion Bureau of Statistics, 1967.

Pissarides, C. The role of relative wages and excess demand in the sectoral flow of labour. *R. E. Studies* 45 (October 1978) 453-468.

Razin, A. A note on the elasticity of derived demand under decreasing returns. *AER* 64 (September 1974) 697-700.

Rees, A. Wage determination and involuntary unemployment. *JPE* 59 (April 1951) 143-153.

Reza, A. Labour supply and demand, absenteeism, and union behaviour. *R. E. Studies* 42 (April 1975) 237-248.

Russel, R. On the demand curve for a factor of production. *AER* 54 (1964) 726-732.

Sargent, T. Estimation of dynamic labor demand schedules under rational expectations. *JPE* 86 (December 1978) 1009-1044.

Sato, R. and T. Koizumi. Substitutability, complementarity and the theory of derived demand. *R. E. Studies* 37 (January 1970) 107-118.

Schaafsma, J. On estimating the time structure of capital-labor substitution in the manufacturing sector: a model applied to 1949-1972 Canadian data. *SEJ* 44 (April 1978) 740-751.

Skolnik, M. An empirical analysis of the substitution between engineers and technicians in Canada. *RI/IR* 25 (April 1970) 284-399.

Stoneman, P. The effect of computers on the demand for labour. *EJ* 85 (September 1975) 590-608.

Swan, N. Difference in the response of the demand for labour to variations in output among Canadian regions. *CJE* 5 (August 1972) 373-385.

Thornton, R. The elasticity of demand for public school teachers. *IR* 18 (Winter 1979) 86-91.

Thurow, L. *Generating Inequality.* New York: Basic Books, 1975.

Thurow, L. Disequilibrium and the marginal productivity of capital and labor. *R. E. Stats.* 50 (February 1968) 23-31.

West, E. and R. Hafer. J.S. Mill, unions, and the wages fund recantation. *QJE* 92 (November 1978) 603-620.

Woodland, A. Substitution of structures, equipment and labor in Canadian production. *IER* 16 (February 1975) 171-187.

Yeung, P. A note on the rule of derived demand. *QJE* 86 (August 1972) 511-517.

B. Minimum Wage Legislation

Adie, D. Teenage unemployment and real federal minimum wages. *JPE* 81 (March/April 1973) 435-441.

Adie, D. The lag in effect of minimum wages on teenage unemployment. *IRRA* (December 1971) 38-46.

Adie, D. and G. Chaplin. Teenage unemployment effects of federal minimum wages. *IRRA* (December 1970) 117-127.

Ashenfelter, O. and R. Smith. Compliance with the minimum wage law. *JPE* 87 (April 1979) 333-351.

Badenhorp, L. Effects of the $1 minimum wage in seven areas. *MLR* 81 (July 1958) 737-743.

Barth, P. The minimum wage and teenage unemployment. *IRRA* (December 1969) 296-310.

Bayliss, F. Union policy toward minimum wage legislation in post war Britain. *ILRR* 11 (October 1957) 72-84. Comment by Bowlby and reply 12 (October 1958) 113-119.

Benewitz, M. and R. Weitraub. Employment effects of a local minimum wage. *ILRR* (January 1964). Comment by Gutman and reply (January 1965).

Blum, F. Social and economic implications of the F.L.S.A.: an interpretation in terms of social cost. *IRRA* (December 1956) 167-183.

Blum, F. The economics of minimum wages. *AER* (September 1947).

Brecher, R. Minimum wage rates and the pure theory of international trade. *QJE* 88 (February 1974) 98-116.

Bronfenbrenner, M. Minimum wages, unemployability and relief. *SEJ* (July 1943).

Brozen, Y. The effect of statutory minimum wage increases on teenage employment. *Journal of Law and Economics* 12 (April 1969) 109-122.

Brozen, Y. Minimum wage rates and household workers. *Journal of Law and Economics* 5 (October 1962) 103-110.

Brozen, Y. and M. Friedman. *The Minimum Wage, Who Really Pays?* Washington: Free Press Society, 1966.

Campbell, C. and R. Campbell. State minimum wage laws as a cause of unemployment. *SEJ* 35 (April 1969) 323-332. Comment by E. Jones and R. White and reply 37 (January 1971) 366-373.

Colberg, M. Minimum wage effects on Florida's economic development. *Journal of Law and Economics* 3 (October 1960) 106-117.

Cotterill, P. and W. Wadycki. Teenagers and the minimum wage in retail trade. *JHR* 11 (Winter 1976) 69-85.

Donner, A. and F. Lazar. *Minimum Wage Policy.* Ottawa: Department of Manpower and Immigration, 1976.

Donner, A. and F. Lazar. *An Analysis of the Low Wage Labour Market in Canada.* Toronto: Donner and Lazar Research Associates, 1975.

Douty, H. Minimum wage regulation in the seamless hosiery industry. *SEJ* (October 1941).

Elder, P. The 1974 amendments to the Federal minimum wage law. *MLR* 97 (July 1974) 33-37.

Fonlenay, A. de and G. Wasskelte. *An Economic Analysis of the Minimum Wage.* Ottawa: Research Projects Group, Strategic Planning and Research, 1976.

Gallaschi, H. Jr. Minimum wages and the farm labour market. *SEJ* 41 (January 1975) 480-491.

Gardner, B. Minimum wages and the farm labor market. *American Journal of Agricultural Economics* (August 1972) 474-476.

Gavett, T. Youth unemployment and minimum wages. *IRRA* (December 1970) 106-117.

Goldfarb, R. Quantitative research on the minimum wage. *MLR* 98 (April 1975) 44-46.

Goldfarb, R. The policy content of quantitative minimum wage research. *IRRA* (1974) 261-268.

Gramlich, E. Impact of minimum wages on other wages, employment and family incomes. *BPEA* (No. 2, 1976) 409-462.

Gutman, R. Employment effects of a local minimum wage. *ILRR* 18 (January 1965) 246-250.

Henricks, H. Effects of the 25 cent minimum wage on employment in the seamless hosiery industry. *Journal of American Statistical Association* (March 1940) 13-23.

Johnson, H. Minimum wage laws: a general equilibrium analysis. *CJE* 2 (November 1969) 599-603.

Katz, A. Teenage employment effects of state minimum wages. *JHR* 8 (Spring 1973) 250-256.

Katzen, L. The case for minimum wage legislation in South Africa. *South African Journal of Economics* 29 (September 1961) 195-217.

Kau, J. and P. Rubin. Voting on minimum wages. *JPE* 86 (April 1978) 337-342.

Kaufman, J. and T. Foran. The minimum wage and poverty. *Towards Freedom From Want.* Madison, Wis.: Industrial Relations Research Association, 1968.

Kaun, D. The fair labor standards act: an evaluation in terms of its stated goals. *South African Journal of Economics* 33 (June 1965) 131-145.

Kaun, D. Minimum wages, factor substitutions and the marginal producer. *QJE* 79 (August 1965) 478-486.

Keyserling, L. *The Role of Wages in a Great Society.* Washington: Conference on Economic Progress, 1966.

King, A. Minimum wages and the secondary labor market. *SEJ* 41 (October 1974) 215-219.

Kosters, M. and F. Welch. The effects of minimum wages on the distribution of changes in aggregate employment. *AER* 62 (June 1972) 323-332.

Kruger, D. Minimum wages and youth employment. *IRRA* (December 1970) 128-135.

Leffler, K. Minimum wages, welfare and wealth transfers to the poor. *Journal of Law and Economics* 21 (October 1978) 345-358.

Lester, R. Employment effects of minimum wages. *ILRR* 13 (June 1960).

Levitan, S. Minimum wages—a tool to fight poverty. *Labor Law Journal* (January 1966) 53-60.

Lianos, T. Impact of minimum wages upon the level and composition of agricultural employment. *American Journal of Agricultural Economics* (August 1972) 477-484.

Lovell, M. The minimum wage, teenage unemployment and the business cycle. *WEJ* 10 (December 1972) 414-427. Comments by A. Fisher and D. Adie and L. Gallaway and reply 11 (December 1973) 514-537.

Macesich, G. and C. Stewart. Recent Department of Labor Studies of minimum wage effects. *SEJ* 26 (April 1960) 281-290.

Mattila, J. The effects of extending minimum wages to cover household maids. *JHR* 8 (Summer 1973) 365-382.

Maurice, S. Monopsony and the effects of an externally imposed minimum wage. *SEJ* 41 (October 1974) 283-287.

McCulloch, J. The effect of a minimum wage law on the labour-intensive sector. *CJE* 7 (May 1974) 316-318.

McKenna, J. *The Long-Run Impact of the Thirty Cent Revision in Ontario's Minimum Wage in Five Industries.* Toron. : Research Branch, Ontario Ministry of Labour, 1973.

Migné, J. Salaire Minimum ou quand le diable se fait moine. *RI/IR* 32 (No. 3, 1977) 310-320.

Mincer, J. Unemployment effects of minimum wages. *JPE* 84 Part 2 (August 1976) S87-S104.

Mixon, J. The minimum wage and voluntary labor mobility. *ILRR* 32 (October 1978) 67-73.

Moloney, J. Some effects of the fair labor standards act upon southern industry. *SEJ* (July 1942) 15-21.

Moore, T. The effect of minimum wages on teenage unemployment rates. *JPE* 79 (July/August 1971) 897-902.

Peterson, J. Research needs in minimum wage theory. *SEJ* 29 (July 1962).

Peterson, J. Employment effects of state minimum wages for women: three historical cases re-examined. *ILRR* 12 (April 1959) 406-422.

Peterson, J. Employment effects of minimum wages, 1938-1950. *JPE* 65 (October 1957) 412-430.

Peterson, J.M. and C.T. Stewart Jr. *Employment Effects of Minimum Wage Rates.* Washington: American Enterprise Institute for Public Research, 1969.

Ragan, J. Minimum wages and the youth labor market. *R. E. Stats.* 59 (May 1977) 129-136.

Reynolds, L. and P. Gregory. *Wages, Productivity and Industrialization in Puerto Rico.* Homewood, Ill.: Richard D. Irwin Co., 1965.

Schweinberger, A. Employment subsidies and the theory of minimum wage rates in general equilibrium. *QJE* 92 (August 1978) 361-374.

Shkurti, W. and B. Fleisher. Employment and wage rates in retail trade subsequent to the 1961 amendments of the Fair Labor Standards Act. *SEJ* 35 (July 1968) 37-48.

Silberman, J. and C. Durden. Determining legislative preferences on the minimum wage. *JPE* 84 (April 1976) 317-329.

Steindl, F. The appeal of minimum wage laws and the invisible hand in government. *Public Choice* 14 (Spring 1973) 133-136.

Stigler, G. The economics of minimum wage legislation. *AER* 36 (June 1946) 358-367.

Tolles, N. American minimum wage laws: their purpose and results. *IRRA* (December 1959) 116-133.

Uri, N. and J. Mixon. The distribution of changes in manufacturing employment and the impact of the minimum wage. *Journal of Econometrics* 7 (February 1978) 103-114.

Waisglass, H. Questions of public policy for the consideration of periodic revisions in the minimum wage. *RI/IR* 28 (July 1973) 629-632.

Webb, S. Economic theory of a legal minimum wage. *JPE* 20 (December 1912) 973-998.

Weiss, H. Economic effects of a nationwide minimum wage. *IRRA* (December 1956) 154-166.

Welch, F. Minimum wage legislation in the United States. *Evaluating the Labor-Market Effects of Social Programs,* O. Ashenfelter and J. Blum (eds.). Princeton: Princeton University Press, 1976.

West, E. The minimum-wage debate—some new developments. *The Labour Gazette* (March 1977) 106-108.

West, E. Toward a comprehensive economic theory of minimum-wage laws. *Canadian Perspectives in Economics.* Toronto: Collier-MacMillan, 1972.

Whittingham, F. Minimum Wages in Ontario. Kingston: Queen's University Industrial Relations Centre, 1970.

Whittingham, F. and H. Fantil. *The Short-Run Impact of the Thirty Cent Revision in Ontario's Minimum Wage on Five Industries.* Toronto: Ontario Department of Labour Research Branch, 1970.

Zaidi, M. *A Study of the Effects of the $1.25 Minimum Wage under the Canadian Labour (Standards) Code.* Study No. 16, Task Force on Labour Relations. Ottawa: Privy Council Office, 1970.

Zucker, A. Minimum wages and the long-run elasticity of demand for low wage labor. *QJE* 87 (May 1973) 267-277.

Part III

Interaction of Supply and
Demand in Alternative
Market Structures

Chapter 9

Wages and Employment Under Competition

Once labour demand and the various aspects of labour supply are determined, we can analyse their interaction in determining the equilibrium price and quantity of labour—wages and employment, respectively. In this chapter we analyse the interaction of labour supply and demand when the firm is competitive in both the product market in which it sells its output, and the labour market in which it purchases labour inputs. In subsequent chapters we relax each of these assumptions, and analyse the situation when the firm is not competitive in the product and labour market. Throughout the analysis we are assuming that labour is selling its services competitively: later we will analyse the situation of collective bargaining via unionization.

In dealing with the interaction of supply and demand in various market structures, it is important to be specific about the level of aggregation that is being analysed. In this section we deal with the level of aggregation of the individual firm, and consequently focus on the firm as the decision-making unit. Later we will deal with higher levels of aggregation such as the occupation, industry, region and economy as a whole.

CATEGORIZING FIRM BEHAVIOUR IN PRODUCT AND LABOUR MARKETS

Because the demand for labour is derived from the output produced by the firm, the way in which the firm behaves in the product market can have an impact on the demand for labour, and hence ultimately on the wage and employment decision. In general, the product market behaviour of the firm is categorized according to the degree of competitiveness of the firm. In decreasing order of degree of competition in selling its output, the four main categories are: (1) competitive, (2) monopolistic-competitive, (3) oligopolistic, and (4) monopolistic. In addition, for the oligopolistic category there are a variety of sub-categories, corresponding to the various ways in which the firms react to the actions of the few other firms in the industry.

Whereas the way in which the firm behaves in the product market affects its derived demand for labour, the way in which it behaves in the labour market affects the supply curve for labour that the firm faces. In essence, the supply curve of labour to an individual firm shows the amount of homogeneous labour (e.g. labour of a particular occupational category) that the firm could employ at various possible wage rates. Analogous to the four

146

main ways of classifying the firm's behaviour in the product market, there are four main ways of classifying the firm's behaviour in the labour market. In decreasing order of the degree of competition it faces in hiring labour, these four categories are: (1) competitive, (2) monopsonistic-competitive, (3) oligopsony, and (4) monopsony. (The "opsony" ending is traditionally used to denote non-competitive conditions in factor markets.) In addition, there are a variety of sub-categories of oligopsony corresponding to the various ways in which firms can react to each other in their hiring decisions.

The product and labour market categorizations are independent in that there is no necessary relationship between the structure of the product market in which the firm sells its output and the labour market in which it buys labour services. The extent to which the firm is competitive in the product market (and hence the shape of its derived demand for labour curve) need not be related to the extent to which the firm is a competitive buyer of labour (and hence the shape of the supply curve of labour that it faces). The two *may* be related, for example if it is a large firm and hence dominates both the labour and product markets, but they need not be related. Hence for *each* product market structure, the firm can behave in at least four different ways as a purchaser of labour. Thus there are at least sixteen different combinations of product and labour market structure that can bear on the wage and employment decision at the level of the firm. More combinations are possible when one considers the sub-categories within oligopoly and oligopsony.

In general, however, the essence of the wage and employment decision by the firm can be captured by an examination of the polar cases when the firm is a competitive seller of its product and a competitive buyer of labour (the competitive norm), and when the firm is a monopolist on the product market, and a monopsonist in the labour market. This chapter focuses on the competitive norm: subsequent chapters deal with monopoly in the product market and monopsony in the labour market.

COMPETITIVE NORM

In the competitive norm the firm is a competitive seller of its output on the product market and a competitive buyer of labour in the labour market. In essence, the firm is so small relative to both markets that it can sell all of the output it wants at the going price of the product, and it can buy all of the labour it wants at the going wage rate. The firm is both a price- and wage-taker: it cannot influence either the product price or the wage rate.

This situation is depicted in Figure 9.1(a) and (b) for two competitive firms. In both cases, their supply schedules for a given homogeneous type of labour are perfectly elastic (horizontal) at the competitive wage rate, w_c. The firms are wage-takers not wage-setters, and consequently can employ all of the labour they want at this competitive wage rate.

For the moment, the wage rate for this specific, homogeneous type of

Figure 9.1   Competitive Norm

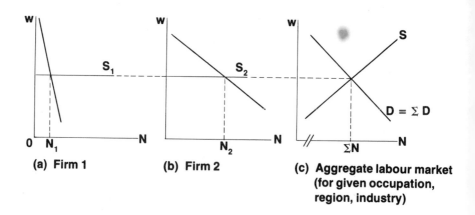

(a) **Firm 1**   (b) **Firm 2**   (c) **Aggregate labour market
                                                                    (for given occupation,
                                                                    region, industry)**

labour is taken as given or predetermined by the interaction of supply and demand in a more aggregate labour market as depicted in Figure 9.1(c). This aggregate labour market could be a regional labour market in a particular industry for a particular occupational category of labour. For example, it could be the Halifax labour market for junior accounting clerks in the manufacturing sector. By assuming that the firms are in the same region and industry and are hiring the same homogeneous occupational type of labour, we are able to minimize the intervening influence of these factors on the wage determination process, and to thereby focus on the issue of wage and employment determination at the disaggregate or microeconomic level of the firm. In subsequent chapters on wage structures, these assumptions are relaxed sequentially and the resultant wage structures analysed.

The demand schedules for labour in the two firms are simply the schedule of the *value* of the marginal products of labour, defined as the marginal physical product of labour times the price at which the firms can sell their products. (These were derived formally in Chapter 8.) Since the firms are assumed to be competitive sellers of their products, then their product prices are fixed at p_1^* and p_2^*. Only if the firms are selling the same output would their product prices have to be the same; otherwise p_1^* need not equal p_2^*. The magnitude and the elasticity of the demand for labour also are depicted as being different simply to highlight that the competitive wage is the same irrespective of these factors. The demand schedules simply determine the level of employment in each firm: in this case N_1 and N_2 units of labour, respectively in firms one and two.

In summary, when the firm is a competitive buyer of labour, it faces a perfectly elastic supply of labour at the competitive wage. When the firm is a competitive seller of its output on the product market, it regards the price at which it sells its output on the product market as fixed, and its derived demand for labour schedule is the value of the marginal product of labour, defined as the marginal physical product of labour times the fixed price at which the firm sells its output. Because the labour supply schedule to the firm is perfectly elastic at the competitive wage rate, the interaction of the firm's labour supply and demand schedules determine the employment level of the firm for that particular type of labour—wages are determined elsewhere, for example, in the aggregate industry labour market for that particular type of labour.

SHORT RUN VERSUS LONG RUN

The previous analysis was based on the long-run assumption that the firm could get all of the labour it needed at the competitive wage rate. That is, in order to expand its work-force it need only hire additional workers at the going wage rate: there is no need to increase wages to attract additional workers.

In the short run, however, even a firm that is competitive in the labour market may have to raise its wages in order to attract additional workers. In such circumstances the firm's short-run labour supply schedule could be upward sloping, as depicted by the schedule S_s in Figure 9.2. In the short run, in order to expand its work-force so as to meet an increase in the demand for labour from D to D', the firm may have to pay higher wages, perhaps by

Figure 9.2   Short Run and Long Run Labour Supply Schedules to Firm

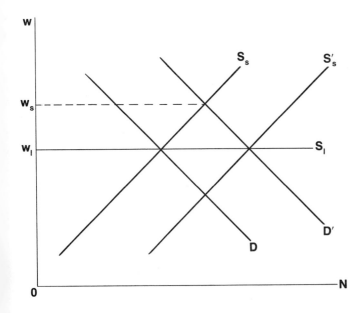

paying an overtime premium to its existing work-force or by paying higher wages to attract local workers within the community. The resultant expansion of the work-force can be depicted as a movement up the short-run supply curve in response to the new higher wage of w_s, occasioned by the increase in the demand for labour from D to D'.

In the longer run, however, a supply influx of other workers will be forthcoming because the firm is paying a greater-than-competitive wage (i.e. $w_s > w_c$) for that particular type of labour. The supply influx may not be instantaneous, but may occur in the long run because it may come from other firms or perhaps from outside of the labour force, and such adjustments take time.

The new supply influx in response to the higher wage could be depicted by the S_s' supply schedule of labour. The supply influx would depress the temporarily high, short-run wage of w_s back to its long-run equilibrium of w_c. Thus the long-run supply of labour schedule to the firm, S_l, can be thought of as a locus of long-run equilibrium points, traced out by various shifting short-run supply schedules of the firm, as the firm tries to expand its work-force.

In essence, temporary wage increases above the competitive norm are consistent with the firm being a competitive buyer of labour in the long run. In fact, short-run wage increases may be a sign that the market is behaving competitively, in that they can be a market signal for the supply response that ensures that the market is competitive, in the longer run.

QUESTIONS

1. It is unreasonable to assume in any analysis of the labour market that labour is homogeneous, given the array of workers with their variety of characteristics. Discuss.
2. Monopoly and monopsony go hand in hand. Discuss.
3. "Given the variety of ways of classifying the firm's behaviour in the product and labour markets, and the various possible types of collusive action on the part of labour, we really have no theory of labour market behaviour. Rather, we have a series of *ad hoc* explanations corresponding to the variety of ways employers and employees can act in the labour market. This is more description than good theory." Discuss.
4. Based on the demand schedules as given in Figure 9.1, what would happen to the respective labour demand schedules for firms 1 and 2 if they both became monopolists in their respective product markets? What would happen to the wages they pay? What would happen to the labour demand schedule in the aggregate labour market, and hence the wage and employment in that market?
5. For Figure 9.1, make up a hypothetical example for firms one and two with their differing labour demand schedules and indicate the reasons for the shape of their particular schedules.

6. What would happen to the analysis of this chapter if firm two in Figure 9.1 began to dominate the aggregate labour market and became a wage-setter rather than a wage-taker?
7. The competitive norm is unrealistic because it predicts that all firms will pay the same wage for the same type of labour and we know that this is not so. Discuss.

Chapter 10

Wages and Employment With Non-Competitive Product Markets

In the previous chapter we analysed the wage and employment decisions of firms that were both competitive buyers of labour services and competitive sellers of their output in the product market. In this chapter we relax one of those assumptions—that of being a competitive seller of its output—and we analyse the situation when the firm sells its output in non-competitive markets. Since the demand for labour is derived from the demand for the services produced by the firm, then this non-competitive behaviour of the firm will affect its labour market decisions. Throughout this chapter we still assume that the firm is a competitive buyer of labour in the labour market.

MONOPOLY

Characteristics and Implications for the Labour Market

The polar case of non-competitive behaviour in the product market is that of monopoly. In this situation the firm is so large relative to the size of the product market that it can influence the price at which it sells its product: it is a price-setter, not a price-taker. In the extreme case of monopoly, the monopolist comprises the whole industry: there are no other firms in the industry. Thus, the industry demand for the product is the demand schedule for the product of the monopolist.

As is well known from standard microeconomic theory, the relevant decision-making schedule for the profit-maximizing monopolist is not the demand schedule for its product, but rather its marginal revenue schedule. In order to sell an additional unit of output, the monopolist has to lower the price of its product. Assuming that it cannot differentiate its homogeneous product to consumers, the monopolist will also have to lower the price on all units of its output, not just on the additional units that it wishes to sell. Consequently, its marginal revenue — the additional revenue generated by selling an additional unit of output—will fall faster that its price, reflecting the fact that the price decline applies to intra-marginal units of output. The marginal revenue schedule for the monopolist will therefore lie below and to the left of its demand schedule. By equating marginal revenue with marginal cost so as to maximize profits, the monopolist will produce less output and charge a higher price (as given by the demand schedule, since this is the price that consumers will pay) than if it were a competitive firm on the product market.

152

This scenario on the product market has implications for the derived demand for labour. Since the monopolist's marginal revenue schedule lies below its demand schedule, then the monopolist's derived demand for labour schedule also lies below the schedule that would prevail if the firm behaved as a competitive firm in the product market. As given by Equation 8.6 in Chapter 8, the labour demand schedule for the competitive firm on the product market is given by:

$$w^* = MPP_N \cdot p_q^* = VMP_N \text{ [competitor]} \tag{8.6}$$

This was derived from the more general equation

$$w^* = MPP_N \cdot MR_Q = MRP_N \text{ [monopolist]} \tag{8.4}$$

which applies to the monopolist since its output price is not fixed. Rather, for the monopolist, marginal revenue is the relevant factor.

The difference between Equations 8.4 and 8.6 highlight the fact that when the monopolist hires more labour to produce more output, not only does the marginal physical product of labour fall (as is the case with the competitor), but also the marginal revenue from an additional unit of output, MR_Q, falls. This latter effect occurs because the monopolist, unlike the competitor, can sell more output only by lowering the product price and this in turn lowers revenue. Because both MPP_N and MR_Q fall when N increases in Equation 8.4, then the monopolist's demand for labour falls faster than it would if it behaved as a competitive firm in the product market, in which case only MPP_N would fall, as given in Equation 8.6.

The difference between the labour demand schedule for a monopolist and the schedule that would prevail if the firm were competitive in the product market is illustrated in Figure 10.1. For illustrative purposes the supply schedule of labour is depicted as upward sloping, perhaps reflecting a short-run situation whereby the firm has to raise wages temporarily to attract additional labour. The labour demand schedule for the competitive firm on the product market would be $D_c = MPP_N \cdot p_Q = VMP_N$. The labour demand schedule for the monopolist is $D_m = MPP_N \cdot MR_Q = MRP_N$. Since $MR_Q < p_Q$ then D_m lies below D_c.

The interaction of the labour supply and demand schedules determine the equilibrium wage and employment of the firm. For the monopolist this is w_m and N_m respectively. If this firm were competitive in the product market, its wages and employment would be w_c and N_c respectively. Thus the monopolist pays a lower wage, $w_m < w_c$, and employs less labour, $N_m < N_c$, than if it were competitive in the product market. In addition it pays labour a wage less than the value of the marginal product of its labour since $w_N < VMP_M$ at N_m. This latter difference has been termed a measure of the Pigouvian exploitation of labour, equal to $VMP_M - w_m$ per worker or $(VMP_M - w_m)N_m$ for the firm's total work-force.

If the monopolist in the product market were competitive in the labour market, then it would face a perfectly elastic labour supply schedule at the

Figure 10.1   **Monopolist Demand for Labour**

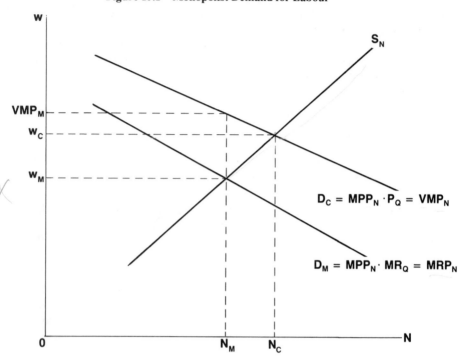

going wage rate. In such circumstances it would pay the competitive wage rate and its reduced labour demand schedule ($D_m < D_c$) would imply that the monopolist employs less labour than it would if it behaved competitively in the product market, and that it pays a wage equal to the marginal revenue product of labour, but less than the value of the marginal product of labour.

Mathematical Exposition: Monopoly

The labour demand schedule for the monopolist can be derived more formally and the results explicitly compared to that of the competitive firm. As in Equation 8.1 of Chapter 8, the profit function of the monopolist is simply revenues minus cost, or

$$\pi = pQ - wN - rK \tag{10.1}$$

and the production function

$$Q = Q(N,K), \text{ where } \partial Q/\partial N > 0 \tag{10.2}$$

Unlike the competitive firm where product prices are fixed, $p = p^*$, for the monopolist, prices are negatively related to output. That is,

$$p = p(Q) = p(Q(N,K)), \text{ where } \partial p/\partial Q < 0. \tag{10.3}$$

Substituting Equations 10.2 and 10.3 into Equation 10.1 yields

$$\pi = p(Q(N,K)) \cdot Q(N,K) - wN - rK \tag{10.1'}$$

The monopolist maximizes profits by employing an additional unit of labour until there are no further profits from employing more labour; that is, until $\partial \pi/\partial N = 0$. From Equation 10.1' this implies

$$\partial p/\partial Q \cdot \partial Q/\partial N \cdot Q + p\partial Q/\partial N = w \tag{10.4}$$

The last term, $p\partial Q/\partial N$, on the left-hand side of this expression, is simply the value of the marginal product of labour. Therefore Equation 10.4 can be rewritten as

$$\partial p/\partial Q \cdot \partial Q/\partial N \cdot Q + VMP_N = w. \tag{10.4'}$$

In the competitive case with $p = p^*$ this would reduce to the familiar competitive demand schedule where $w = VMP_N$.

The left-hand side of Equation 10.4 is the marginal revenue product of labour, MRP_N; that is, the partial differential of revenue with respect to labour. Thus

$$MRP_N = \partial p/\partial Q \cdot \partial Q/\partial N \cdot Q + VMP_N \tag{10.5}$$

Since $\partial p/\partial Q < 0$, $\partial Q/\partial N > 0$, and $Q > 0$, then $\partial p/\partial Q \cdot \partial Q/\partial N \cdot Q < 0$ and therefore $MRP_N < VMP_N$. This occurs because as the monopolist uses more labour to produce more output ($\partial Q/\partial N > 0$), it must lower its product price to sell the additional output ($\partial p/\partial Q < 0$), and this price adjustment will apply to all of the firm's output ($Q > 0$).

Monopoly and the Elasticity of Demand for Labour

At this point it may be worth digressing on a common misconception concerning the elasticity of demand for the output and hence the derived demand for labour from a monopolist. By definition, a monopolist is the only producer of a particular product or service. Consequently it is tempting to think of the demand for the monopolist's output as being price inelastic (and hence its derived demand for labour as being inelastic) because consumers are unable to purchase the particular output elsewhere.

This ignores the fact, however, that consumers need not always consume the particular output produced by the monopolist. Consumers can usually purchase alternative near substitutes, and will do so as the price charged by the monopolist increases. In essence, the monopolist is the industry, and the demand for industry output need not be inelastic, but will depend on such factors as the cost and availability of substitutes from other industries.

Not only is it the case that the demand for the output of the monopolist need not be inelastic: in fact, the monopolist will operate on the elastic portion of its demand schedule. This can be demonstrated rigorously as follows.

As previously given in Equation 10.1', the profit function for the monopolist is

$$\pi = p(Q)Q - wN - rK \tag{10.6}$$

The monopolist maximizes profits by selling output until there are no additional profits to be made: that is, until $\partial\pi/\partial Q = 0$. Differentiating Equation 10.6 partially with respect to Q and setting this equal to zero, yields

$$\partial p/\partial Q \cdot Q + p = w\,\partial N/\partial Q + r\,\partial K/\partial Q \tag{10.7}$$

That is, marginal revenue equals the marginal cost of an additional unit of output. Defining the elasticity of output with respect to price as $\theta_{Qp} = \partial Q/\partial p \cdot p/Q$, then $1/\theta = \partial p/\partial Q \cdot Q/p$ and therefore $p/\theta = \partial p/\partial Q \cdot Q$. Substituting this into Equation 10.7 and defining the right-hand side as marginal cost, yields

$$p(1 + 1/\theta) = MC \tag{10.8}$$

Assuming that the marginal cost of output is positive, $MC > 0$, then for the monopolist

$$p(1 + 1/\theta) > 0 \tag{10.9}$$

This will be true only when the monopolist operates on the elastic portion of its demand curve: that is, when $\theta < -1$. (This latter statement can be proven by multiplying both sides by $1/p$, subtracting one from both sides, and then inverting and hence reversing the sign.)

Unfortunately it is not easy to give an intuitive explanation for why the monopolist will operate on the elastic portion of its demand curve. However, only on the elastic portion is marginal revenue positive, and as long as marginal costs are positive this is where the monopolist will operate. Marginal revenue is positive only on the elastic portion of the demand schedule because only here will a price reduction lead to a sufficiently large increase in quantity demanded so as to increase total revenues so that marginal revenues are positive.

Wages of Monopolists

In theory, the previous analysis has little implication for the wages that monopolists will pay relative to the wages paid by firms that are competitive in the product market. This is so because the firm's behaviour in the product market need not be related to the way the firm behaves in the labour market. Specifically, if the firms are competitive in the labour market then they all face a perfectly elastic supply schedule for labour in the labour market; that is, they are wage-takers, not wage-setters. In such circumstances the monopolist pays the same competitive wage as all other employers.

There are reasons to believe, however, that wages paid by a monopolist may differ from those paid by firms that are competitive in the product market. Without analysing these factors in the context of a formal model, they can be enumerated qualitatively. In some circumstances, these factors serve to imply that monopolists will pay more than the competitive wage; in other circumstances, the opposite prevails.

One factor suggesting that the monopolist would pay greater-than-competitive wages is that the monopolist has monopoly profits, and labour — especially if organized — may be able to appropriate some of these profits. Alternatively stated, the monopolist may be under less pressure to be cost-conscious and hence may more readily yield to wage demands. Being sensitive to their public image, monopolists may also pay higher wages as a way of buying the image of being a good employer. This may especially be the case if the monopolist is regulated and subject to the review of a regulatory agency.

By virtue of simply being a large firm (even though it may be a small employer of certain types of labour), monopolists may also pay high wages. This could be the case, for example, if large firms must use formal methods to evaluate job applicants and hence they pay a high wage so as to have a queue of applicants from which to formally evaluate. In addition, large firms may have to pay a wage premium to compensate for the rigid work schedules and mass production techniques associated with large size. Finally, by virtue of their size, large firms may have to follow administratively determined wage policies: unable to pay each worker its marginal product, such firms may pay wages approximating the productivity of the more productive workers within the group. In this way they minimize the risk of losing their more productive workers at a cost of having to pay slightly higher than average wages.

The previously discussed factors suggest why monopolists may pay high wages if they are competitive buyers of labour. Each of these factors, however, could also be associated with lower-than-average wages being paid by monopolists. For example, although monopoly profits could enable the monopolist to pay high wages, they could also enable them to resist wage demands, perhaps by holding out longer against strike activity. In terms of preserving its public image, especially if regulated, monopolists may want to be a model employer by paying high wages, but they may also want to appear as cost conscious to the consuming public and to regulatory agencies. By virtue of their size, monopolists may also be able to pay lower-than-average wages, for example, if their size provided employment security or ample opportunities for advancement, or if turnover was less costly to them because of the availability of standby work-forces.

Other factors could also be at work to enable monopolists to pay lower wages. Their reduced demand for labour would imply lower wages if there was some inelasticity to their supply curve for labour, which could be the case in the short run or if the monopolist also dominated the local labour market. In addition, since the monopolist will always operate on the elastic portion of the demand schedule for its product, this factor may impart some elasticity to its derived demand for labour and this means that wage demands may be tempered somewhat by the threat of a substantial employment reduction.

Clearly the various factors that affect the wage determination process of monopolists do not yield unambiguous predictions on whether a monopolist will pay above or below average wages. Consequently, as is so often the case in economics, we must appeal to the empirical evidence to ascertain the net impact of the variety of factors. This evidence will be examined in a subsequent chapter on inter-industry wage differentials where the degree of concentration in the product market is viewed as a determinant of wages.

The previous discussion also highlights a weakness in this area of analysing wage determination in firms that are not competitive in the product market. Specifically, we have no adequate consistent theory of such a wage determination process, especially as it relates to the regulatory environment that is prevalent in such monopolistic sectors as the transportation, communications and utilities industries. Consequently, we rely on *ad hoc* theories — or stories, may be the more appropriate term — that are all too often devised to describe the results. Clearly, this is an area in need of further theoretical research in labour market economics.

MONOPOLISTIC COMPETITION

In between the polar cases of competition and monopoly on the product market are a variety of intermediate cases. Firms can be monopolistic-competitive, a situation characterized by many firms the actions of which do not affect other firms, but products which are differentiated in some way giving the firm some discretion in its price-setting. In such circumstances the demand for the firm's product is not perfectly elastic, as is the competitive case, but rather has a slight degree of inelasticity reflecting the fact that if the firm raises its price slightly it will not lose all of its market, and if it lowers its price slightly it will not gain all of the market.

In such circumstances the firm has a slight degree of discretion with respect to being able to pass wage increases on to customers in the form of price increases. Such cost increases need not put these firms out of business: they will retain a segment of the market given that their product is differentiated in some fashion. The degree of differentiation of their product determines the degree to which wage cost increases can be passed on to the consumer. If its product is not well differentiated, then this firm approaches the competitive norm, in which case a wage cost increase confined to the firm (and not to other firms in the industry) could put the firm out of business. If the product is well differentiated, then this firm approaches the monopolistic norm, in which case it can be thought of perhaps as a local industry.

The end results of monopolistic competition are qualitatively the same as for monopoly, since the firm has a degree of inelasticity to the demand schedule for its product. Consequently, it has a derived marginal revenue schedule with all of the implications that this has for wage determination. While qualitatively similar to monopoly, the situation of monopolistic competition is quantitatively different because there are limits imposed by other firms with similar, albeit perhaps not identical, products and services.

To a certain degree, in the short run at least, most firms can be thought of as having a slight degree of discretion with respect to price setting. Specifically, they could raise their prices slightly without losing all of their market instantly. Custom, habit persistence, lack of knowledge, and transactions costs would ensure that these firms retain some of their customers. In the longer run, however, such firms may not want to exercise these quasi-monopoly powers because of the entailed loss of customers. In essence, once the optimal degree of such quasi-monopoly powers are exercised, then the firm will be as cost conscious with respect to wages as would other firms. In other words, monopoly power—even a slight degree of monopoly power—may enable firms to pay a higher than average wage. But once this wage premium is paid, they will respond as do other firms to changes in the wages they face.

OLIGOPOLY WITH A KINKED DEMAND CURVE

Between the polar cases of monopoly and competition lies a variety of product market structures termed oligopoly. Such industries are characterized by few firms that produce sufficiently similar products that the actions of one firm will affect the other firms. Consequently the firms will react to the actions of the other firms. In theory, there are infinite ways in which the firms can react; consequently, there are infinite ways to categorize oligopoly situations. (This in fact is one of the criticisms of oligopoly theory: is it a theory, or a set of *ad hoc* descriptions of various situations?)

One of the more interesting situations from the point of view of its implications for labour market behaviour is that of oligopoly with a kinked demand curve. This situation is depicted in Figure 10.2(a). At the going market price of the product, p_0, the oligopolist's demand curve is kinked. This occurs because there is an asymmetry between how the other oligopolists will respond to price increases and decreases on the part of this particular firm. For price increases the other firms do not react; consequently, the firm loses a substantial share of the market as depicted by the elastic portion of the demand schedule above the price p_0. For price decreases, however, the other firms would respond by lowering their own prices; consequently this firm does not gain a substantial share of the market as depicted by the inelastic portion of the demand schedule below the price p_0.

The marginal revenue schedule of the oligopolist is therefore discontinuous over some range of price changes. The discontinuous portion occurs because, when the oligopolist lowers its price below p_0, its marginal revenue

**Figure 10.2   Product Demand and Labour Demand For
             Oligopolist With Kinked Demand Curve**

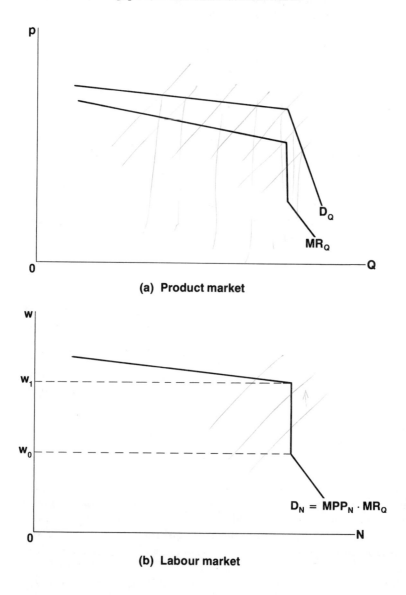

(a) Product market

(b) Labour market

drops not only because it has to lower its price for even its intramarginal units
of output, but also because the other oligopolists will respond with price
cuts.

The implications of this phenomenon for the derived demand for labour of the oligopolist is depicted in Figure 10.2(b). Reflecting the shape of the firm's product demand, the derived demand for labour (being the marginal physical product of labour times the marginal revenue from additional output) will also have an elastic upper portion, a discontinuous portion, and an inelastic lower portion.

The discontinuity or kink in the derived demand schedule for labour reflects the fact that there is a range of wage changes, w_0 to w_1, for which the oligopolist would not change its price (and hence output and hence derived demand for labour). This is so because price increases would lead to a large decrease in market share since the other oligopolists would not increase their prices. Conversely, price decreases would not lead to a large increase in market share because these price decreases would be met by other oligopolists. Because of the dire consequences no matter which way they change their price, oligopolists would try to absorb wage changes before altering their price, and hence output, and hence employment decisions. For this reason there is a range of wage changes that would not be associated with employment changes for the oligopolist.

This absorption power of oligopolists has implications for minimum wages (as well as other forms of wage fixing) because it implies that minimum wage increases for a limited range (e.g. from w_0 to w_1 in Figure 10.2(b)) may be absorbed by oligopolists rather than passed on to consumers in the form of higher product prices and hence reductions in the derived demand for labour. If all oligopolists were affected equally, however, then it is more likely that they would all respond to this common wage-cost increase with a common price increase, and the usual adverse employment effect would ensue. Consequently the minimum wage increase may not have an adverse employment effect in situations where workers are employed in oligopolistic firms that employ disproportionately large amounts of low-wage workers.

Similarly union wage increases, over a certain range, may not lead to adverse employment effects if they are confined to specific oligopolistic firms. As with the minimum wage, if all of the oligopolistic firms were affected similarly, they would probably all react with a common price increase and the usual adverse employment effect would ensue. This is one situation when it may be advantageous for unions to divide and conquer, gaining wage increases selectively in particular oligopolistic firms that would be reluctant to respond with price increases. Rather, the wage-cost increases may be absorbed from oligopoly profits.

CONCLUDING OBSERVATIONS ON NON-COMPETITIVE PRODUCT MARKETS

Clearly the way in which a firm behaves in the product market can affect the way it behaves in the labour market. Since the firm's demand for labour is derived from the demand for the product or service produced by the firm, then whether the firm is a price-setter or price-taker can influence its employment and *possibly* wage determination. ⊶

The term *possibly* is used with respect to the wage determination process because as long as the firm is competitive in the labour market—and it can be competitive in the labour market and not competitive in the product market—then it would have to pay at least the going wage for labour. This fact is important because it suggests that there may be an upward bias towards higher wages in firms that are not competitive in the product market. This upward bias occurs because non-competitive forces in the product market usually have an indeterminant impact on the wages they would pay to their employees. However, the forces of competition in the labour market would ensure that non-competitive firms in the product market do not pay below the competitive wage. These same forces, however, may be ignored by non-competitive firms that pay greater-than-competitive wages, perhaps out of monopoly or oligopolistic profits.

For example, if a monopolist did not pay a competitive wage, it may not be able to recruit any work-force. Consequently, the forces of competition in the labour market ensure a competitive floor on wages paid by the monopolist. However, if the monopolist paid a greater-than-competitive wage out of monopoly profits, the same forces of competition need not ensure a competitive ceiling. That is, the excess supplies of applicants could be ignored by the monopolist, who is under less pressure to be cost conscious. Because competitive pressures in the labour market ensure a floor, but not necessarily a ceiling on wages paid in non-competitive sectors of the product market, there may be an upward bias to wages paid in these sectors.

QUESTIONS

1. Strictly speaking, the analysis depicted in the diagram of Figure 10.1 is incorrect since the supply of labour schedule would not be the firm's relevant decision-making schedule, if it affected the wage rate. Discuss.
2. It is deceptive to say that monopolist firms do not behave as competitive firms. Both are simply maximizing profits subject to the constraints they face. However, the monopolist simply faces different constraints and this leads to different outcomes. Discuss.
3. Pigouvian exploitation of labour would not persist in the long run because employees would simply move to places where they were paid the value of the marginal product of their labour. Discuss.
4. Since the monopolist, by definition, is the only producer of its output, consumers cannot substitute other outputs, and consequently the demand for the product produced by the monopolist is price-inelastic. This in turn makes the monopolist's derived demand for labour inelastic, which in turn means that the monopolist will pay a greater-than-competitive wage. Discuss.

5. Discuss the possible impact of monopoly profits on the wages paid by monopolists.
6. It is not possible to say on theoretical grounds whether monopolists will pay higher or lower wages than competitive firms. Discuss.
7. In the field of industrial organization, considerable advances have been made in analysing the impact of various regulatory constraints, imposed by regulatory agencies, on the price and output decision of regulated firms, especially in the transportation, communications and utilities industries. The field of labour market economics, however, has not kept pace in analysing the impact of these various constraints for the wage and employment decision of such regulated firms. Correct this imbalance... and if successful, submit your paper to a reputable economics journal.
8. We really have no theory of non-competitive pricing. Rather, we have a series of *ad hoc* stories corresponding to all of the different possible cases between the competitive and monopolistic norms. Consequently it is more fruitful to examine the implications of these two polar norms and to treat the non-competitive cases as gravitating towards one or other of the norms. Discuss.
9. Illustrate the situation of Figure 10.2 by setting up a hypothetical product demand schedule for this oligopolist and derive the marginal revenue schedule. Explain why the large drop in marginal revenue occurs where it does and discuss the implication of this drop for the firm's labour demand schedule.
10. Wage fixing, for example via minimum wage or union wage increases, may not have an adverse employment effect if the employer is an oligopolist with a kinked demand curve for its product. This is especially the case if it applies disproportionately to one or a few of the oligopolists rather than to all. Discuss.
11. Competition in the labour market ensures a competitive floor on wages but not necessarily a competitive ceiling. Competition on the product market is necessary to ensure a competitive ceiling. Consequently there is an upward bias to the wages paid by firms that are not competitive in the product market. Discuss.

REFERENCES AND FURTHER READINGS

[This section does not contain references to the extensive literature on the role of non-competitive product market conditions on the determination of aggregate money wages. This is contained in the references in Chapter 17 on Wage-Price-Unemployment Trade-Offs and the Phillips curve. Related references on inter-industry wage determination also are contained in Chapter 15.]

Alcian, A. and R. Kessel. Competition, monopoly and the pursuit of pecuniary gain. *Aspects of Labor Economics*. Princeton: Princeton University Press, 1962.

Dalton, J. and E. Ford. Concentration and professional earnings in manufacturing. *ILRR* 31 (April 1978) 379-384.

Dalton, J. and E. Ford. Concentration and labor earnings in manufacturing and utilities. *ILRR* 31 (October 1977) 45-60.

Hendricks, W. The effect of regulation on collective bargaining in electric utilities. *Bell Journal of Economics* 6 (Autumn 1975) 451-465.

Jones, J. and L. Laudadio. Wage differentials and market imperfection: some cross section results in Canadian manufacturing industries. *RI/IR* (No. 3, 1975) 408-421.

Landon, J. The effect of product market concentration on wage levels. *ILRR* 23 (January 1970) 237-247.

Levinson, H. Unionism, concentration and wage changes. *ILRR* 20 (January 1967) 198-205.

Ross, S. and M. Wachter. Wage determination, inflation and the industrial structure. *AER* 63 (September 1973) 675-692.

Schwartzman, D. Monopoly and wages. *Canadian Journal of Economics and Political Science* 26 (August 1960) 428-438.

Wachtel, H. and C. Betsey. Employment and low wages. *R. E. Stats.* 54 (May 1972) 121-129.

Weiss, L. Concentration and labour earnings. *AER* 56 (March 1966) 96-117.

Chapter 11

Monopsony in the Labour Market

Chapter 9 examined the wage and employment decision under the competitive norm, when the firm is both a competitive seller of its output in the product market and a competitive buyer of labour in the labour market. Chapter 10 relaxed one of those assumptions—that of a competitive seller of its output—and examined the labour market implications when the firm is a non-competitive seller of its output, but still a competitive buyer of labour in the labour market. In this chapter the assumption of being a competitive buyer of labour is relaxed. So as to trace out the implications of this single change, termed monopsony, the firm is still assumed to be a competitive seller of its product. The results of relaxing both assumptions simultaneously —that of competition in the labour market and the product market—follow in a straightforward fashion from the results of each separate case.

SIMPLE MONOPSONY

When a firm is a monopsonist it is so large relative to the size of the local labour market that it influences the wage at which it hires labour. It is a wage-setter, not a wage-taker. In order to attract additional units of labour, the monopsonist has to raise wages; conversely, if it lowers the wage rate slightly, it will not lose all of its work-force.

Consequently the monopsonist faces an upward sloping labour supply schedule rather than a perfectly elastic labour supply schedule at the going wage, as was the case when the firm was a competitive buyer of labour. This labour supply schedule shows the average cost of labour for the monopsonist because it indicates the wage that must be paid for each different size of the firm's work-force. Since this same wage must be paid for each homogeneous unit of labour, then the wage paid at the margin becomes the actual wage paid to all of the workers, and this same average wage is paid to all.

The firm's labour supply or average-cost-of-labour schedule is not its relevant decision-making schedule. Rather, the relevant schedule is its *marginal* cost of labour which lies above its average cost. This is so because when the firm has to raise wages to attract additional units of labour, in the interest of maintaining internal equity in the wage structure it also has to pay that higher wage to its existing work-force (intra-marginal workers). Thus the marginal cost of adding an additional worker equals the new wage plus the addition to wage costs imposed by the fact that this new higher wage must be paid to the existing work-force. Consequently, the marginal cost of adding an additional worker is greater than the average cost, which is simply the wage.

165

This situation can be depicted by a simple hypothetical example. Suppose the monopsonist employed only one worker at a wage of one dollar per hour. Its average cost of labour would be the wage rate of one dollar. This would also be its marginal cost: that is, the extra cost of hiring this worker. If the monopsonist wanted to expand this type of work-force, however, it would have to pay a higher wage of, for example, 1.20 dollars to attract an additional worker. Its average cost of labour is the new wage of 1.20 dollars (i.e. (1.20 + 1.20)/2); however, the marginal cost of adding the new worker is the new wage of 1.20 dollars *plus* the additional .20 per hour it has to pay the first worker in order to maintain internal equity in the wage structure. Thus the marginal cost of the second worker is 1.40 dollars per hour, which is greater than the average cost or wage of 1.20 dollars. If a third worker cost 1.40 dollars, then the average cost or wage of the three workers would be 1.40 dollars, while the marginal cost of adding the third worker would be 1.80 dollars, composed of 1.40 dollars for the third worker plus the additional .20 dollars for each of the other two workers. (This example is further extended

Figure 11.1   Monopsony

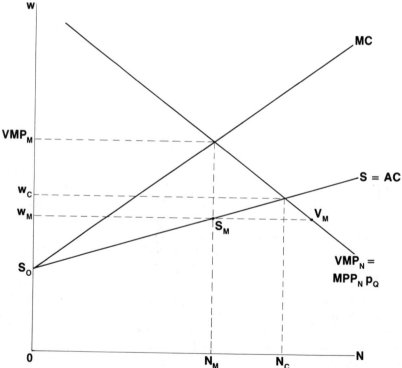

in the first three columns of Table 11.1, which is presented later to show the impact of minimum wages on a monopsony situation.)

The monopsony situation is illustrated diagramatically in Figure 11.1. The essence of monopsony is that the firm faces an upward sloping supply schedule for labour and hence has a marginal cost of labour schedule that lies above the supply or average cost schedule. The firm maximizes profits by hiring labour until the marginal cost of an additional unit of labour just equals the marginal revenue generated by the additional unit of labour. Marginal revenue is given by the VMP schedule in this assumed case of the firm being a competitive seller of its product. This equality of marginal cost and VMP occurs at the employment level N_m.

The VMP curve for the monopsonist is not really its demand curve for labour in the sense of showing the various quantities of labour that will be demanded at various wage rates. This is so because the monopsonist does not pay a wage equal to the VMP of labour. For example, in Figure 11.1 at the wage w_m, the quantity of labour demanded is N_m, not w_mV_m, as would be the case if VMP were a demand schedule equating w with VMP. In essence, the demand for labour is determined by the interaction of the MC and VMP schedules and this depends on the shape of the supply schedule (and hence the MC schedule) as well as the VMP schedule. This line of reasoning is analogous to that underlying the fact that a product market monopolist has no supply curve for its product.

IMPLICATIONS OF MONOPSONY

The level of employment, N_m, associated with monopsony is lower than the level, N_c, that would prevail if the monopsonist behaved as a competitive buyer of labour, equating the supply of labour with the demand. The monopsonist restricts its employment somewhat because hiring additional labour is costly since the higher wages have to be paid to the intra-marginal units of labour.

For N_m units of labour, the monopsonist pays a wage of w_m as given by the supply schedule of labour. The supply schedule shows the amount of labour that will be forthcoming at each wage and, for a wage of w_m, then N_m units of labour will be forthcoming. This wage is less than the wage, w_c, that the monopsonist would pay if it employed the competitive amount of labour N_c. The monopsonist wage is also less than the value of the marginal product of N_m units of labour. That is, the monopsonist pays a wage rate that is less than the value of the output produced by the additional unit of labour (although the value of that output does equal the marginal cost of producing it). This monopsony profit or difference between wages and the value of marginal product of labour has been termed a measure of the monopsonistic exploitation of labour, equal to $VMP_m - w_m$ per worker or $(VMP_m - w_m)N_m$

for the monopsonist's work-force. This monopsony profit accrues to the firm because its wage bill, $w_m N_m$, is less than the market value of the marginal output contributed by the firm's labour force, $VMP_m N_m$.

Because the value of the marginal product of labour for the monopsonist is greater than the value of the marginal product if that firm hired competitively ($VMP_m > VMP_c$, the latter of which equals w_c) then welfare to society would be increased by transferring labour from competitive to monopsonistic labour markets. This seemingly paradoxical result — an increase in welfare by expanding non-competitive markets relative to competitive markets — occurs simply because the value of the marginal product of labour is higher in the monopsonistic market. In effect, transferring labour is akin to breaking down the barriers giving rise to monopsony: it is allocating labour to its most productive use.

Although monopsony leads to a wage less than the value of the marginal product of labour, it is also true that intra-marginal workers are receiving a seller's surplus; that is, the wage they are paid, w_m, is greater than their reservation wage as indicated by the supply schedule. The existing work-force up until N_m units of labour is willing to work for the monopsonist for a wage that is less than the wage, w_m, they are paid. The wage that they are willing to work for is illustrated by the height of the labour supply schedule, which reflects their preferences for this firm and their opportunities elsewhere. However, to the extent that they are all paid the same wage, w_m, then the existing work-force receives a seller's surplus or economic rent equal to the triangle $S_o S_m w_m$.

This is why the term monopsonist exploitation of labour should be used with care. It is true that the monopsonist pays a wage less than the value of the marginal product of labour. However, it is also true that the monopsonist pays a wage greater than the reservation wage (opportunity cost, supply price) that intra-marginal employees could get elsewhere for their labour. This seller's surplus or economic rent received by employees may be acceptable if the employees are low paid and have low alternative wages elsewhere because of being isolated or because of discrimination reducing their other alternatives. However, the seller's surplus may be less acceptable if the employees are high paid and if they would be perfectly willing to work for a wage equal to their next best alternative. Efficient resource allocation requires only that they be paid a wage equal to their next best alternative. A higher wage has implications only for distributive equity, not allocative efficiency. It may be taxed away without affecting the efficient allocation of resources.

A final implication of monopsony is that there will be equilibrium vacancies (equal to $V_m - S_m$ in Figure 11.1) at the wage paid by the monopsonist. In other words the monopsonist would report vacancies at the wage it pays, but it will not raise wages to attract additional labour to fill these vacancies. In this sense the vacancies are at equilibrium, since there are no automatic forces that will reduce the vacancies. The monopsonist would like to hire additional labour *at the going wage* since the value of the marginal product exceeds the wage cost of an additional unit. However, because the higher wage would have to be paid to intra-marginal units of labour, the value of the marginal product just equals the marginal cost, and that is why there are no forces to reduce the vacancies. The monopsonist is maximizing profits by having vacancies. It does not reduce the vacancies because it would have to raise wages to do so and the marginal cost of doing so is more than the marginal revenue.

CHARACTERISTICS OF MONOPSONISTS

As long as there is some inelasticity to the supply schedule of labour faced by a firm, then that firm has elements of monopsony power. To a certain extent most firms may have an element of monopsony power in the short run, in the sense that they could lower their wages somewhat without losing all of their work-force. However, it is unlikely that they would exercise this power in the long run because it would lead to costly problems of recruitment, turn-over, and morale. Facing an irreversible decline in labour demand, however, firms may well allow their wages to deteriorate as a way of reducing their work-force.

In the long run, monopsony clearly will be less prevalent. It would occur when the firm is so large relative to the size of the local labour market that it influences wages. This could be the case, for example, in the classic one industry towns in isolated regions. Such firms need not be large in an absolute sense: they are simply large relative to the size of the small local labour market, and this makes them the dominant employer. Monopsony may also be associated with workers who have particular preferences to remain employed with the monopsonist. In such circumstances, wages could be lowered and they would stay with the monopsonist because their skills or preferences are not transferable.

Thus a mining company could be a monopsonist, even if it were reasonably small, if it were located in an isolated region with no other firms competing for the types of labour it employed. The same company could even be a monopsonist for one type of labour — for example, miners — while having to compete for other types of labour — for example, clerical workers. Conversely, an even larger mining company may be a competitive employer of miners it it were situated in a less isolated labour market and had to compete with other firms. It is size relative to the local labour market that matters, not absolute size.

Monopsony may also be associated with workers who have special-ized skills (specific human capital) that are useful mainly in a specific firm, or with workers who have particular preferences to remain employed with a specific firm. Because their skills or preferences are not completely transferable, such workers are tied to a single employer with a degree of monopsony power. The reserve clause in professional sports, for example, effectively ties the professional employee to a specific employer (team), giving the employer a degree of monopsony power. At a minimum the employer need pay a salary only slightly higher than the players next-best-alternative salary, which would be considerably less. In practice a much higher salary is usually paid in order to extract maximum performance. When reserve clauses are inapplicable and players are free agents, as for example when different leagues compete, the resultant salary explosions attest to the fact that the competitive salary is much higher than the monopsonist salary.

The professional sports example illustrates the important fact that, although monopsonists pay less than they would if they had to compete for labour, they need not pay low wages. In fact, unique specialized skills are often associated with high salaries, albeit they may even be higher if there was more competition for their rare services. Monopsony does not imply low wages: it only implies wages that are lower than what they would be if there were competition for the particular skills.

PERFECT MONOPSONISTIC WAGE DIFFERENTIATION

The previous discussion focused on what could be labelled *simple monopsony* —a situation where the monopsonist did not differentiate its work-force but rather paid the same wages to all workers of the same skill, both marginal and intra-marginal workers. In terms of Figure 11.1, all workers were paid the wage, w_m, even though intra-marginal workers would have worked for a lower wage as depicted by their supply price. The resultant seller's surplus or economic rent (wage greater than the next-best-alternative) is appropriated by the intra-marginal workers.

This highlights another implication of monopsony. The monopsonist may try to appropriate this seller's surplus by differentiating its otherwise homogeneous work-force so as to pay each worker only their reservation wage. If the monopsonist were able to do this for *each and every* worker, the result could be labelled *perfect monopsonistic wage differentiation*. In this case the supply schedule would be its average cost of labour *and* its marginal cost, because it would not have to pay the higher wage to the intra-marginal workers.

In fact there is an incentive for the monopsonist to try to expand its work-force by means that would make the cost of expansion peculiar only to the additional workers. In this fashion the monopsonist could avoid the rapidly rising marginal cost associated with having to pay higher wages to intra-marginal workers. Thus monopsonists may try to conceal the higher wages paid to attract additional labour so as not to have to pay their existing work-force the higher wage. Or they may try to use non-wage mechanisms, the costs of which are specific to only the new workers. Moving allowances, advertising or other more expensive job search procedures, and paying workers for paper qualifications that are largely irrelevant for the job, are all ways in which monopsonists may try to expand their work-force without raising wages for all workers.

IMPERFECT MONOPSONISTIC WAGE DIFFERENTIATION: APPLICATION TO SEX DISCRIMINATION

There may also be situations where monopsonists are unable to differentiate *each* worker so as to pay each only their reservation wage, but are able to differentiate between broad groups of otherwise homogeneous workers. This situation could be termed *imperfect monopsonistic wage differentiation*. In such circumstances the monopsonist only has to pay the same wage *within* groups: different wages can persist *between* groups. Such may be the case, for example, with respect to male and female workers, the example that will be pursued in this section.

The conditions necessary for imperfect monopsonistic discrimination are first that the markets for the different types of labour can be separated (otherwise the low wage workers would simply move to the high wage market), and second that there are different supply elasticities in each market (otherwise there are no monopsony profits for the firm to exploit). The importance of these two factors as preconditions for monopsony will become clearer as the analysis progresses.

The situation of imperfect monopsony is depicted in Figure 11.2 for a hypothetical example of a male and female work-force for the firm. For illustrative purposes, males and females are assumed to be equally productive so that there is one VMP schedule for the combined male and female work-force. However, the employer is able to segment or differentiate the male and female work-force from each other. In other words, while there is internal competition within each work-force, there is not competition between the male and female work-forces. The lower supply schedule for females relative to males reflects their lower reservation wage, which in turn may reflect poor employment opportunities elsewhere as well as a low subjective evaluation of their own labour market worth.

Although the labour supply schedules in Figure 11.2 appear parallel, the wage elasticities for different employment levels may be different, whether the curves are parallel or not. Specifically, wage elasticity is defined as $\theta = \partial N/\partial w \cdot w/N$, and this depends not only on the slope of the supply schedule, $\partial N/\partial w$, but also on where the firm is on the supply schedule, w/N. For females, as will be demonstrated later, w is lower than males and N is higher; consequently w/N is smaller and female labour supply therefore more inelastic.

This lower elasticity for females could prevail for a variety of reasons. Females may have fewer employment opportunities elsewhere and they may be tied to the area of their husbands' employment. Household responsibilities and commuting problems may tie them to a single particular local firm. Household and institutional discrimination, especially in educational institutions, may mean that they have been unable to accumulate continuous work

Figure 11.2   Imperfect Monopsonistic Wage Differentiation Between Males and Females

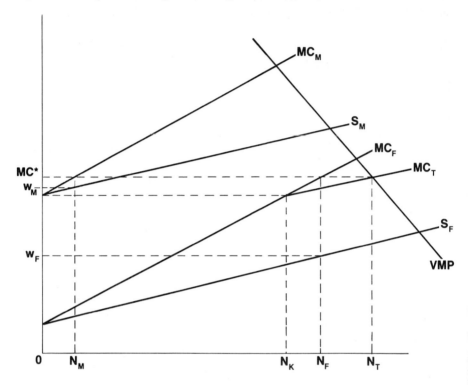

experience or labour-market-oriented skills that would lead to competition for their services. In such circumstances, female labour supply to an individual firm may be more inelastic than male labour supply.

Since the supply schedules for both males and females are upward sloping, the employer will have a derived marginal cost schedule which lies above each supply schedule. This reflects the fact that the employer has to pay higher wages to expand each work-force, and because of competition *within* each group it has to pay these higher wages to the intra-marginal workers within the group. The total marginal cost schedule, mc_T, is obtained by *horizontally* summing the male and female marginal cost schedules, because this indicates the total amount of labour than can be obtained for a given marginal cost. In other words as the firm expands its homogeneous work-force, it would do so first by hiring only females because their marginal cost is below that of males. However, at some point, N_k in Figure 11.2, the marginal cost of female labour would just equal that of male labour and the firm would expand by hiring a mixture of males and females, always keeping its marginal cost as low as possible. At this point, N_k, the total marginal cost schedule is kinked downwards, reflecting the fact that it is a weighted average of the male and female marginal cost schedules.

The profit maximizing employer will hire labour until the marginal cost (MC_T) just equals marginal revenue (VMP_N). This occurs at the employment level N_T in Figure 11.2. This total work-force will consist of N_m males and N_f females because only here will the marginal cost of females just equal the marginal cost of males, and both will equal the common equilibrium marginal cost, MC^* (i.e. $MC_f = MC_m = MC^*$).

Male wages, w_m, are given by the height of the male supply schedule for N_m units of male labour, and female wages, w_f, are given by the height of the female supply schedule for N_f units of female labour. Male wages exceed female wages for the same assumed homogeneous type of labour and this is an equilibrium condition since the firm is maximizing profits by equating marginal cost with marginal revenue. Even though female wages are always lower than male wages over the relevant range of the supply schedules in this diagram, the firm would not hire exclusively females because the marginal cost of doing so is not always below that of males. And it is the marginal cost of labour, not always the wage, that is relevant for profit maximization.

Imperfect monopsonistic wage differentiation of this form can explain what otherwise appears to be a contradiction in the theory of discrimination: the persistence of a male-female wage differential for equally productive workers, and the persistence of a mixed work-force. These phenomenon were contradictions to competitive theory because, under competition, firms would hire only low wage females and this would increase the demand for females relative to males until the male-female wage differential disappeared. If some firms could resist competitive pressures and satisfy their desire to discriminate by paying higher wages to males, then males would gravitate to these employers and females would gravitate to non-discriminating employers. Discrimination would thereby lead to all-male or all-female work-forces in different firms (and presumably the lower cost female firms expanding relative to the higher cost male firms). That male-female wage differentials and mixed work-forces seem to persist, therefore, appears at odds with competitive pressures. They are consistent, however, with imperfect monopsonistic wage differentiation.

Even here, however, there should be competitive pressures at work to break down the segmentation that enables males and females to be considered as two separate pools of labour, with females having a lower reservation wage. In essence, competition from other employers, facilitated by improved labour market information, should serve to raise the wage opportunities for females with other firms, and this would raise the female labour supply schedule of Figure 11.2, mitigating against monopsonistic wage discrimination.

MATHEMATICAL EXPOSITION

The results of the previous section can be demonstrated more rigorously by the use of mathematics. The profit function for the monopsonist is:

$$\pi = pQ(M,F) - w_m(M)M - w_f(F)F \qquad (11.1)$$

The firm is still assumed to be a competitor in the product market, so that p is fixed. However, reflecting the fact that monopsonists are wage-setters and have to raise wages to attract additional labour, male and female wages are positively related to their respective employment levels. The profit maximizing firm employs additional labour until $\partial\pi/\partial M = \partial\pi/\partial F = 0$ which, for males, implies

$$p\partial Q/\partial M = w_m + \partial w_m/\partial M \cdot M \qquad (11.2)$$

— that is, the value of the marginal product of male labour (left-hand side) equals its marginal cost (right-hand side). Marginal cost in turn is the male wage rate plus the adjustment in that wage rate for the M intra-marginal units of male labour.

The wage elasticity of supply of male labour to the firm is defined as

$$\theta_m \equiv \partial M/\partial w_m \cdot w_m/M \qquad (11.3)$$

Inverting, multiplying by w_m and adding w_m to each side yields

$$w_m(1 + 1/\theta_m) = w_m + \partial w_m/M \cdot M \qquad (11.4)$$

— which is the right-hand side of Equation 11.2. Substituting Equation 11.4 into 11.2 yields:

$$p\partial Q/\partial M = w_m(1 + 1/\theta_m) \qquad (11.5)$$

The same derivation for females yields:

$$p\partial Q/\partial F = w_f(1 + 1/\theta_f) \qquad (11.6)$$

Under profit maximization, the value of the marginal product of males and females are equal; that is, $p\partial Q/\partial M = p\partial Q/\partial F$. Therefore, from Equations 11.5 and 11.6

$$w_m(1 + 1/\theta_m) = w_f(1 + 1/\theta_f) \qquad (11.7)$$

For $w_m > w_f$, it must be the case that $(1 + 1/\theta_m) < (1 + 1/\theta_f)$. Subtracting one from each side yields $1/\theta_m < 1/\theta_f$, and multiplying by θ_f yields $\theta_f/\theta_m < 1$, which implies $\theta_f < \theta_m$. That is, for $w_m > w_f$ it must be the case the $\theta_m > \theta_f$: at their equilibrium levels of employment, male labour supply to the firm must be more elastic than female labour supply.

Equation 11.7 also illustrates why the labour supply elasticities have to be different for the male-female wage differential to persist. If $\theta_f = \theta_m$ then $w_m = w_f$.

MINIMUM WAGES AND MONOPSONY

Monopsony also has interesting implications for the employment impact of an exogenous wage increase, for example, from minimum wages, unionization, equal pay laws or other forms of wage fixing. Specifically, over a specified range, an exogenous wage increase may actually *increase* employment in a monopsonistic firm. This seemingly paradoxical result can be illustrated by an example of a minimum wage increase faced by a monopsonist. The proposition first will be demonstrated rigorously, and then explained heuristically and by way of an example.

Formal Exposition

Figure 11.3 illustrates a monopsonistic labour market with w_0 being the wage paid by the monopsonist for N_0 units of labour with a value of marginal product of VMP_0. With the imposition of an exogenous wage increase, perhaps from minimum wages, to w_1, the new labour supply schedule to the

Figure 11.3   Monopsony and a Minimum Wage

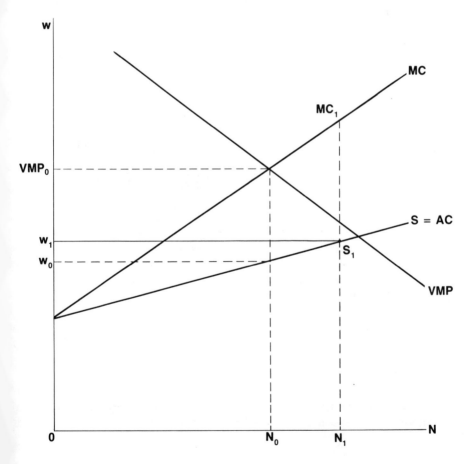

firm becomes horizontal at the minimum wage. This is so because the firm cannot hire at wages below the minimum wage. Thus the firm's labour supply schedule becomes w_1S_1S: to the right of S_1 it becomes the old supply schedule because firms can pay higher than the minimum wage.

The relevant marginal cost schedule, therefore, becomes $w_1S_1MC_1MC$. It is the same as the labour supply schedule for the horizontal portion w_1S_1 because both marginal and intra-marginal workers receive the minimum wage and consequently marginal cost equals average cost equals the minimum wage. Similarly, to the right of S_1 the marginal cost schedule becomes the old marginal cost schedule MC_1MC reflecting the relevance of the portion of the old supply schedule S_1S. The jump in marginal cost between S_1 and MC_1 occurs because when the firm expands its work-force beyond N_1 units of labour it has to raise wages to do so and the wage increase applies to all intra-marginal workers who previously were receiving the minimum wage.

After the imposition of the new minimum wage, the monopsonist would equate MC with MR (i.e. VMP) and hence employ N_1 units of labour at the minimum wage w_1. Wages have increased from w_0 to w_1 and, paradoxically, employment has increased from N_0 to N_1. In fact, for wage increases up to VMP_0, employment would increase, reaching a maximum increase for wages at the intersection of the supply and VMP schedules.

Heuristic Explanation

Why would wage increases ever lead to employment increases on the part of the firm? It really does not make intuitive sense that a firm would ever respond to a wage increase by employing more labour. The answer to this seeming paradox lies in the fact that the minimum wage negates or makes redundant a certain portion of the firm's supply and marginal cost of labour schedule. Faced with the new constraint of the minimum wage, the firm no longer need concern itself, at least up to a point, with the fact that if it wants more labour it will have to raise wages and pay these higher wages to all workers. In other words it is no longer inhibited in its employment expansion by the rapidly rising marginal cost of such expansion. Consequently it will expand employment because although the wage it pays is higher, the marginal cost of expansion is lower since it already pays the minimum wage to its intra-marginal workers.

This does not mean that the monopsonist would welcome a minimum wage increase because then it wouldn't have to worry about the rising marginal cost of labour. The minimum wage obviously reduces profits to the monopsonist, otherwise it would have self imposed a minimum wage without the need for legislation. The monopsonist is simply responding to a different set of constraints: the minimum wage constraint simply leads to more employment, at least over a limited range of wage increases.

TABLE 11.1

HYPOTHETICAL EXAMPLE OF MONOPSONIST RESPONDING TO MINIMUM WAGE

Units of Labour	No Minimum Wage		Minimum Wage		Value of Marg. Prod.
	Wages	Marg. Cost	Wages	Marg. Cost	
N (1)	S=AC (2)	MC (3)	w_1S_1S=AC (4)	$w_1S_1MC_1MC$ (5)	VMP (6)
1	1.00	1.00	2.00	2.00	3.00
2	1.20	1.40	2.00	2.00	2.50
3	1.40	1.80	2.00	2.00	2.30
4	1.60	2.20	2.00	2.00	2.20
5	1.80	2.60	2.00	2.00	2.00
6	2.00	3.00	2.00	2.00	1.80
7	2.20	3.40	2.20	3.40	1.60

Hypothetical Example

The response of a monopsonist to a minimum wage increase is illustrated in the hypothetical example of Table 11.1. The symbols refer to those in Figure 11.3. The firm's labour supply schedule is given in column (2) with hypothetical increments of .20 dollars per hour necessary to attract an additional worker. The resultant marginal cost schedule is given in column (3), rising faster than the average wage cost because of the necessity to pay intra-marginal workers the extra wage. In the absence of the minimum wage the monopsonist would equate MC with VMP and hence employ four workers.

With the imposition of a minimum wage equal to 2.00 dollars per hour, the firm's labour supply schedule becomes as in column (4). For the seventh worker the minimum wage is redundant, since that worker would not work for less than 2.20 dollars per hour, as indicated earlier in column (1). With the minimum wage the firm's new marginal cost of labour schedule becomes as in column (5). It is constant at the minimum wage for up until six workers because the firm simply pays the minimum wage to all workers. There is a large jump in MC associated with the seventh worker, however, because to acquire the seventh worker the firm has to pay not only the 2.20 dollars for that worker but also an additional .20 dollars for each of the previous six workers for a total of 3.40 dollars (i.e. 2.20 + 6(.20)).

Given the new marginal cost schedule associated with the minimum wage, the firm will equate MC with VMP by employing five workers. The minimum wage increase results in an increase in employment for four to five workers.

Monopsony profits before the minimum wage were (VMP−w)N = (2.20−1.60)4 = 2.40 dollars per hour. After the minimum wage they are reduced to zero in this particular case because the minimum wage was set exactly equal to the VMP of the fifth unit of labour. (In Figure 11.3, for example, there still would be some monopsony profits even after the minimum wage.)

Practical Importance

While in theory minimum wage increases can lead to employment increases in situations of monopsony, in practice the importance of this factor depends on the extent to which monopsony is associated with workers who are paid below minimum wages. Earlier it was pointed out that monopsonists may well pay high wages even though these wages are not as high as they would be if there were more competition for these workers. Low wage labour markets that are most dramatically affected by minimum wages tend to be in the garment and textile trades and in the service sector, especially hotels, restaurants and theatres. Employers in these sectors tend to be small and the pool of low wage labour from which they draw large. Consequently, the conditions giving rise to monopsony are not prevalent. There may be isolated instances of one industry towns where the minimum wage would have an impact on otherwise monopsonistic wage determination. However, it is unlikely that these conditions are sufficiently prominent to negate the usual adverse employment effect that economic theory predicts will emanate from minimum wage increases.

EVIDENCE OF MONOPSONY

Empirical evidence on the prevalence of monopsony is both scant and at times contradictory. In an early study, Bunting (1962) computed concentration ratios of the percentage of the local labour force employed by the largest firms in 1948. He finds little evidence of monopsony power associated with concentration.

Some more recent studies, however, have found evidence of monopsony in some particular labour markets. Landon and Baird (1971) test for the existence of monopsony in the market for U.S. teachers by regressing the starting salary of teachers on a measure of monopsony (number of school districts in the county) and a variety of variables designed to control for ability to pay (per capita income and the percentage of income raised locally) and willingness to pay (tax rate). The starting salary of teachers was used to approximate a homogeneous group of minimally qualified teachers. All variables were statistically significant except for the tax rate. The regression coefficient for the monopsony variable indicated that a one percent increase in the number of school districts in the county gave rise to a 116 dollar increase in the starting salary for teachers. That is, the more competition for the teachers, the greater their salary: conversely the less competition and the greater the monopsony, the less their salary.

If these results are correct, one policy implication is that decentralization would lead to higher starting salaries because of the increased competition, while consolidation of school districts would lead to reduced salaries because the consolidated districts would act like monopsonists. Thus one would expect school boards and taxpayers to support consolidation so as to have more bargaining power against teachers. Conversely one would expect teachers to support decentralization to increase the competition for their services.

In a study of the market for nurses in the U.S., Cohen (1972) regresses the wages of registered nurses relative to an index of competitive wages in the community on variables reflecting monopsony power of the firm. An index of competitive wages was used to control for regional and other factors that could legitimately affect wages. The monopsony variables included a concentration ratio indicating the percentage of beds in the area provided by the four largest hospitals, and a dummy variable to reflect the existence of a nursing school in the area. Theoretically one would expect wages to be negatively related to the concentration variable (because concentration implies monopsony power) and the nursing school variable (because of the attachment of nurses to areas with a nursing school). The regression results confirmed these expectations. Registered nurses receive lower salaries, relative to the competitive wage in the community, in areas that are dominated by a small number of hospitals and where a nursing school is present. The latter variable simply reflects the fact that nurses are often reluctant to leave an area that has a nursing school: their resultant immobility, and hence excess supply in such an area, depresses their wages.

Additional empirical evidence of monopsony in the market for nurses in the U.S. is found in other studies, notably Hurd (1973), Yett (1970), and Link and Landon (1976). These studies suggest that some of the perennial shortage of nurses may be explained by the prevalence of monopsony power in hospitals.

Although the empirical evidence is by no means conclusive, there does appear to be evidence of monopsony in at least some particular labour markets. Further evidence for newspaper printing employees and construction workers is found in Landon (1970) and Landon and Pierce (1971). The extent to which these results can be generalized, even within the occupations where some monopsony was found, remains an open question. In addition, the extent to which it was monopsony power, rather than other factors, that reduced wages could be open to debate.

In theory, however, it is unlikely that monopsony can be an extremely important factor in the long run. Improved communications, labour market information, and labour mobility make the isolated labour market syndrome, necessary for monopsony, unlikely at least for large numbers of workers. It is also true that as these factors improve over time, monopsony should diminish.

QUESTIONS

1. Combine the results of Chapter 10 on monopoly in the product market with Chapter 11 on monopsony in the labour market and illustrate the wage and employment determination process. Is it necessary that monopoly be accompanied by monopsony? Is it possible that the two conditions could go together?
2. If the monopsonist is a wage-setter and not a wage-taker then it can set wages in whatever fashion it wants. Discuss.
3. Monopsonists are at a disadvantage relative to competitive buyers of labour because, when the monopsonist wants to expand its work-force, it has to raise wages while the competitive buyer can get all the labour it wants at the going wage. Discuss.
4. The monopsonist has an upward sloping labour supply schedule because when it expands its work-force it has to use better quality labour and hence has to pay a higher wage. Discuss.
5. The monopsonist's demand for labour depends on its elasticity of labour supply. Illustrate this proposition in Figure 11.1 by drawing both a more elastic and a more inelastic supply schedule through the point S_m.
6. Explain why the monopsonist has no unique demand schedule for labour.
7. Is it possible for a multi-million dollar professional sports player to be subject to monopsonistic exploitation of labour? Is it possible for workers who are subject to monopsonistic exploitation of labour to be receiving an economic rent on the sale of their labour market services? Could workers who are receiving an economic rent for their services ever be considered disadvantaged workers?
8. Monopsonists are not necessarily evil: they are simply acting like any other firms when they maximize profits subject to constraints. It is just that the constraints they face are different and this enables them to make a monopsony profit per worker equal to the difference between the wage they pay and the value of the marginal product of labour. The solution to this problem is therefore to alter the constraints faced by monopsonists. Discuss.
9. If the economic rent of $S_oS_mw_m$ in Figure 11.1 were taxed away from the workers, what would happen to the equilibrium employment of the monopsonist? Specifically, would these workers go elsewhere if only their earnings in this particular employment were taxed? Similarly, if the monopsonist appropriates this surplus, what would happen to its employment?
10. Discuss various ways in which monopsonists may try to differentiate their work-force so as to appropriate any economic rent or seller's surplus of their workers.
11. Based on your knowledge of professional sports contracts, discuss ways in which monopsony behaviour may be exhibited.

12. One of the conditions necessary for monopsonistic wage discrimination against females as a group is that their labour supply to the firm must be more inelastic than that of males, at their respective wages and employment. Would you expect this to be the case, and why?

13. Based on the diagram of Figure 11.2, the slopes of the male and female labour supply schedules appear to be the same. How is it then that female labour supply must be more inelastic than male labour supply for the wages of females to be less than the wages of males in this situation of imperfect monopsonistic wage discrimination?

14. Based on the respective supply schedules of males and females in Figure 11.2, if other firms began to compete with this monopsonist for labour, what type of labour would they probably hire and what would this do to the respective supply schedules of this monopsonist? Specifically, would it be able to keep differentiating its pools of labour in the face of such competition?

15. The equilibrium of Figure 11.2 is unstable in the long run because, if the monopsonist is paying males a higher wage than equally productive females, it would obviously try to replace its costly male work-force with a less costly female work-force. Discuss.

16. Indicate how imperfect monopsonistic wage discrimination between males and females can explain the persistence of a male-female wage differential for equally productive workers and the persistence of a mixed work-force within a firm. Could monopsony explain the persistence of these phenomenon throughout the aggregate economy?

17. In the case of imperfect monopsonistic wage differentiation (as illustrated in Figure 11.2), would the monopsonist ever hire an all female work-force? Why are the male and female marginal cost schedules not vertically summed to get a total marginal cost schedule? Would this monopsonist ever report vacancies of male and female labour at the going wage and, if so, exactly what is the measure of the vacancies for each?

18. The fact that a minimum wage, over a specific range, may actually increase employment for a monopsonist illustrates the proposition that a monopsonist does not have a demand curve for labour in the usual sense. For if it did, then a wage increase would have to be accompanied by a reduction in employment. Discuss.

19. Explain heuristically why a minimum wage increase, over a certain range, would lead to a monopsonist actually increasing employment. Given this possibility, could the monopsony argument be relied upon to negate the critics of minimum wage legislation who argue that minimum wages will have an adverse employment effect and hence harm some of the very people it was designed to help? Could minimum wages ever be applied selectively to monopsony situations? Could wage fixing via unionization be applied more selectively?

20. Based on Figure 11.2, trace through the impact of equal pay for equal work legislation, assuming that the firm could not lower male wages.

21. Based on Figure 11.3, discuss the favourable impact on resource allocation of setting a minimum wage at the intersection of the S and VMP schedules. Heuristically, in what sense are resources allocated more efficiently at that point than at the monopsonist's equilibrium? If the monopsonist followed a policy of perfect wage differentiation in the absence of the minimum wage, what would be the implications for resource allocation? Compare the income distribution consequences of the two alternatives of minimum wages and perfect wage differentiation.

22. Based on the data of Table 11.1, how many units of labour would the monopsonist employ if it acted as a perfectly discriminating monopsonist? What are the consequences for efficient resource allocation?

23. Trace through the implications of the firm acting as an oligopsonist with a kinked supply curve; that is, where wage increases would be met by other oligopsonists but wage decreases would not, so that substantial losses of employment would result.

24. According to Link and Landon (1976, p. 151), "clear evidence of a relation between depressed wage levels and monopsony or oligopsony can be isolated empirically in labour markets such as nursing where highly specialized training is required, where the cross-elasticity of supply between occupations is small, where substantial inter-area variations in monopsony power are present, and where limited geographic mobility exists in the labour market". Discuss how each of these factors could lead to monopsony or oligopsony power being exercised.

25. Cohen (1972, p. 43) estimated the following equation to test for the existence of monopsony in the nursing market:

$$w_N/w_C = 3.69 - 0.30CR - 0.02NS$$

where w_n is the starting wage of registered nurses (in dollars per hour), w_c is an index of competitive wages in the area, CR is a concentration ratio giving the percentage of beds in the area provided by the four largest hospitals, and NS is a dummy variable coded one if the hospital has a nursing school, zero otherwise.

   Use this equation to predict the starting salaries of registered nurses in the following three cases, assuming throughout that the competitive wage index is unity (approximately the sample mean):
   (a) competitive case when CR = .20 and NS = 0;
   (b) typical case when CR = .60 and NS = 0;
   (c) oligopsony case when, for example, CR = .80 and NS = 1;
   (d) monopsony when, for example, CR = 1.00 and NS = 1.

REFERENCES AND FURTHER READINGS

Altman, S. *Present and Future Supply of Registered Nurses.* Washington: Dept.
of Health, Education and Welfare, 1971. Chapter II, Appendix A.

Altman, S. The structure of nursing education and its impact on supply.
Empirical Studies in Health Economics, H. Klarman (ed.). Baltimore:
Johns Hopkins Press, 1970.

Archibald, G. The factor gap and the level of wages. *Economic Record* 30
(November 1954) 187) 187-199.

Arrow, K. and W. Capron. Dynamic shortages and price rises: the engineer-
scientist case. *QJE* (May 1959) 292-307.

Baily, M. Dynamic monopsony and structural change. *AER* 65 (June 1975)
338-349.

Bronfenbrenner, M. Potential monopsony in labor markets. *ILRR* 9 (July
1956) 577-588.

Bunting, R. *Employer Concentration in Local Labor Markets.* Chapel Hill,
N.C.: University of North Carolina Press, 1962.

Cohen, H. Monopsony and discriminating monopsony in the nursing
market. *Applied Economics* 4 (March 1972) 39-48.

Craig, P. Monopsony in manpower. *Yale Law Journal* (March 1953).

Devine, E. Analysis of manpower shortages in local government. New
York: Praeger, 1970.

Devine, E. Manpower shortages in local employment. *AER Proceedings* 59
(May 1969) 538-546.

Ehrenberg, R. Heterogeneous labor, minimum hiring standards, and job
vacancies in public employment. *JPE* 81 (November/December 1973)
1442-1450.

Falero, F. A note on monopsony, minimum wages and unemployment.
American Economist (Fall 1966).

Fellner, W. Prices and wages under bilateral monopoly. *QJE* 61 (1947).

Hall, W. Unionization, monopsony power, and police salaries. *IR* 16
(February 1977) 94-100.

Hieser, R. Wage determination with bilateral monopoly in the labour
market: a theoretical treatment. *ER* 36 (March 1970) 55-72.

Hirshleifer, J. An exposition of the equilibrium of the firm: symmetry
between product and factor analysis. *Economica* 29 (August 1962)
263-268.

Hurd, R. Equilibrium vacancies in a labor market dominated by non-profit
firms: the shortage of nurses. *R. E. Stats.* 55 (May 1973) 234-240.

Landon, J. and R. Baird. Monopsony in the market for public school
teachers. *AER* 61 (December 1971) 966-971. Comment by R.
Thornton and reply, *ILRR* 28 (July 1975) 574-578.

Landon, J. and W. Peirce. Discrimination, monopsony, and union power in
the building trades: a cross sectional analysis. *IRRA Proceedings 24*
(December 1971) 254-261.

Link, C. and J. Landon. Market structure, nonpecuniary factors and professional salaries: registered nurses. *Journal of Economics and Business* 28 (Winter 1976) 151-155.

Link, C. and J. Landon. Monopsony and union power in the market for nurses. *SEJ* 41 (April 1975) 649-659.

Maurice, S. Monopsony and the effects of an externally imposed minimum wage. *SEJ* 41 (October 1974) 283-287.

Nelson, P. The elasticity of labor supply to the individual firm. *Econometrica* 41 (September 1973) 853-866.

Persky, J. and H. Tsang. Pigouvian exploitation of labor. *R. E. Stats.* 56 (February 1974) 52-57.

Robinson, J. *The Economics of Imperfect Competition.* London: Macmillan, 1933, Reprinted 1965, 211-228.

Rottenberg, S. The baseball players' labor market. *JPE* (June 1956) 242-258.

Yett, D. The chronic shortage of nurses: a public policy dilemma. *Empirical Studies in Health Economics,* H. Klarman (ed.). Baltimore: Johns Hopkins Press, 1970.

Yett, D. Causes and consequences of salary differentials in nursing, *EI* 7 (March 1970) 78-99.

Chapter 12

Institutionalism, Dualism and Radicalism

Throughout this section we have emphasized the interaction of supply and demand in alternative market structures as being crucial in determining wages and employment. There have always been schools of thought, however, that have de-emphasized, and at times attacked, the notion of these market forces as being important factors in wage and employment determination. The severity of the criticism of the economic factors has ranged from saying that they play an important but minor role, to saying that they are distinctly subservient to other political-institutional factors, to the more radical critiques that argue that the economic framework simply masks the forces of power and class conflict that are the real determinants of wages and employment.

While it is always hazardous to try to categorize alternative perspectives and paradigms, they are labelled here as institutionalism, dualism, and radicalism. While there are some basic differences between these perspectives, they have as a common thread a critique of the neoclassical paradigm. In what follows an attempt will be made to summarize each of these schools of thought with respect to their criticism of neoclassical theory, their own contribution, and their own strengths and shortcomings.

INSTITUTIONALISM

The institutionalist tradition in labour economics is one that plays down the economic forces and emphasizes the roles of individuals, institutions, custom and socio-political factors. It tends to emphasize descriptive realism as being more important than abstract, theoretical reasoning. The case-study and real-world observations are emphasized as being important in understanding the behaviour of the labour market.

The institutionalist tradition is evident in the work of Lester (1946) who attacked the assumptions of economics and its emphasis on marginal analysis as being unrealistic. He argued for empirical testing of the assumptions often employed in economics. For example, in responding to interviews and questionnaires, employers said that they did not use marginal analysis in their everyday business decisions and that they seldom responded to wage increases by reducing employment. Lester interpreted this as a rejection of conventional economic analysis.

Conventional economics was not without its defence. Machlup (1946) stressed the fact that it was the predictions and not the assumptions of theory that mattered, and that simplifying assumptions were necessary to deduce generalizations about labour market behaviour. For example, the assumption of perfect mobility is a simplifying assumption that enables predictions about long-run wage differentials. It can be relaxed, and the implication for wage differentials examined. In addition, it may not be so unrealistic if one remembers that all that is required for the implications of economic analysis is that some workers at the margin of decision (not all workers) be mobile or, at times, have the threat of mobility.

The neoclassical paradigm can also be defended on the basis that it is operational and leads to empirically verifiable propositions. In defending the use of abstractions such as profit maximization on the part of firms and income maximization on the part of individuals, Rottenberg (1956, p.45) states: "complex motivation in real life does not destroy the truism of simple motivational behaviour in the abstract neoclassical model of the labour market. Other things equal, it can be a correct description of real life behaviour to say that workers make job choices with reference to relative prices".

The institutional tradition is also evident in the work of Arthur Ross (1956). He argued that wages are determined by "conscious human decision rather than by impersonal market forces" and that to understand union wage policy we must understand the internal political aspect of the union—"what kind of organism it is, how it functions, and what is the role of leadership". Above all, Ross emphasized the interdependence of the wage structure and the importance of "equitable comparisons" as a criteria for wage determination.

The institutionalist tradition has continued in the writings of those who emphasized the importance of segmentation in labour markets. These writings in particular were the forefront of the more current work on dual labour markets. Kerr (1954), for example, coined the phrase "Balkanization of labour markets" to describe what he felt was a trend towards the increased segmentation of the labour market into a variety of non-competing groups. In his view firms were becoming increasingly divorced or insulated from the competitive forces of the external labour market. They recruited from this labour market only at the lower "ports of entry". Most jobs were filled from internal promotion from the firm's "internal labour market". Consequently, administered rules and internal company policies governing the internal labour market were more important than competitive economic forces that were important only for the seldom-used external labour market.

Dunlop (1957) also emphasized the importance of segmentation with the concepts of "job clusters" and "wage contours". Job clusters were occupational groupings with common wage-making characteristics so that wages within the clusters were highly interdependent. The clusters were linked together by technology, administrative rulings of the firm, or social custom. Wage contours referred to the stable wage relationships between certain firms that were linked together by similar product markets, labour markets, or custom. Thus the wages of an individual worker was dependent upon the job cluster of the occupation and on the wage contour of the firm. These clusters and contours defined the relevant comparisons for the actual wage determination process. Key wage settlements spilled over onto other jobs within the same cluster and onto other firms within the same contour. Thus, institutional forces which determined the nature of the job clusters, wage contours, key settlements and spillover effects were seen as being of prime importance in the wage determination process.

The institutionalist framework, with its impressive list of contributors, has given insight into the real-world behaviour of labour markets. It has been rich in classification and in describing the peculiarities of the labour market. However, it has not really provided an *analysis* of the basic forces that lie behind the every day actions of labour and management. Consequently, it has seldom given rise to empirically testable implications that are capable of empirical confirmation or refutation. As such its contribution has not been cumulative. Rather, its insights have been incorporated into labour market analysis in a rather *ad hoc* fashion, often to explain particular anomalies.

In recent years, a literature has emerged applying Hirschman's (1970) concepts of exit and voice to the labour market. Exit refers to the traditional competitive response of leaving unsatisfactory market situations for more acceptable ones; voice refers to alternative means (e.g. complaint, protest or suggestions) to improve unsatisfactory market situations. While the concepts of exit and voice can be subject to many of the criticisms of institutional economics, they do provide some interesting insights into labour market behaviour.

According to Hirschman, traditional economics regards exit, or the threat of exit, as the basic pressure that ensures that competition will provide goods and services efficiently: if they are not so provided, then customers will exit and shop elsewhere. There are situations, however, where exit is not feasible, perhaps because it is a costly process or because of brand loyalty. In such circumstances, consumers may use voice ranging from constructive suggestion to severe protest. Most important, the possibility of exit reduces the necessity to use voice. From a policy perspective, Hirschman's analysis therefore implies that the usual economic solution of attaining efficiency through increased competition (exit) works against the possibility of attaining efficiency through mechanisms involving voice.

This has interesting implications for the analysis of labour markets since it suggests that increased competition and mobility (exit)—the panacea of economists — may reduce the use of voice as a way of handling labour market problems. As Freeman (1976) points out, collective bargaining can be viewed as the institutional embodiment of voice in the labour market. It therefore can serve as a viable alternative to the costly use of exit as a way of handling labour market problems.

Johnson's (1975) perspective on the impact of unions can also be viewed in the context of exit versus voice. Traditional economic analysis regards the union as a causal factor gaining higher wages for union members, largely through the threat of exit (withdrawal of services). Johnson raises the possibility, however, that causality works the other way. That is, for various reasons some firms and industries simply pay a greater-than-competitive wage, usually because it is important for them to reduce turnover and to have a queue of applicants from which to hire. Workers that are fortunate enough to be hired in this sector will not use exit to improve their situation because they cannot do better elsewhere. Because exit is not effective for them, they turn to voice in the form of collective bargaining and unionization to achieve other objectives (e.g. due process), knowing that they will be remaining in the firm for a long time. In essence, high wages reduces exit and encourages voice, raising the intriguing possibility that high wages leads to unionization rather than vice versa.

Clearly the exit, voice, and loyalty concepts raise some interesting issues, especially with respect to the comparative efficiency of various forms of exit as opposed to voice and loyalty as general ways of achieving efficiency and reconciling efficiency objectives with other objectives. In particular, it raises the possibility that many institutional arrangements can be regarded as efficient ways of utilizing voice in the labour market.

DUALISM

The institutionalist tradition has also re-emerged in recent years in the works of a number of economists who characterize the labour market as being segmented into two main parts, the primary or core, and the secondary or peripheral labour market. An excellent review of this literature, with emphasis on its applicability to the Canadian environment and its usefulness in analysing Canadian human resource issues, is contained in Smith (1976).

Characteristics of Segmented Markets and Their Work-force

The characteristics of the primary and secondary labour markets are given in Doeringer and Piore (1971, p.165):

> Jobs in the primary market possess several of the following characteristics: high wages, good working conditions, employment stability, chances of advancement, equity, and due process in the administration of work rules. Jobs in the secondary market, in contrast, tend to have low wages and fringe benefits, poor working conditions, high labour turnover, little chance of advancement, and often arbitrary and capricious supervision. There are distinctions between workers in the two sectors which parallel those between jobs: workers in the secondary sector, relative to those in the primary sector, exhibit greater turnover, higher rates of lateness and absentee-

ism, more insubordination, and engage more freely in petty theft and pilferage.

Of crucial importance in the analysis of segmented labour markets is the role of the internal labour market of individual firms in the primary sector. Within each internal labour market, well-developed hierarchies and stable employment relationships develop that are of mutual benefit to both management and workers. The job security and opportunities for career advancement that are so important to workers are also of value to management as ways of retaining a work-force that has accumulated enterprise specific skills and informal on-the-job training. In such circumstances, firms will try to reduce turnover cost by paying high wages, granting job security, and providing career advancement.

Within the internal labour market, the allocation of labour is determined by administrative rules and custom. Competitive forces, emphasized by neoclassical economics, have only a minor influence in determining broad limits within which administered and customary wage and employment policies are carried out.

Reasons for Segmentation

Reasons for the segmentation of labour markets are difficult to disentangle from the characteristics of the markets because cause and effect are interrelated. In essence, segmentation prevails because it produces characteristics in workers that sustain the segmentation. A veritable Catch 22 situation prevails as workers are trapped in the secondary labour market in part because of their poor work habits: their poor work habits in turn result in part from their being employed in the secondary labour force. Cause and effect are unclear. But what is clear is the cumulative nature of the problem and the inherent difficulty of breaking out of the secondary labour market. In essence, segmentation becomes self-perpetuating.

To a large extent segmentation is historically determined and is sustained by forces of custom and tradition. Well established patterns emerge and these become accepted norms. As Doeringer and Piore (1971, p.85) state with respect to the wage determination process: "Any wage rate, set of wage relationships, or wage-setting procedure which prevails over a period of time tends to become customary; changes are then viewed as unjust or inequitable, and the work group will exert economic pressure in opposition to them". Thus segmentation becomes self-perpetuating through the forces of custom and tradition.

Institutional and legal factors can also foster segmentation in labour markets. Unions, especially craft unions, can create barriers to entry into the primary (often unionized) labour market via such devices as the hiring hall, nepotism and lengthy apprenticeship programs. Professional associations also create barriers to entry and prevent competition via occupational licensing and the control of paraprofessional substitutes. Discrimination can be an

effective barrier preventing minority groups from moving from the secondary to the primary labour market.

Social legislation may foster segmentation, usually as an unintended
side effect. For example, termination of employment legislation, experience
rating under unemployment insurance, ceilings on the payroll tax used to
finance social security — all of which result in quasi-fixed costs being associated with each employee — encourage firms to work their existing work-
force longer hours (to spread the fixed costs) rather than to hire additional
employees which would result in additional fixed costs. The existing work-
force becomes protected from the competition of other workers because of
these legislated fixed costs associated with hiring additional workers. These
legislated quasi-fixed costs are compounded by the normal fixed costs associated with the recruitment, hiring and training of new workers. To a certain
extent employers may minimize these quasi-fixed costs by contracting out
for work in the secondary labour market which does not have these high fixed
costs, often because the legislation is inapplicable to small employers and to
the self-employed. In essence, legislation that results in quasi-fixed costs of
employment fosters segmentation by discouraging employers from hiring
potential recruits from the secondary labour market, especially if their work
habits are such that turnover may be high and hence the fixed costs are lost.

The impact of such legislation in fostering segmentation is illustrated
most dramatically in the so-called "black markets" that are alleged to have
developed as a way of avoiding the legislation. Especially in response to the
difficulty of laying off workers, but also in response to minimum wage and
other legislation, employers have at times responded by purchasing semi-
finished inputs from households or by contracting out to households to do
specific tasks (e.g. sew on buttons, assemble a minor part). Veritable "cot-
tage industries" develop which are not covered by legislation that creates
fixed costs of employment, nor by safety laws, child labour laws, nor any
other labour standards for that matter. In addition, the job of quality control,
supervising, and monitoring the labour input is left up to the household, with
firms simply buying or not buying the output. Markets develop and operate in
unusual forms, and employers and employees adjust to legislation in subtle
fashions!

Policy Implications of Segmented Labour Markets

Concern for issues of public policy arise from the segmented labour market
analysis for reasons of both distributive equity and allocative efficiency.
Equity concerns arise because workers trapped in the secondary labour
market tend to be disadvantaged workers, often caught in a vicious circle of
poverty, and experiencing other problems associated with discrimination and
poor working conditions. Efficiency concerns arise because of the costs
associated with immobility of labour and barriers to entry.

As Smith (1976, p.27) points out, as a general policy prescription the

dual and segmented labour market analysis suggests a re-emphasis towards
the structural aspects of labour demand and away from the structural aspects
of labour supply (i.e human capital theory) as well as aspects of the level of
aggregate demand (i.e. macroeconomic full employment policies). Macroeconomic full employment policies to raise the level of aggregate demand
are dismissed as helping mainly workers in the primary labour market, with
at best a minor trickling-down effect on those in the secondary market, and a
loosening of the barriers that prevent workers from moving from the secondary to the primary market. As Smith (1976, p.28) concludes: "policies to
maintain high, stable levels of aggregate demand have beneficial but limited
effects in the dual theory".

Similarly, human capital policies that alter the structure of labour
supply are not regarded by dual labour market analysts as viable ways of
improving the earnings of workers in the secondary labour markets. Thus
improved education, training, mobility and labour market information—the
traditional human capital factors—are dismissed largely on the grounds that
they do little to improve earnings because they do not necessarily enable
those in the secondary labour market to enter the primary labour market. In
essence, improving the characteristics of workers via human resource development will do little if this is not accompanied by policies that alter the
structure of labour demand so that these workers obtain jobs in the primary
labour market.

After rejecting aggregate demand (full employment) and structural
supply (human capital) policies, proponents of the dual labour market
analysis suggest the structure of labour demand as being the most important determinant of the wages and working conditions of workers in the
secondary labour market. The structure of labour demand is reflected in the
characteristics of the industry, occupation, region and firm in which workers
find themselves. That is, the structure of labour demand in the secondary
labour market reflects declining demand, low profitability, fierce competition
in the product market, and competitive pressures from other sources of
labour supply. Thus it is the characteristics of markets more than the characteristics of the workers themselves that are taken as being responsible for the
low wages of the working poor in the secondary labour market.

Proponents of dual labour market analysis, therefore, recommend de-
emphasizing human resource policies — the panacea of the 1960s — and
recommend improvements in the characteristics of the markets in which low
wage workers find themselves. This could be done basically in two ways.
One is to *extend* the protection, high wages and good working conditions of
workers in the primary labour market to workers in the secondary labour
market. This could be accomplished by wage fixing (e.g. minimum wages,
equal pay laws), labour standards legislation, the encouragement of
unionization and collective bargaining in the secondary labour market, and by
policies such as unemployment insurance that would increase the bargaining

power of workers in the peripheral sector. Wherever these policies have adverse side effects, perhaps on the employment opportunities of low wage workers, they would have to be rectified by complementary programs, such as perhaps public employment.

A second device to improve the labour market situation in which low wage workers find themselves is to break down the barriers that prevent movement from the secondary to the primary labour market. In particular, anti-discrimination laws may be effective, as would the removal of unnecessary educational or occupational licensing requirements. In general, however, not much hope is held out for these policies because there is the possibility that even if secondary sector workers get jobs in the primary sector, they will still be treated as secondary workers. In addition, many of the protective features and job security of the primary labour market are regarded as desirable, and removing these features would be like "throwing out the baby with the bath water". Hence, the emphasis on extending the benefits of the primary labour market into the secondary labour market.

Strengths and Weaknesses of Dualism

An overall evaluation of the usefulness of dual labour market analysis is both difficult and perhaps premature. It may be premature because much of the work appeared in the 1960s and sufficient time has not passed to judge its usefulness. Nevertheless, it is a continuation of the institutionalist tradition that has always been a part — at times the only part — of labour market analysis.

On the positive side, the dualist (and institutionalist) approach has often exposed observers to the harsh realities of the operations of labour markets and has emphasized that low wages may be a result of the characteristics of the labour market in which workers operate as well as (or rather than) the characteristics of the workers themselves. This highlights the fact that the poverty of the working poor may be a fault of the economic system as well as (or rather than) of individual workers themselves. Dualism has also provided a wealth of descriptive information, classification devices and, most importantly, insights into the real-world operation of labour markets, especially for the working poor.

These very contributions, however, are at the root of the weaknesses of dual labour market analysis. In its over-concern for descriptive detail, and in documenting reality, the dual labour market analysis has fallen short of providing a coherent and systematic analysis of the basic causal forces that underly the every day actions of labour market participants. The emphasis on descriptive case studies and the in-depth analysis of particular local labour markets also has suffered from an inability to generalize the results. In essence, the dual labour market analysis has been long on description and classification and short on cumulative theoretical analysis from which one could derive testable implications capable of empirical acceptance or refutation.

To a certain extent this may be an unfair criticism since it comes from the very paradigm—neoclassical economics with its emphasis on cumulative theory and empirical implications capable of empirical scrutiny—that the dual labour market analysis criticizes. Nevertheless, unless dual labour market analysis moves beyond description and classification, it is unlikely to do more than supplement more traditional economic analysis as a way of understanding labour market behaviour.

As an example, one of the fundamental weaknesses of dual labour market analysis is its failure, at least at this stage, to explain how the barriers between the primary and secondary labour markets can persist in the long run against competitive forces. Why can't workers move, in the long run, from the secondary to the primary labour market, and why don't employers recruit in the secondary labour market knowing that they could obtain abundant labour at low wages? It is not enough to *describe* the barriers: it is also necessary to *explain* why they exist and how they can persist over time. Without a theory of cause and effect, policy prescriptions are, at best, hazardous.

This suggests that a fruitful approach would be to try to explain the causal factors that give rise to the institutional barriers that separate the primary and secondary labour markets. In other words, whereas economics traditionally regards institutional factors and administrative policies as constraints (and then analyses their impact, especially on efficiency), perhaps more understanding could be had by regarding them as rational (and perhaps efficient) outcomes of employer and employee interaction, given the peculiarities of the labour market. In formal terms, what may be needed is an endogenous theory of institutions and administrative arrangements, rather than simply regarding them as exogenously given. This was suggested in our earlier discussion of the importance of voice as opposed to exit, and it is in the spirit of the work of Addison and Burton (1978, p.221), who have argued that the "labour market phenomena that have been labelled as 'institutional', non-market phenomena by institutionalists—comparative group monitoring and collective bargaining, internal labour markets and seniority practices— may be seen...as institutional arrangements adopted by market participants because of the efficiency of such arrangements".

RADICALISM

An alternative perspective on labour market economics is found in the recent radical neo-Marxian writings as discussed, for example, in the works of Barry Bluestone (1968, 1970), Samuel Bowles (1972), Richard Edwards, Michael Reich and Thomas Weisskopf (1972), Herbert Gintis (1970, 1971), David Gordon (1971, 1972), Bennet Harrison (1972), and Howard Wachtel (1971, 1972). Probably the best summary of the radical perspective, giving an explicit comparison with the orthodox neoclassical and the dual labour market perspectives, is contained in Gordon (1972).

As Gordon (1972, p.53) points out:

> Radical economic theory ... has not yet been pulled together into a fully embellished theoretical system. Individual strands of radical economic analysis have begun to interweave, but many of the features of the eventual fabric have not become entirely clear. So far, much of the analysis has not even been precisely formulated, much less published; it continues to flow through conversations, letters and unpublished notes.

This makes a review of the radical perspective difficult; nevertheless, some common threads interweave through their analysis.

Following Marx, radicals emphasize that *economic classes* emerge as a result of the particular way in which productive activity is organized: under capitalism, the working class and capitalists emerge, with each group developing a strong subjective identification with their own class. Because of technological change and growth, an *economic surplus* develops over and above the subsistence level necessary to sustain and maintain the economic system. *Class conflict* arises over the division of this economic surplus. Under the current state of capitalism, this surplus tends to be appropriated by the capitalist owners of the means of production and they use the surplus to ensure their continued *power*. In particular, they use the instruments of the *state* (e.g. police, education, granting agencies, tax-transfer schemes) to ensure that effective power remains in their hands. These policies could include the granting of concessions to the working class, largely as a way to buy support, co-opt insurgence, and defuse protest.

Over time, however, capitalism develops *internal contradiction:* in essence, it contains the seeds of its self-destruction. In particular, competition, efficiency and the specialization of labour are necessary for the survival of capitalism, but these very factors dehumanize and alienate the work-force, strengthening the class consciousness amongst exploited workers. Eventually, their plight will become intolerable and they will act in a concerted fashion to gain the effective power necessary to improve their position.

Radicals, therefore, emphasize the importance of class power in economic relationships. In particular, Gordon (1972, p.64) argues that there are really two stages in the determination and distribution of income. First, the share of total income that goes to workers as opposed to capitalists depends on the relative power of the two groups. Second, once that share is determined by power relationships, then the amount that a given worker gets within the working class depends on the individual's productivity, which in turn varies with the personal characteristics and capacities of the worker (as emphasized by human capital theory) and the characteristics of the job (as emphasized by dualism). Thus, to the conventional concepts of the quality of labour supply as emphasized by human capital theorists, and the structure of labour demand as emphasized by dual labour market analysts, radicals have added the concept of class power as an important factor in the determination and distribution of income. To cite Gordon (1972, p.65): "The worker's final wage thus depends *both* on his individual productivity *and* on the relative power of the class to which he belongs. The radical theory thus combines the radical concept of class with orthodox notions of supply and demand".

As a general policy prescription, therefore, radicals tend to emphasize the importance of the development of class consciousness amongst workers and of fundamental changes in the power relationships between workers and capitalists. Specific policies to change these power relationships are not usually spelled out clearly, but what is clear is the radicals' belief that most of the policy recommendations that flow from traditional economic analysis, or from the dual labour market perspective, are ineffective without radical changes in power relationships.

AN OVERALL ASSESSMENT

Any overall assessment of the various competing paradigms — neoclassical, institutional, dual, and radical — is made difficult by the political overtones that surround any perspective. In addition, some of the writings — those of Lester Thurow (1969) for example — are difficult to categorize because they contain elements of various paradigms. The matter is further complicated by the fact that the dual and new radical perspectives have not been subject to the test of time. And when they are judged, it is probably through the perspective of the reigning paradigm — neoclassical economics — with its emphasis on cumulative theory that yields implications capable of empirical acceptance or rejection. The extent to which this is a fair test is an open question, especially since the empirical testing itself is geared to the neoclassical paradigm with its emphasis on marginal analysis.

Each of the perspectives certainly does give insights into our understanding of labour market behaviour. Neoclassical economics, with its emphasis on income and relative prices as they affect various facets of labour supply and labour demand in alternative market structures, certainly has provided a systematic and consistent theoretical explanation for various aspects of observed labour market behaviour. This is especially the case when it has been modified to incorporate realistic factors such as uncertainty, transaction costs, and lack of information. Institutionalism, with its emphasis on the importance of individuals, institutions, custom and socio-political factors, has reminded us of the importance of these factors, especially as they interact in that most peculiar of markets — the labour market. In addition, some perspectives of voice versus exit, for example, have suggested the possibility that certain institutional features of the labour market are rational efficient responses to peculiarities of the labour market. Dualism has continued the institutional tradition and has focused on the structure of labour demand that segments the labour market into essentially two non-competing groups in the primary and secondary labour markets. Radicalism adds the importance of power relationships in a system of inherent class conflict.

While there certainly is no consensus as to which paradigm provides us with the greatest understanding of labour market behaviour, there is certainly more agreement that the insights from all of the paradigms have been useful. As a general proposition it is probably correct to say that the basic neoclassical economic paradigm has not been replaced — at least not yet — by any of the alternatives. Nevertheless, they have been useful in pointing out its weaknesses and in pressuring it to analyse institutional phenomenon, labour market segmentation, and power relationships — all of which are particularly important in labour markets. The extent to which the neoclassical paradigm is sufficiently adaptable remains an open — and interesting — question.

QUESTIONS

1. "By emphasizing descriptive realism, especially with respect to the assumptions of economics and the motivation of labour and management, institutional labour economics must be correct and therefore more useful in our understanding of labour market behaviour." Discuss.

2. "Because it assumes perfect information, perfect mobility and zero transaction costs, conventional microeconomics has no applicability to the labour market." Discuss.

3. Discuss the meaning of the following terms as used in labour market analysis: internal versus external labour markets; job clusters; wage contours, key settlements and spillover effects; and exit, voice, and loyalty.

4. Briefly outline the characteristics of the primary and secondary labour markets, and the characteristics of the workers in each. Is there a parallel in the literature on product markets as described in the field of industrial organization?

5. Discuss the main forces that give rise to the segmentation of the primary from the secondary labour market, according to the proponents of dual labour markets. Over time would we expect these forces to increase or decrease, and why?

6. Document a variety of internal administrative rules or company personnel policies that apply to the internal labour market. To what extent might these be an efficient response to the peculiarities of the labour market rather than simply inefficient institutional constraints?

7. Compare and contrast the *general* policy implications that flow from each of the following paradigms—neoclassical, institutional, dual, and radical. What would each say about the usefulness of the following specific policies:

(a) minimum wage legislation;
(b) equal pay legislation;
(c) unemployment insurance;
(d) training programs;
(e) job creation in the public sector.

8. "It is tempting to argue that each of the various labour market paradigms has a role and that different paradigms may be necessary to analyse different phenomenon. However, it is intellectually unsatisfactory to utilize paradigms in such an *ad hoc* fashion so as to 'fit the facts' of each case. If a set of forces are important then they should apply as basic determinants of a variety of phenomenon at a variety of levels". Discuss.

9. The use of voice has been suggested as an alternative to exit as a way of dealing with some labour market problems. Discuss various forms of exit and voice and discuss their costs and benefits.

10. "One of the problems of relying on voice is that the free market will provide an insufficient amount of voice because it has public good characteristics; that is, the benefits of voice are available to a wide group of persons (while the costs may be born by those who provide the voice) and the market does not automatically extract payment from those who benefit, to reward those who bear the cost." Discuss the extent to which this is true. To the extent that it is true, are there institutional arrangements to make all those who benefit pay so as to reward those who bear the cost?

11. In his evaluation of the usefulness of the dual labour market approach in the Canadian context, David Smith (1976, p.3) suggests that it highlights the following areas for further research: barriers to job choice arising from restrictions to entry into many types of jobs; the effect on job choice of behavioural traits induced by the work environment and peer groups; the extent to which on-the-job training is more of a socialization process than a costly investment, and the role of discrimination in this process; analysis of types of internal labour markets created by economic organizations and the integration of this analysis with economic theory developed primarily for external labour markets. Discuss briefly how our understanding of each of these areas could be furthered by the application of dual and/or conventional labour market analysis.

REFERENCES AND FURTHER READINGS

Addison, J. and J. Burton. Wage adjustment processes: a synthetic treatment. *BJIR* 16 (July 1978) 208-223.

Alexander, A. Income, experience and the structure of internal labour markets. *QJE* 88 (February 1974) 63-85.

Bishop, C. Hospitals: from secondary to primary labour market. *IR* 16 (February 1977) 26-34.

Bluestone, B. Low wage industries and the working poor. *Poverty and Human Resources Abstracts* (March/April 1968).

Bluestone, B. The tripartite economy: labour markets and the working poor. *Poverty and Human Resources* (July/August 1970).

Bosanquet, N. and P. Doeringer. Is there a dual labour market in Great Britain? *EJ* 83 (June 1973) 421-435.

Bowles, S. Unequal education and the reproduction of the social division of labour. *The Capitalist System,* R. C. Edwards, M. Reich and T. E. Weisskopf, eds. Englewood Cliffs, N.J.: Prentice-Hall, 1972.

Cain, G. The challenge of dual and radical theories of the labour market to orthodox theory. *AER Proceedings.* 65 (May 1975) 16-22.

Doeringer, P. and M. Piore. *Internal Labour Markets and Manpower Analysis.* Lexington, Mass.: Heath, 1971.

Doeringer, P. and M. Piore. Unemployment and the "dual" labour market. *Public Interest* 38 (Winter 1975) 67-79.

Donner, A. and F. Lazar. An econometric study of segmented labour markets and the structure of unemployment: the Canadian experience. *IER* 14 (1973) 312-327.

Dunlop, J. The task of contemporary wage theory. *The Theory of Wage Determination,* J. Dunlop, ed. New York: St. Martin's Press, 1957.

Edwards, R., M. Reich and T. Weisskopf. *The Capitalist System.* Englewood Cliffs, N.J.: Prentice-Hall, 1972.

Flanagan, R. Segmented market theories and racial discrimination. *IR* 12 (October 1973) 253-273.

Freeman, R. Individual mobility and union voice in the labour market. *AER Proceedings* 66 (May 1976) 361-368.

Gintis, H. Education, technology, and the characteristics of worker productivity. *AER Proceedings* (May 1971) 266-279.

Gintis, H. New working class and revolutionary youth. *Review of Radical Political Economics* (Summer 1970) 43-73.

Gordon, D. *Theories of Poverty and Underemployment.* Lexington, Mass.: Heath, 1972.

Harrison, B. Additional thoughts on the dual labour market. *MLR* 95 (April 1972) 37-39.

Harrison, B. *Education, Training and the Urban Ghetto.* Baltimore: Johns Hopkins, 1972.

Hirschman, A. *Exit, Voice and Loyalty.* Cambridge, Mass.: Harvard University Press, 1970.

Johnson, G. Economic analysis of trade unionism. *AER Proceedings* 65 (May 1975) 23-28.

Kerr, C. The balkanization of labour markets. *Labour Mobility and Economic Opportunity,* E. Wight Bakke et al., eds. Cambridge, Mass.: M.I.T. Press, 1954.

Klitgaard, R. The dual labour market and manpower policy. *MLR* 94 (November 1971) 45-48.

Lester, R. Shortcomings of marginal analysis for wage-employment problems. *AER* 36 (March 1946) 63-82.

Mace, J. and G. Wilkinson. Are labour markets competitive—a case study of engineers. *BJIR* 15 (March 1977) 1-17.

Machlup, F. Marginal analysis and empirical research. *AER* 36 (September 1946) 519-554.

Mellow, W. Equilibration in the labor market. *SEJ* 45 (July 1978) 192-204.

Miyazaki, H. The rat race and internal labour markets. *Bell Journal of Economics* 8 (Autumn 1977) 394-418.

Osterman, P. An empirical study of labour market segmentation. *ILRR* 28 (July 1975) 508-523.

Piore, M.J. Fragments of a "sociological" theory of wages. *IRRA* (December 1972) 286-295.

Rees, A. and G. Shultz. *Workers and Wages in an Urban Labor Market.* Chicago: University of Chicago Press, 1970.

Ross, A. Do we have a new industrial feudalism? *AER* 48 (December 1958) 903-920.

Ross, A. *Trade Union Wage Policy.* Berkeley: University of California Press, 1956.

Rottenberg, S. On choice in labor markets. *ILRR* 9 (January 1956) 183-199. Comment by R. Lampman and reply, 9 (July 1956) 629-641.

Smith, David. *The Dual Labour Market Theory: A Canadian Perspective.* Kingston: Queen's University Industrial Relations Centre, 1976.

Thurow, L. *Poverty and Discrimination.* Washington: Brookings, 1969.

Wachtel, H. Capitalism and poverty in America: paradox or contradiction? *AER Proceedings* 62 (May 1972) 187-194.

Wachtel, H. Looking at poverty from a radical perspective. *Review of Radical Political Economics* (Summer 1971) 1-19.

Wachter, M. Primary and secondary labour markets: a critique of the dual approach. *BPEA* (No. 3, 1974) 637-694.

Williamson, O., M. Wachter and J. Harris. Understanding the employment relation: an analysis of idiosyncratic exchange. *Bell Journal of Economics* 16 (Spring 1975) 252-278.

Part IV

Wages and Wage Structure

Chapter 13

Wages: Topics, Fringe Benefits, Purposes

In previous chapters we discussed labour demand and various aspects of labour supply and how they interact in alternative market structures to determine wages and employment. In the four chapters of this section of the text we focus on one aspect of that interaction — wages.

TOPICS OF WAGE DETERMINATION

The main topics of wage determination involve the determination of the level and of changes in real wages, the general level of money wages, and the variety of wage structures that exist. The latter is the subject matter of this section, with the former two topics being discussed briefly in a subsequent chapter on the wage-price-unemployment relationship. Since the topics of real wages and the general level of money wages are more the subject matter of macroeconomics, their comprehensive treatment is left to macro texts and courses.

In addition to these general aspects of wage determination there are a variety of applied topics in the area. They include wage fixing legislation (minimum wages, equal pay, fair wage laws on government contracts, and extension legislation), wage parity, wage comparability and wage arbitration, union impact, and wage-price guidelines. Many of these topics have already been discussed; others will be dealt with in the remainder of the text.

The various aspects of labour supply are obviously interrelated. In particular, real wages are simply money or nominal wages divided by the price level. In turn, the general level of money wages is simply an average of all of the individual wages in an economy. Individual wages in turn reflect the variety of wage structures that are the result of different ways of classifying workers, the main ones being by occupation, industry, region, establishment, and by personal characteristics such as sex, race, age or immigrant status.

Even the wage structures themselves overlap considerably. For example, industry and occupational designations are often similar and the wage of an occupational group may reflect heavily the industry or perhaps the region that tends to predominate the occupation. Both inter-occupational wage differentials (between occupations) and intra-occupational wage differentials (within occupations) may reflect personal characteristics of the work-force as well as their education and labour market experience. Thus it is often difficult to talk of a concept such as an occupational wage structure by itself without reference to other wage determining factors.

TOTAL COMPENSATION AND FRINGE BENEFITS

Any analysis of wages and wage structures is complicated by the fact that wages are only one aspect of the total compensation associated with a job. In particular, fringe benefits (indirect labour costs) are a large and increasing component of total compensation.

This is illustrated in Table 13.1, adapted from Ostry and Zaidi (1979). Between 1957 and 1975-76 fringe benefits as a percentage of direct labour costs (wages) increased from 16.4 to 31.1 per cent. This approximate doubling in percentage terms tended to occur across most of the categories of fringe benefits, so that the ranking of the components remained the same, with pay for time not worked, and pension and welfare plans being the largest component, although the latter grew the slowest.

Ostry and Zaidi (1979, pp. 207-8) also indicate that there is substantial industry and regional variation in fringe benefits as a percentage of wage costs. For example, in 1975-76 the percentages ranged from 36.5 per cent in the chemical industry to 23.7 per cent in light manufacturing. Contrary to some public opinion the figure for the government sector was a below average 28.5 per cent. On a regional basis, Ontario and Quebec had the highest fringe benefits as a percentage of wages and the Prairies were the lowest.

While interesting in their own right, the data on fringe benefits are also interesting for what they imply about wage structures. In particular, wage structures and their changes over time may not reflect what is happening to total compensation, given the industrial and regional variation in fringe benefits and their changes over time. This could be particularly important, for example, in analysing the inter-industry wage differential between the public and private sectors and its changes over time. At the very least, qualitative statements concerning fringe benefits should accompany state-

Table 13.1
FRINGE BENEFITS:[1] COMPONENTS AND CHANGES OVER TIME

Fringe Benefit Categories	$ Per Worker		% of Wages	
	1957	1975-76	1957	1975-76
Pay For Time Not Worked	287	1823	6.7	14.8
Pension and Welfare Plans	272	1267	6.4	9.8
Payments Required By Law[2]	87	413	2.0	3.4
Bonuses, Profit-Sharing, Other	55	346	1.3	3.1
Total Fringe Benefits	701	3849	16.4	31.1

Notes: [1]Figures are for all industries. Separate figures for manufacturing and non-manufacturing are not dramatically different.

[2]Includes workmen's compensation, unemployment insurance and Canada/Quebec pension plans.

Source: Ostry, S. and M. Zaidi. *Labour Economics in Canada,* 3rd ed. Toronto: Macmillan, 1979, pp. 202-203.

ments about our various wage structures and their changes over time.

The existence and growth of fringe benefits are an interesting phenomenon to try to explain, especially given the basic economic proposition that unconditional cash transfers (e.g. wages) are more efficient than transfers-in-kind (e.g. fringe benefits). This economic proposition follows from the fact that recipients who receive cash could always buy the transfers-in-kind if they wanted them, but they are better off because they could buy other things if they wanted them more. Applied to fringe benefits, why wouldn't employees and employers prefer wage compensation since it would enable employees to buy whatever fringe benefits they want rather than being given some they may not value?

There are obviously a variety of possible reasons for the existence and growth of fringe benefits. They are usually not taxed and, as taxes have increased over time, this increasingly makes fringe benefits a preferred form of compensation. (This does raise the question, however, of why governments should want to offer tax advantages to fringe benefits over wages.) There may be economies of scale, and administrative economies for group purchases through the employer of such things as pension and insurance plans. However, many of these economies still could be had through completely voluntary group plans. There is the possibility that workers think they are receiving fringe benefits free in the sense that, if they did not have the fringe benefits, their wages would not rise by a corresponding amount. This possibility, of course, can be true in times of wage controls to the extent that fringe benefits are exempt or more difficult to control. More likely, workers simply prefer fringe benefits because it is an easy way of purchasing benefits that they value. In some cases, like increased vacations and holidays with pay, it is a way of institutionalizing the increased purchase of more leisure that accompanies their growing wealth.

Employers may have accepted the increased role of fringe benefits for reasons that are beneficial to them. Paid vacations and holidays, for example, enable the planning of the production process more than if the workers desire for increased leisure came in the form of lateness, absenteeism, work slow-downs, or turnover. Similarly, workmen's compensation and unemployment insurance and health insurance can reduce the need for employers to have contingency plans for workers in industrial accidents or subject to layoffs or health problems. In addition, some fringe benefits may alter the behaviour of workers in a fashion that is preferred by the employer. Subsidized cafeterias can reduce long lunch hours and keep employees in the plant, the provision of transportation can ensure that workers get to work on time, and company health services can reduce absenteeism and provide a check on a worker's health.

Governments may also prefer fringe benefits (and hence grant favourable tax treatment) because they may reduce pressures for government expenditures elsewhere. Employer-sponsored pensions may reduce the need for public pensions; contributions to the Canada (or Quebec) Pension Plan may reduce the need for public care for the aged, at least for the aged who have worked; and increased contributions for unemployment insurance directly reduce the amount the government has to pay to this fund. In addition, many fringe benefits are part and parcel of the whole package of increased social security, and hence the reasons for their growth are caught up with the reasons for the growth of the whole welfare state.

PURPOSES OF WAGES AND WAGE STRUCTURES

The discussion of wage determination is made more complicated— and often emotive—by the fact that wages and wage structures are called upon to serve a variety of purposes in our economy. Wage structures are the relative prices of labour that are utilized to allocate labour to its most productive and efficient use and to encourage human capital development — education, training, mobility, job search — into areas yielding the highest return. In addition wages are an important component of family income and hence may have an important role to play in the achievement of an equitable distribution of income. Our macroeconomic objectives of full employment, price stability and a viable balance of payments can also be affected by wage developments, just as wage determination is affected by the macroeconomic environment.

There is a complex nexus between wages and productivity. Usually we think of high wages being the result of high productivity that can come about, for example, through various forms of human capital formation, or through technological change. (With respect to the latter factor, wage increases are one way of distributing the gains of general productivity improvements: price reductions are another.) However, there is the possibility of cause and effect working the other way as well. That is, high wages may induce productivity improvements through improved morale, health, and intensity of work effort, as well as by reductions in absenteeism and turnover. In addition wage increases may induce efficient changes elsewhere in the system — changes that should have occurred earlier but that would not occur without the shock induced by a wage change.

The matter is further complicated by the fact that wages and wage structures serve a social role, in that prestige is associated with wages; hence, the importance of *relative* positions in the wage hierarchy and the importance of key comparison groups. The social role of wages is further heightened by the fact that labour services are inseparable from the person who provides the services: hence, the importance of the human element in labour market analysis.

Clearly wages and wage structures are called upon to serve a variety of often conflicting roles in our economic system in particular, and in our social system in general. Perhaps this is why there is so much emotive conflict over various policies — minimum wages and wage-price guidelines for example — that affect wages. While it may be unrealistic to expect to resolve these conflicts, it is feasible to utilize economics to illustrate the impact of alternative policies, to elucidate the tradeoffs that are involved, and to suggest alternative and complementary policies.

REFERENCES AND FURTHER READINGS

Bailey, W. and A. Schwenk. Employer expenditures for private retirement and insurance plans. *MLR* 95 (July 197˙ 15-19.

Bauman, A. Measuring employee compensation in U.S. industry. *MLR* 93 (October 1970) 17-24.

Ehrenberg, R. *Fringe Benefits and Overtime Behavior.* Lexington, Mass.: D.C. Heath, 1971.

Ehrenberg, R. The impact of the overtime premium on employment and hours in U.S. industry. *WEJ* 9 (June 1971) 199-207.

Ehrenberg, R. Absenteeism and the overtime decision. *AER* 60 (June 1970) 352-357.

Employee Benefits Costs in Canada, 1975-1976. Toronto: Thorne Riddell Associates, 1976.

Folk, H. Effects of private pension plans on labor mobility. *MLR* 86 (March 1963) 285-288.

Garbarino, J. Fringe benefits and overtime as barriers to expanding employment. *ILRR* 17 (April 1964) 426-442.

Garbarino, J. and R. MacDonald. The fringe barrier hypothesis and overtime behavior. *ILRR* 19 (July 1976) 562-569. Comment by R. MacDonald and reply 19 (July 1966) 562-572.

Hameed, S. Employment impact of fringe benefits in Canadian manufacturing sector: 1957-1965. *RI/IR* 28 (No. 2, 1973) 380-396.

Hawkesworth, R. Fringe benefits in British industry. *BJIR* 15 (November 1977) 396-402.

Jain, H. and P. Janzen. Employee pay and benefit preferences. *RI/IR* 29 (No. 1, 1974) 99-110. Also, 32 (No. 3, 1977) 449-451.

Johnson, A. and R. Meljus. Multi-employee pensions and labor mobility. *Harvard Business Review* (September/October 1963) 147-161.

Kalamotousakis, G. Statistical analysis of the determinants of employee benefits by type. *American Economist* (Fall 1972) 139-147.

Laudadio, L. and M. Percy. Some evidence of the impact of non-wage labour cost on overtime work and employment. *RI/IR* 28 (No. 2, 1973) 397-404.

Lawler, E. and E. Levin. Union officers' perception of members' pay preferences. *ILRR* 21 (July 1968) 509-518.

Lester, R. Benefits as a preferred form of compensation. *SEJ* 33 (April 1967) 488-495.

Mabry, B. The economics of fringe benefits. *IR* 12 (February 1973) 95–106.

Macdonald, B. The design of a fringe benefit costing program. *RI/IR* 28 (October 1973) 799–807.

McCormick, B. Methods of wage payment, wages structures and the influence of factor and product markets. *BJIR* 15 (July 1977) 246–266.

Milkovich, G. and M. Delaney. A note on cafeteria pay plans. *IR* 14 (February 1973) 112–116.

Oi, W. Labor as a quasi-fixed factor of production. *JPE* 70 (December 1962) 538–555.

Pencavel, J. Alternative methods of remuneration, *Research in Labor Economics*, R. Ehrenberg (ed.). Greenwich, Conn.: JAI Press, 1977.

Perlman, R. Observations on overtime and moonlighting. *SEJ* 32 (October 1966).

Rice, R. Skill, earnings and the growth of wage supplements. *AER* 61 (May 1966) 583–592.

Rosen, S. On the interindustry wage and hours structure, *JPE* (April 1969) 249-273.

Scanlon, B. Effects of pension plans on labor mobility and hiring older members. *Personnel Journal* 44 (January 1965).

Schultz, L. Ruminations on the benefit package. *RI/IR* 28 (No. 4, 1973) 849–858.

Solnick, L. Unionism and fringe benefit expenditures. *IR* 17 (February 1978) 102–107.

Tandan, N. *Workers with Long Hours.* Special Labor Force Study No. 9, Series A. Ottawa: Information Canada, 1972.

Taylor, J. Toad or butterfly?: a constructive critique of executive compensation practices. *ILRR* 21 (July 1968) 491–508.

Wand, R. Manhour behaviour in U.S. manufacturing: a neo-classical interpretation. *JPE* 76 (February 1968).

Chapter 14

Occupational Wage Structures

As the *Canadian Classification and Dictionary of Occupations* (1971)—hereafter termed the CCDO — indicates, the term occupation denotes the "kind of work performed" (p. xiii); that is, "the term 'occupation' is used to refer to a number of jobs that have the same basic work content, even though they may be found in a number of different establishments or industries" (p. xv).[1]

The occupational wage structure refers to the wage structure between various occupations or occupation groups. The occupation groups can be broadly defined, as for example, one of the 23 CCDO two-digit major groups such as managerial, clerical, sales, service or processing. Or they can be narrowly defined occupations, such as one of the 6700 seven-digit occupations, for example, typist (4113-126) or arc-welder (8335-138).

The average wage in an occupation, and the changes in that wage relative to the wages in other occupations will reflect the forces of labour supply and demand in the occupations. Before analysing the basic determinants of these forces, it may be worth highlighting, at the outset, the differences between the various concepts of labour supply that have been developed so far. These concepts differ, reflecting different levels of aggregation—the individual, firm, occupation, or region. (See, for example, Kruger (1968, pp. 40–48)).

The *individual's* labour supply schedule reflects the income-leisure choice decision on the part of the individual. Its shape depends upon the relative importance of income and substitution effects induced by a wage change. The labour supply schedule that the *firm* faces for a given occupation reflects the extent to which the firm is a wage-setter or a wage-taker. Monopsonistic firms face an upward sloping labour supply schedule, whereas competitive buyers of labour face a perfectly elastic supply of labour schedule at the going wage rate as that wage is determined in the more aggregate labour market for the occupation. That wage rate for the *occupation*, and its relation to wages in other occupations, is the subject of this chapter.

---

[1] Current occupational definitions in Canada are given in the Canada Department of Manpower and Immigration, *Classification and Dictionary of Occupations* (1971) as well as in the Canada Bureau of Statistics (1971), *Occupational Classification Manual, Census of Canada*, which is based on the CCDO classification scheme, adapted for census purposes. While the current concepts are more accurate in the sense of portraying the current occupational distribution, they do not always utilize the occupation groups that were commonly employed in earlier censuses. Meltz and Stager (1979a) discuss these differences.

DETERMINANTS OF OCCUPATIONAL SUPPLY AND DEMAND

Figure 14.1 illustrates the occupational wage differential (skill differential) that exists between two hypothetical occupations, for example skilled welders and unskilled labourers. The demand schedules for each occupation are simply the aggregation of the demand schedules of the various firms that utilize each type of labour. They could be large or small, elastic or inelastic, depending on the circumstances. For example, the hypothetical demand schedule for skilled workers is depicted as small simply because few welders are used in the various firms, and it is depicted as relatively inelastic because there are few good substitute inputs for welders. In addition, the demand for the output produced by welders (especially in non-residential construction) tends to be price inelastic, and welding costs tend to be a small proportion of the total cost of producing the output. The opposite situation prevails for labourers and their occupational demand schedule tends to be large and elastic in this example.

The supply schedules for each of the occupations are upward sloping, reflecting the fact that higher wages are required to attract additional workers into the occupations, away from other occupations, or from non-labour market activities. The higher wages are often necessary to attract additional workers because of different worker preferences for the various occupations, or because of increasing costs associated with acquiring the skills necessary to do the work. Those who prefer the occupation or who have a natural talent for doing the work would enter at the lower wages; higher wages would be necessary to attract those who did not have a preference for the occupation or who could do the work only by a more costly acquisition of the skills.

The supply schedule, therefore, can be thought of as reflecting a ranking of actual and potential workers in the occupation, where those who most prefer the occupation or who have an innate talent for it are ranked at the beginning (and hence require a lower wage to enter), and those who least prefer the occupation or for whom the acquisition of the skills would be more costly are ranked at the end (and hence require the higher wage to enter). If all preferences were identical and there were no increasing costs associated with entering the occupation, then the supply schedule would be perfectly elastic at the going wage for the occupation.

The degree of elasticity of the supply schedule to each occupation also depends on the responsiveness of alternative sources of labour supply which, in turn, depends upon such factors as labour market information and mobility, training requirements, immigration, and the general state of the economy. For example, in the short run, the labour supply schedule to an occupation may be inelastic (and hence a demand increase would lead to more of a wage increase than an employment increase) for a variety of reasons: potential recruits to the occupation are not yet aware of the high wages; they have to be trained to enter the occupation; fulfilling some of the occupational demand through immigration takes time; and the labour market is presently tight, so there is no ready surplus of labour from which to draw.

In the long run, however, most of these factors would adjust to the new demands and the labour supply schedule to the occupation would be more elastic. It may not be perfectly elastic if the new sources of supply are more costly than the original sources. However, in the long run if all of the supply responses had sufficient time to adjust, and if the new sources of supply were not more costly than the original sources, then any inelasticity to the labour supply in an occupation would reflect the different preferences of workers, which would result in a need to raise wages to attract workers who do not have a strong preference for the occupation.

REASONS FOR INTER-OCCUPATIONAL WAGE DIFFERENTIALS

Given the basic determinants of occupational supply and demand, economic theory predicts that the forces of competition will ensure an equal present value of net advantage at the margin in the long run across all occupations. If this does not prevail, then competition ensures that workers at the margin of decision will move from jobs of low net advantage to ones of high net advantage. This does allow for considerable variation in the occupational wage structure to reflect such factors as the non-pecuniary aspects of the job, the human capital skills brought to the job, intra-marginal rents for scarce talents, short-run adjustments, and non-competitive forces. It also suggests that wage controls will encourage adjustments in such things as non-pecuniary fringe benefits or skill acquisition until the equality of net advantage is restored.

Thus the occupational wage differential portrayed in Figure 14.1 could persist even in the long run and in the face of competitive forces. In such circumstances, however, it would reflect a compensating wage differential for differences between the occupations in the non-pecuniary aspects of the job, differences in human capital costs associated with each job, or economic rents associated with scarce talents. In the short run it could also reflect short-run adjustments, and even in the long run it could reflect the absence of competitive forces.

Each of these factors will be discussed in turn. In order to focus on the effect of the one factor by itself we will assume that all other aspects of the job are the same, so that the resulting occupational wage differential reflect only the one set of factors under examination.

Non-pecuniary Aspects of Job

Occupations differ in their non-pecuniary characteristics, such as pleasantness, safety, responsibility, fringe benefits, seasonal or cyclical stability, and the certainty of their return. Occupational wage differentials may exist therefore, to compensate for these non-pecuniary differences. As Adam Smith (1937, p.100) observed over two hundred years ago:

> The five following are the principal circumstances which, so far as I have been able to observe, make up for a small pecuniary gain in some employments, and counter-balance a great one in others: first, the agreeableness or disagreeableness of the employments themselves; secondly, the easiness and cheapness, or the difficulty and expense of learning them; thirdly, the constancy or inconstancy of employment in them; fourthly, the small or great trust which must be reposed in those who exercise them; and fifthly, the probability or improbability of success in them.

Thus, all other factors equal (e.g. human capital requirements, short-run adjustments, and non-competitive forces), an occupation may pay a wage premium to compensate for the fact that it is unpleasant, unsafe, or entails unstable or uncertain returns, or has poor fringe benefits. For example, miners would get a premium for working underground as opposed to above ground, policemen and firefighters would get a premium because of the danger of their work, and workers in many construction occupations would get a wage premium because of the seasonal and cyclical nature of the job.

In essence, each of these non-pecuniary aspects of the job has a price. This is so because employees have a *demand* for various non-pecuniary attributes of the job and employers can *supply* these non-pecuniary aspects associated with their jobs. The interaction of this supply and demand for these non-pecuniary characteristics determines their price, although this price is really a shadow or implicit price in the form of a compensating wage. Workers don't explicitly pay employers, for example, fifty dollars a month for a safer work environment, but they could pay that amount implicitly in the form of lower wages relative to an identical job without the safe work environment.[2]

Empirically it is difficult to isolate the compensating wage differential that is associated with different non-pecuniary aspects of occupations because, in the real world, other things are not held constant. In particular, many low wage jobs also have unpleasant, unsafe working conditions with uncertain returns and poor fringe benefits. What economic theory predicts, however, is that even within this group of low wage jobs with low non-pecuniary benefits, there will be compensating wage differentials to reflect the differences in the already low non-pecuniary aspects of the job.

---

[2] This suggests that the hedonic technique (e.g. Lucas (1977)) may be a useful way of estimating the shadow price (compensating wage) for each of the characteristics associated with a job. In essence, wages could be regressed on the various job characteristics (as well as human capital characteristics of workers, to control for these factors) with the estimated regression coefficients reflecting the wage compensation that the market determines as being necessary to compensate for variation in the characteristics of the job.

Human Capital Requirements

Occupational wage differentials could also reflect differences in the human capital requirements associated with different jobs. Thus wage premiums may be paid in specific occupations for the particular skills workers bring to those occupations. These skills could be acquired through costly investments in human capital, in which case the wage premium reflects a compensation for the cost of human capital formation. A competitive wage premium would be one that just yields a competitive rate of return on the investment in human capital.

Based on Canadian data, for example, Wilkinson (1966, p.556) finds that "discounted returns to various levels of education within jobs are roughly the same — which may mean that an equalization process has been occurring". He emphasized (p. 572) "the tendency for individuals to move into jobs or education levels where, according to the discount rate they are using, the net present value of earnings are the largest".[3]

Thus, other things being equal, workers with a university degree would receive a higher wage relative to those without a degree. Apprentices receive low wages in the apprenticeship phase as they acquire training, and they receive higher wages when they are craftsmen utilizing their skills.

The importance of human capital factors in influencing the Canadian occupational wage structure is illustrated in Meltz and Stager (1979). Utilizing regression analysis, they show that a large portion of the inter-occupational wage structure during each of the census years 1941, 1951, 1961, and 1971 can be explained by inter-occupational differences in the education and experience (age) of workers in each occupation, with occupations requiring higher education and experience paying higher wages.

Endowed Talents and Economic Rents

Individuals may also be *endowed* with skills that are valued in the marketplace, in which case the wage premium that is paid to them reflects their natural embodiment of these skills rather than their costly acquisition of the skills. The individual may be endowed with a skill that is useful in a variety of occupations (e.g. strength, dexterity or intelligence) or one that is unique to one or a few (e.g. ability to sing or put the puck in the net).

Economic theory predicts an equality of net advantage *at the margin* associated with each job. Competition ensures this equality at the margin. However, this does not prevent some members of an occupation from receiving an economic rent defined as the difference between what they are paid in their occupation and what they would earn in their next best alternative. This economic rent or seller's surplus is illustrated in Figure 14.1 (a) as

---

[3] B. Wilkinson, *Studies in the Economics of Education*, Economics and Research Branch, Ottawa: Canada Department of Labour, 1965, page 556. Reproduced by permission of the Minister of Supply and Services Canada.

Figure 14.1   Occupational Wage Differential

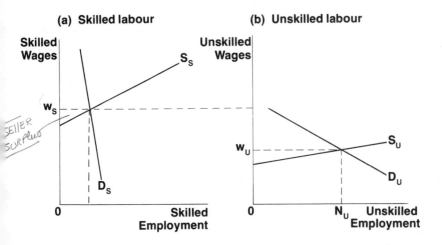

(a) Skilled labour   **(b) Unskilled labour**

the area of the triangle below the market wage w_s and above the supply schedule S_s. This is an economic rent or seller's surplus because the reservation wage depicting what workers could get in alternative occupations (including non-labour market activities) is given by the height of the labour supply schedule. However, the actual wage, w_s, is determined by the interaction at the margin of the supply and demand schedules. To the extent that this actual wage is paid to all workers in the occupation, intra-marginal workers receive an economic rent and hence have a strong preference to remain in this occupation. Because it is a surplus payment over and above what is necessary to keep the worker in the occupation, it can be taxed away without affecting the allocation of resources to the occupation.

It is because of the existence of economic rents and the high returns to a scarce talent that the prediction of economic theory — equality of net advantage at the margin across all occupations — becomes deceptive, even though it is true. The phrase may imply that all occupations are equally advantageous and that none are any more attractive than others. Clearly this is not true: many occupations can be more attractive than others, but they can be unattainable because of the talents they require. Competitive forces simply ensure that no *additional* gains in net advantage can be made by leaving or entering an occupation: the equality is at the margin. Competitive forces do not ensure that all occupations are equally attractive or that people in some occupations would not prefer to be in others that are presently unattainable to them.

For example, the average salary of a professional hockey player may be ten times that of a university professor. Even if all university professors wanted to be hockey players, they may not possess the talent to do so. There could be an equality of net advantage at the margin —that is no *additional* net advantage to be had — even though all university professors longed to be hockey players. It would be deceptive to say that both occupations were equally advantageous: it is more accurate to say that no additional advantages are to be had by occupational mobility. The net advantages associated with being a hockey player may be unattainable to most and in this sense there are no additional gains in net advantage to be had. Thus it must be emphasized that economic theory predicts an equality of net advantage at the margin, which means simply that no additional net advantage can be attained by further occupational change.

Short-Run Adjustments

The equality of net advantage at the margin predicted by competitive economic theory is one that would prevail in the long run, defined as the time period that is sufficiently long for all adjustments that are going to occur to have occurred. Thus occupational wage differentials could reflect, in part at least, the price signal that induces the supply response that is part of the long-run adjustment process.

For example, assume that the wages of a particular skilled job are twice those of an unskilled job. This is an equilibrium wage differential in the sense that there are no competitive forces that would alter the differential: there is an equality of net advantage at the margin for each occupation. Now assume a permanent exogenous increase in the demand for skilled workers, perhaps because of technological change. In the short run, the supply schedule to the skilled occupation may be fairly inelastic because of a long training period required to do the skilled work. Thus wages would rise in this occupation and this would be a short-run signal for workers in other occupations to acquire the skills necessary to work in the skilled occupation. The old equality of net advantage has now tipped in favour of the skilled occupation because the wage advantage has increased: there now are gains in net advantage to be had by acquiring the skills necessary to work in the skilled occupation.

In response to the short-run wage premium in the skilled occupations, new workers will enter this occupation and this increased supply will reduce the wage premium until it is just large enough to restore an equality of net advantage at the margin: that is, until no further gains in net advantage are possible. This wage adjustment process may be buttressed by the fact that mobility into this skilled occupation may reduce the supply of labour in the other occupations, and this would serve to increase their wages.

The new equality of net advantage may or may not be associated with the old occupational wage differential whereby skilled workers received twice the wage of unskilled workers. This depends on the preferences of workers in the occupations (i.e. on the slopes of the supply schedules to each occupation). If the skilled occupation had an upward sloping supply schedule, and therefore higher wages were necessary to attract the additional workers, the new skill differential may be greater than two to one. The skilled workers who were already in the occupation (intra-marginal workers) would receive an additional rent because they were willing to work in the occupation at the old wage but now receive the new higher wage that was necessary to expand the occupation.

Non-competitive Factors

Up to this point we have focused on how the forces of competition would ensure an equality of net advantage at the margin across all occupations and how this could give rise to inter-occupational wage differentials to reflect such factors as non-pecuniary differences, requirements for human capital or natural talents, and short-run adjustments. The occupational wage structure may also reflect the fact that in some instances the forces of competition may be weakened or absent. In such circumstances, non-competitive factors prevent the complete supply response that would ensure that wages adjust to ensure an equality of net advantage at the margin.

The extreme version of the importance of non-competitive factors is in the dual or segmented labour market as discussed earlier. According to that perspective, competition has only a minor influence on wage structures, with the forces of custom and tradition and administered rulings being much more important.

Even within the neoclassical economic perspective, as well as the dual labour market one, there are forces that can thwart some of the impact of competition. In particular, occupational licensing on the part of professional associations, by regulating entry into the profession, can effectively lead to a reduction in the supply of labour to the occupation and hence artificially high salaries. Unions, especially craft unions through the hiring hall and apprenticeship requirements, can also control supply to an occupation. Discrimination may also exclude people from some occupations and crowd them into others, raising wages in the former and depressing them in the latter.

Other policies may work directly on wages rather than indirectly through the supply of labour. Minimum wage legislation would affect low wage occupations and equal pay for equal work laws would affect wages in female-dominated occupations. Wage controls would have an ambiguous effect. To the extent that low wage workers are exempt then the occupational wage structure may narrow; however, to the extent that it is more difficult to enforce at high income levels, then the structure may widen. Legislation setting fair wages in jobs on government contracts may fall differently on different occupations: in particular, its effect may be most important on occupations in construction jobs where such laws are more prominent. Wage extension legislation that extends the results of negotiated wage settlements throughout an industry may also affect occupations differently. Any or all of these factors may thwart the forces of competition, and this would be reflected in the wage structure between occupations.

Unions may also have an impact on the occupational wage structure, with their effect depending upon the differential impact of the union by occupation and on the extent to which the occupation is unionized. To the extent that unions have obtained larger relative wage gains for their less skilled members — perhaps through equal absolute wage increases — then they may have narrowed the occupational wage structure. However, if the extent of unionization (and professional associations) is greater in high wage occupations then this would widen the occupational wage structure. This is compounded by the fact that if union wages lead to an adverse employment effect, then some of those so affected may compete for jobs in the low wage occupations, widening the structure even further. The impact of unions on the occupational wage structure, therefore, is ultimately an empirical proposition.

Clearly, there are a variety of socio-legal-institutional factors that can work against the forces of competition in the labour market. In fact, many of these factors arose as a response to the results of competitive market forces. Since their impact falls differently on different occupations, they will obviously affect the inter-occupational wage structure.

MEASURES OF WAGE STRUCTURE

Before analysing how the Canadian wage structure has changed over time, it is necessary to discuss various ways of measuring wage structures. Although there exists a variety of measures corresponding to the various statistical measures of dispersion, perhaps the two most common that are used to measure the occupational wage structure are the skill differential, and the coefficient of variation.

Skill Differential

The skill differential simply relates the wages of a particular representative occupation group to that of another representative group. For example, two particular occupations, or groups of occupations, could be chosen as representatives of skilled and unskilled occupations. The average wages of the skilled and unskilled occupations, w_s and w_u respectively, could then be compared as absolute differences $w_s - w_u$, proportionate differences $(w_s - w_u)/w_u$, or as ratios w_s/w_u or w_u/w_s.

While the *absolute* differences may convey important information (for example, the wage benefits that can be expected from human capital formation), they do not standardize or control for the wage level itself. Thus an absolute wage gap may grow over time simply because the level of wages are increasing over time. To standardize for the level of wages, a *relative* measure of dispersion is needed, such as the proportionate wage advantage of skilled workers or the ratio of skilled to unskilled wages. Since both contain the same information (once you know one you can solve for the other by algebraic manipulation), the ratio is often used because of its simplicity.

One problem with the skill differential is that it can be sensitive to the particular occupations chosen as reference groups. Thus the ratio of the wages of janitors to welders may behave very differently from the wages of labourers to press operators, as unskilled and skilled occupations respectively. To a certain extent this can be mitigated by the judicious selection of reference groups that are representative, or by using more aggregate occupation groups. Nevertheless, the problem still remains that reference group comparisons, while expositionally simple, may not be representative of changes in the whole structure. For this reason the wages in a particular occupation are often compared to the average wage in all occupations (e.g. Meltz and Stager (1979)).

Coefficient of Variation

A more comprehensive measure of the occupational wage structure is given by the coefficient of variation, defined as the standard deviation divided by the mean. In formulae terms, the coefficient of variation of an occupational wage structure of n occupations is

$$CV = [\sum_{i=1}^{n} (w_i - \bar{w})^2/n]^{1/2} /\bar{w}$$

Computation of the coefficient of variation, therefore, requires the following steps. For each occupation, subtract the average wage of that occupation, w_i, from the overall average wage in all occupations, $\bar{w}$. Square each of these n differences, sum them over the n occupations, and divide by the number of occupations, n. Then take the square root of this number to get the standard deviation of the series. Divide by the overall average wage of all occupations to get the coefficient of variation.

Clearly the coefficient of variation is a comprehensive measure since it takes account of all elements of the occupation and it takes account of changes throughout the distribution. In addition, it controls for the average wage level in the sense that it will not increase over time simply because average wages are increasing over time. (This is accomplished when the standard deviation is divided by the overall mean.)

Unfortunately, the virtues of the coefficient of variation also give rise to its problems. By yielding a single unique number that comprehensively takes account of all changes throughout the distribution, it does not indicate *where* the change has occurred. Thus a smaller coefficient of variation is consistent with the occupational wage structure becoming uniformly more narrow, or wages just below or above the average becoming closer to the average, or those below the average becoming closer to the average, and this outweighing the effect of those above the average rising even further above the average.

The coefficient of variation is a summary measure of dispersion and, as a summary measure, it may mask important changes. In addition it is a summary statistic that has no intuitive or heuristic meaning by itself. What is meant, for example, by a coefficient of variation of .52? While it is a more comprehensive measure than the skill differential, it does not convey the readily understandable information, for example, contained in the simple statement that the ratio of the wages of welders to labourers is 3/1.

Clearly, there is no unique best measure of the dispersion of the occupational wage structure. Trade-offs are involved and the appropriate measure depends on the information one is trying to show. It is important, however, to know how the various measures are derived. Only then can one know the strengths and weaknesses and hence the appropriateness of the measure.

SECULAR OR LONG-RUN CHANGES IN THE OCCUPATIONAL WAGE STRUCTURE

Of particular interest in analysing the occupational wage structure is the extent to which it has changed over the long run. Has it narrowed or widened, where have the major changes occurred in the structure, and what are the reasons for these changes?

Empirical Evidence

The most comprehensive study of the long-run changes in the Canadian occupational wage structure is contained in Meltz and Stager (1979a), which also reviews other studies in Canada, the United States, and the United Kingdom. Their empirical work is based largely on census data for the years 1931, 1941, 1951, 1961, and 1971, and taxation data from 1971-1974.

While it is hazardous to try to summarize their results (and the original study should be consulted for the details), the following conclusions appear to emerge. In general, there was a tendency for the Canadian inter-occupational wage structure to narrow from 1931 to 1951, and to remain roughly constant and perhaps even widen slightly from 1951 to 1971. However, the current occupational wage structure is still more narrow than in the early period of 1931. While this is the overall trend for all occupations, individual occupations showed marked differences in their trends, reflecting the different supply and demand conditions.

With respect to where in the wage structure the major changes occurred, at least since 1951, the data seem to indicate that the extremes have become more extreme (rather than the changes being uniform throughout the distribution). That is, since 1951 the very high wage occupations have become relatively higher wage, and the very low wage occupations have become relatively lower wage, and this has helped to end the narrowing (and perhaps contributed to the widening) of the overall inter-occupational wage structure since 1951. This may be changing in recent years with the slower growth in earnings of some high income professionals.

Meltz and Stager (1979a) also review the earlier Canadian studies and find them generally to be consistent with their own findings, in spite of the different data sources. With respect to a broader comparison with a variety of studies based on the United States and United Kingdom, Meltz and Stager (1979a, p. 4) conclude:

> The findings of these studies were generally similar among these countries, particularly for the 1940–1950 period. In the United States, the pattern of wage differentials appears to have been as follows: narrowing between 1900 and 1920; widening in the 1920–1932 period; little change in the 1930s depression; pronounced narrowing during the 1940s (particularly in World War II); stability in the 1950s and 1960s—with some evidence of widening towards the end of the 1960s. For the other countries included in the summary, the pattern is similar with two exceptions: there is some evidence of stability (rather than widening) in the 1920s, and of widening in the 1950s and 1960s — notably in Canada and the United Kingdom.[4]

Reasons for Long-Run Pattern

The reasons for the long-run changes in the occupational wage structure basically can be summarized under changes in the supply and demand conditions of the occupations, changes in wage-fixing practices, and possibly changes in the content of jobs.

Demand Factors

Changes in the demand for different occupations often are not regarded as important determinants of occupational differentials in the long run, because demand changes would lead to short-run wage changes, which would in turn lead to supply responses. As long as labour supply to an occupation is fairly elastic in the long run, demand changes would lead to changes in employment, not wages.

However, there may be times when demand changes can lead to more permanent changes in the occupational wage structure. If, for example, demand increases are continuous and not fully anticipated, they may give rise to a constant series of wage increases to attract additional labour. The maturation of industrialization that has gone on since the 1930s, for example, may be associated with a slower growth in the demand for skilled craft workers and an increase in the demand for the less skilled blue and white collar jobs associated with automation and mechanization. It is tempting to think of industrialization as increasing the demand for skilled workers relative to unskilled, but this need not be the case, especially in the more mature

---

[4] N. Meltz and D. Stager, *The Occupational Structure of Earnings in Canada, 1931–1975*, Anti-Inflation Board Report, Ottawa: Supply and Services, 1979, page 4. Reproduced by permission of the Minister of Supply and Services Canada.

phases of industrialization. Automation and mechanization may place a premium on a few key skills required to construct and operate the facilities; nevertheless, the bulk of the demand increase may be for the less skilled occupations in operation and maintenance. In essence, the maturation of industrialization may be associated with a substitution of unskilled blue and white collar industrial workers for the more skilled craft workers, and this may have been a factor contributing to the compression of the occupational wage structure that has occurred, at least until the 1950s.

Meltz and Stager (1979a) also discuss how short-run, empirical changes in the demand for labour (to be discussed later) may give rise to permanent, long-run changes in the occupational wage structure because of a "ratchet effect". Cyclical increases in the demand for *skilled* labour tend to widen the wage structure; however, when the demand dissipates, the wage structure returns to its normal long-run pattern. However, cyclical increases in the demand for *unskilled* labour tends to narrow the wage structure and for socio-political-institutional reasons there is built-in resistance to the re-establishment of the old wider structure. In essence, short-run widening tends to be temporary and short-run narrowing tends to become institutionalized as permanent. Hence the term "ratchet effect", and hence the built-in bias for the occupational wage structure to narrow over time.

Demand factors also may permanently affect the occupational wage structure if there are different supply elasticities to different occupations. In particular, if the long-run supply to less skilled occupations is more inelastic than the long-run supply to the more skilled occupations, then even equal demand increases in both would lead to greater wage increases in the less skilled occupations and hence a narrowing of the wage structure. It is possible, for example, that the labour supply schedule is relatively inelastic for low wage occupations (higher wages are necessary to attract additional workers) because of a reluctance to do unskilled work and because of a preference for a more pleasant work environment which is usually associated with skilled jobs. This could be reinforced by a ratchet effect if workers who become exposed to the skill develop a reluctance to return to unskilled trades.

Supply Factors

On the supply side, there are reasons to believe that much of the long-run narrowing of the occupational wage structure, at least up until the 1950s, can be explained by exogenous increases in the supply of skilled workers and decreases in the supply of unskilled. Changes in these factors since the 1950s may also explain the cessation of the narrowing and the possible recent widening.

Increases in the supply of skilled labour have been associated with a variety of factors. Most aspects of human capital formation — training, education, mobility and labour market information — have become cheaper to the *individual* with massive government provision or support of these programs, and they have become more affordable with our increased family income over time. Improved communication in general, and employment services in particular, have improved information and mobility. Immigration has been increasingly restricted to skilled occupations and many supply restrictions (the hiring hall, occupational licensing, apprenticeship schemes) have been reduced or made redundant with the ascendency of mass production and industrial units over craft units.

In addition to this exogenous increase in the supply of skilled workers which would serve to reduce skilled wages, there has been a decrease in the supply of unskilled workers which would serve to raise the wages of unskilled workers. Immigration has been reduced over time and it has increasingly become skill oriented, therefore reducing this pool of unskilled labour. With the diminution of the farm population, rural to urban migration is no longer a source of unskilled labour. Legislation limiting child labour and establishing compulsory school attendance has reduced the supply of young unskilled labour. Social programs that reduce the incentive to work — welfare, unemployment insurance, public pensions — may also reduce the supply of unskilled labour.

Minimum Wages, Unions and Job Content
Minimum wage laws may also have increased over time to raise the wages of unskilled workers relative to skilled workers. Unions may also serve to compress the occupational wage structure, especially if they follow policies of equal absolute, rather than relative, gains for their members. The increased importance of industrial as opposed to craft unions would serve to strengthen the tendency of unions to compress the occupational wage structure.

Finally, the content of jobs themselves may have changed over time, narrowing the distinction between skilled and unskilled work. As stated by Reynolds and Taft (1956, p. 357):

> There are indications that many skilled occupations are becoming less skilled, arduous and responsible with the improvement of mechanical equipment and working conditions. . . . At the other end of the ladder there are fewer and fewer jobs which are entirely unskilled. Labourers now work with an increasing amount of mechanical equipment, which both lends some element of skill to their work and raises their productivity. Narrowing of the differential in job content between skilled and unskilled work may be partly responsible for, or at any rate may help to legitimize, a narrower differential in wage rates.

Summary of Reasons for Long-Run Changes
These various factors—an increase in the demand for unskilled workers, an increase in the supply of skilled and decrease in the supply of unskilled workers, and minimum wages, unions and changes in job content—may all

serve to explain the narrowing of the occupational wage structure that appears to have gone on through much of the 1900s. Some of these factors may also explain why the narrowing appears to have stopped since the 1950s and may even be widening in recent years.

In particular, dramatic demographic changes, documented earlier, have occurred in the composition of our labour force. Specifically, there have been large influxes of female workers, particularly married women, and of younger workers as the baby boom population entered the labour market. In general, many of these workers were unskilled and this increase in the supply of unskilled may have contributed to a widening of the occupational wage structure. In addition, there is the possibility that the cessation of the narrowing in the 1950s and 1960s may reflect the long-run forces working themselves out. That is, prior to the 1950s, the occupational wage structure may have been narrowing as a result of a series of unanticipated transitory demand increases (associated for example with World War II and with post-war demand) and the long-run supply responses never fully worked themselves out until after the 1950s.

SHORT-RUN OR CYCLICAL CHANGES IN OCCUPATIONAL WAGE STRUCTURES

In addition to its long-run trend patterns, the occupational wage structure exhibits pronounced changes in the short run over the business cycle or in response to unusual events such as war. In particular, the occupational wage structure or skill differential tends to narrow in tight labour markets associated with periods of prosperity or war, and the wage structure tends to widen in recessions. As with the long-run changes, these cyclical changes must be explicable by changes in the demand and supply of labour, or in changes in wage fixing or job content over the business cycle.

Reasons for Widening During Recession

During a recession there is a maintenance of the demand for skilled labour but a decrease in the demand for unskilled workers, and hence a widening of the skill differential. As Oi (1962) points out, this occurs because skilled workers are associated with greater fixed recruiting and hiring costs than unskilled workers. Firms are therefore reluctant to lay off their skilled workers for fear of losing the fixed costs by not being able to rehire their skilled workers when prosperity returns. In addition, as Reder (1955) points out, recessions are associated with shorter production runs and skilled workers are better able to adapt to the variety of tasks associated with shorter production runs.

During a recession there is also an increase in the supply of unskilled workers relative to skilled workers. This occurs, as Reder (1955) indicates, because skilled workers, who were retained for reasons discussed earlier, are moved down the internal queue or occupational ladder, having the same effect as an increase in the supply of unskilled workers and therefore depressing unskilled wages even further. Many of the unskilled workers, on the other hand, are laid off and enter the reserve of unemployed where they exert a further depressing influence on unskilled wages because the firm can always hire unskilled workers from the queue of unemployed.

In essence, unskilled wages are kept low because of the reduction in the demand for unskilled workers and because of the competition from skilled workers and from the reserve of unemployed. This leaves unskilled workers with no bargaining power to get a compensating wage for the usually unpleasant nature of unskilled jobs.

Reasons for Narrowing During Prosperity

During periods of tight labour markets, associated for example with prosperity or war, the previous scenario is reversed. Demand for unskilled workers rises relative to the demand for skilled workers, and the supply of skilled workers increases. Unskilled wages therefore rise more rapidly than skilled wages and the occupational wage structure narrows.

The demand for unskilled workers rises more rapidly than the demand for skilled workers because the firm already has the reserve of skilled workers that it retained during the previous recession. There is, therefore, no need to raise skilled wages to attract additional skilled workers from the outside. However, the firm will increase its demand for unskilled workers from the external labour market and will have to raise unskilled wages to attract these workers from the small pool of unemployed that has dwindled because of the tight labour market. This would also enable unskilled workers to obtain the compensating wage differential that would normally be associated with the unpleasant nature of many unskilled jobs.

Periods of prosperity are also associated with longer production runs that enable production processes to be broken down into a series of repetitive tasks that can be done by unskilled labour. This may also increase the demand for unskilled relative to skilled labour.

On the supply side, during periods of tight labour markets there is an increase in the supply of skilled workers relative to unskilled. According to Reder (1955), this occurs because hiring and job standards are relaxed and firms utilize many of their unskilled workers to perform skilled tasks. In effect, the content of the skilled jobs becomes diluted and a lower wage rate in these skilled occupations results.

These short-run changes can have longer-run effects in that, once unskilled workers are exposed to doing some of the skilled tasks, they may accumulate experience and on-the-job training in these tasks. In addition, they may develop a preference for some of the better working conditions that are often associated with skilled tasks. Thus a short-run narrowing of the occupational wage structure may encourage a longer-run narrowing, even though the initial short- run stimuli are gone. As indicated earlier, this may account for some of the long-run narrowing that has occurred.

SOME CONCLUDING OBSERVATIONS

The occupational wage structure has exhibited both long-run trend patterns and short-run variation. It seems possible to explain both the long- and short-run patterns by basic forces of supply and demand, coupled with institutional factors such as minimum wages and unions. Nevertheless, to a certain extent the explanations appear as *ad hoc* responses that have been devised after the fact, to explain the facts. Consequently, the explanations have not been subject to rigorous empirical tests based on data that was not used to derive the explanation itself.

What is needed on the theoretical side is a more consistent theoretical explanation that will encompass *all* aspects of occupational wage structures: the reasons for their magnitude at any given point in time, their long-run changes over time, and their short-run changes over business cycles and in response to unusual events. What is needed on the empirical side is more discriminating empirical tests that will enable the rejection of some hypotheses and the acceptance of others. Until the theory can be improved and the evidence tested more rigorously, we should regard with caution our various explanations for the behaviour of occupational wage structures. Without an adequate theoretical explanation, policy prescriptions are, at best, hazardous.

QUESTIONS

1. Discuss the interrelationship between occupational wage structures and other wage structures, particularly wage differentials by industry, region and personal characteristics. Why does the interrelatedness make it difficult to talk about such a thing as a pure occupational wage differential? Illustrate by an example.
2. Discuss the differences between inter- and intra-occupational wage differentials.
3. Discuss the various factors that determine the shape of the labour supply schedule for an occupation. Give an example of an occupation that may have an elastic supply schedule and one that may have an inelastic one, and indicate why this is so. If both occupations received an equal increase in the demand for their labour, what would happen to the skill differential between the two occupations?
4. "Economic theory predicts that all occupations yield an equal net advantage. This is patently not so and therefore economic theory is wrong." Discuss.
5. Discuss the expected impact on wages, and hence the wage structure, of each of the following policies:

  (a) an increase in unionization;

  (b) an increase in public subsidies to education, training, job search and mobility;

  (c) wage-price controls;

  (d) child labour laws;

  (e) laws governing the minimum age one can leave school;

  (f) a reduction in rural-urban migration;

  (g) a reduction in immigration;

  (h) an exogenous influx into the labour force of younger workers and married women;

  (i) an increase in workmen's compensation;

  (j) an increase in industrial safety regulations;

  (k) a reduction in the seasonal nature of construction work and a more even phasing of construction activity over the business cycle;

  (l) more strict control of entry into the medical profession;

  (m) a reduction of featherbedding on the part of unions.

6. Just as in computing the aggregate price index where it is important to net out the effect of quality change over time, so in computing the aggregate wage index we should net out changes in the quality of labour and in the characteristics of jobs. Otherwise we won't know how much, if any, an increase in the aggregate wage level is attributable to quality change or to changes in the work environment as opposed to a pure wage increase. How do you think these factors—labour quality and job environment—have changed over time, and how would this affect our aggregate wage level?

7. "The purpose of human resource programs is to increase the elasticity of labour supply to an occupation". Discuss.

8. "One of the problems in recent years is that the occupational wage structure has narrowed so much that there is little incentive to acquire skills or to engage in job search or mobility". Discuss.

9. Discuss the strengths and weaknesses of the coefficient of variation and the skill differential as measures of the occupational wage structure. Discuss some alternative measures. Make up a hypothetical example of an occupational wage structure and compute the coefficient of variation. Compute the skill differential for each occupation, defined as the ratio of the wage in each occupation to the average wage of all occupations.

10. Discuss the possible long-run narrowing of the occupational wage structure that has gone on over the last fifty years. Why may this narrowing have stopped, at least between 1950 and 1970? What do you think the structure would be like in the future and why?

11. Discuss the reasons for the short-run fluctuations in the skill differential over the business cycle and in response to tight labour markets associated with war. How might these factors also alter the long-run wage structure?

12. "We really don't have a consistent theory that can explain both the long-run and short-run changes in the occupational wage structure. Rather, we have a series of *ad hoc* explanations (stories?) that have often arisen, after the facts, to explain the facts". Discuss.
13. "There is little policy interest in analysing occupational wage structures because they have no normative significance by themselves. They are simply the result of the interplay of various market and institutional forces. If these forces are undesirable, then they should be curbed for that reason, not because of any impact that they may have on the occupational wage structure. For this reason, when told that occupational wage structures have narrowed over the last fifty years and that they narrow at the peak of the business cycle, an appropriate response is—so what?" Discuss.

REFERENCES AND FURTHER READINGS

Adam, J. Wage differentials in Czechoslovakia. *IR* 11 (May 1972) 157–171.
Addison, J. The composition of manual worker wage earnings. *BJIR* 14 (March 1976) 56–69.
Bahral, U. Wage differentials and specification bias in estimates of relative labor prices. *R.E. Stats.* 44 (November 1962) 473–481.
Bell, P. Cyclical variations and trends in occupational wage differences in American industry. *R.E. Stats.* 33 (November 1951) 329–337.
Blackmore, D. Occupational wage relationships in metropolitan areas, 1961–1962. *MLR* 86 (December 1963) 1426–1431.
Boskin, M. A conditional logit model of occupational choice. *JPE* 82 (March/April 1974) 389–398.
Bruce, C. and J. Cheslak. Sources of occupational wage differentials in a competitive labour market. *RI/IR* 33 (No. 4, 1978) 621–640.
Bumber, H. Changes in occupational wage differentials. *ILR* (February 1964).
Butler, A. and K. Kim. The dynamics of wage structures. *SEJ* 39 (April 1973) 588–600.
Douty, H. Sources of occupational wage and salary dispersion within labor markets. *ILRR* 15 (October 1961) 67–74.
Dunlop, J. and M. Rothbaum. International comparisons of wage structure. *ILR* 71 (April 1955) 347–363.
Dunlop, J. Cyclical variation in wage structure. *R.E. Stats.* 21 (February 1939) 30–39.
Evans, R. Wage differentials, excess demand for labor and inflation: a note. *R.E. Stats.* 45 (February 1963) 95–98.
Fisher, A. Education and relative wage rates. *ILR* 25 (June 1932) 742–764.
Fisher, M. The human capital approach to occupational differentials. *International Journal of Social Economics* 1 (No. 1, 1974) 40–62.
Friedman, M. The supply of factors of production. *Price Theory: A Provisional Text,* Chicago: Adline, 1966, 199–225.

Goldner, W. Labor market factors and skill differentials in wage rates. *IRRA* (September 1957) 207-216.

Gunter, H. Changes in occupational wage differentials. *ILR* 89 (February 1964) 136-155.

Gustman, A. and M. Segal. The skilled-unskilled wage differentials in construction. *ILRR* 27 (January 1974) 261-275.

Hawkesworth, R. The movement of skill differentials in the U.K. engineering industry. *BJIR* 16 (November 1978) 277-286.

Hershkowitz, M. and Z. Sussman. Growth, induced changes in final demand, educational requirements, and wage differentials. *R.E. Stats.* 53 (May 1971) 169-175.

Hildebrand, G. and G. Delehanty. Wage levels and differentials. *Prosperity and Unemployment,* R. and M. Gordon (eds.). New York: Wiley, 1966.

Hugh-Jones, E. (ed.). *Wage-Structure in Theory and Practice.* Amsterdam: North-Holland, 1966.

Kanninen, T. Occupational wage relationships in manufacturing. *MLR* 76 (November 1953) 1171-1178.

Keat, P. Long run changes in the occupational wage structure, 1900-1956. *JPE* 68 (December 1960) 584-600.

Kerr, C. Wage-relationships—the comparative impact of market and power forces. *The Theory of Wage Determination,* John Dunlop (ed.). New York: St Martin's Press, 1957, 173-193.

Knowles, K. and D. Roberts. Differences between the wages of skilled and unskilled workers, 1880-1950. *Bulletin of the Oxford Institute of Statistics* 13 (April 1951) 109-127.

Lebergoth, S. Wage structures. *R.E. Stats.* 29 (November 1947) 274-285.

Loveridge, R., K. Hancock and K. Moore. Occupational wage structure in Australia since 1914. *BJIR* 10 (March 1972) 107-122.

Lucas, R. Hedonic wage equations and psychic wages in the returns to schooling. *AER* 67 (September 1977) 549-558.

Lydall, H. *The Structure of Earnings.* London: Oxford University Press, 1968.

Maher, J. The wage pattern in the United States, 1946-1957. *ILRR* 15 (October 1961) 3-20.

Mansfield, E. A note on skill differentials in Britain, 1948-1954. *R.E. Stats.* 39 (August 1957) 348-351.

Mansfield, E. Wage differentials in the cotton textile industry. *R.E. Stats.* 37 (February 1955) 77-82.

McCaffree, K. The earnings differential between white collar and manual occupations. *R.E. Stats.* 35 (February 1953) 20-30.

Meltz, N. *Changes in the Occupational Composition of the Canadian Labour Force, 1931-1961.* Canada Dept. of Labour. Ottawa: Queen's Printer, 1965.

Meltz, N. *Manpower in Canada 1931-1961.* Manpower and Immigration. Ottawa: Queen's Printer, 1969.

Meltz, N. and D. Stager. *The Occupational Structure of Earnings in Canada, 1931-1975*. Anti-Inflation Board Report. Ottawa: Supply and Services, 1979a.

Meltz, N. and D. Stager. Trends in the occupational structure of earnings in Canada 1931-1971. *CJE* 12 (May 1979b) 312-315.

Muntz, E. The decline in wage differentials based on skill in the United States. *ILR* 71 (June 1955) 575-592.

Ober, H. Occupational wage differentials, 1907-1947. *MLR* 71 (August 1948) 127-134.

Oi, W. Labor as a quasi-fixed factor of production. *JPE* 70 (December 1962) 531-555.

Organization for Economic Cooperation and Development. *Wages and Labor Mobility.* Paris, 1965.

Ostry, S. A note on skill differentials. *SEJ* 29 (January 1963) 231-234.

Ostry, S., H. Cole and K. Knowles. Wage differentials in a large steel firm. *Bulletin of the Oxford University Institute of Statistics* 20 (August 1958) 217-64.

Oxnam, D. The relation of unskilled to skilled wage rates in Australia. *Economic Record* 26 (June 1950) 112-118.

Ozanne, R. A century of occupational differentials in manufacturing. *R.E. Stats.* 44 (August 1962) 292-299.

Peitchenis, S. Occupational wage differentials in Canada, 1939-1965. *Australian Economic Papers* 8 (June 1969) 20-40.

Perlman, R. A note on the measurement of real wage differentials. *R.E. Stats.* 41 (May 1959) 192-195.

Perlman, R. Forces widening occupational wage differentials. *R.E. Stats.* 40 (May 1958) 107-115.

Raimon, R. The indeterminateness of wages of semi-skilled workers. *ILRR* 6 (January 1953) 180-194.

Reder, M. Wage structure theory and measurement. *Aspects of Labor Economics.* Princeton: Princeton University Press, 1962.

Reder, M. The theory of occupational wage differentials. *AER* 45 (December 1955) 833-852.

Reynolds, L. and C. Taft. *The Evolution of Wage Structure.* New Haven: Yale University Press, 1956.

Rice, R. Skill, earnings, and the growth of wage supplements. *AER* 61 (May 1966).

Rosen, S. Unionism and the occupational wage structure in the United States. *IER* 11 (June 1970) 269-286.

Rothbaum, M. and H. Ross. Two views on wage differences: intra-occupational wage diversity. *ILRR* 7 (April 1954) 367-384.

Routh, G. Interpretations of pay structure. *International Journal of Social Economics* 1 (No. 1, 1974) 13-39.

Sackley, A. and T. Gavett. Blue-collar/white-collar pay trends: analysis of occupational wage differences. *MLR* 94 (June 1971) 5-12.

Salkener, L. *Toward a Wage Structure Theory.* New York: Humanities Press, 1964.

Schoeplein, R. Secular changes in the skill differential in manufacturing, 1952-1973. *ILRR* 30 (April 1977) 314-324.

Segal, M. Occupational wage differentials in major cities during the 1950s. *Human Resources in the Urban Economy,* M. Perlman (ed.). Baltimore: Johns Hopkins Press, 1963.

Sellier, F. The effect of inflation on the wage structure of France. *The Theory of Wage Determination,* J. Dunlop (ed.). New York: St. Martin's Press, 1957.

Smith, A. *The Wealth of Nations.* Toronto: Random House, 1937.

Steiber, J. Occupational wage differentials in the basic steel industry. *ILRR* 12 (January 1959) 167-181.

Turner, H. Trade unions, differentials, and the levelling of wages. *Manchester School of Economics and Social Studies* 21 (September 1952) 227-282.

Turner, H. Inflation and wage differentials in Great Britain. *The Theory of Wage Determination,* J. Dunlop (ed.). New York: St. Martin's Press, 1957.

Walker, J. Occupational wage relationships in 17 labor markets, 1955-1956. *MLR* (December 1956) 1419-1426.

Walsh, W. The short-run behaviour of skilled wage differentials. *ILRR* 30 (April 1977) 302-313.

Wilkinson, B. Present values of lifetime earnings for different occupations. *JPE* 74 (December 1966) 556-572.

Chapter 15

Inter-Industry Wage Differentials

As the Canadian *Standard Industrial Classification* (1970) manual indicates, industrial designations refer to the principal kind or branch of economic activity of establishments in which individuals work. The industries may be broadly defined sectors, as, for example, agriculture, mining, manufacturing, construction, transportation, trade and public administration. Or they may be more narrowly defined. For example, within the non-durable manufacturing sector there are food and beverage, tobacco, rubber, textile and paper industries. The inter-industry wage structure indicates the wage differential between industries, however broadly or narrowly defined.

THEORETICAL DETERMINANTS OF INTER-INDUSTRY WAGE DIFFERENTIALS

The average wage in an industry will reflect a variety of factors, including the occupational composition and personal characteristics of the work-force, and the regional domination of some industries. Consequently, pure inter-industry wage differentials are difficult to calculate because they reflect other wage structures, notably those by occupation, region and the personal characteristics of the work-force.

If we could net out the effect of these other wage structures, however, so that we were comparing wages across industries for the same occupation, the same type of worker, and the same region, then the relatively pure inter-industry wage differential would reflect only the different characteristics of the industry. Many of these different wage determining characteristics are similar to the ones analysed as determinants of the inter-occupational wage structure — non-pecuniary aspects of the jobs in each industry, short-run adjustments, and non-competitive forces. If there are no differences in any of these aspects, competitive forces should ensure that all industries pay the same wage for the same type of labour.

This is illustrated in Figure 15.1(a), which deals with a given homogeneous type of labour that differs only in so far as it is employed in either industry 1 or 2. If there are no differences between the industries in the non-pecuniary aspects (e.g. safety, pleasantness) or in their non-competitive aspects (e.g. monopoly, unionization), then economic theory predicts an equality of compensation between the two sectors in the long run. This is ensured by the mobility of labour towards higher paying industries, or by the entry of new firms into lower paying industries. In the short run, of course, this may not occur and hence there is some inelasticity to the supply of

Figure 15.1   Interindustry Wage Structure for a Given Homogeneous Type of Labour

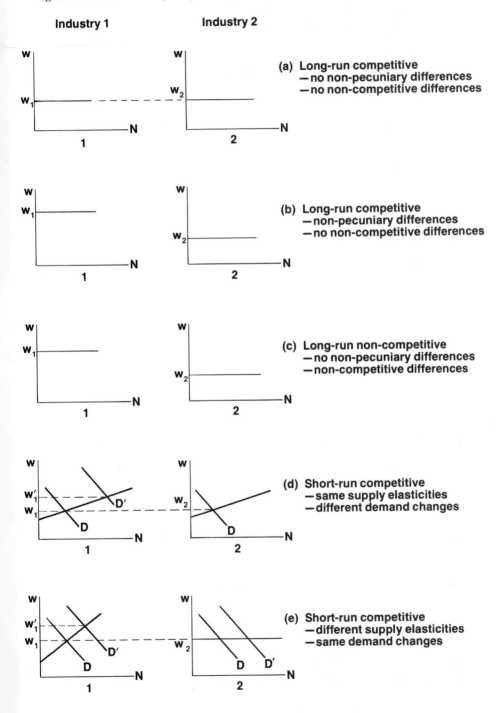

labour, as in Figures 15.1(d) and 15.1(e). In the long run there may also be some inelasticity to the extent that non-pecuniary or non-competitive differences are related to the employment in the industry.

The basic general determinants of the inter-industry wage structure, therefore, are non-pecuniary and non-competitive differences between the industries in the long run, and adjustment factors in the short run. Each of these will be examined in turn.

Non-pecuniary Aspects

Industries, like occupations, can differ in the non-pecuniary aspects of the job. Some industries, for example, may be associated with unpleasant or unsafe work conditions, or with seasonal or cyclical employment. These conditions would require a compensating wage payment to attract workers into the industry. Thus workers in the same occupation and region, and with the same demographic characteristics could receive different wages for being in different industries. This is illustrated in Figure 15.1(b) where Industry 1 is required to pay the compensating wage premium.

Casual empiricism does not always confirm the expectation that compensating wage premiums would have to be paid to attract workers to less desirable industries. On the surface it appears that industries with undesirable working conditions are often associated with low wages rather than a compensating wage premium. This is certainly the story portrayed in our earlier discussion of dual labour market analysis.

Unfortunately, in the real world, it is difficult to disentangle all of the wage influencing forces at work. The poor wages *and* working conditions in some industries may be a result of other factors, such as a declining demand or a lack of unionization. Economics simply predicts that even within the low wage sector of our economy, and when all other factors are held constant, inter-industry wage differentials could exist to compensate for inter-industry differences in the non-pecuniary aspects of the jobs in the various industries. Even this proposition, however, may be disputed by many, especially proponents of the dual labour market analysis. In addition, empirical testing is made difficult because of the near impossibility of controlling for the various other wage determining factors.

Non-competitive Factors

There also may be a variety of non-competitive factors that could affect the inter-industry wage structure. The degree of monopoly power of the firms in the industry may affect wages; however, as discussed in Chapter 10, theoretical considerations alone do not indicate unambiguously whether monopolistic firms would pay higher or lower wages than firms in competitive industries. To the extent that both have to compete in the same labour market, irrespective of the way they compete in the product market, then non-competitive industries would not be able to pay *below* the going wage. However, their non-competitive conditions may enable them to pay *more* than the going wage: hence, the presumption that non-competitive industries may pay higher wages for the same type of labour.

The ability of non-competitive sectors to pay higher wages will more likely be translated into higher *actual* wages by non-competitive institutional forces in the labour market itself. Such devices include wage fixing laws (minimum wages, equal pay, fair wage laws and extension legislation), occupational licensing, and unions (to be discussed in a subsequent separate chapter). To the extent that these factors affect different industries in a different manner, they will also affect the inter-industry wage structure.

Minimum wage laws would obviously affect low wage industries, such as personal services (laundries, hotels, restaurants and taverns), retail trade, and parts of non-durable manufacturing, especially clothing. Equal pay laws would affect those industries with a high proportion of females (and which also are often low wage), for example, non-durable manufacturing, retail trade, services and finance, insurance and real estate. Fair wage laws and wage extension laws tend to be most important in the construction sector. Occupational licensing and unionization tend to be more prominent in high wage industries — in part, of course, because they may have raised wages in those industries.

Figure 15.1(c) illustrates the situation where Industry 1 pays a higher wage for the same type of labour as in Industry 2 because of non-competitive factors. Industry 1, for example, may have monopoly profits that were converted into higher wages because of a high degree of unionization. This may persist in the long run because the non-competitive forces prevent the forces of competition from equalizing wages.

The forces of competition, however, may work in a subtle fashion over the long run. In particular, coupled with having to pay a higher wage, firms in Industry 1 would be able to recruit the "cream of the crop" within each occupation and they may even be able to change the non-pecuniary aspects of their job, for example, by requiring more responsibility or more rigorous work assignments. Hence, skill differentials and non-pecuniary differentials can change in response to the non-competitive differentials (unless of course they are controlled by the non-competitive factors), and the extent to which the inter-industry wage differential reflects pure non-competitive forces becomes more difficult to evaluate.

Short-Run Demand Changes

Just as with the occupational wage structure, the inter-industry wage structure may reflect short-run changes in the demand for labour, derived from changes in the demand for the output of a particular industry. Thus a short-run increase in the demand for the output of a particular industry may lead to an increase in the derived demand for labour in that industry. To the extent that the supply of labour to the industry is somewhat inelastic in the short run (it may take time to attract new workers), then that industry would experience wage increases.

In the long run, however, the supply of labour to the industry would probably be fairly elastic as the short-run wage increases would attract new workers. Unlike the supply of labour to an *occupation,* which may be inelastic because of training cost, preferences for other occupations, or because of innate talents for particular skills, the long-run supply of labour to an *industry* should be fairly elastic because there are usually minimal costs to changing industries (unlike changing occupations or regions), and because preferences for particular industries are probably less strong than preferences for a particular occupation or region.

To the extent that the supply of labour to an industry is perfectly elastic in the long run, changes in the demand for labour would lead to employment changes, not wage changes in the industry. However, to the extent that non-pecuniary returns may decrease or non-competitive factors increase as employment increases in an industry, the supply of labour to the industry may be somewhat inelastic even in the long run. In these circumstances, long-run changes in demand may lead to changes in the inter-industry wage structure as well as to employment changes

Short-run changes in aggregate demand associated with business cycle fluctuations may also have a differential impact across industries. This could emanate from the fact that aggregate demand changes very often imply different disaggregate demand changes by industry (Figure 15.1(d)): construction, for example, is cyclically sensitive. The different impact across industries may also emanate from the differing abilities of industries to expand or contract their work-forces without changing wages—the differing supply elasticities illustrated in Figure 15.1(e). Thus, even faced with the same demand change, industries may respond with different wage changes to expand or contract their work-force. Low wage industries, for example, may have a fairly elastic supply determined by minimum wages, downward wage rigidity, and by competitive pressures exerted by the pool of unemployed. For them, fluctuations in demand would simply lead to employment changes, whereas higher wage industries may have to adjust their wage policy. If this were the case, the inter-industry wage structure would be positively related to the business cycle, expanding during economic expansions and contracting during economic contractions.

The prediction that *inter-industry* wage structures would be *positively* related to cyclical conditions is not in contradiction to our earlier prediction that the *inter-occupational* wage structure would be *negatively* related to the business cycle. As long as we are dealing with pure wage structures, the two are independent and they can therefore respond to the same cyclical pressures differently.

In particular, with respect to the inter-occupational wage structure, it is the higher skilled wages that remain relatively fixed over the cycle for reasons outlined earlier. Therefore, the skill differential w_s/w_u will decrease during prosperity because w_u increases and w_s remains relatively constant. However, with respect to the inter-industry wage structure it is the low wage industry that has the rigid wages for reasons outlined earlier. Therefore, the inter-industry wage differential w_h/w_l (with h and l being high and low wage industries respectively) would increase when w_h increases and w_l remains constant during prosperity. This is illustrated by a hypothetical example in the questions at the end of the chapter.

EMPIRICAL EVIDENCE

The previously discussed theoretical determinants of industry wages should explain the magnitude of inter-industry wage differentials and the reasons for their changes over time, both in the long run and the short run. Unfortunately, this is an area where there is little consensus on how to interpret the empirical results. This in part reflects the continuing debate between institutionalists and neoclassical economists over the relative importance of market and non-market forces in the wage determination process. And it reflects the difficulty in empirical work of controlling for the effect of intervening variables so that one is examining a relatively pure inter-industry wage differential.

Magnitude of Inter-industry Wage Differentials

Empirical evidence does suggest the existence and persistence of inter-industry wage differentials for the same type of labour. Based on extensive analysis of Canadian data, Kumar (1974, p.33) concludes: "In Canada, some industries pay higher wage rates than others to workers of similar skill: significant inter-industry differentials exist for unskilled labour as well as for skilled workers. . . . There has been little change in the relative position of industries in the inter-industry wage hierarchy". Ostry and Zaidi (1979, p.353) also document the stability of the ranking of industries in terms of their wages, but they indicate that in the long run (e.g. over forty years) there is considerable pliability. Thus high wage industries tend to remain high wage industries, although their position can change over long periods of time. This reflects the fact that the long-run determinants of inter-industry wage differentials — non-pecuniary characteristics of the industries and non-competitive factors that may affect industries differently — are likely to change only slowly.

Wage equations, estimated from multiple regression analysis, also typically find the worker's industry to be an important determinant of his wage, even after controlling for the effect of such wage determining factors as education, experience, sex, occupation and region. Based on U.S. data, for example, Betsey and Wachtel (1972, p.127) conclude that "there is substantial variation in wage earnings across industry categories, after the effects of personal characteristics have been eliminated".

Empirical Determinants of
Inter-industry Wage Differentials

While there appears to be agreement that inter-industry wage differentials do prevail, there is not agreement on whether these differences are *pure* inter-industry differentials or whether they reflect skill differentials that are not fully controlled for, compensating differentials for differences in the non-pecuniary aspects of the job in each industry, or wage differentials that arise because of non-competitive factors.

On the question of the impact of skill differentials on inter-occupational wage differentials, it is nearly impossible, given the nature of available data, to fully control for this factor. And yet it is crucial to control for skill differentials because, for theoretical reasons outlined earlier, high wage industries would probably be able to recruit the "cream of the crop" for each occupation. Utilizing a specific occupation group such as unskilled labour or maintenance mechanic may go a long way to *reduce* the effect of different skills levels, but does it completely *eliminate* the effect? Is an unskilled labourer in the furniture industry the same as an unskilled labourer in petroleum refineries, especially if petroleum refineries have to pay high wages for other reasons (e.g. unions extracting monopoly profits) and therefore will be able to hire the best workers for each occupation? Even multiple regression analysis that controls for differences in skill levels by a variety of human capital and personal characteristics variables, may omit less quantifiable factors the importance of which could vary across industries.

In spite of these reservations stemming from the inability of the data to enable the estimation of a pure inter-industry wage differential that fully controls for skill differentials, it is unlikely that skill differentials could account for the *large* inter-industry differentials that persist. Non-pecuniary differences in the nature of the jobs in the industries could be important; however, low wage industries also tend to be associated with poor working conditions and unstable employment (e.g. Kumar (1974, pp. 54-61)). Non-competitive conditions in the product market of the industry could be important; however, there appears to be no empirical consensus on the effects of various measures of industry concentration on wages in the industry. Differences in the extent and impact of unionization could be important, especially in industries with monopoly profits, and Kumar's (1974, pp. 62-65) work bears this out in Canadian data.

Clearly the extent to which the inter-industry wage structure can be explained on purely economic grounds remains an open question. In part this reflects the inability to utilize existing data to *fully* control for the effect of other wage structures; consequently, the inter-industry wage structure may reflect such factors as skill differences, discriminatory wage differentials, and union-non-union wage differentials. Certainly economists have *not* been able to demonstrate empirically that once all the legitimate wage determining factors are controlled for, there is no remaining pure wage differentials across industries.

Changes in the Inter-industry Wage Structure

While economists have not been very successful in explaining the factors that determine the *magnitude* of the inter-industry wage structure, they have been more successful in documenting how it has *changed* over time. As indicated earlier, the ranking has been relatively stable throughout much of the post World War II period in Canada, although it is more flexible over a longer period of time. The long-run determinants of the inter-industry wage structure, such as non-pecuniary aspects and non-competitive factors, and other wage structures (e.g. occupation and region) that are related to the industry wage structure, change very slowly over time.

In addition, as indicated in Kumar (1974, p. 24) and Ostry and Zaidi (1979, p. 355), the dispersion of the inter-industry wage structure in Canada has also been fairly constant over the long run, an observation that has been documented for other industrialized countries. Thus, the inter-industry wage structure is fairly stable not only in that the dispersion has been fairly constant, but also in that industries tend to maintain their approximate ranking within the constant structure.

In the shorter run, over the business cycle, Ostry and Zaidi (1979, p. 355) find the inter-industry wage structure to be positively related to the business cycle: that is, to widen in boom periods and contract in recessions. This is consistent with the theoretical explanation, outlined earlier, based on the rigidity of wages in low wage industries.

SUMMARY AND CONCLUDING OBSERVATIONS

Empirically, there are a number of generalizations that can be made about inter-industry wage differentials. They are large, although the magnitude of a pure differential after controlling for other factors remains elusive. In particular, we do not know how much of the inter-industry wage structure can be attributed to a pure differential, and how much to such factors as non-pecuniary and non-competitive differences, or to short-run adjustments.

Over the long run, the inter-industry wage structure has been relatively constant, both in the sense of a constant dispersion, and a relatively constant ranking of industries within the hierarchy, although in the very long run the ranking has exhibited some pliability. This reflects the fact that the basic determinants of the inter-industry wage structure, such as non-pecuniary and non-competitive factors, change very slowly. In addition, as emphasized by dual labour market analysts, custom and tradition may make it very difficult for wage structures to change, even if some of the basic determinants change.

Over the short run, in response to business cycle changes, the inter-industry wage structure tends to be pro-cyclical, expanding in expansions and contracting in contractions. This probably reflects a greater degree of wage rigidity for all occupations in low wage industries.

While we have been reasonably successful in documenting the magnitude and changes of inter-industry wage structures, we have been less successful in empirically verifying the explanations for these magnitudes and their changes over time. As Ostry and Zaidi (1979, p. 370) conclude after a thorough review of Canadian evidence and the results of other (often contradictory) studies: "The wage structure.... is by and large consistent with expectations in its relationships with some explanatory variables, while not so consistent with others".

Our inability to consistently explain the reasons for the magnitude and changes in inter-industry wage structures reflects both empirical and theoretical problems. On the empirical side, the available data simply does not enable one to fully control for the impact of the variety of factors at work affecting inter-industry wages and their structure. Consequently, empirical generalizations are often made on the basis of rough associations, and explanations for the phenomenon often are provided in an *ad hoc* fashion.

On the theoretical side, the weakness stems from the fact that many of our explanations for the magnitude and the changes in the inter-industry wage structure are ones that are derived from the facts, after the fact. Thus they cannot be subject to empirical testing: since the "theory" is derived from the data, it is bound to be verified. If rejected by a new set of data, however, a new theoretical story emerges. In addition, the theory is not always formulated so as to explain all aspects of inter-industry wage differentials — for example, their magnitude and how that magnitude changes in the long run and the short run — nor to be consistent with other observable phenomenon, such as inter-occupational wage differentials.

Clearly this is an unsatisfactory state of affairs, and it is one that has contributed to the schism between neoclassical economists who tend to follow the dictum "theory is truth — don't be fooled by the facts", and institutionalists and others who have amassed an array of facts without a satisfactory explanation for them. Progress is needed on both fronts.

QUESTIONS

1. Discuss how the inter-industry wage structure is intricately mixed with a variety of other wage structures and why this makes it so difficult to estimate a pure inter-industry wage differential.
2. "In a competitive economy, there can be no such thing as a pure inter-industry wage differential in the long run". Discuss.
3. Modify Figure 15.1(a) to reflect the fact that Industry 1 becomes more easy to unionize as employment expands. What would happen to the inter-industry wage structure and how would it change over time if the demand for labour in the two industries increased the same?
4. Modify Figure 15.1 to reflect each of the following factors, and depict the change in the inter-industry wage structure:
   (a) the industry becomes unionized, but the industry is so competitive on the product side that unions are unable to get wage gains;

(b) the industry becomes monopolized, but the firms still compete in a perfectly competitive labour market;

(c) the industry becomes monopolized, and the union is able to appropriate some monopoly profits in the form of wage increases.

5. "Even if labour were not mobile, the action of firms would ensure that the inter-industry wage structures reflected competitive forces". Discuss.

6. "The dual labour market literature has amply documented that industries with poor working conditions are also low wage industries. Therefore, compensating premiums do not exist and traditional labour market analysis must be replaced by an analysis grounded in the realities of the system". Discuss.

7. Would you expect wages to be higher or lower in monopolistic industries than competitive industries and why?

8. "Even if laws or unions can fix wages in an industry above the competitive rate, the resulting queue of applicants will enable employers to hire better quality labour or change the non-pecuniary aspects of the job so as to restore an equality of net advantage". Discuss.

9. Why might the supply of labour to an industry be inelastic in the short run, but elastic in the long run? Could it ever be inelastic in the long run?

10. Why might we expect, roughly speaking, that the supply of labour to an occupation is more inelastic than the supply of labour to an industry?

11. How would you expect the inter-industry wage structure to change over the business cycle? Is this consistent with the behaviour of inter-occupational wage differentials over the cycle?

12. "A theory that requires high skilled wages to be fairly rigid over the business cycle (to explain the cyclical behaviour of the occupational wage structure), but requires wages in low wage industries to be fairly rigid over the cycle (to explain the cyclical behaviour of the inter-industry wage structure), has problems". Discuss.

13. Consider an economy of only two industries, one high wage and the other low wage. Each employs the same number of workers, equally divided between two groups, skilled and unskilled. Skilled workers are identical with each other in the two industries and so are unskilled workers. The low wage industry pays its skilled labour $4.00 per hour, and its unskilled labour $2.00 during both a recession and an expansion; that is, it has a rigid wage structure. The high wage industry pays its skilled labour $8.00 per hour in both a recession and an expansion, but it pays unskilled labour $2.00 during recession and $6.00 during expansion; that is, its skilled wages are rigid.

    For the whole economy, calculate the inter-occupational wage differential (ratio of skilled to unskilled wages) in both the recession and the expansion. Calculate the inter-industry wage differential (ratio of high to low industry) for both skilled and unskilled workers in both the recession and the expansion. Why does the inter-occupational wage differential contract in the expansion and the inter-industry differential widen?

14. Document the main empirical generalizations that we have concerning the inter-industry wage structure and its changes.

15. Why might you expect the inter-industry wage structure to be fairly constant over time, and for the ranking of industries within the hierarchy to change only slowly?

16. The inter-industry wage structure reflects both dispersion and ranking within that dispersion. Illustrate how dramatic changes could occur in the ranking of industries without altering the wage structure.

17. "A theory of inter-industry wage differentials must be able to explain why differentials exist and why they change over time, both in the long run and the short run. In addition, it must be consistent with other theories and it must be capable of empirical acceptance or rejection". Discuss with respect to the current state of inter-industry wage theory.

18. What do you think are the greatest gaps in our understanding of inter-industrial wage structures? How would you propose to fill those gaps?

19. "Even if we knew the determinants of the overall inter-industry wage structure, and why it changed, this would be of little policy value since there is not much we could or should do to change that structure. It is the result of the interplay of a variety of market forces and what we want to do is to make sure that the market forces are legitimate (e.g. non-discriminatory, not artificial). Once that is done, then the inter-industrial wage structure is what it is, and nothing more should be done". Discuss.

REFERENCES AND FURTHER READINGS

Allen, B. Market concentration and wage increases: U.S. manufacturing, 1947-1964. *ILRR* 21 (April 1968) 353-366.

Anderson, C. Wage spillover mechanisms: a U.S.-Canadian analysis. *IR* (May 1972) 172-183.

Bailey, W. and A. Sckmenk. Wage differences in manufacturing. *MLR* 94 (May 1971) 16-19.

Behman, C. Wage determination process in U.S. manufacturing. *QJE* 82 (February 1968) 117-142.

Behman, S. Wage changes, institutions and relative factor prices in manufacturing. *R.E. Stats.* 51 (August 1969).

Benson, S. On union rivalries and the minimum differentiation of wage patterns. *R.E. Stats.* 41 (February 1959).

Blumenthal, T. The effect of socio-economic factors on wage differentials in Japanese manufacturing industries. *Economic Studies Quarterly* 17 (September 1966) 53-67.

Bowlby, R. The inter-industry wage structure and productivity. *ILRR* 7 (October 1953).

Brogan, R. and E. Erickson. Capital-skill complementarity and labour earnings. *SEJ* 42 (July 1975) 83–88.

Brown, D. Expected ability to pay and the inter-industry wage structure in manufacturing. *ILRR* 16 (October 1962) 45–62.

Cullen, D. The interindustry wage structure, 1899–1950. *AER* 46 (June 1956) 353–369.

Derious, E., J. Crossley and W. Maunder. Wage rate indexes by industry, 1948–1965. *Economica* 35 (November 1968).

Dunlop, J. Productivity and the wage structure. *Income, Employment and Public Policy.* New York: Norton, 1949.

Eckstein, O. The wage-price process in modern industry. *R.E. Studies* (October 1964).

Eckstein, O. and T. Wilson. The determination of money wages in American industry. *QJE* 76 (August 1962) 379–414. Comment by T. McGuire and L. Rapping 81 (November 1967) 684–690.

Eisemann, D. Inter-industry wage changes 1938–1947. *R.E. Stats.* 38 (November 1956).

Garbarino, J. A theory of interindustry wage structure variation. *QJE* 64 (May 1950) 282–305.

Haddy, P. and M. Correll. British inter-industrial earnings differentials, 1924–1955. *EJ* 68 (March 1958) 104–111.

Haddy, P. and A. Tolles. British and American changes in inter-industry wage structure under full employment. *R.E. Stats.* 33 (November 1957) 408–414.

Haworth, C. and D. Rasmussen. Human capital and inter-industry wages in manufacturing. *R.E. Stats.* 53 (November 1971) 376–379.

Kumar, P. *Relative Wage Differentials in Canadian Industries.* Kingston: Queen's University Industrial Relations Centre, 1975.

Kumar, P. Differentials in wage rates of unskilled labour in the Canadian manufacturing industries. *ILRR* 26 (October 1972) 631–645.

Landon, J. The effect of product market concentration on wage levels: an intra industry approach. *ILRR* 23 (January 1970) 237–247.

Levinson, M. Pattern bargaining: a case study of the automobile workers. *QJE* 74 (May 1960) 296–317.

Lutz, M. Quit rates and the quality of the industrial wage structure. *IR* 16 (February 1977) 61–70. Comment by J. W. Mixon and reply 18 (Winter 1979) 122–125.

Lutz, M. The evolution of the industrial earnings structure: the geological theory. *CJE* 9 (August 1976) 473–491.

Maher, J. The wage pattern in the United States, 1946-1957. *ILRR* 15 (October 1961) 3–20. Comment by M. Benowitz and A. Spiro and reply 16 (October 1962) 122–133.

Masters, S. An inter-industry analysis of wages and plant size. *R.E. Stats.* 51 (August 1969) 341-345.

McGuire, T. and L. Rapping. Inter-industry wage change dispersion and the "spillover" hypothesis. *AER* 56 (June 1966) 493-501.

McGuire, T. and L. Rapping. The role of market variables and key bargains in the manufacturing wage determination process. *JPE* (September/October 1968) 1015-1068.

Meyers, F. and R. Boulby. The inter-industry wage structure and productivity. *ILRR* 7 (October 1953) 92-102.

Mills, D. Explaining pay increases in construction, 1953-1972. *IR* 13 (May 1974) 196-201.

Organization for Economic Cooperation and Development. *Wages and Labour Mobility.* Paris, 1965.

Ostry, S. Inter-industry earnings differentials in Canada, 1945-1956. *ILRR* 12 (April 1959) 335-352.

Ostry, S. and M. Zaidi. *Labour Economics in Canada*, 3rd ed. Toronto: Macmillan, 1979.

Papola, T. and V. Bharadway. Dynamics of industrial wage structure: an inter-country analysis. *EJ* 80 (March 1970) 72-90.

Perlman, R. Value productivity and the inter-industry wage structure. *ILRR* 10 (October 1956) 26-39.

Pessarides, C. The role of relative wages and excess demand in the sectoral flow of labour. *R.E. Studies* 45 (October 1978) 453-468.

Phelps, B. and M. Browne. Earnings in industries of the United Kingdom, 1948-1959. *EJ* 62 (September 1962) 517-549.

Reuber, G. Wage adjustments in Canadian industry. *R.E. Studies* 37 (October 1970) 449-468.

Rosen, S. On the inter-industry wage and hours structure. *JPE* 77 (April 1969) 249-273.

Ross, A. and W. Goldner. Forces affecting the inter-industry wage structure. *QJE* 64 (May 1950) 254-281.

Ross, C. The construction wage stabilization program. *IR* 17 (October 1978) 308-314.

Ruppe, R. Wages, prices, and imports in the American steel industry. *R.E. Stats.* 52 (February 1970) 34-46.

Sawhney, P. and I. Herrnstadt. Inter-industry wage structure variation in manufacturing. *ILRR* 24 (April 1971) 407-419.

Schweitzer, S. Factors determining the inter-industry structure of wages. *ILRR* 22 (January 1969) 217-225.

Shulenburger, D. A contour theoretic approach to the determination of negotiated wage change in the building construction industry. *EI* 41 (July 1978) 395-410.

Slichter, S. Notes on the structure of wages. *R.E. Stats.* 32 (February 1950) 80-91.

Sluper, R. Labour mobility over the life cycle. *BJIR* 13 (July 1975) 194–214.

Stewart, C. Wage structure in an expanding labour market: the electronics industry in San Jose. *ILRR* 21 (October 1967) 73–91.

Tylecote, A. Determinants of changes in the wage hierarchy in United Kingdom manufacturing industry 1954–1970. *BJIR* 13 (March 1975) 65–77.

Ulman, L. Labor mobility and the industrial wage structure in the post-war United States. *QJE* 67 (February 1965) 73–97.

Vanderkamp, J. Industrial mobility: some further results. *CJE* 10 (August 1977) 462–472.

Vroman, W. Manufacturing wage behavior with special reference to the period 1962–1966. *R.E. Stats.* 52 (May 1970) 160–167.

Wabe, S. and D. Leech. Relative earnings in U.K. manufacturing. *EJ* 88 (June 1978) 296–313.

Wachtel, H. Workers management and inter-industry wage differentials in Yugoslavia. *JPE* 80, Part 1 (May/June 1972) 540–560.

Wachter, M. Cyclical variation in the inter-industry wage structure. *AER* 60 (March 1970) 75–84.

Wachter, M. Relative wage equations for United States manufacturing industries, 1947–1967. *R.E. Stats.* 52 (November 1970) 405–410.

Weiss, L. Concentration and labor earnings. *AER* (March 1956) 96–117.

Williams, C.G. Changes in the skill mix and their effect on the railroad industry's wage level. *ILRR* (October 1966) 88–91.

Chapter 16

Regional Wage Structures and Geographic Mobility

The existence of pronounced regional wage differentials is a well documented fact in Canada as in most economies. Ostry and Zaidi (1979, p. 376), for example, indicate that average hourly earnings in manufacturing in 1975 varied from $4.56 per hour in Quebec to $6.55 per hour in British Columbia and that the relative ranking of regions has remained fairly stable over time. In descending order from high to low wage, the ranking has been British Columbia, Ontario, and the Prairies, with Quebec and the Atlantic Provinces alternating at the bottom.

As with most wage structures, however, what is less well known are the reasons for the differentials and the extent to which a pure geographic wage differential would persist in the very long run. The problem is compounded by the fact that regional wage structures tend to reflect a variety of other wage structures, notably those by industry, occupation and personal characteristics of the workers; hence, it is difficult to isolate what could be considered a pure inter-regional wage differential, independent of other wage differentials. The low wage position of Quebec, for example, occurs in part because of the preponderance of low wage, labour-intensive, light manufacturing industries in that province.

ECONOMIC DETERMINANTS OF REGIONAL WAGE DIFFERENTIALS

Economic theory predicts that the forces of competition would ensure an equality of net advantage at the margin associated with identical jobs in each region. That is, if the non-wage aspects of employment were the same, competition would ensure that expected wages (i.e. wages times the probability of being employed) for the same job would be the same across all regions. Competitive forces could operate in the form of workers moving from the low wage regions to the high wage regions, or in the form of firms moving from high wage regions to low wage regions to minimize labour cost. As workers leave the low wage region, the reduced supply would raise wages, and as firms enter the low wage region, the increased demand would also increase wages. The converse would happen in the high wage region and the process of the mobility of labour and/or capital would continue until an equality of net advantage were restored in the long run.

244

To the extent that different people have different geographic prefer-ences, the supply of labour for a given occupation in a particular region may not be perfectly elastic. That is, for a region to expand its work-force, higher wages may have to be paid to attract workers from other regions. This could obviously be the case in the short run, but it may also be the case in the long run to the extent that geographic preferences exist. In such circumstances, some workers may be receiving location rents in the sense that they would prefer to remain in a particular region even if wages were lower.

The equality of net advantage at the margin predicted by economic theory does allow for considerable variations in the inter-regional *wage* structure; however, that variation would have to reflect compensating differ-ences, short-run adjustments, or non-competitive factors. Each of these will be discussed in turn.

Compensating Differences

The compensating differences are most obvious and they include wage compensation for such factors as cost of living, remoteness, and climate. They may even include compensation for non-priced externalities such as pollution and congestion. Obviously the compensating factors need not work in the same direction. Urban workers may receive a wage premium to compensate for pollution or congestion externalities, or a higher cost of living: they would obviously not receive it for remoteness.

In addition, the compensating factors need not be valued the same by all workers. The compensating wage is paid to get the marginal worker into the region. Intra-marginal workers may not require the full compensating factor — after all, they were in the region in the first place, even before the compensating wage was paid the marginal worker — and yet because of competition for their services, they are paid the full compensating premium. As indicated earlier, these intra-marginal workers would be receiving loca-tion rents because of their geographic preference.

Short-Run Adjustments

Short-run inter-regional wage differentials could also be present. In fact such short-run differentials are signals that are necessary to induce the mobility that will lead to a long-run equilibrium. The key questions concerning the appropriateness of the economic explanation for short-run wage differentials then becomes: does mobility move in the direction predicted by economics (that is, from low to high wage regions), and does this process serve to reduce the differential?

The adjustment process can take a long time because the costs of geographic mobility can be large, involving not only the direct costs of moving, but also the psychic costs associated with such factors as leaving a familiar cultural, linguistic and geographic environment. In addition, the factors giving rise to the adjustments may change slowly but continuously over time. For example, the decline of the fishing and maritime trade may be a slow but constant sequence of demand declines, reducing the derived demand for labour in the Maritime region. The supply response would be very slow, usually involving younger workers who would not have built up as strong regional attachments as older ones. By the time the supply response has occurred, a further demand decline occurs, and the adjustment process continues.

In essence, a long-run equality of wages is not achieved because of a series of short-run adjustments that continue in the same direction. Even if they are fully anticipated by workers, their supply response cannot be immediate. The system may be in constant long-run disequilibrium, although in a series of short-run equilibrium. Thus inter-regional wage differentials could persist for a long period of time, although economics predicts that the forces of competition (mobility of capital and labour) should respond to these differentials, and that this should serve to reduce them.

Non-competitive Factors as Barriers to Mobility

Not only is geographic mobility hindered by the *natural* barriers that arise because of the high direct and psychic costs of moving, but also it can be hindered by artificial barriers and by public policies that have an indirect, and perhaps unintentional, impact on mobility.

Occupational licensing, for example, can hinder geographic mobility. As Safarian (1974, p.81) illustrates, in Canada there is considerable provincial variation in the certification and licensing requirements of various trades and crafts. Some provinces may not recognize training done in other jurisdictions, others may have residency requirements, and others may even require citizenship. In addition, trade unions that control hiring (i.e. have the "hiring hall") can require that people who have worked in the zone be hired first, hence discouraging others from entering the zone. While these policies do achieve other objectives, they also reduce the effectiveness of inter-regional mobility as a force to reduce inter-regional wage differentials.

Social transfer programs that try to reduce income disparities will obviously have different regional impacts and this could reduce regional mobility. In such circumstances governments are faced with a basic dilemma: as they use transfer programs to reduce income inequality, they reduce part of the incentive for people to engage in regional mobility, unless the transfer programs are conditional upon geographic mobility. Regional expansion policies can encourage capital to move into low income areas, but this also reduces the mobility of labour from that region and hence reduces some of the market forces that would reduce inequalities. Obviously these policies can achieve other important objectives — most noticeably, perhaps, a more equitable distribution of regional income — but they do have the effect of reducing the effectiveness of geographic mobility as a force to reduce geographic wage differences.

MIGRATION DECISION

As the previous section indicates, economic theory predicts that the forces of competition would serve to reduce pure regional wage differentials so that they reflected compensating differences, short-run adjustments, or non-competitive factors. Those forces of competition were the movement of capital from high to low wage areas, and the movement of labour from low to high wage areas.

This latter movement — geographic mobility or migration — can be treated as a human capital decision, the determinants of which are discussed in Chapter 7. That is, geographic mobility will occur as long as the marginal benefits exceed the marginal costs to the individuals making the decision. Benefits can include such factors as expected income (which in turn can be a function of earnings and job opportunities as well as transfer payments), climate, and the availability of social services. Costs can include the usual costs of information seeking and moving, as well as the psychic costs associated with geographic moves. In addition the migration decision may depend on one's ability to finance the move — a problem that is particularly acute in human capital theory because one cannot legally use human capital (e.g. the larger expected earnings) as collateral to finance any necessary loan.

The human capital framework provides a variety of empirically testable propositions concerning the mobility decision. Other things being equal, relative to older workers, younger workers would tend to engage in more job mobility because they have a longer benefit period from which to recoup the costs, their opportunity cost (forgone income) of moving is lower as are their direct costs if they do not have a home to sell or family to move, and their psychic costs are probably lower because they have not established long ties in their community. In addition, they may not be locked in by seniority provisions or pensions that are not portable.

Although older persons who are about to retire may move to get the benefits of a better climate, potential workers would move towards job opportunities: that is, to areas of low unemployment or to centres where there is a large stock of jobs available. In addition, economic theory predicts that geographic mobility would be pro-cyclical, increasing at the peak of a business cycle when job opportunities are more abundant, and decreasing in a recession when jobs are scarce.

Mobility in and out of Quebec would be expected to be lower than in other regions of Canada because of language and cultural differences. In addition, as Grant and Vanderkamp (1976, p. 87) indicate, distance is an inhibiting factor because it increases moving costs and uncertainty as well as the psychic costs associated with being uprooted from one's familiar environment.

EMPIRICAL EVIDENCE ON INTERNAL MIGRATION

Empirical evidence tends to verify the implications of migration as a human capital decision. In the Canadian context, this is evident in the work of Anderson (1967), Courchene (1970, 1974), Grant and Vanderkamp (1976), Laber and Chase (1971), McInnis (1970), and in the extensive work of John Vanderkamp (1968, 1971, 1972, 1973, and 1976).

In one of the more current Canadian studies, Grant and Vanderkamp (1976) confirm that migrants typically move from low income, high unemployment regions to high income, low unemployment regions, and that they are more likely to move to a nearby region so as to minimize the moving and psychic costs associated with a more distant move. They also confirm that mobility is greater for younger than older workers, migration to and from Quebec tends to be substantially lower than for other regions, and migration increases in prosperity and decreases in recession.

With respect to the impact of migration, they find that it does improve the income position of the migrant considerably and that it reduces regional disparities. Grant and Vanderkamp (1976, pp. 88—89) conclude: "The overall impression is one of a labour market adjustment process that works in the right direction; but the adjustment is rather sluggish and by no means the caricature of frictionless market adjustments.... It is quite clear that the migration process contributes to the elimination of regional disparities". They attribute much of the slowness of the adjustment process to the large distances in Canada, to the language and cultural differences, and to the fact that many of the demand changes that set off the adjustments (for example, the decline in coal-mining, shipbuilding and fishing in the Maritimes) have been protracted and continuous.

Clearly both the causes and consequences of the migration decision are in line with the predictions of economic theory. That is, geographic mobility responds to the costs and benefits associated with migration, and the process of migration tends to reduce the regional disparities that induced the migration decision. The extent to which the process would ever completely eliminate *pure* regional earnings differentials remains an open and probably empirically unverifiable proposition, given the near impossibility of completely controlling for the impact of other wage structures, as well as compensating factors, short-run adjustments, and non-competitive forces.

INTERNATIONAL MIGRATION

The decision to migrate internationally also can be viewed as a human capital decision that depends upon benefits and costs. In this decision, the non-economic constraints are even more important, however, because immigration is strictly regulated and hence subject to political decisions of the host economy. These political decisions, however, often are a function of the economic environment.

In Canada, for example, immigration currently is regulated through a point system whereby a large percentage of the points are given for such factors as education, training, previously arranged employment, and possession of skills that are in high demand and short supply. Clearly the control of immigration is highly job-oriented and it can be turned on and off depending upon economic conditions. As Ostry and Zaidi (1979, p. 17) indicate with respect to Canada: "selective immigration has become a more deliberate and conscious instrument of manpower policy, intended to serve as an adjustment mechanism by relieving selective shortages in particular skills or areas. . . . Year-to-year fluctuations in level at least appear to be influenced by economic conditions of this country."

Peitchinis (1975, pp. 42, 43) cites empirical evidence to indicate that immigration has been pro-cyclical in Canada, at least since 1950. That is, in prosperous times immigration tends to be large, and in periods of recession and high unemployment it is small. This is attributed to the fact that in periods of high unemployment, immigration officials may tighten up on the influx, and new immigrants may be less prone to enter. The importance of the economic environment is further illustrated by the fact that new immigrants have chosen to settle in the more prosperous regions and urban centres of Canada.

As with the internal migration decision, international migration is strongly influenced by economic factors in the direction predicted by economic theory. What is less clear is the impact of immigration itself on wage differentials. To the extent that recent Canadian immigration has been restricted to skilled groups, this augmentation of skilled labour should serve to reduce skill differentials. In addition, since immigration has gone to the more prosperous regions, it should serve to reduce inter-regional wage differentials.

BRAIN DRAIN

From a policy perspective, one of the most interesting and controversial aspects of international migration is the issue of the so-called brain drain. The problem arises because countries, especially less developed ones, may lose their most skilled labour to the more developed countries. It is the skilled workers that tend to leave because they can afford to do so, they have the knowledge of foreign opportunities (perhaps acquired while studying abroad), and they can usually amass sufficient points to enter the host country.

The problem is especially acute with countries that heavily subsidize the education and training of their workers. In such circumstances, the home countries bear the cost of the education, and the skilled emigrant reaps all of the benefits in the form of higher earnings in the host country. In many circumstances these skilled workers are the very persons that the developing economy can least afford to lose.

The brain drain often occurs when students from less developed economies go to more developed economies for advanced education and training. The psychic costs associated with the cultural and environmental change have already been incurred, and the direct cost of education or training is often borne by the home country. By definition, the income opportunities are greater in the more developed host country and hence the temptation to stay.

Estimates of Canada's net gain from the brain drain are given in Wilkinson (1965) for the period 1951-61. He estimated that Canada gained approximately $6 billion from the human capital embodied in immigrants (i.e. it would have cost $6 billion to provide the equivalent education in Canada), and cost roughly $1-2 billion through emigration to the U.S. Thus, on net Canada gained approximately $4-5 billion from this aspect of the brain drain.

For countries that are net losers of highly skilled labour, there are some possible remedies, but they all involve other problems. Having the individuals themselves pay for their own education and training would at least ensure that they were paying the costs for the benefits they could receive if they emigrate. However, especially in developing economies, this may hinder large numbers of otherwise poor people from acquiring the education or training. Placing an "exit tax" equal to the amount of the human capital cost borne by the state is theoretically possible, but practically difficult to enforce, and it may be politically unpopular as it becomes compounded with issues of human rights. Recruiting your own students abroad and encouraging their return is a policy that is utilized, but it does have costs and it may be vacuous if viable job opportunities cannot be provided. Providing job opportunities at high wages, of course, is easier said than done, especially in countries that have followed a conscious policy of minimizing wage differentials, possibly for equity reasons. Clearly, as in so many elements of public policy, a variety of delicate trade-offs are involved.

QUESTIONS

1. Discuss the problems associated with calculating what could be considered a pure inter-regional wage differential. What does economic theory imply about the existence of such a differential?
2. Discuss the competitive forces that should work to reduce inter-regional wage differentials.
3. The economic model of migration has been criticized for predicting that the forces of competition would reduce regional disparities. Some have argued that disparities would increase as the best people leave for the better job alternatives, and as capital flows to the already expanding sector. Discuss.

4. "Equality of net advantage at the margin does not imply that everyone is equally happy with their geographic location". Discuss.
5. It could be argued that market forces will not prevent cities from growing beyond a socially optimal size because pollution or congestion externalities associated with city growth are not accounted for through the market mechanism. Discuss the extent to which wage adjustments may reflect these externalities. Will the wage adjustments ensure a socially optimal city size?
6. "Even though we may not be able to make empirical statements about the magnitude of a pure geographic wage differential, we can empirically test how the geographic wage structure will *change* in response to changes in its determinants". Discuss.
7. "Long-run changes in the demand for labour should not affect the inter-regional wage structure to the extent that they are fully anticipated". Discuss.
8. Discuss the variety of artifical barriers that can impede geographic mobility in a country like Canada. Should these barriers be removed?
9. Discuss the ways in which government social transfer programs may decrease or increase geographic mobility. To the extent that they decrease mobility, should they be removed? Are there ways of mitigating their adverse effects on geographic mobility?
10. Discuss the extent to which the migration decision is a human capital decision. To the extent that it is a human capital decision, what does this tell us about the determinants of migration? Derive some empirically testable hypotheses from the human capital model of migration.
11. "Internal and international migration are essentially different decisions because international migration involves political boundaries and therefore controls which take it out of the economic realm". Discuss.
12. Would you expect geographic mobility to be greater for younger or older workers and why?
13. Discuss the extent to which empirical evidence for Canada supports the economic analysis of the migration decision, both internally and internationally.
14. What impact would immigration be expected to have on wage structures in the host country?
15. Discuss what is meant by the brain drain, why it arises, and possible solutions to the problem.

REFERENCES AND FURTHER READINGS

A. Regional Wage Structures

Behman, S. Interstate differentials in wages and unemployment. *IR* 17 (May 1978) 168-188.

Bell, F. The relation of the region, industrial mix and production functions to metropolitan wage levels. *R.E. Stats.* 49 (August 1967) 368–374.

Benham, L, A. Maurize and M. Reder. Migration, location and remuneration of medical personnel: physicians and dentists. *R.E. Stats.* 50 (August 1968) 332–347.

Block, J. Regional wage differentials: 1907–1946. *MLR* 66 (April 1948) 371–377.

Borts, G. The equalization of returns and regional economic growth. *AER* (June 1960) 319–347.

Chernick, S. *Interregional Dispersion in Income.* Staff Study No. 14. Ottawa: Economic Council of Canada, 1966.

Coelho, P. and M. Ghali. The end of the north-south wage differential. *AER* 61 (December 1971) 932–937. Comment by M. Ladenson and reply 63 (September 1973) 754–762.

David, L. and H. Ober. Inter-city wage differences, 1945–1946. *MLR* (June 1948).

Denton, F. *An Analysis of Interregional Differences in Manpower Utilization and Earnings.* Staff Study No. 15. Ottawa: Economic Council of Canada, 1966.

Douty, H. Wage differentials: forces and counterforces. *MLR* (March 1968) 74–81.

Economic Council of Canada. *People and Jobs: A Study of the Canadian Labour Market.* Ottawa: Information Canada, 1976.

Fuchs, V. Hourly earnings differentials by region and size of city. *MLR* 90 (January 1967) 22–26.

Fuchs, V. and R. Perlman. Recent trends in Southern wage differentials. *R.E. Stats.* 42 (August 1960) 292–300.

Gallaway, L. The north-south wage differential. *R.E. Stats.* 45 (August 1963) 264–272.

Gallaway, L. Labor mobility, resource allocation, and structural unemployment. *AER* 53 (September 1963) 698–701.

Gallaway, L. and R. Cebula. Differentials and indeterminacy in wage rate analysis: an empirical note. *ILRR* 26 (April 1973) 991–995.

Gatons, P. and R. Cebula. Wage-rate analysis: differentials and indeterminacy. *ILRR* 25 (January 1972) 207–212.

Hanna, F. *State Income Differentials.* Durham, North Carolina: Duke University Press, 1959.

Hanna, F. Contribution of manufacturing wages to regional differences in per capita income. *R.E. Stats.* 33 (February 1951) 18–28.

Hanushek, E. Regional differences in the structure of earnings. *R.E. Stats.* 55 (May 1973) 204–213.

Johnson, G. Wage theory and inter-regional variations. *IR* 6 (May 1967) 321–337.

Lester, R. Effectiveness of factory labor: south-north comparisons. *JPE* 54 (February 1946) 60–75.

Marcis, R. Joint estimation of the determinants of wages in subregional labour markets in the U.S., 1961-1972. *Journal of Regional Science* 14 (Aug. 1974) 259-268.

McInnis, M. The trend of regional income differentiation in Canada. *CJE* 1 (May 1968) 440-470.

Morony, J. Factor prices, factor proportions and regular factor endowments. *JPE* 78 (January/February 1970) 158-164.

Polzen, P. State and regional wage differences. *SEJ* 38 (January 1972) 371-378.

Reza, A. Geographical differences in earnings and unemployment rates. *R.E. Stats.* 60 (May 1978) 201-208.

Saville, L. Earnings of skilled and unskilled workers in New England and the South. *JPE* 62 (October 1954) 390-405.

Scully, G. The north-south manufacturing wage differential, 1869-1919. *Journal of Regional Science* 11 (August 1971) 235-252.

Scully, G. Interstate wage differentials: a cross section analysis. *AER* 59 (December 1969) 757-773.

Segal, M. Regional wage differences in manufacturing in the postwar period. *R.E. Stats.* 43 (May 1961) 148-155.

Sickle, J. Regional economic adjustments: the role of geographical wage differentials. *AER* 44 (May 1954) 381-392.

Stiglitz, J. Wage determination and unemployment in LDC's. *QJE* 88 (May 1974) 194-227.

Ulman, L. Labour mobility and the industry wage structure in the postwar United States. *QJE* (February 1965) 73-97.

Wonnacott, R. Wage levels and employment structure in United States regions: a free trade precedent. *JPE* 72 (August 1964) 414-419.

Zaidi, M. Structural unemployment, labor market efficiency and the intra-factor allocation mechanism in the United States and Canada. *SEJ* 35 (January 1969) 205-213. Comment by B. Mabry and reply 39 (October 1972) 307-310.

B. Geographic Mobility, Migration and the Brain Drain

Anderson, I. *Internal Migration in Canada, 1921-1961.* Staff Study No. 13. Ottawa: Economic Council of Canada, 1966.

Batchelder, A. Occupational and geographic mobility: two Ohio area case studies. *ILRR* (July 1965) 570-583.

Bellante, D. The North-South differential and the migration of heterogeneous labor. *AER* 69 (March 1979) 166-175.

Berry, R.A. and R. Soligo. Some welfare aspects of international migration. *JPE* 77 (September/October 1969) 778-794.

Bhagwati, J. (ed.). *The Brain Drain and Taxation.* Amsterdam: North-Holland, 1976.

Bhagwati, J. and M. Partington. *Taxing the Brain Drain.* Amsterdam: North-Holland, 1976.

Bhagwati, J. et. al. The brain drain: a symposium. *Journal of Development Economics* 2 (September 1975) 193-378.

Bowles, S. Migration as investment: empirical tests of the human investment approach to geographical mobility. *R.E. Stats.* 52 (November 1970) 356-362.

Bramhall, D. and H. Bryce. Interstate migration of labor force age population. *ILRR* 22 (July 1969) 576-583.

Bunting, R. A test of the theory of geographic mobility. *ILRR* 15 (October 1961) 75-82.

Burton, J. and J. Parker. Interindustry variations in voluntary labor mobility. *ILRR* 22 (January 1969) 199-216.

Comay, Y. The migration of professionals: an empirical analysis. *CJE* 5 (August 1972) 419-429.

Comay, Y. Influences on the migration of Canadian professionals. *JHR* 6 (Summer 1971) 333-344.

Comay, Y. Determinants of return migration: Canadian professionals in the U.S. *SEJ* 37 (January 1971) 318-322.

Comay, Y. The benefits and costs of study abroad and migration. *CJE* 3 (May 1970) 300-308.

Courchene, T. *Migration, Income and Employment: Canada 1965-1968.* Montreal: Howe Research Institute, 1974.

Courchene, T. Interprovincial migration and economic adjustment. *CJE* 3 (November 1970) 550-576.

Crowley, R. An empirical investigation of some local public costs of in-migration to cities. *JHR* 5 (Winter 1970) 11-23.

Denton, F. and B. Spencer. Some aspects of economic adjustments through migration flows. *EJ* 84 (December 1974) 868-885.

Farber, S. A directional flow migration model. *SEJ* 45 (July 1978) 205-217.

Farber, S. A labour shortage model applied to the migration of college professors. *JHR* 10 (Fall 1975) 482-499.

Fein, R. Educational patterns in Southern migration. *SEJ* 32, (July 1965) 106-124.

Fields, G. Labor force migration, unemployment and job turnover. *R.E. Stats.* 68 (November 1976) 407-415.

Folk, H. Effects of private pension plans on labor mobility. *MLR* 86 (March 1963) 285-288.

Friedland, T. Geographic mobility in the legal services industry. *SEJ* 42 (July 1975) 141-144.

Gallaway, L. Age and labor mobility patterns. *SEJ* 36 (October 1969) 171-180.

Gallaway, L. Labor mobility and structural unemployment. *AER* 53 (September 1963) 694-716.

George, M. *Internal Migration in Canada.* 1961 Census Monograph. Ottawa: Dominion Bureau of Statistics, 1970.

Grant, E. and J. Vanderkamp. *The Economic Causes and Effects of Migration: Canada 1965-1971.* Ottawa: Economic Council of Canada, 1976.

Graves, P. Income and migration revisited. *JHR* 14 (Winter 1979) 112–119.

Green, A. *Immigration and the Postwar Canadian Economy.* Toronto: Macmillan, 1976.

Greenwood, M. Research on internal migration in the United States. *Journal of Economic Literature* 13 (June 1975) 397–433.

Greenwood, M. Lagged response in the decision to migrate. *Journal of Regional Science* 10 (December 1970) 375–384.

Greenwood, M. The determinants of labor migration in Egypt. *Journal of Regional Science* 9 (August 1969) 283–290.

Kaluzny, R. Determinants of household migration. *R.E. Stats.* 57 (August 1975) 269–274.

Kau, J. and C. Sirmans. New, repeat, and return migration: a study of migrant types. *SEJ* 43 (October 1976) 1144–1148. Comment by J. Da Vanzo and reply 44 (January 1978) 680–689.

Laber, G. Human capital and Southern migration. *JHR* 8 (Spring 1973) 223–241.

Laber, G. and R. Chase. Interprovincial migration in Canada as a human capital decision. *JPE* 79 (July/August 1971) 795–804.

Ladinsky, J. The geographic mobility of professional and technical manpower. *JHR* (Fall 1967) 475–494.

Lainos, T. Labor mobility and market imperfections. *Canadian Journal of Agricultural Economics* 18 (November 1970) 97–108.

Langley, P. The private gains to long distance migration in the United States. *EJ* 89 (March 1979) 120–126.

Lansing, J. and J. Morgan. The effects of geographic mobility on income. *JHR* (Fall 1967) 449–460.

Lebergoth, S. Long-term factors in labor mobility and unemployment. *MLR* 82 (August 1959) 876–881.

Levy, M. and W. Wadycki. The influence of family and friends on geographic labor mobility: an international comparison. *R.E. Stats.* 55 (May 1973) 198–203.

Liu, B. Differential net migration rates and the quality of life. *R.E. Stats.* 57 (August 1975) 329–337.

Long, L. On measuring geographic mobility. *Journal of the American Statistical Association* 65 (September 1970) 1195–1203.

Miller, A. The migration of employed persons to and from metropolitan areas of the U.S.A. *Journal of the American Statistical Association* (December 1967) 1418–1432.

Miller, E. Is out-migration effected by economic conditions? *SEJ* 39 (January 1973) 396–405.

Mincer, J. Family migration decisions. *JPE* 86 (October 1978) 749–776.

Muth, R. Migration: chicken or egg? *SEJ* 37 (January 1971) 295–306.

Comment by W. Mazek and J. Chang and reply 38 (July 1972) 133-142.

Myers, G. Migration and the labour force. *MLR* 97 (September 1974) 12-16.

Navratil, R. and J. Doyle. The socioeconomic determinants of migration and the level of aggregation. *SEJ* 43 (April 1977) 1547-1559.

Nickson, M. *Geographic Mobility in Canada, October 1964-October 1965.* Special Labour Force Studies No. 4. Ottawa: Dominion Bureau of Statistics, 1967.

Organization of Economic Cooperation and Development. *Wages and Labour Mobility.* Paris: Organization for Economic Cooperation and Development, 1965.

Ostry, S. and M. Zaidi. *Labour Economics in Canada,* 3rd Ed. Toronto: Macmillan, 1979.

Palmer, G. *Labor Mobility in Six Cities.* New York: Social Science Research Council, 1954.

Parai, L. *Immigration and Emigration of Professional and Skilled Manpower during the Post-War Period.* Special Study No. 1. Ottawa: Economic Council of Canada, 1965.

Parnes, H. *Research on Labor Mobility.* New York: Social Science Research Council, 1955.

Parnes, H. Labor force participation and labor mobility. *A Review of Industrial Relations Research.* Madison, Wisconsin: Industrial Relations Research Association, 1970, 1-78.

Parnes, H. and R. Spitz. A conceptual framework for studying labor mobility. *MLR* 29 (November 1969) 55-58.

Peitchinis, S. *The Canadian Labour Market.* Toronto: Oxford University Press, 1975.

Polachek, S. and F. Horvath. A life cycle approach to migration. *Research in Labor Economics,* R. Ehrenberg (ed.). Greenwich, Conn.: JAI Press, 1977.

Porter, A. Inflation, wage behaviour and labor mobility. *RI/IR* 24 (No. 3, 1969) 498-519.

Preston, L. Research on internal migration in the United States. *Journal of Economic Literature* 13 (June 1975) 397-433.

Raimon, R. Labor mobility and wage inflexibility. *AER* 54 (May 1964) 133-144.

Raimon, R. Interstate migration and wage theory. *R.E. Stats.* 44 (November 1962) 428-438.

Rodriguez, C. On the welfare aspects of international migration. *JPE* 83 (October 1975) 1065-1072.

Romans, J. Benefits and burdens of migration (with special references to the brain drain). *SEJ* 40 (January 1974) 447-455.

Rosenbluth, G. Wage rates and the allocation of labour. *CJE* 1 (August 1968) 566-582.

Saben, S. Geographic mobility and employment status. *MLR* (August 1964) 873-881.

Safarian, E. *Canadian Federalism and Economic Integration.* Toronto: University of Toronto Press, 1974.

Sahota, G. An economic analysis of internal migration in Brazil. *JPE* 76 (March/April 1968) 218-245.

Samuel, T. *The Migration of Canadian-Born between Canada and the United States of America, 1955 to 1968.* Ottawa: Department of Manpower and Immigration, 1969.

Scanlon, B. Effects of pension plans on labor mobility and hiring older members. *Personnel Journal* 44 (January 1965).

Schroeder, L. Interrelatedness of occupational and geographical labour mobility. *ILRR* 29 (April 1976) 405-411.

Schwartz, A. Migration, age, and education. *JPE* 84 (August 1976) 701-720.

Schwartz, A. Interpreting the effect of distance on migration. *JPE* 81 (September/October 1973) 1153-1169.

Scott, A. The brain-drain: is a human capital approach justified? *Education, Income, and Human Capital,* W. Lee Hansen (ed.). New York: National Bureau of Economic Research, 1970.

Scott, A. The recruitment and migration of Canadian social scientists. *CJE* 33 (November 1967) 495-508.

Scott, A. and H. Grubel. The international flow of human capital. *AER* 56 (May 1966) 268-274. Comment by N. Aitken and reply 58 (June 1968) 539-547.

Scott, A. and H. Grubel. The international movement of human capital: Canadian economists. *CJE* 2 (August 1969) 375-388.

Sjaastad, L. The costs and returns of human migration. *JPE* 70 (October 1962) S80-S93.

Sommers, P. and D. Suits. Analysis of net interstate migration. *SEJ* 40 (October 1973) 193-201.

Starr, S. In search of a rational immigration policy. *CPP* 1 (Summer 1975) 328-342.

Steinnes, D. Causality and migration. *SEJ* 45 (July 1978) 218-226.

Stone, L. *Migration in Canada: Regional Aspects.* 1961 Census Monograph. Ottawa: Dominion Bureau of Statistics, 1969.

Sureal, E. and H. Hamilton. Some raw evidence on educational selectivity in migration to and from the South. *Social Forces* (May 1965) 536-547.

Tarner, J. Metropolitan area intercounty migration rates: a test of labor market theory. *ILRR* 18 (January 1965) 213-223.

Thomas, G. Regional migration patterns and poverty among the aged in the South. *JHR* 8 (Winter 1973) 73-84.

Ulman, L. Labor mobility and the industrial wage structure in the postwar United States. *QJE* (February 1965) 73-97.

Usher, D. Public property and the effects of migration upon other residents of the migrants' countries of origin and destination. *JPE* 85 (October 1977) 1001-1020.

Vanderkamp, J. The role of population size in migration studies. *CJE* 9 (August 1976) 508–516.

Vanderkamp, J. *Mobility Behaviour of the Labour Force.* Special Study No. 16. Ottawa: Economic Council of Canada, 1973.

Vanderkamp, J. Return migration: its significance and behaviour. *WEJ* 10 (December 1972) 460–466.

Vanderkamp, J. Migration flows, their determinants and the effects of return migration. *JPE* 79 (September/October 1971) 1012–1031.

Vanderkamp, J. The effect of out-migration on regional employment. *CJE* 3 (November 1970) 541–549.

Vanderkamp, J. Interregional mobility in Canada: a study of the time pattern of migration. *CJE* 1 (August 1968) 595-608.

Wadycki, W. Alternative opportunities and interstate migration. *R.E. Stats.* 56 (May 1974) 254-257.

White, H. Matching, vacancies and mobility. *JPE* 78 (January/February 1970) 97-105.

Wilkinson, M. European migration to the United States. *R.E. Stats.* 52 (August 1970) 272–279.

Yezer, A. and L. Thurston. Migration patterns and income change. *SEJ* 42 (April 1976) 693–702. Comment by J. Da Vanzo and reply 44 (October 1977) 391–394.

Young, G. The choice of dependent variable for cross-section studies of migration. *CJE* 8 (February 1975) 93-100.

Part V

Unemployment and the
Wage-Price-Unemployment
Trade-Offs

Chapter 17

Wage-Price-Unemployment Trade-Offs and the Phillips Curve

Previous chapters dealt with a variety of wage *structures,* in particular the occupational, industrial and regional wage structures. In this chapter, we deal with the aggregate wage *level* and its determinants, in particular how it is affected by other macroeconomic variables such as inflation and unemployment. Usually this topic is analysed at the macroeconomic level of aggregation of the economy as a whole; however, increasing attention is being paid to its microeconomic foundations — that is, how aggregate wage changes ultimately are the results of decisions made by individual workers and firms. In addition, the empirical estimation of the determinants of aggregate wage changes are often made at the more disaggregate level of the industry, or for particular wage contracts, as well as the economy as a whole.

The focus of our analysis is on the labour market dimensions of the issue. Since this is essentially a topic of macroeconomics, a more complete treatment is left to texts and courses in macroeconomics. This is also necessitated by the fact that, despite the wealth of studies in this area, it is one where there is not a consensus on all of the issues. Consequently, it is difficult to present a textbook treatment of the state of the art. Rather, an attempt will be made to provide a conceptual framework that highlights many of the relevant issues. Our framework follows that utilized by Sawyer (1975) in the Canadian context.

DETERMINANTS OF AGGREGATE MONEY WAGE CHANGES

Unemployment Rate

In his classic article based on data from the United Kingdom for the period 1861-1957, Phillips (1958) estimated a negative relationship between money wage changes and unemployment in the economy as a whole — the so-called Phillips curve, or the wage-unemployment trade-off as depicted in Figure 17.1. The negative relationship was explained on the basis that the unemployment rate was a measure of excess demand or supply in the labour market. Low unemployment would reflect excess demand or supply in the labour, and when there is excess demand for something its price rises — hence the high $\dot{w}$ when U is low. Conversely, high unemployment reflects an excess supply of labour, and when there is excess supply of something its price falls — hence the negative $\dot{w}$ when U is high. For institutional reasons, money

Figure 17.1 Phillips Curve

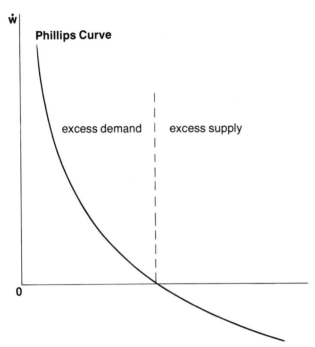

Note: $\dot{w}$ = percentage change in money wages over a given time period
$= (w_t - w_{t-1})/w_{t-1}$
U = unemployment rate in percent

wages may be rigid downwards and hence $\dot{w}$ may seldom be negative (although it was in some periods in the historical data used by Phillips in the United Kingdom). In such circumstances the Phillips curve would approach but not fall below the horizontal axis.

This simple Phillips curve approach suggests one determinant of the change in the level of aggregate money wages, that determinant being the tightness of the labour market as reflected, for example, in the aggregate unemployment rate. In empirical work other measures of labour market tightness, such as the job vacancy rate, also have been used. Reid and Meltz (1979) discuss the relationship between the vacancy rate and the unemployment rate as measures of labour market tightness, and they indicate why the vacancy rate may be a better measure, at least in recent years.

Unfortunately, the negative relationship between $\dot{w}$ and U as embodied in the Phillips curve could not explain recent events where there seemed to be no trade-off between $\dot{w}$ and U; rather, the economy was experiencing *both* high $\dot{w}$ and U. Part of the problem was in the weak microeconomic foundations of the early Phillips curve literature; in essence, it was not grounded in a theory of the behaviour of firms and workers, and hence it did not predict well when other factors altered their behaviour, notably when expected inflation diverged dramatically from actual inflation in recent years. To try to explain this shift in the Phillips curve, variables in addition to the unemployment rate were discussed as determinants of money wage changes.

Inflation: Actual and Expected

The role of inflation—especially the divergence between actual and expected inflation—in the wage determination process can be illustrated in a simple labour market model. Figure 17.2 illustrates an aggregate labour market in short-run equilibrium with the equilibrium wage rate w_0 and employment N_0 being determined by the intersection of labour demand and supply. Labour demand is a function of the aggregate price level (denoted by p_0 in parenthesis) because, as indicated earlier, the labour demand schedule for firms is the marginal revenue product of labour, defined as the marginal physical product times the price at which the product is sold. Hence, an increase in the price of output, other things being equal, will increase the derived demand for labour.

The aggregate labour supply schedule is also depicted as a function of the price level, to the extent that wage demands reflect inflation. That is, the labour supply schedule indicates the money wage level that is required to bring forth various quantities of labour to the labour market: it can be thought of as the asking wage of labour. An increase in inflation would increase the asking wage by exactly the same amount of the inflation (i.e. shift the labour supply schedule vertically upwards by the amount of the inflation — both wages and prices being measured in the same units on the vertical axis) *if* the inflation were fully anticipated, *if* there are no lagged adjustments in wage demands, and *if* there were no money illusion on the part of labour (i.e. if labour bargained in terms of real wages and not nominal wages). However, if any of these assumptions are violated — that is, if expected inflation is less than actual inflation, or if wage adjustments lag price adjustments, or if labour tends to bargain more in terms of nominal wages rather than real wages—then the labour supply schedule in Figure 17.2 would shift vertically upwards by less than the amount of the inflation.

In fact it is the adjustment of the labour supply schedule (i.e. the way in which wage demands respond to inflation) that is crucial in determining the relationship between money wages, prices, and unemployment. In particular, when wage demands are less than price increases—for any of the reasons cited earlier — then real wages will fall, employment will increase, and unemployment will decrease; that is, there will be a negative relationship between the rate of change in money wages and inflation on the one hand, and unemployment on the other hand. This could well be the case in the short run when one may expect wage demands to lag inflation. However, in the

Figure 17.2   Labour Market Adjustment to Inflation

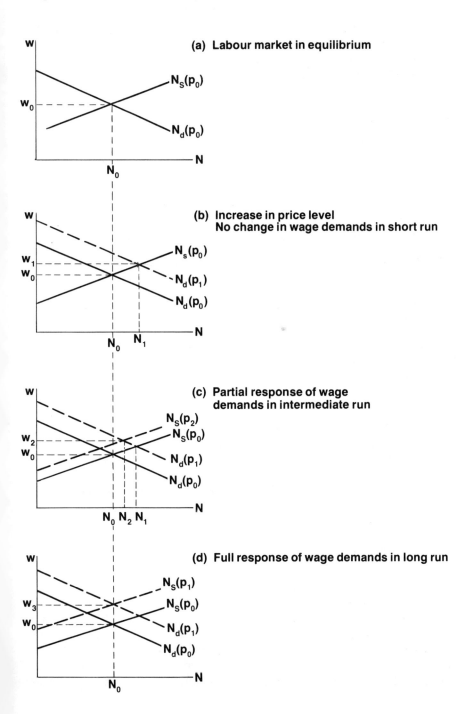

longer run, when wage demands would more fully reflect inflation, then the aggregate labour supply schedule would shift vertically upwards by the amount of the inflation (money wage demands would just equal inflation), real wages would stay the same, and hence employment and unemployment would remain at these old levels. In the long run there would be no trade-off between inflation and unemployment. This scenario giving rise to a trade-off between inflation and unemployment in the short run but not in the long run is illustrated step by step in Figure 17.2.

Figure 17.2(a) illustrates the labour market in equilibrium at a given price level p_0. Money wages are w_0, real wages are w_0/p_0, employment is N_0, and the unemployment rate (not shown) associated with an employment level of N_0 is U_0.

Figure 17.2(b) illustrates the short-run response of the labour market to an increase in the aggregate price level. Reflecting this increase in the price for their products, the derived demand for labour on the part of firms will increase (recall that $N_d = MPP_n \cdot p_Q$ so that N_d increases as p_Q increases). Assuming in the short run that there is no increase in the asking wage on the part of labour (i.e. the N_s schedule does not shift upwards), then money wages will simply increase from w_0 to w_1, reflecting the increased demand for labour. Real wages drop from w_0/p_0 to w_1/p_1 since $w_1 < p_1$. This higher money wage increases employment from N_0 to N_1 and this results in a reduction of unemployment from U_0 to U_1 (not shown in the diagram). That is, in the short run there is a negative relationship between unemployment and the rate of increase of money wages (the Phillips curve) or inflation (the price-unemployment trade-off curve).

Real wages in Figure 17.2(b) have fallen. This is so because the increase in the wage level from w_0 to w_1 is less than the increase in the price level from p_0 to p_1. This can be seen on the diagram whereby at any given employment level, say N_0, the vertical increase in the N_d schedule (that is $p_1 - p_0$) is greater than the increase in money wage $w_1 - w_0$. Thus, $w_1/p_1 < w_0/p_0$. In fact, it is because of this fall in real wages that firms will hire the additional labour, enabling employment to increase and unemployment to decrease.

Real wages have decreased because money wage demands have not kept up with inflation. As indicated earlier this could be the case for a variety of reasons. The inflation may have been *unanticipated*; that is, expected inflation was less than actual inflation, and wage demands are based on expected inflation. Wage demands may simply have *lagged* the inflation, a realistic possibility given that wage contracts can be fixed for a long period of time. Labour may also be under *money illusion* (that is, labour bargained in terms of money wages rather than real wages)—a possibility that could carry over from times when inflation was low, so that money and real wages were similar. In the job search context—often utilized as a micoeconomic foundation for the wage-price-unemployment relationship — the money illusion notion would suggest that unemployed job seekers would receive their reservation wage or money wage demand sooner in periods of inflation with its associated higher money wage offers on the part of firms. In essence, job seekers are fooled into accepting a job sooner (reducing search unemployment) because they receive their reservation wage sooner in periods of inflation. Whatever the reason — unanticipated inflation, lagged wage demands, or money illusion—wage demands are less than inflation in the short run, and this wage rigidity leads to increased employment and reduced unemployment in periods of inflation.

Over time, however, this situation is unlikely to prevail in the longer run. Wage demands will soon begin to reflect the inflation. It will become anticipated and hence expected inflation will approach actual inflation. The wage lags may become shorter as contracts become shorter, so that wages can adjust more rapidly to changing circumstances. Any money illusion that may have prevailed becomes dissipated as workers realize that their real wages have become eroded by inflation: in the job search context, workers adjust their reservation wage upwards to reflect the inflation.

This is reflected in Figure 17.2(c). The labour supply schedule itself shifts upwards, reflecting the higher money wage demands associated with each level of employment. As long as the wage demands are less than the inflation, real wages will still decrease (i.e. $w_2/p_1 < w_0/p_0$) and employment will therefore increase from N_0 to N_2. The increase in employment, however, is less than the increase that would have occurred had money wage demands not risen to reflect the inflation: that is, $N_2 < N_1$. In this intermediate run situation, when money wage demands *partially* but not fully reflect the inflation, there is still a trade-off between inflation and unemployment, but it is not as great as the trade-off in the short run when wage demands do not reflect inflation.

In the long run, however, we would expect that anticipated inflation would equal actual inflation, there would be no lags in the wage response to inflation, and there would be no money illusion. In such circumstances money wages would rise exactly by the amount of the inflation. The labour supply schedule would shift vertically upwards by exactly the amount of the inflation. Since the increase in money wages, w_3-w_0, , is exactly equal to the increase in the price level, p_1-p_0, real wages would be the same (i.e. $w_3/p_1=w_0/p_0$) and employment would remain at N_0. That is, in the long run there is no trade-off between inflation or money wage changes on the one hand and unemployment on the other hand. The Phillips curve (relationship between $\dot{w}$ and U) and the inflation-unemployment trade-off curve (relationship between $\dot{p}$ and U) would be vertical at the long run equilibrium level of unemployment U_0 (the natural or full employment unemployment rate).

It may even be the case that wage demands may overshoot actual inflation in a particular time period. That is, expected inflation may exceed actual inflation, or wage demands may reflect a catch-up process from previous years. In such circumstances, real wages would increase, employment will fall, and unemployment will increase beyond the long-run or equilibrium level of unemployment, even though the economy is expanding and experiencing inflationary demand increases. That is, high inflation may be associated with high unemployment, rather than there being a trade-off between the two. In terms of a Phillips curve or inflation-unemployment diagram, the economy may be operating to the right of the long-run, equilibrium level of unemployment and will continue to do so until the high unemployment moderates wage demands. Later we will see how wage-price controls could in theory prevent this costly stage of high unemployment *and* high inflation, albeit they may have other costs, not the least of which is the unfairness to labour if their wage demands were based on a catch-up for past inflation rather than an anticipation of future inflation. Controls can reduce future inflation, but they can't compensate for past inflation.

This simplistic but realistic labour market adjustment process does highlight the simultaneity between wages, prices and unemployment. It doesn't matter what sets off the process — wage increases or price increases — they are intricately related. This process illustrates — as suggested by Phelps (1967) and Friedman (1968) — how there may be a trade-off between inflation and unemployment in the short run, but why there is less of a trade-off, if any at all, in the long run. The microeconomic foundations of this process arise because of short-run wage rigidities that could be attributed to unanticipated inflation, lags in the wage determination process, or money illusion in the bargaining or job search process. In the long run such rigidities are not as great or are completely absent and the market will reflect real forces.

The simultaneity in the process illustrates the danger of regarding the determinants of inflation, money wage changes, and unemployment in any unique causal ordering. They all are interrelated and they all respond to the causal forces that are involved when buyers and sellers of labour interact in the labour market. The picture is even more complex when, as the general equilibrium analysis of macroeconomics illustrates, activities in the labour market are both influenced by and have an influence on other markets.

From the point of view of the determinants of aggregate money wages — the point that we were originally discussing in this chapter — this suggests the expected inflation rate to be an important determinant of aggregate money wages (as well as vice versa). In empirical work, the expected inflation rate usually is estimated from the past history of inflation.[1] The

---

[1] Empirical studies may also employ a "catch-up" variable to reflect the difference between past wages and past inflation. Depending on the nature of the data, however the catch-up factor may be captured by other variables. As Reid (1979) points out, if past wages did lag past inflation (so that a catch-up would be in order), then real wages will have fallen, employment will increase, and unemployment decrease. Thus an unemployment variable in the wage equation would reflect the catch-up process, with a low unemployment rate reflecting pressure to catch-up.

unemployment rate is also an important determinant of money wage changes mainly as an indicator of a short-run equilibrium adjustment process, to the extent that money wage demands are not perfectly synchronized with the actual inflation rate of any given year. In the long run, to the extent that money wages adjusted perfectly to the inflation, then unemployment and money wages would be affected by *real* factors in the economy. The real forces affecting the long run or equilibrium *unemployment rate* in the economy will be discussed in the next chapter. One of the real forces affecting *money wages* (and real wages) is productivity.

Productivity and the Wage-Price-Productivity Nexus: Mathematical Exposition

At an informal level, the relationship between productivity and wages is obvious. If labour is more productive, its value is greater in the market-place and it will be rewarded in the form of higher wages. The firm's labour demand schedule was derived earlier as the locus of points for which the wage rate equals the marginal physical product of labour times the price at which the output is sold. An increase in the productivity of labour, other things held constant, would therefore increase the demand for labour and hence the wage rate.

As indicated in Sawyer (1975, pp. 323-4), the positive relationship between wages and the productivity of labour can be illustrated more formally. In a Cobb-Douglas production function, output Q is related to the inputs of labour, N, and capital, K: that is,

$$Q = \alpha N^\beta K^\gamma \tag{17.1}$$

The marginal productivity of labour can be derived as

$$\partial Q/\partial N = \beta \alpha N^{\beta-1} K^\gamma = \beta(Q/N) = \beta A \tag{17.2}$$

where A is defined as Q/N, the average product of labour. As indicated in our earlier discussion of the demand for labour, the marginal productivity of labour equals the real wage rate. Therefore,

$$w/p = \beta A \tag{17.3}$$

and

$$w = \beta A p \tag{17.4}$$

Taking the total differential of w, substituting in for the values of the partials, dividing the left-hand side by w and the right-hand side by βAP yields:

$$\partial w/w = \partial \beta/\beta + \partial A/A + \partial p/p \tag{17.5}$$

That is,

$$\dot{w} = \dot{\beta} + \dot{A} + \dot{p} \tag{17.6}$$

Equation 17.6 indicates that the rate of change of money wages equals the change in labour's share,[2] $\dot{\beta}$; the change in productivity, $\dot{A}$; and the inflation rate $\dot{p}$. This relationship prevails in the long run when there are no wage rigidities, so that such things as productivity changes and price changes are reflected fully in wage changes. This illustrates our earlier assertion that the rate of change of real wages depends on changes in real factors. That is, if labour's share does not change, then the rate of change in real wages will equal the rate of change of productivity; that is $\dot{w} - \dot{p} = \dot{A}$ when $\beta = 0$.

Equation 17.6 provides considerable information about the wage and price determination process that is especially useful in discussing wage-price guidelines. It illustrates that money wage increases can be equal to the *sum* of inflation plus productivity increase, and that labour's share would not increase. That is, if $\dot{w} = \dot{p} + \dot{A}$ then $\dot{\beta} = 0$ (labour's share would not increase). This is important because one could easily make the mistake of thinking that if wage increases exceeded inflation by the amount of the productivity increase, then labour is receiving *all* of the gains of the productivity increase. This is not so: labour's share would not increase under such circumstances. In fact all factors of production can have an increase in their real return equal to the productivity increase and there would be no change in factor shares.

If the rate of change in money wages is less than the rate of change of prices and productivity, that is, if $\dot{w} < \dot{p} + \dot{A}$, then labour's share β must be falling (i.e. $\dot{\beta} < 0$). Conversely, if the rate of change in money wages exceeds the rate of change of prices and productivity, then labour's share is increasing.

Rewriting Equation 17.6 as

$$\dot{p} = \dot{w} - \dot{A} - \dot{\beta} \tag{17.7}$$

illustrates the interrelationship of the wage and inflation process. It also indicates how declining productivity can have inflationary pressures; that is, a decline in $\dot{A}$ leads to an equal increase in $\dot{p}$ if $\dot{w}$ does not adjust downwards.

Other Determinants of Money Wage Changes

In addition to the long-run factors of productivity, inflation, and labour's share, and the short-run impact of the unemployment rate, other variables have been suggested as determinants of money wage changes. In many cases, these variables are included (a) to control for certain factors, given the particular nature of the data set employed in the empirical work, or (b) to act as a proxy for other variables for which data was not available. In other cases, they are included in a more or less *ad hoc* fashion, often without a careful theoretical rationale, simply to reflect institutional features that are believed to affect money wage changes. While these factors may truly have

---

[2] From Equation 17.4, $w = \beta Ap$. Multiplying each side by N, and dividing by pQ yields $\frac{wN}{pQ} = \frac{\beta ApN}{pQ}$. Substituting Q/N for A yields $\frac{wN}{pQ} = \beta$. That is, β equals labour's share of real output defined as wN/pQ.

an exogenous effect, they may also simply reflect a common set of underlying forces. Hence, the importance of an appropriate theoretical foundation to sort out cause and effect — the crucial linkage for most policy purposes.

The rate of increase of wages in the United States, for example, may be regarded as a determinant of wage changes in Canada. This could occur through wage spillovers from key groups in the United States, through international unions, multinational corporations, or pressures for wage parity. Again, the extent to which U.S. wages would exert an independent influence, as opposed to Canadian and U.S. wages moving together in response to a common set of forces, would be a difficult issue to disentangle.

Profits have been regarded as a determinant of wage changes largely on the belief that high profits reflect a greater ability to pay or a higher opportunity cost of resisting wage demands and engaging in a strike. They could also reflect short-run demand changes over a business cycle, as well as the residual result of the working out of the wage-price relationship. Again, cause and effect becomes difficult to disentangle without a well-specified theoretical rationale.

Changes in unionization also have been regarded as an independent determinant of money wages, a possibility that emerges especially if one regards power relationships as being important, for example in determining labour's share. Currently this has been emphasized because of the recent rapid increase in unionization in the public sector — a sector where market forces may not serve as an effective check in curbing wage demands. While unions can undoubtedly have an impact on the wages of their members, their impact on the rate of *change* of the *aggregate* wage level is a much more complicated matter. This depends on such general equilibrium effects as their impact on the wages of non-union members, and on how employers adjust to wage increases emanating from unionization.

Market imperfections also have been discussed, especially in the context of insulating wages from competitive pressures. In the context of dual labour market analysis, for example, aggregate money wage changes could emanate from institutional changes, and from changes in administrative practices, or segmentation of the labour market. This would be facilitated by the ability to pass wage cost increases on to consumers via administrative pricing in non-competitive product markets. To a certain extent the belief in these market imperfections and non-competitive forces — most notably monopoly power in the product market and union power in the labour market — were part of the rationale for wage-price controls and guidelines. The exact manner in which these imperfections would affect the wage and inflation process, however, was seldom spelled out clearly. In particular, while imperfections could explain why the price and wage *levels* are higher than they would be in the absence of the imperfections, they do not explain the *changes* in prices and wages, unless one believes that the imperfections themselves change rapidly.

This is not to say that market imperfections do not have an important role in the inflation and wage determination process. Earlier, in fact, we discussed how such imperfections as imperfect forecasting (i.e. unanticipated inflation), lags, and money illusion could give rise to a negative relationship between aggregate money wages and unemployment, at least in the short run. Imperfections can be important: but it is crucial to specify exactly how they work in any theory of aggregate wage determination.

Unusual events — in particular, large wage settlements in specific sectors of the economy — often have been discussed as important determinants of aggregate money wage changes in the economy as a whole. The belief is that unusually high settlements in specific sectors have set off a chain reaction, spilling over into other sectors. In Canada, such key settlements allegedly have included Seaway workers in the late 1960s, construction trades in the 1960s and early 1970s, and the public sector in the 1970s.

While it can be tempting to regard these settlements as setting off inflationary wage settlements elsewhere, there is a danger in such *ad hoc* theorizing about the impact of peculiar events. Certainly they can affect the magnitude of wages in a particular sector, and hence they can affect the wages of that sector relative to other sectors, at least in the short run. Nevertheless, the mechanism whereby this affects aggregate wages in the economy as a whole is not clear. What appears to be a spillover effect may simply be a variety of sectors responding to the same set of economic forces. And even if there are purely institutional spillover effects, it is not clear that they will persist in the long run. There will always be a group that stands out as receiving unusually large settlements in a given short period of time. Some of the gain may reflect a catch-up, some may reflect a short-run demand increase, and some may be a purely transitory gain that will be dissipated over time. Unusually high wage settlements in a particular sector may be a *symptom* of any of a variety of factors: it is another matter, however, to argue that they are the *cause* of general increases in aggregate money wages.

EMPIRICAL EVIDENCE

From a theoretical point of view we have seen how such factors as productivity and inflation can affect aggregate money wage changes, and how the unemployment rate may also be a determinant, especially in the short run, when wage demands may not be synchronized with actual inflation in a given time period. With less, if any, of a theoretical rationale, other determinants have been added, including such factors as wages in the U.S., profits, unionization, and a series of unusual events.

Empirical studies in Canada on the determinants of aggregate money wages (i.e. the Phillips curve) include Archibald (1969); Auld, Christophides, Swidinsky and Wilton (1979); Beare (1973); Bodkin, Bond, Reuber, and Robinson (1966); Cousineau and Lacroix (1977, 1978); Kaliski (1972); Marion (1969); McFetridge (1972); Reid and Meltz (1979); Reuber (1970); Rowley and Wilton (1973a, 1973b, 1974a, 1974b, 1977); Smith (1976); Sparks and

Wilton (1971); Swidinsky (1972); Turnovsky (1972); Vanderkamp (1966, 1972); and Zaidi (1969, 1970). While there exists a wealth of studies, the results are difficult to summarize, in part because of differences in methodology and data sets. However, some generalizations appear to emerge.

In the short run there is a trade-off between the rate of change of wages (or inflation), and unemployment; however, in the long run there is much less of a trade-off if any at all. Expectations and lags are important; hence, it takes a long time for the impact of inflation to work its way through the economic system to affect such factors as wage demands and unemployment. However, in the long run, people and institutions do adjust in a fairly rational fashion and their actions do reflect the inflation — adjusting for the past inflation and anticipating future inflation. Hence, the aggregate level of money wages in any one period cannot be viewed in isolation from the inflation and unemployment of other periods — past, present and future.

Empirical studies on the impact of the wage-price controls instituted in Canada in October, 1975 also indicate that controls did reduce the rate of increase of money wages relative to what they would have been in the absence of controls. Reid (1979), for example, indicates that during the approximately three year period after the imposition of controls in Canada, the annual rate of change of money wages was reduced by about 8.5 percentage points relative to the period immediately preceding controls. That is, during the first three quarters of 1975 prior to controls, wage settlements were averaging 17.5 per cent, and during the following three years of controls, wage settlements dropped to an average increase of 9.0 per cent. Of this 8.5 percentage point reduction, approximately 4.5 percentage points were attributable to controls and 4.0 percentage points attributable to a general reduction that would have gone on simply because of the state of the economy. That is, the rate of increase of money wages would have moderated even without controls; however, controls appear to have further moderated wage increases. Reid indicates that these results are broadly consistent with other Canadian studies on the impact of controls, notably Auld, Christophides, Swidinsky and Wilton (1977), and Cousineau and Lacroix (1978).

A variety of interesting policy implications follow from these empirical generalizations. Given the importance of lags and expectations, it is hazardous to base policy on a snapshot picture at a point in time. Wage controls, for example, may be unfair if they prevent a catch-up for past inflation and they may be ineffective to the extent that wage settlements after controls would simply catch-up for any losses during controls. On the other hand, if wage and price controls can break the cycle of expectations, they may dampen any inflationary wage-price spiral and they may enable the economy to move towards an equilibrium level of unemployment without experiencing severe levels of unemployment that could result from wage demands exceeding inflation. In other words, controls accompanied by the appropriate monetary and fiscal policies may enable the bypassing of a costly phase of high unemployment that would be necessary to moderate wage demands.

In addition, the empirical generalizations indicate that to the extent that there is little or no trade-off between wage changes (or inflation) and unemployment in the long run (i.e. the Phillips curve is vertical at the long-run rate of unemployment), then we should focus our attention on the determinants of this long-run level of unemployment in the economy. The various facets that affect our aggregate unemployment rate — including demographic and institutional factors that may have shifted outwards the Phillips curve — are the subject of the next chapter.

QUESTIONS

1. Discuss the theoretical rationale, if any, for the use of the unemployment rate as a determinant of the rate of increase in aggregate money wages.
2. Distinguish between the Phillips curve and the inflation-unemployment trade-off curve.
3. In the econometric estimation of aggregate money wage equations, the unemployment rate is often entered in reciprocal form (i.e. $1/U$), with an expected positive sign, to capture the non-linear relationship whereby the Phillips curve is convex to the orgin. Illustrate why this is the case, and why a positive sign would reflect a negative relationship between $\dot{w}$ and U.
4. The original Phillips curve literature was often criticized for simply reflecting an unstable empirical relationship without any theoretical rationale for the relationship. Consequently, the policy implications were often wrong, and when the underlying causal determinants changed, the old empirical relationship no longer predicted well. This illustrates the importance of theory for accurate prediction and for policy prescriptions. Discuss.
5. Trace out the Phillips curve and the price-unemployment curve, both in the short run and the long run, from the adjustment process portrayed in Figure 17.2. What if the asking wage of labour increased by more than the inflation rate of a given year, perhaps because of a catch-up process or because of an anticipation of even higher inflation in the future? Illustrate this in Figure 17.2, and illustrate the new point in the Phillips curve and the inflation-unemployment trade-off. What if this were prevented by a wage-price control problem that restricted wage increases to the inflation of that year? (Illustrate on the diagram and on the trade-off curves). Could this provide a rationale for a controls program to move the economy towards its long-run equilibrium without experiencing a phase of high unemployment necessary to moderate wage demands? Does it matter if the original wage demands in excess of

actual inflation were based on a catch-up for past inflation, or an expectation of future inflation? What if the controls were not accompanied by the appropriate monetary and fiscal policies to curb inflationary pressures? What if inflation continued in spite of the wage controls, perhaps because the price-markup over labour costs were increased?

6. Illustrate how the adjustment process of Figure 17.2 could arise from a job search process whereby job seekers face a distribution of money wage offers and have an acceptance or reservation wage in money terms. That is, they will continue to remain unemployed and search (sample the distribution of money wage offers) until they receive their reservation wage. Indicate how an increase in aggregate demand and its accompanying increase in the aggregate price level may reduce search unemployment in the short run, but may not reduce it in the long run when the reservation wage adjusts to the inflation.

7. "Any microeconomic theory of behaviour that requires wage rigidities due to such things as unanticipated inflation, wage lags or money illusion in the collective bargaining or job search process, could only explain phenomenon in the short run, not in the long run". Discuss.

8. Derive Equation 17.6 from the production function of Equation 17.1 and the assumption that labour is paid a real wage equal to its marginal productivity.

9. "If inflation is 6 per cent and productivity 2 per cent, and if money wages increase by 8 per cent, then labour receives *all* of the productivity increase and nothing is left over for other factors of production". Discuss.

10. Discuss the extent to which non-competitive forces such as monopolies and powerful unions could lead to wage and price inflation.

11. Assume that the following short-run *hypothetical* Phillips curve is estimated econometrically:

$$\dot{w} = 2.5 + .9\dot{p}e - .25U$$

where $\dot{w}$ is the annual rate of change in money wages, $\dot{p}e$ is the annual expected inflation rate, and U is the unemployment rate. All variables are expressed in percentage terms and their averages over the sample period are 10 for $\dot{w}$, 10 for $\dot{p}e$, and 6 for U. The estimated coefficients are all significantly different from zero, and the coefficient of $\dot{p}e$ is not significantly different from one, according to conventional significance tests.

(a) What is the expected rate of change of money wages that would result if expected inflation were 10 per cent and the unemployment rate 6 per cent?

(b) What would happen if the unemployment rate were raised to 10 per cent?

(c) What would happen if expected inflation were moderated to 5 per cent?

(d) What does the coefficient for the inflation-expectations variable imply about the rational expectations of labour?

(e) What does the coefficient of the unemployment rate variable imply about the shape of the Phillips curve?

(f) Plot a Phillips curve assuming expectations of inflation of 5 per cent. Plot a Phillips curve assuming expectations of inflation of 10 per cent. What happens to the Phillips curve if expectations of inflation increase from 5 to 10 per cent?

(g) Assume that the short-run aggregate price equation was estimated as $\dot{p} = 2 - .25U + 1.1\dot{w}$ and that, in the long run, actual inflation equals expected inflation: that is, $\dot{p} = \dot{p}e$. Utilize the short-run Phillips curve and aggregate price equations, and the long-run equilibrium condition to solve for the long-run Phillips curve. Compare the shape of the long-run and short-run Phillips curves. Solve for the long-run or natural rate of unemployment as a function of money wages.

REFERENCES AND FURTHER READINGS

A.   Phillips Curve and the Wage-Price-Unemployment Relationship

Alkerlof, G. Relative wages and the rate of inflation. *QJE* 83 (August 1969) 353-374.

Allen, B. Market concentration and wage increases: U.S. manufacturing, 1947-1964. *ILRR* (April 1968) 353-366.

Archibald, G. The Phillips curve and the distribution of unemployment. *AER* 59 (May 1969) 124-134.

Ashenfelter, O., G. Johnson and J. Pencavel. Trade unions and the rate of change of money wages in United States manufacturing industry. *R.E. Studies* 39 (January, 1972) 27-54.

Ashenfelter, O., and J. Pencavel. Wage changes and the frequency of wage settlements. *Economica* 42 (May 1975).

Barron, J. Search in the labour market and the duration of unemployment. *AER* 65 (December 1975) 934-942.

Barrett, N., G. Gerardi and T. Hart. Quarterly price and wage behaviour in U.S. manufacturing. *QJE* 88 (August 1974) 385-408.

Beare, J. Wage and price change relationships in post-war Canada. *CJE* 6 (May 1973) 260-266.

Behman, S. Wage determination process in U.S. manufacturing. *QJE* 82 (February 1968) 117-142.

Behman, S. Labor mobility, increasing labor demand and money wage rate increases in United States manufacturing. *R.E. Studies* 31 (October 1963) 253-266.

Bellante, D. and M. Jackson. Cycle neutral unemployment rates and aggregate wage change. *SEJ* 41 (July 1974) 87-95.

Berg, S. and T. Dalton. Sectoral employment and shifts in the aggregate Phillips curve. *SEJ* 41 (April 1975) 543-601.

Bhatia, R. Profits and the rate of change in money earnings in the United States, 1935-1959. *Economica* 29 (August 1962) 255-62.

Bhatia, R. Unemployment and the rate of change of money earnings in the United States, 1900-1958. *Economica* 28 (August 1961). 286-96.

Black, S. and H. Kelejian. The formulation of the dependent variable in the wage equation. *R. E. Stats* 39 (January 1972) 55-59.

Bodkin, R. *The Wage-Price-Productivity Nexus.* Philadelphia: University of Pennsylvania Press, 1966.

Bodkin, R. An analysis of the trade-offs between full employment, price stability and other goals. *Canadian Economic Policy Since the War*, S. Kaliski (ed.). Canadian Trade Committee, 1966.

Bodkin, R., E. Bond, G. Reuber, and T. Robinson. *Price Stability and High Employment.* Special Study No. 5. Ottawa: Economic Council of Canada, 1966.

Bodkin R. and A Lerner. *Two Lectures on the Wage-Price Problem.* Vancouver: UBC Economics, 1974.

Bowen, W. *The Wage Price Issue.* Princeton: Princeton University Press, 1960.

Bowen, W. and R. Berry. Unemployment conditions and movements of the money wage level. *R. E. Stats.* 65 (May 1963) 163-172.

Brechling, F. The trade-off between inflation and unemployment. *JPE* 76 (July/August 1968) 712-737.

Brenner, R. The death of the Phillips curve reconsidered. *QJE* 91 (August 1977) 389-418.

Bruce, C. The wage spiral: Canada 1953-1970. *EJ* 95 (June 1975) 372-376.

Bruno, M. Exchange rates, import costs and wage-price dynamics. *JPE* 86 (June 1978) 379-403.

Crispo, J. (ed.). *Wages, Prices, Profits and Economic Policy.* Toronto: University of Toronto Press, 1967.

Corry, B. and D. Laidler. The Phillips relation: a theoretical explanation. *Economica* 34 (May 1967) 189-197.

Couling, K. and D. Metcalf. Wage unemployment relations: a regional analysis for the U.K., 1960-1965. *Oxford Institute of Economic Statistics Bulletin* 29 (February 1967) 31-39.

Dicks-Mireaux, L. and J. Dow. The determinants of wage inflation: the United Kingdom, 1946-1956. *The Journal of the Royal Statistical Society* Series A, 22 (1959).

Donner, A. Labour turnover, expectations and the determination of money wage changes in U.S. manufacturing. *CJE* 5 (February 1972) 16-34.

Dow, J. C. and L. Dicks-Mireaux. Excess demand for labour. *Oxford Economics Paper* N.S. 10 (February 1959).

Dowling, J. Wage determination in two-digit manufacturing industries. *Quarterly Review of Economics and Business* 13 (Spring 1972) 27-36.

Eagly, R. Market power as an intervening mechanism in Phillips curve analysis. *Economica* 32 (February 1965) 48-64.

Eatwell, J., J. Llewellyn and R. Tarling. Money wage inflation in industrial countries. *R. E. Studies* 41 (October 1974) 515-523, and comment by R. Thomas 43 (October 1976) 551-552.

Eckstein, O. Money wage determination revisited. *R. E. Studies* 35 (April 1968) 133-143.

Eckstein, O. and T. Wilson. The determination of money wages in American industry. *QJE* 76 (August 1962) 379-414.

Fellner, W. Phillips type approach or acceleration? *BPEA* (No. 2, 1971) 469-483.

Flanagan, R. Wage interdependence in unionized labour markets. *BPEA* (No. 3, 1976) 635-682.

Flanagan, R. The U.S. Phillips curve and international unemployment rate differentials. *AER* 63 (March 1973) 114-131. Comments by M. Barrett and reply 65 (March 1975) 225-231, comments by R. Avelsson et. al. 67 (March 1977) 218-224.

France, R. Wages, unemployment and prices in the United States, 1890-1932, 1947-1957. *ILRR* 15 (January 1962) 171-190.

Fried, J. Inflation-unemployment trade-offs under fixed and floating exchange rates. *CJE* 6 (February 1973) 43-52.

Friedman, M. Nobel lecture: Inflation and unemployment. *JPE* 85 (June 1977) 451-472.

Friedman, M. The role of monetary policy. *AER* 58 (March 1968) 1-17.

Garbarino, J. Unionism and the general wage level. *AER* 40 (December 1950) 893-96.

Goldman, B. and J. Maxwell. *Wage Developments in Canada: The Pressure to Catch-up.* Montreal: C. D. Howe Research Institute, 1975.

Gordon, D. A neo-classical theory of Keynesian unemployment. *SEJ* 12 (December 1974) 431-459.

Gordon, R. Wages, prices, and unemployment, 1900-1970. *IR* 14 (October 1975) 273-301.

Gordon, R. Wage-price controls and the shifting Phillips curve. *BPEA* (No. 2, 1971) 385-421.

Green, C. The employment ratio as sign of aggregate demand pressure. *MLR* 100 (April 1977) 25-32.

Greer, D. Market power and wage inflation: a further analysis. *SEJ* 41 (January 1975) 466-479.

Gronan, R. Information and frictional unemployment. *MLR* 61 (June 1971) 290-301.

Grossman, H. The cyclical pattern of unemployment and wage inflation. *Economica* 41 (November 1974) 403-13.

Grossman, H. Aggregate demand, job search and employment. *JPE* 81 (November-December 1973) 1353-1369.

Hall, R. The process of inflation in the labour market. *BPEA* (No. 2, 1974) 343-410.

Hall, R. Prospects for shifting the Phillips curve through manpower policy. *BPEA* (N0. 3, 1971) 659-702.

Hamermesh, D. Wage bargains, threshold effects and the Phillips curve. *QJE* 84 (August 1970) 501-517. Comment by A. Gustman and reply, 86 (May 1972) 332-341.

Hamermesh, D. Market power and wage inflation. *SEJ* 39 (October 1972) 204-212.

Hansen, B. Excess demand, unemployment, vacancies and wages. *QJE* 84 (February 1970) 1-24.

Hines, A. The Phillips curve and the distribution of unemployment. *AER* 62 (March 1972) 155-160.

Hines, A. Wage inflation in the United Kingdom, 1948-1962: a disaggregated study. *EJ* 79 (March 1969) 66-89.

Hines, A. Unemployment and the rate of change of money rates in the United Kingdom, 1862-1963: a reappraisal. *R. E. Stats.* 50 (February 1968) 60-67.

Hines, A. Trade unions and wage inflation in the United Kingdom, 1893-1961. *R.E. Studies* 31 (October 1964) 221-242.

Holmes, J. and D. J. Smyth. The relation between unemployment and excess demand for labour. *Economica* 37 (August 1970) 311-315.

Holt, C. Improving the labour market trade-off between inflation and unemployment. *AER* 59 (May 1969) 135-146.

Holt, C., C. MacRae, S. Schweitzer and R. Smith. *The Unemployment Inflation Dilemma: A Manpower Solution.* Washington: Urban Institute, 1971.

Holt, C., C. MacRae, S. Schweitzer and R. Smith. Manpower proposals for phase III. *BPEA* (No. 3, 1971) 703-734.

Jackson, D., H. Turnover and F. Wilkinson. *Do Trade Unions Cause Inflation?* Cambridge: Cambridge University Press. 1972.

Jackson, M. and E. Jones. Unemployment and occupational wage changes in local labour markets. *ILRR* 26 (July 1973) 1135-1145.

Johnson, G. The determination of wages in the union and nonunion sectors. *BJIR* 15 (July 1977) 211-225.

Johnson, S. and P. Smith. The Phillips curve, expectations and stability. *Quarterly Review of Economics and Business* 13 (Autumn 1973) 85-91.

Kahn, L. Union strength and wage inflation. *IR* 18 (Spring 1979) 144-155.

Kaliski, S. and D. Smith. Inflation, unemployment and incomes policy. *CJE* 6 (November 1973) 574-591.

Karen, D. and M. Spiro. The relation between wages and unemployment in U.S. cities, 1955-1965. *Manchester School of Economics and Social Studies* 38 (March 1970) 1-14.

Klein, L. and R. Ball. Some econometrics of determinants of absolute prices and wages. *EJ* 69 (September 1959) 465-482.

Koshal, R. and L. Gallaway. The Phillips curve for West Germany. *Kyklos* 24 (March 1971) 346-349.

Kotowitz, J. *The Effect of Direct Taxes on Wages.* Anti-Inflation Board Report. Ottawa: Supply and Services, 1979.

Kuh, E. A productivity theory of wage levels — an alternative to the Phillips curve. *R. E. Studies* 34 (October 1967) 333-360.

Kuska, E. The simple analysis of the Phillips curve. *Economica* 33 (1966) 462-467.

Laidler, D. and D. Purdy. *Inflation and Labour Markets.* Toronto: University of Toronto Press, 1974.

Levinson, H. Unionism, concentration and wage changes: toward a unified theory. *ILRR* 20 (January 1967) 198-205.

Lipsey, R. The relationship between unemployment and the rate of change of money wage rates in the United Kingdom, 1862-1957: a further analysis. *Economica* 27 (February 1960) 1-31.

Lipsey, R. and P. Steiner. The relationship between profits and wage rates. *Economica* 28 (May 1961) 137-159.

Lucas, R. and E. Prescott. Equilibrium search and unemployment. *Journal of Economic Theory* 7 (1974) 188-209.

Lucas, R. and L. Rapping. Price expectations and the Phillips curve. *AER* 59 (June 1969) 342-350.

Lucas, R. and L. Rapping. Real wages, employment and inflation. *JPE* 77 (September/October 1969) 721-754.

Lucas, R. and L. Rapping. Unemployment in the great depression: is there a full explanation? *JPE* 80 (January/February 1972) 186-191.

Marion G. Le rôle des fonction de production dans les relations d'arbitrage salaire, emploi et prix. *CJE* 2 (November 1969) 536-545. Comment by J. Beare and reply 3 (November 1970) 607-614.

Marion, G. La demande excédentaire de travail et la variation des salaires dans l'industrie manufacturiere au Canada. *CJE* (August 1968) 519-539.

McCaffree, K. A further consideration of wages, unemployment, and prices in the United States, 1948-1958. *ILRR* 17 (October 1963) 60-74.

McCallum, B. Wage rate changes and the excess demand for labour. *Economica* 41 (August 1974) 269-277.

McGuire, T. and L. Rapping. The supply of labor and manufacturing wage determination in the United States. *IER* 11 (June 1970) 258-268.

McGuire, R. and L. Rapping. The role of market variables and key bargains in the manufacturing wage determination process. *JPE* 76 (October 1968) 1015-1036.

MacRae, C. The relation between unemployment and inflation in the Laffer-Johnson model. *Journal of Business* 45 (October 1972) 513-518.

Metcalf, D. The determinants of earnings changes: a regional analysis of the U.K., 1960-1968. *IER* 12 (June 1971) 273-282.

Mehra, Y. Spillover in wage determination in U.S. manufacturing industries. *R. E. Stats*. 68 (August 1976) 300-312.

Meyer, B. A comparison of the U.S. and Canadian wage adjustment mechanisms: 1948-1967. *RI/IR* 29 (December 1974) 846-856.

Mitchell, D. Union wage determination. *BPEA* (No. 3, 1978) 537-592.

Mitchell, E. Explaining the international pattern of labor productivity and wages. *R. E. Stats*. 50 (November 1968) 461- 69.

Modigliani, F. and E. Tarantelli. A generalization of the Phillips curve for a developing country. *R. E. Studies* 40 (April 1973) 203-224.

Morley, J. Prices, wages, unemployment and inflation. *ILRR* 108 (October 1973) 329-343.

Mortensen, D. Job search, the duration of unemployment and the Phillips curve. *AER* 60 (December 1970) 847-862. Comment by P. Gayer and R. Goldfarb and reply 62 (September 1972) 714-719.

Packer, A. and S. Park. Distortions in relative wages and shifts in the Phillips curve. *R. E. Stats*. 55 (February 1973) 16-22.

Parker, M. Incomes policy: some further results on the determination of the rate of change of money wages. *Economica* 37 (November 1970) 384-401.

Perry, G. Determinants of wage inflation around the world. *BPEA* (No. 2, 1975) 403-448.

Perry, G. Inflation versus unemployment: the worsening trade-off. *MLR* 94 (February 1971) 68-71.

Perry, G. *Unemployment, Money Wage Rates and Inflation*. Cambridge, Mass.: M.I.T. Press, 1966.

Perry, G.I. The determinants of wage rate changes and the inflation-unemployment trade-offs for the United States. *R. E. Studies* 31 (October 1964) 287-308.

Phelps, E. Money-wage dynamics and the labor-market equilibrium. *JPE* 76 (July/August 1968) 678-711.

Phelps, E. Phillips curves, expectations of inflation and optional unemployment over time. *Economica* 34 (August 1967) 254-281.

Phillips, A. The relation between unemployment and the rate of change of money wage rates in the United Kingdom, 1861-1957. *Economica* 25 (November 1958) 283-299. Comment by G. Routh 36 (1959) 299-315.

Pierson, G. The effect of union strength and the U.S. Phillips curve. *AER* 58 (June 1968) 456-467.

Raynauld, A. Relations d'arbitrage et politique économique. *RI/IR* 28 (No. 1, 1973) 1-16.

Rees, A. The Phillips curve as a menu for policy choice. *Economica* 37 (August 1970) 227-238.

Rees, A. and M. Hamilton. Post-war movements of wage levels and unit labor costs. *The Journal of Law and Economics* 5 (October 1963) 41-68.

Rees, A. and M. Hamilton. The wage-price-productivity perplex. *JPE* 75 (February 1967) 63-70.

Reid, F. and N. Meltz. Causes of shifts in the unemployment-vacancy relationship. *R. E. Stats.* 61 (August 1979) 470-475.

Reuber, G. Wage adjustments in Canadian industry. *R. E. Studies* 37 (October 1970) 449-468.

Reuber, G. The objectives of Canadian monetary policy, 1941-1961. *JPE* 72 (April 1964) 109-132.

Robb, A.L. and W. Scarth. Wage inflation and the distribution of unemployment. *RI/IR* 29 (No. 2, 1974) 332-340.

Ross, S. and M. Wachter. Wage determination, inflation and the industrial structure. *AER* 63 (September 1973) 675-692.

Rowley, J. and D. Wilton. *The Determination of Wage Change Relationships.* Ottawa: Economic Council of Canada, 1977.

Rowley, J. and D. Wilton. Quarterly models of wage determinants. *QJE* 88 (November 1974) 671-680.

Rowley, J. and D. Wilton. Empirical foundations for the Canadian Phillips curve. *CJE* 7 (May 1974) 240-259.

Rowley, J. and D. Wilton. Quarterly models of wage determination: some new efficient estimates. *AER* 63 (June 1973) 380-389.

Rowley, J. and D. Wilton. Wage determination: the use of instrumental assumptions. *IER* 14 (June 1973) 525-529.

Salop, S. Systematic job search and unemployment. *R. E. Studies* 40 (1973) 191-201.

Sawyer, J. *Macroeconomics: Theory and Policy in the Canadian Economy.* Toronto: Macmillan, 1975, Chap. 13.

Sculley, G. Static vs. dynamic Phillips curves. *R. E. Stats.* 61 (August 1974) 387-389.

Sellakaerts, W. and M. Chossudovsky. A comparison of optional and actual policies for high employment and price stability under external inflational conditions: the Canadian experience. *SEJ* 41 (October 1974) 206-214.

Siebert, C. and M. Zaidi. The short-run wage-price mechanism in U.S. manufacturing. *WEJ* 9 (September 1971) 278-88.

Smith, Douglas. Labour market institutions and inflation. *BJIR* 14 (March 1976) 35-42.

Smith, Douglas. Wage linkages between Canada and the United States. *ILRR* 29 (January 1976) 258-268.

Smyth, D. Unemployment and inflation: a cross-country analysis of the Phillips curve. *AER* 61 (June 1971) 426-429.

Soffer, B. The effects of recent long-term wage agreements on general wage level movements: 1950-1957. *QJE* 73 (February 1959) 36-60.

Sparks, G. and D. Wilton. Determinants of negotiated wage increases. *Econometrica* 39 (September 1971) 739-750.

Swan, N. and D. Wilton (eds.). *Inflation and the Canadian Experience.*

Kingston: Industrial Relations Centre, Queen's University, 1971.

Swidinsky, R. Trade unions and the rate of change of money wages in Canada, 1953-1970. *ILRR* 25 (April 1972) 363-375.

Taylor, J. Staggered wage setting in a macro model. *AER Proceedings* 69 (May 1979) 108-113.

Taylor, J. Hidden unemployment, hoarded labor and the Phillips curve. *SEJ* 37 (July 1970) 1-16.

Thomas, R. and P. Stoney. A note on the dynamic properties of the Hines inflation model. *R. E. Studies* 37 (April 1970) 286-294.

Toyoda, T. Price expectations and the short-run and long- run Phillips curves in Japan, 1956-1968. *R. E. Stats.* 54 (August 1972) 267-274.

Turner, H.A. and D. Jackson. On the determination of the general wage level - a world analysis. *EJ* 80 (December 1970) 827-849. Comment by J. Knight and R. Mabro and reply 82 (June 1972) 677-693, and an interchange 83 (June 1973) 520-526.

Turnovsky, S. The expectations hypothesis and aggregate wage equation: empirical evidence for Canada. *Economica* 39 (February 1972) 1-17.

Vanderkamp, J. Wage adjustment, productivity and price change expectations. *R. E. Studies* 39 (January 1972) 61-72.

Vanderkamp, J. The Phillips relation: a theoretical explanation - a comment. *Economica* 35 (1968) 179-184.

Vanderkamp, J. Wage and price level determination: an empirical model for Canada. *Economica* 33 (May 1966) 194-218.

Vrooman, W. Manufacturing wage behavior with special reference to the period 1962-1970. *R. E. Stats.* 52 (May 1970) 160-167.

Wachter, M. The changing cyclical responsiveness of wage inflation. *BJIR* (No. 1, 1976) 115-168.

Watanabe, T. Price changes and the rate of changes of money wage earnings in Japan, 1955-1962. *QJE* 80 (February 1966) 31-47.

Waud, R. Inflation, unemployment, and economic welfare. *AER* 60 (September 1970) 631-644. Comment by G. Tullock and reply 62 (December 1972) 1004-1006.

Wiles, P. Cost inflation and the state of economic theory. *EJ* (June 1973) 377-398.

Williamson, J. Phillips curves, expectations of inflation and optimal unemployment over time: comment. *Economica* 25 (1968) 283-287.

Wise, D. Labor force composition and the Phillips curve. *EI* 13 (June 1975) 297-302.

Zaidi, M. Unemployment, vacancies and conditions of excess demand for labour in Canada. *Applied Economics* 2 (1970) 101-112.

Zaidi, M. The determination of money wage rate changes and unemployment-inflation "trade-offs" in Canada. *IER* 10 (June 1969) 207-219.

B.　Wage-Price Guidelines and Incomes Policy

Ackley, G. Observations on phase II price and wage controls. *BPEA* (No. 1, 1972) 173-190.

Anton, F. *Wages and Productivity: The New Equation.* Toronto: Copp Clark, 1969.

Auld, D., L. Christophides, R. Swidinsky and D. Wilton. The impact of the Anti Inflation Board on negotiated wage settlements. *CJE* 12 (May 1979) 195-213.

Bailey, M. Contract theory and the moderation of inflation by recession and by controls. *BPEA* (No. 3, 1976) 585-634.

Bosworth, B. Phase II: the U.S. experiment with an incomes policy. *BPEA* (No. 2, 1972) 343-384.

Brunner, K. and A. Meltzer (eds.). *The Economics of Price and Wage Controls.* New York: North-Holland, 1976.

Christian, J. Bargaining function and the effectiveness of the wage-price guideposts. *SEJ* 37 (July 1970) 51-65.

Clegg, H. *How to Run an Income Policy.* London: Heinemann, 1971.

Cluff, A. The cyclical behavior of labor productivity: implications for an incomes policy. *Quarterly Review of Economics and Business* 12 (Autumn 1972) 35-43.

Crispo, J. (ed.). *Wages, Prices, Profits and Economic Policy.* Toronto: University of Toronto Press, 1968.

Feige, E. and D. Pearce. The wage-price control experiment—Did it work? *Challenge* (July/August 1973) 40-44.

Ferguson, C. Wages, productivity and the guidelines. *ER* 47 (June 1971) 217-229.

Feidler, E. The price-wage stabilization program. *BPEA* (No. 1, 1972) 199-210.

Goodwin, C. (ed.). *Exhortion and Controls: The Search for a Wage-Price Policy, 1945-1971.* Washington: Brookings Institution, 1975.

Gordon, R.J. The response of wages and prices to the first two years of controls. *BPEA* (No. 3, 1973) 765-779.

Gordon, R.J. Wage-price controls and the shifting Phillips curve. *BPEA* (No. 2, 1972) 385-421.

Haythorne, G. Prices and incomes policy: the Canadian experience. *ILR* 108 (December 1973) 485-503.

Hunter, L. British incomes policy, 1972-1974. *ILRR* 29 (October 1975) 67-84.

Jefferson, C., K. Sams and D. Swann. The control of incomes and prices in the United Kingdom, 1964-1967: policy and experience. *CJE* 1 (May 1968) 269-294.

Kaliski, S. and D. Smith. Inflation, unemployment and incomes policy. *CJE* 6 (November 1973) 574-591.

Lerner, A. Employment theory and employment policy. *AER* 57 (May 1967) 1-18.

Lipsey, R. and J. Parkin. Income policy: a reappraisal. *Economica* 37 (May 1970) 115-138.

McKee, A. Wage-price guidelines —Canada's approach. *Review of Social Economy* 30 (March 1972) 14-29.

Mitchell, D. Phase II wage controls. *ILRR* 27 (April 1974) 351-375.

Mitchell, D. Incomes policy and the labour market in France. *ILRR* 25 (April 1972) 315-335.

Mitchell, D. British incomes policy, the competitive effect, and the 1967 devaluation. *SEJ* 37 (July 1970) 88-92.

Mitchell, D. A simplified approach to income policy. *ILRR* 22 (July 1969) 512-527.

Nowlan, D. On wage-price guidelines. *CJE* 1 (August 1968) 644-647.

Perry G. Controls and income shares. *BPEA* (No. 1, 1972) 191-194.

Perry, G. Wages and the guideposts. *AER* 57 (September 1967) 897-904. Comments by P. Anderson, M. Wachter and A. Throop and reply 59 (June 1969) 351-369.

Pitchford, J. The usefulness of the average-productivity wage adjustment rule. *ER* 47 (June 1971) 226-255.

Reid, F. The effect of controls on the rate of wage change in Canada. *CJE* 12 (May 1979) 214-227.

Reid, F. *An Analysis of U.S. Wage Controls and Implications for Canada.* Anti Inflation Board Report. Ottawa: Supply and Services, 1978.

Reid, F. The response of wages to the removal of controls: the American experience. *RI/IR* 32 (No. 4, 1977) 621-628.

Reid, F. Canadian wage and price controls. *CPP* 2 (Winter 1976) 104-113.

R. E. Stats. Symposium: the future of U.S. wage-price policy. 54 (August 1972) 213-231.

Robinson, D. Implementing an incomes policy. *IR* 8 (October 1968) 73-90.

Sheahan, J. *The Wage-Price Guideposts.* Washington: Brookings Institution, 1967.

Shultz, G. and R. Aliber (eds.). *Guidelines, Informal Controls and the Market Place.* Chicago: University of Chicago Press, 1966.

Smith, D. *Incomes Policies: Some Foreign Experiences and their Relevance for Canada.* Special Study No. 4. Ottawa: Economic Council of Canada, 1966.

Sturmthal, A. Incomes policies in the light of international experience: further comments. *RI/IR* 23 (April 1968) 221-233.

Sturmthal, A. European experiences with incomes policy. *IRRA* (December 1966) 106-149.

Ulman, L. Wage-price policies: some lessons from abroad. *IR* 8 (May 1969) 195-213.

Ulman, L. and R. Flanagan. *Wage Restraint: a Study of Incomes Policies in Western Europe.* Berkeley: University of California Press, 1971.

Wallack, S. Wage-price guidelines and the rate of wage changes in U.S.

manufacturing, 1951-1966. *SEJ* 32 (July 1971) 33-47.

Wallis, K. Wages, prices and incomes policy: some comments. *Economica* 38 (August 1971) 304-310.

Zaidi, M. Inflation, employment and incomes policy. *International Journal of Social Economics* 1 (No. 2, 1974).

Chapter 18

Unemployment

With the possible exception of the Consumer Price Index, no single aggregate statistic gets as much attention as our unemployment rate. In spite of this importance, there is not a great deal of knowledge about what is meant by our unemployment figures. How are they measured? What are the different types of unemployment and how can they be cured, if they should be cured? How useful is the summary statistic of an aggregate unemployment rate? Are there alternative or complementary measures? These questions are the focus of this chapter.

WAYS OF MEASURING UNEMPLOYED

In Canada, measurement of the unemployed can be obtained from the Labour Force Survey, the Census, or from the number of registrants or claimants in the Unemployment Insurance Commission. While there are these alternative measures, and different ones can be useful for different purposes, the unemployment measure according to the Labour Force Survey is the one that receives the most attention: it is the one that is so often quoted by the press and utilized for general policy purposes.

Labour Force Survey

As indicated in the section on defining the labour force in Chapter 4 on Labour Force Participation, the Labour Force Survey in Canada is conducted monthly by Statistics Canada. According to the Revised Labour Force Survey, utilized since January, 1976, people are categorized as unemployed if they did not have work but they were available for and actively seeking work. In their thorough discussion of the old and new Labour Force Surveys, Ostry and Zaidi (1979, pp. 4-8) indicate some minor exceptions to this general principle. For example, the unemployed also includes persons who were available for work but who were not seeking work because they were on lay-off for six months or less, or they had a new job to start within four weeks. Nevertheless, the general principle remains: to be counted as unemployed, one has to be available for and actively seeking work. That is, in general circumstances, it is necessary to engage in active job search to be classified as unemployed.

Persons are categorized as employed if they did any work for pay or profit, including unpaid work on a family farm or business, or if they normally had a job but were not at work because of such factors as bad weather, illness, industrial dispute, or vacation. The employed plus the unemployed make up the labour force, and the unemployment rate is defined as the number of unemployed divided by the labour force.

Census

The Canadian Census, conducted every ten years since 1871, also provides information on the unemployed, at least since 1921. Rather than being based on a sample of the population, the Census is based on the whole relevant population, with detailed information coming from approximately one-third of this population. Consequently Census data is more comprehensive and provides detailed information on such factors as unemployment by industry, and occupation, as well as a wealth of demographic and economic information on the respondents. For this reason the Census data has proven useful in detailed statistical and econometric analysis of labour market behaviour. However, as our earlier discussion on defining the labour force indicated in Chapter 4, the usefulness of the Census data is limited by the fact that it is conducted only once every ten years and its reliability on labour force issues may be questioned because of the fact that it covers so many issues in addition to labour force activity.

As indicated by Statistics Canada, *Background Information on the 1971 Census Labour Force Data*, a comparison of the methodologies and results of the Census with the Labour Force Survey conducted at the same time illustrates some interesting findings with respect to the nature of the questionnaire and the accompanying responses. While the overall participation and unemployment rates were not too dissimilar, for females the Census unemployment rate was 8.9 per cent compared to the corresponding Labour Force Survey rate of only 5.0 per cent. This discrepancy occurred because the Census question was direct and suggestive with respect to search activity, asking if the person looked for work, for example, by contacting a Canada Manpower Centre or newspaper. This suggestiveness with respect to search activity may have prompted many women who really weren't looking for work to respond that they did look for work (and therefore are classified as unemployed), perhaps because they checked some want ads in the paper. Hence, the high female unemployment rate in the Census. The Labour Force Survey question, on the other hand, was more indirect and suggestive with respect to non-search activity, asking what the person did most of the week: for example, looked for work, or kept house. By specifically suggesting "kept house" as an alternative, the Labour Force Survey may have encouraged some women who actually looked for work (and hence should be included in the unemployed) to give the socially acceptable response of having kept house, thereby being counted as outside of the labour force rather than unemployed. Hence the lower female unemployment rate, according to the Labour Force Survey.

Which is correct? The Labour Force Survey probably undercounted by missing females who were marginally attached to the labour force and who were looking for work, even if only in a casual fashion. The Census probably overstated the number of unemployed females by including some who really weren't looking for work. Hopefully the new Labour Force Survey in current use will give a more accurate picture, since it asks a chain of questions that should put its results with respect to females in between those of the old Labour Force Survey and the Census; that is, the new questions do not immediately ask if the person kept house, nor do they prod the respondent by immediately suggesting a variety of search activities.

Unemployment Insurance Claimants

A third data source — unemployment insurance claimants — can be used to obtain estimates of the unemployed. However, these estimates are not commonly available and they are not the figures that one finds so often quoted in the press or utilized for general policy purposes. Comparisons of the number of unemployed according to unemployment insurance figures versus Labour Force Survey figures are given in Naemark (1973) and Cook, Jump, Hodgins and Szabo (1976).

While the number of unemployed according to the Labour Force Survey may be similar to the number claiming unemployment insurance or registered in an unemployment insurance office, the two series need not be similar. The number of unemployment insurance claimants may exceed the Labour Force Survey number because some people may be collecting unemployment insurance but not actively seeking work. These people could range from persons on maternity leave who are legally entitled to collect unemployment insurance, to persons who traditionally do seasonal work and collect unemployment insurance for part of the year, to outright cheaters who simply don't bother looking or who may even be working illegally. Such persons may be collecting unemployment insurance, but they need not indicate that they are actively seeking work to the confidential Labour Force Survey questionnaire.

On the other hand, the number of unemployed according to the Labour Force Survey could exceed the number of unemployment insurance claimants. New job seekers, for example, may not be eligible, or the long-term unemployed may have exhausted their benefit period. Some may not be covered by unemployment insurance; others may not register because then they would have to accept a job. They (or their parents who are often the respondents) may still indicate on a Labour Force Survey questionnaire that they are actively seeking work.

Clearly the two series need not move together since they indicate somewhat different things. Because, from a policy perspective, what is wanted is an indicator of the number of persons who are available for work and actively seeking work, then the Labour Force Survey figures are the ones that are commonly used.

TYPES OF UNEMPLOYMENT

Assuming that the Labour Force Survey figures give an accurate portrayal of the number of unemployed who truly are available for and actively seeking work, we can categorize this amount of unemployment according to its proximate cause. Since there are various causes, there are various types of unemployment, the usual categories being frictional, structural, demand deficient, seasonal, and insurance induced. Each of these will be discussed in turn, with an emphasis on illustrating the main characteristics of each type of unemployment rather than on providing a rigorous definition. As will become evident in the ensuing discussion, the distinctions are often not clear-cut, either conceptually or practically.

Frictional Unemployment

Frictional unemployment can be thought of as unemployment that would prevail even in a well-functioning labour market. It results even if jobs and workers are matched in the sense that workers are qualified and willing to fill the jobs; they simply have to be brought together. For this reason, frictional unemployment is often associated with job search activity within a given labour market. As such, it may be of short duration, but optimal search may go on for a long period of time if the unemployed are younger persons with a low opportunity cost of time and a long expected benefit period from which to recoup the costs of search, and if the cost of job search is reduced by unemployment insurance benefits.

Frictional unemployment may coexist with unfilled vacancies in the same labour market. In fact one possible definition of frictional unemployment is the amount of unemployment that corresponds to the number of vacancies that could be filled by the unemployed in an individual labour market. (See, for example, Vanderkamp, 1968.) That is, in an individual labour market, if labour supply is defined as employed plus unemployed (working or looking), and labour demand is defined as employed plus vacancies, then when there is no excess demand or supply (supply equals demand), the number of unemployed equals the number of job vacancies. These unemployed could fill the vacancies by the definition of their being in the individual labour market. This frictional unemployment, equal to the number of vacancies, exists even though the individual labour market is in equilibrium in the sense that labour supply equals demand.

An alternative way to view frictional unemployment is to regard it as unemployment that is optimal in the sense that it has been reduced until the social cost of reducing it is no longer worth the social benefits. (See, for example, Lipsey, 1965.) Such frictional unemployment should not be reduced any further; it is a sign that the labour market is operating efficiently, given the fact that matching job seekers with job vacancies is a costly process. If the benefits of reducing the unemployment were worth the costs, broadly defined to include social as well as private benefits and costs, then the unemployment would be categorized as structural.

Structural Unemployment

Structural unemployment results when the skills or location of the unemployed are not matched with the characteristics of the job vacancies. Workers and vacancies are considered to be in different labour markets, either by virtue of geography or because they are not matched with respect to qualifications and characteristics. The analogy that is often used is that of matching square pegs to round holes. Proposed solutions to structural unemployment usually involve improving the human capital characteristics of the workers by education or training programs, or improving the job matching process itself by mobility, labour market information, or job search. They could also include adapting the characteristics of the jobs themselves by altering entrance requirements, rearranging the basic job components to adapt to changing available skills, and even job enrichment and job enlargement.

The distinction between frictional and structural unemployment can be blurred conceptually, and in practice it can be difficult to clearly delineate the two. Nevertheless, there are differences in degree if not in kind. Frictional unemployment is a result of the matching process; structural unemployment occurs when there is mismatching. Frictional unemployment is associated with job search in an individual labour market; structural unemployment involves more costly solutions, ranging from retraining for a job within the individual labour market to job search and relocation in other labour markets. Frictional unemployment can be regarded as optimal in that the cost of reducing it just equals the benefits; structural unemployment implies that the benefits exceed the cost and that therefore it should be reduced until it is only frictional. What the two have in common is that they are related to the characteristics of the workers and the job, not to the general state of aggregate demand in the economy. Even here, though, the distinction between demand deficient unemployment and non-demand deficient unemployment (frictional, structural) may become blurred as the characteristics of the work-force and of jobs themselves may be related to the aggregate state of the economy.

Demand Deficient Unemployment

Demand deficient unemployment exists when there is insufficient aggregate demand in the economy to provide jobs. It is not a matter of workers engaging in normal job search or lacking the correct skills or being in the wrong labour market; rather it is a matter of insufficient aggregate demand to generate sufficient job vacancies. Therefore, job vacancies would fall short of the number of unemployed job seekers. That is, defining labour supply as employed plus unemployed and labour demand as employed plus vacancies, then insufficient demand, defined as being less than supply, would imply vacancies being less than the number unemployed.

Demand deficient unemployment is usually associated with adverse business cycle conditions; hence, the term cyclical unemployment is often used. However, it may also be associated with a chronic (as opposed to short-term cyclical) insufficiency of aggregate demand as occurred, for example, in the Great Depression of the 1930s. Since the cause of such unemployment is a deficiency of aggregate demand, its cures usually involve macroeconomic policies to increase consumption, investment, exports, or government spending, or to decrease imports and taxes. Monetary, fiscal, and exchange rate policies are the traditional macroeconomic instruments.

Seasonal Unemployment

Seasonal unemployment is often associated with insufficient demand in a particular season. In this sense it can be considered as demand deficient unemployment; nevertheless, it is different in the sense that it is not a shortage of *aggregate* demand from the economy as a whole, but rather a shortage of demand in a particular season. The patterns are usually predictable over the year and specific to particular industries. For example, seasonal unemployment is usually heavy in the winter months in construction, agriculture and the tourist trade.

To a certain extent seasonal unemployment may also have a structural component to it in the sense that many of the seasonal jobs could be adapted to employ more people over the slow season. Some construction jobs could be modified so as to be more continuous throughout the year. Tourist facilities can likewise adapt, for example, as winter ski areas become summer schools in other sports or crafts. A structural component to seasonal unemployment is also exhibited by the fact that in some industries like agriculture, migrant labour often moves to other labour markets, following the seasonal patterns of demand.

Clearly the fact that such adaptation of jobs and workers can and does go on illustrates that seasonal unemployment is not immutable. It is related to the costs and benefits of reducing such unemployment, and the private market will respond to changes in these costs and benefits. To the extent, for example, that the cost to employers and employees of seasonal unemployment is reduced by the availability of unemployment insurance benefits, then one may expect more seasonal unemployment. Again, the types of unemployment—in this case seasonal and insurance induced—can be difficult to distinguish.

Aggregate unemployment rates are often referred to as seasonally adjusted or unadjusted. The seasonally unadjusted figures simply show the unemployment rate as it is in a particular month, unadjusted for seasonal fluctuations. The seasonally adjusted figures show the unemployment rate that would have prevailed had the particular month not been associated with unusually high or low seasonal demand conditions. Those who are seasonally unemployed are not *removed* from the figures; they are simply averaged in over the year.

Insurance Induced Unemployment

Another category of unemployment — that which is induced by unemployment insurance — has become of increased policy concern, especially in recent years. Chapter 3 on the work incentive effects of alternative income maintenance schemes dealt with the work incentive effects of changes in unemployment insurance. The static, partial equilibrium, work-leisure choice framework indicated that both the income and substitution effects would theoretically reduce incentives to work. That is, potential recipients may be able to afford non-work activities (income effect) and their returns to work are reduced (substitution effect), because as they work they contribute to the unemployment insurance fund and they forgo the opportunity to collect unemployment insurance.

Some who collect the unemployment insurance may not be actually seeking work (and hence may not be recorded in our unemployment figures); nevertheless, many may engage in longer periods of job search, waiting for a better job or not accepting the first job that comes along. In this sense unemployment insurance is often regarded as adding to frictional unemployment.

This process, however, may also have longer-run implications for structural and demand deficient unemployment. In particular, if the period of unemployment is used for human capital formation such as increased training or mobility to another labour market, then it may reduce future structural unemployment. In addition, to the extent that unemployment insurance acts as a built-in stabilizer — taking in large contributions during periods of low unemployment and transferring purchasing power to the unemployed during periods of high unemployment — it may also reduce demand deficient unemployment.

Empirical evidence in Canada indicates that some of our unemployment can be attributed to the availability of unemployment insurance and that some of the recent increase in our unemployment rate can be attributed to the 1971 liberalization of the Unemployment Insurance Act. These changes — discussed in Cook, Jump, Hodgins and Szabo (1976, Chapter 5) — basically involved increased coverage, liberalized eligibility, increased duration and amount of benefits, and the making of benefits taxable and contributions tax deductible.

While their data base and methodology are different, the following studies provide estimates of the percentage point increase in Canada's unemployment rate that are attributed to the 1971 *changes* in the Unemployment Insurance Act: .8, (Grubel, Maki, and Sax (1975, p. 187)); .4 to .7, (Green and Cousineau (1976, p. 114)); .74, (Siedule, Skoules, Newton (1976, p.22)); .7, (Rea (1977, p. 277)); and 1.9, (Reid and Meltz (1979)). In addition, these studies by Grubel, Maki and Sax (1975), Green and Cousineau (1976), and Rea (1977) provide estimates of the *total* impact of unemployment insurance in 1972 (that is, the difference between a situation of unemployment insurance and a hypothetical one with no unemployment insurance) that are approximately twice the impact of the 1971 changes. As these authors indicate, however, such estimates should be taken with caution because it is difficult to predict the hypothetical alternative situation of no unemployment insurance. Dennis Maki (1975, p. 398) also provides regional estimates of the impact of the 1971 revisions to the Unemployment Insurance Act on regional unemployment rates ranging from 0.2 percentage points in Ontario to 1.6 percentage points in the Atlantic Region and British Columbia, with Quebec and the Prairies in between at 0.8 and 1.1 respectively.

While there is considerable variation in the estimates of the total impact of unemployment insurance and of the 1971 changes in the legislation, there is substantial agreement that the impact is positive and that the changes did raise our unemployment rate relative to what it would have been without the legislation. More specifically, the actual unemployment rate of 6.3 per cent in 1972 would have been around 5.6 per cent (utilizing the typical estimated impact of .7 found in many of the studies), and perhaps even lower if the larger estimates of the impact were used. This does not make these changes in unemployment insurance undesirable: it simply points out that the changes affected our aggregate unemployment rate and that this should be considered in interpreting this statistic.

UNEMPLOYMENT RATE AS A SUMMARY STATISTIC

Much of the previous discussion suggests that the unemployment rate may not be telling all that we think it tells us, or perhaps used to tell us, about such things as the aggregate state of the economy, the extent to which the labour market is in equilibrium, the tightness or looseness of the labour market, or the extent of hardship in the population. It is not that the unemployment rate is wrong; rather it may be asking too much of a *single* measure to indicate all these things, especially when dramatic demographic changes have occurred in the labour force and institutional changes have occurred in such things as our unemployment insurance.

There are reasons to suggest that the unemployment rate may *understate* the degree of hardship and loss in the economy, and there are reasons to suggest that it may *overstate* the hardship and loss. For these reasons, complementary indicators have been suggested to supplement the aggregate unemployment rate.

Elements Understating Hardship and Loss

The reported unemployment rate may understate what could be labelled a true unemployment rate because it does not indicate the *hidden unemployed*. The hidden unemployed could include discouraged workers who gave up looking for work and who would therefore be counted as not in the labour force, as they engaged in such activities as household work, early retirement, or even school. As our early discussion of labour force participation indicated, discouraged workers were those who dropped out of the labour force in periods or places of high unemployment. In addition, the hidden unemployed may even include people who drop out of the population that is being surveyed. For example, to the extent that crime increases during periods of high unemployment, these people may be engaging in (unreported) criminal work, or if apprehended they may be in criminal institutions. In neither case would they be part of the labour force. Or, to the extent that vagrancy increases in times of high unemployment, these people usually would not be considered part of the population that is surveyed. Our unemployment figures do not reflect the loss or hardship of these hidden or disguised unemployed.

In addition, our aggregate unemployment figures by themselves do not indicate the extent to which some workers have added themselves to the labour market to maintain a declining family income associated with a high unemployment rate. In other words, it does not indicate the loss of household production or the loss of education on the part of these added workers who may be compelled by the high employment rate to leave the household or educational institutions or early retirement.

Nor does the aggregate unemployment rate capture the fact that many employed people may be involuntarily employed only part-time. People are recorded as employed if they did *any* work during the survey reference period. The fact that some may want to do more work is not reflected.

In addition, a high unemployment rate by itself does not indicate the degree of hardship associated with the fact that most measures of income inequality are greater during periods of high unemployment. Hollister and Palmer (1972) and Maslove and Rowley (1975), for example, indicate that the poor, more than the non-poor, are adversely affected by high unemployment even if this means reduced inflation. On the labour market side this can occur for a variety of reasons: the poor are most likely to be unemployed; secondary workers from poor families are more likely to drop out of the labour force; the wages of the poor fall the most or rise the slowest; and their hours of work are reduced during periods of high unemployment. The unemployment rate by itself does not reflect the fact that poverty is exacerbated in periods of high unemployment.

These various factors suggest that the unemployment rate may understate the true loss and hardship in the economy. In addition, to the extent that these factors worsen in periods of high unemployment — hidden unemployment, the number of added workers, involuntary part-time employment, and poverty all increase — then this underestimate and loss is most severe in periods of high unemployment, when conditions already are severe.

Elements Overstating Hardship and Loss

There are reasons to believe, however, that the unemployment rate may be overstating the degree of hardship and loss in our economy, especially relative to the situation in the 1950s and early 1960s. Many of these reasons hinge on the fact that our unemployment increasingly has fallen on younger workers and married women, and for a variety of reasons there is a belief — held by some, but not all — that the hardship and loss associated with such unemployment is not as severe as that which is associated with the unemployment of males in families where only the male otherwise works.

Increasingly our unemployed consist of females and younger workers, as they have expanded their participation in labour force activities and increasingly are subject to a high incidence or likelihood of being unemployed. (See, for example, Ostry and Zaidi, 1979, pp. 153-4.) The unemployment rate of middle-aged males, on the other hand, has not changed dramatically over the 1950s, 1960s and 1970s, tending to be in the neighbourhood of 4 per cent. To the extent that younger workers and women have alternative sources of income to rely upon, and to the extent that the economic well-being of the family is more dependent upon the employment of males, then there is the possibility that the economic hardship associated with a given unemployment rate is not as great now as when males dominated the labour market. This perspective, of course, can be challenged — and probably will be challenged increasingly — as the participation of women in labour market activities and their contribution to family income becomes regarded as permanent rather than secondary. Nevertheless, under current circumstances, the possibility remains that the economic hardship, at least as far as the family is concerned, is not as great when the wife or a younger member is unemployed, as when the husband is unemployed. As a more general proposition, with the growing proportion of families where *both* the husband and wife work, the unemployment of *either* may result in less hardship than when males tended to dominate the labour market and became unemployed.

This possibility of reduced hardship is buttressed by the fact that many of the unemployed may be looking for part-time jobs. This would be the case especially for married women who also maintain prime responsibility for household tasks. It may also be the case for students who go to school part-time. One may also expect an increase in frictional unemployment associated with the optimal job search of the growing number of younger workers in the labour market. Lengthy job search may be perfectly rational on their part, given their lower opportunity cost of time, and long benefit period from which to recoup these costs, and possible support from family income. The hardship associated with being unemployed may also be reduced, or at least cushioned, by the increased availability of more liberal unemployment insurance benefits.

These possibilities are not meant to play down the hardship associated with being unemployed. It is a serious loss to the economy and more importantly to the individuals and families involved. Nevertheless it is important to be aware that a six percent unemployment rate in the mid 1970s probably would not inflict the hardship that an *identical* rate would have inflicted on families in the mid 1950s. Whether an average unemployment rate of over six percent in the 1970s inflicts more hardship than an average rate of slightly over five percent in the 1960s, or four percent in the 1950s, remains an open question.

COMPLEMENTARY MEASURES

Because of these problems associated with a single aggregate unemployment estimate, some have suggested using complementary measures. In general, these measures are suggested to supplement rather than replace the information contained in the aggregate unemployment rate estimate. These measures include, for example, such things as disaggregate unemployment figures, supplementary information, hardship indices, and sub-employment indices.

Disaggregate unemployment figures simply involve reporting unemployment rates for various sub-groups, for example, prime working-age males, females, younger workers, or new entrants into the labour force. While such estimates are readily available from the Labour Force Survey, and they are published, they tend not to get much public attention nor to be portrayed by the media.

Supplementary information would also be useful on such factors as the degree of job search by the unemployed, the extent to which they are looking for part-time work, the duration of their unemployment, and the reasons they may have given up looking for work. Such information is increasingly available, especially from the Revised Labour Force Survey since 1976; nevertheless, it tends not to get wide publicity to the general public.

Hardship indices are also possible. To the extent that the unemployment of younger workers or married women is regarded as not inflicting as much hardship as the unemployment of married men, one way to construct such an index is to use weights that involve a lower emphasis for youths or married women. Weighing the unemployed by the average *wage* of their peer group, for example, would give more weight to married men since they tend to have higher wages. To the extent that wages are a proxy for the economic loss to the economy, the weighting would also reflect these differential losses.

While such a weighing scheme may reflect the differential hardship or loss, it is certainly not without its problems. It would imply, for example, that low wage disadvantaged workers or females who are discriminated against would receive a lower weight in the hardship index. This may be perverse, for example, if one feels that hardship is minimized if it is shared. In such circumstances one would want to weight inversely to wages to reflect the compound hardship of a low wage individual also being unemployed. Clearly the appropriate weight for hardship is not related to wages in a simple fashion. It is true that the family hardship may not be severe if a young worker with a low potential wage is unemployed; but it may be very severe if a mother in a single-headed family, also with a low potential wage, is unemployed.

Sub-employment indices of various kinds also have been proposed. Sub-employment indices reflect that portion of the labour force that is sub-employed, usually defined to include not only the unemployed, but also discouraged workers, involuntary part-time workers, and full-time workers who do not earn some minimal income. Variations on this theme are possible. Levitan and Taggert (1974), for example, suggest an Employment and Earnings Inadequacy Index which excludes those in households of adequate family income, even though the earnings of one party may be low.

Computation of their index involves the following three steps: compute the sub-employed defined as unemployed plus discouraged workers plus involuntary part-time workers plus employed family heads whose earnings are less than an officially defined poverty level; exclude those in households with adequate family income (perhaps because of assets or income from other family members); and divide by the sum of the labour force and discouraged workers. Their calculations, based on U.S. data for March, 1972, imply an Earnings Inadequacy Index of 11.5 per cent, compared to an unemployment rate of 6 per cent and a sub-employment rate of 15 per cent.

These complementary measures are meant to be illustrative rather than exhaustive. Others are possible, and over time more will probably be proposed, implemented, and perhaps even utilized by the general public. The important point is that they are meant to supplement rather than to replace the aggregate unemployment rate as a measure of cyclical conditions, labour market disequilibrium, and economic loss and hardship.

QUESTIONS

1. (a) Discuss the various ways in which the number of unemployed typically are measured in Canada.
   (b) Which is the measure that receives the most publicity?
   (c) Discuss the strengths and weaknesses of the various measures.
2. Indicate some of the basic changes that were involved in the Revised Labour Force Survey of 1976 compared to the old Labour Force Survey in Canada.
3. The female unemployment rate according to the 1971 Census was

approximately nine per cent compared to a rate of approximately five per cent recorded by the Labour Force Survey for the same time.
   (a) Why?
   (b) Which is correct?
   (c) What does this imply about the importance of structuring questions for survey responses?

4. Indicate the main types of unemployment, their main causes, and the usual policies discussed to curb each type of unemployment.

5. Frictional unemployment is optimal. Discuss.

6. In the late 1950s and early 1960s there was considerable debate over the relative importance of structural versus demand deficient unemployment. Much of the debate waned during the relatively full employment period of the mid and late 1960s. What does this imply about the existence of structural unemployment?

7. There is some renewed interest in the issue of structural unemployment, associated with the demographic changes in the labour force, and with the high unemployment that has occurred even during periods of inflation. Discuss why this may be the case.

8. Why might the so-called *full-employment* unemployment rate have increased over time?

9. Why might we expect younger workers to have higher unemployment rates than older workers, and what does this imply about the changes in our aggregate unemployment rate over time?

10. Historically in Canada, female unemployment rates have been considerably lower than male unemployment rates; however, by the mid 1970s they began to exceed male rates.
   (a) Why might this be the case?
   (b) What does this imply about the time pattern of our aggregate unemployment rate?

11. Indicate some basic differences between frictional and structural unemployment. If possible, provide examples of when it may be unclear as to whether to categorize a worker as frictionally or structurally unemployed.

12. All unemployment can be categorized as frictional, structural, or demand deficient. Discuss.

13. (a) Indicate some of the uses for which our aggregate unemployment rates are often used.
   (b) Why might this single measure increasingly be inadequate for these purposes?
   (c) What are some of the alternatives and what are their strengths and weaknesses?

REFERENCES AND FURTHER READINGS

A. Unemployment

Annable, J. A theory of downward rigid wages and cyclical unemployment. *EI* 15 (July 1977) 326-349.

Azariadis, C. On the incidence of unemployment. *R. E. Studies* 43 (February 1976) 115-126.

Barber, C. Canada's unemployment problem. *CJE* 28 (February 1962) 88-102.

Barnes, W. Job search models, the duration of unemployment and the asking wage: some empirical evidence. *JHR* 10 (Spring 1975) 230-240.

Barrett, N. and R. Morgenstern. Why do blacks and women have high unemployment rates? *JHR* 9 (Fall 1974) 452-464.

Barrett, N. and B. Sodersten. Unemployment flows, welfare and labor market efficiency in Sweden and the U.S. *Swedish Economic Journal* 77 (September 1975).

Berman, B. Alternative measures of structural unemployment. *Employment Policy and the Labour Market*, A. Ross (ed.). Berkeley: University of California Press, 1965.

Bonin, J. and W. Davis. Estimated seasonal components in recorded unemployment in 1970. *ILRR* 25 (April 1972) 383-398.

Brigger, J. Unemployment statistics and what they mean. *MLR* 94 (November 1971) 22-29.

Bruce, C. and J. Marshall. Job search and frictional unemployment. *RI/IR* 31 (No. 3, 1976) 402-414.

Butler, A. Identifying structural unemployment. *ILRR* 20 (April 1967) 441-446.

Cook, P., G. Jump, C. Hodgins, and C. Szabo. *Economic Impact of Selected Government Programs Directed Toward the Labour Market*. Ottawa: Economic Council of Canada, 1976.

Cousineau, J. and C. Green. Structural unemployment in Canada: 1971-1974. Did it worsen? *RI/IR* 33 (No. 2, 1978) 175-192.

Cripps, T. and R. Tarling. An analysis of the duration of male unemployment in Great Britain: 1932-1973. *EJ* 84 (June 1974) 289-316.

Della Valle, P. and B. Meyer. Changes in relative female-male unemployment: a Canadian-United States comparison. *RI/IR* 31 (No. 3, 1976) 417-430.

Demsetz, H. Structural unemployment: a reconsideration of the evidence and the theory. *Journal of Law and Economics* 4 (October 1961) 80-92.

Denton, F. and S. Ostry. *An Analysis of Post-War Unemployment*. Staff Study No. 3, Economic Council of Canada. Ottawa: Queen's Printer, 1964.

Disney, R. Recurrent spells and the concentration of unemployment in Great Britain. *EJ* 89 (March 1979) 109-119.

Donner, A. Regional unemployment rates and total economic growth in Canada, 1953-1968. *RI/IR* 26 (August 1971) 721-725.

Donner, A. and F. Lazar. An econometric study of segmented labour markets and the structure of unemployment: the Canadian experience. *IER* 14 (June 1973) 312-327.

Eaton, R. and P. Neher. Unemployment, underemployment and optimal job search. *JPE* 83 (April 1975) 355-376.

Evans, G. A note on trends in the relationship between unemployment and unfilled vacancies. *EJ* 85 (March 1975) 135-139.

Fearn, R. Cyclical, seasonal and structural factors in area unemployment. *ILRR* 28 (April 1975) 424-431.

Federal Reserve Bank of New York. International comparability of unemployment statistics. *Monthly Review of the Federal Reserve Bank of New York* 43 (March 1961) 47-51.

Feinberg, R. Risk aversion, risk and the duration of unemployment. *R. E. Stats.* 59 (August 1977) 264-271.

Feldstein, M. The economics of the new unemployment. *Public Interest* 33 (Fall 1973) 3-42.

Feldstein, M. Temporary layoffs in the theory of unemployment. *JPE* 84 (October 1976) 937-958.

Fellegi, J., G. Gray and R. Platek. The new design of the Canadian labour force survey. *Journal of American Statistical Association* (1967) 421-454.

Flaim, P. Discouraged workers and changes in unemployment. *MLR* 96 (March 1973) 8-16.

Flanagan, R. The U.S. Phillips curve and international unemployment rate differentials. *AER* 63 (March 1973) 114-131. Comment by N. Barrett and reply 65 (March 1975) 225-231.

Friedman, B. and M. Wachter. Unemployment, Okuns law, labor force and productivity. *R. E. Stats.* 56 (May 1974) 167-176.

Gallaway, L. The full employment-unemployed rate: 1953-1980. *JHR* 5 (Fall 1970) 487-510.

Gallaway, L. Labour mobility, resource allocation and structural unemployment. *AER* 52 (September 1963) 694-716.

Gastworth, J. Estimating the number of hidden unemployment. *MLR* 96 (March 1973) 17-26.

Gilpatrick, E. *Structural Unemployment and Aggregate Demand*. Baltimore: Johns Hopkins Press, 1966.

Gilpatrick, E. On the classification of unemployment: a view of the structural inadequate demand debate. *ILRR* 19 (January 1966) 201-212.

Gilroy, C. Supplemental measures of labour force underutilization. *MLR* 98 (May 1975) 13-23.

Gilroy, C. and R. McIntire. Job losers, leavers and entrants: a cyclical analysis. *MLR* 97 (November 1974) 35-39.

Gordon, D. A neoclassical theory of Keynesian unemployment. *EI* 12 (December 1974) 431-459.

Gordon, R. Has structural unemployment worsened? *IR* 3 (May 1965) 53-77.

Gramlick, E. The distributional effects of higher unemployment. *BPEA* (No. 2, 1974) 293-342.

Green, C. Labour market performance from an employment perspective. *Canadian Public Policy* 3 (September 1977) 315-323. Comment by S. Kaliski 3 (Autumn 1977) 515-517.

Green, G. Comparing total and state insured unemployment. *MLR* 49 (June 1971) 37-48.

Gronan, R. Information and frictional unemployment. *AER* 61 (June 1971) 290-301.

Gruber, W. The use of labour force participation and unemployment rates as a test for structural difficulties. *IRRA* (December 1965) 220-232.

Gujarati, D. The behaviour of unemployment and unfilled vacancies. *EJ* 82 (March 1972) 195-204. Comment by J. Foster and reply 83 (March 1973) 192-202.

Hall, R. The rigidity of wages and the persistence of unemployment. *BPEA* (No. 2, 1975) 301-350.

Hall, R. Why is the unemployment rate so high at full employment? *BPEA* (No. 3, 1970) 369-402.

Hamermesh, D. A disaggregative econometric model of gross changes in employment. *Yale Economics Essays* 9 (Fall 1969) 107-145.

Hansen, B. Excess demand, unemployment, vacancies and wages. *QJE* 84 (February 1970) 1-23.

Hareman, R. Unemployment in Western Europe and the United States. *AER Proceedings* 68 (May 1978) 44-50.

Hartle, D. Seasonal unemployment in Canada, 1951-1957. *CJE* 24 (February 1958) 93-98.

Hollister, R. and J. Palmer. The implicit tax of inflation and unemployment. *Redistribution to the Rich and Poor*, K. Boulding and M. Pfaff (eds.). Belmont, Calif.: Woodsworth, 1972.

Hughes, J. The measurement of unemployment: an exercise in political economy. *IRJ* 7 (Winter 1976/77) 4-12.

Jones, E. The elusive concept of underemployment. *JHR* 6 (Fall 1971) 519-564.

Kaitz, H. Analysing the lengths of spells of unemployment. *MLR* 93 (November 1970) 11-20.

Kaliski, S. Structural unemployment in Canada: the occupational dimension. *CJE* 2 (May 1969) 250-267.

Kaliski, S. Structural unemployment in Canada: towards a definition of the geographic dimension. *CJE* (August 1968) 551-565.

Kaliski, S. Structural unemployment: a new stage in the debate. *Canadian Banker* (Autumn 1967) 72-77.

Katz, A. Schooling, age and length of unemployment. *ILRR* 27 (July 1974) 597-605.

Killingsworth, C. The continuing labor market twist. *MLR* 91 (September 1968) 12-17.

Killingsworth, C. The bottleneck in labour skills. *The Battle Against Unemployment*, A. Okun (ed.). New York: Norton and Co., 1965.

Kleiman, E. Measuring the structural severity of unemployment. *IR* 7 (February 1968) 146-159.

Lazar, F. Regional unemployment rate disparities in Canada. *CJE* 10 (February 1977) 112-129.

Lazar, F. and A. Donner. The dimension of Canadian youth unemployment: a theoretical explanation. *RI/IR* 28 (No. 2, 1973) 295-324.

Lebergoth, S. Annual estimates of unemployment in the United States, 1900-1954. *The Measurement and Behavior of Unemployment*. Princeton, N.J.: Princeton University Press, 1957.

Leigh, D. An empirical investigation of the determinants of the level of unemployment in six major occupations. *WEJ* 10 (December 1972) 384-395.

Leigh, D. and V. Rawlins. Racial differences in male unemployment rates. *R. E. Stats.* 56 (May 1974) 150-157.

Levitan, S. and R. Taggart. Employment earnings inadequacy. *MLR* 96 (October 1973) 19-27.

Levitan, S. and R. Taggart. *Employment and Earnings Inadequacy.* Baltimore: Johns Hopkins Press, 1974.

Lipsey, R. Structural and deficient demand unemployment re-considered. *Employment Policy and the Labour Market*, A. Ross (ed.). Berkeley: University of California Press, 1965, 210-255.

Lovell, M. The minimum wage, teenage unemployment and the business cycle. *WEJ* 10 (December 1972) 414-427.

Mackay, D. and G. Reid. Redundancy, unemployment and manpower policy. *EJ* (December 1972). Comment by T. Lancaster 86 (June 1976) 335-338.

Marston, S. Employment instability and high unemployment rates. *BPEA* (No. 1, 1976) 169-210.

Maslove, A. and J. Rowley. Inflation and redistribution. *CJE* 8 (August 1975) 399-409.

Mattila, J.P. Job quitting and frictional unemployment. *AER* 64 (March 1974) 235-239.

McGregor, A. Unemployment duration and the reemployment probability. *EJ* 88 (December 1978) 693-706.

Mehmet, O. A note on the disguised unemployment hypothesis. *Economia Internazionale* 24 (February 1971).

Mellow, W. Search costs and the duration of unemployment. *EI* 41 (July 1978) 423-430.

Melvyn, P. Youth unemployment in industrialized market economics. *ILR* 116 (July-August 1977) 23-38.

Metcalf, D. Urban unemployment in England. *EJ* 85 (September 1975) 578-589.

Miernyk, W. British and American approaches to structural unemployment. *ILRR* 12 (October 1958) 3-19.

Mincer, J. Determining the number of hidden unemployed. *MLR* 96 (March 1973) 27-30.

Monthly Labor Review. Measuring Unemployment. 102 (March 1979) 13-52.

Morgenstern, R. and N. Barrett. The retrospective bias in unemployment reporting by sex, race and age. *Journal of American Statistical Association* 69 (June 1974) 355-357.

Musgrave, R. Demand versus structural unemployment. *Unemployment in a Prosperous Economy*, W. Bowen and F. Harbison (eds.). Princeton, N.J.: Industrial Relations Centre, 1965.

Moy, J. and Sorrentino, C. Unemployment in nine industrialized nations. *MLR* 98 (June 1975) 9-18.

Naemark, N. Comparing unemployment statistics with data from the Unemployment Insurance Commission. *Canadian Statistical Review* (March 1973).

Niemi, B. The male-female differential in unemployment rates. *ILRR* 27 (April 1974) 331-350.

Ostry, S. *Unemployment in Canada.* 1961 census monograph. Ottawa: Dominion Bureau of Statistics, 1968.

Ostry, S. and M. Zaidi. *Labour Economics in Canada.* 3rd ed. Toronto: Macmillan, 1979.

Owen, J. and L. Belzung. An epilogue to job displacement: a case study of structural unemployment. *SEJ* 33 (January 1967) 395-408.

Perry, G. Changing labor markets and inflation. *BPEA* (No. 3, 1970) 411-441.

Reder, M. Wage structure and structural unemployment. *R. E. Studies* 31 (October 1964) 309-322.

Reder, M. The theory of frictional unemployment. *Economica* 36 (February 1969) 1-28.

Rees, A. The meaning and measurement of full employment. *The Measurement and Behaviour of Unemployment.* Princeton, N.J.: Princeton University Press, 1957.

Rosen, C. Bibliography: hidden unemployment and related issues. *MLR* 96 (March 1973) 31-37.

Salop, S. A model of the natural rate of unemployment. *AER* 69 (March 1979) 117-125.

Sawers, L. Unemployment and the structure of labour demand. *Review of Radical Political Economy* 1 (May 1969) 56-74.

Simler, N. Long-term unemployment, the structural hypothesis and public policy. *AER* 54 (December 1964) 985-1002.

Skolnik, M. and F. Siddiqui. The paradox of unemployment and job vacancies. *RI/IR* 31 (No. 1, 1976) 32-54. Comment by F. Reid and reply 32 (No. 1, 1977) 133-138.

Smith, D.C. Seasonal unemployment and economic conditions. *Employment Policy and the Labour Market*, A. Ross (ed.). Berkeley: University of California Press, 1965.

Smyth, D. and P. Lowe. The vestibule to the occupational ladder and unemployment. *ILRR* 23 (July 1970) 561-565.

Solow, R. What happened to full employment? *Quarterly Review of Economics and Business* 13 (Summer 1973) 7-20.

Stoikov, V. Increasing structural unemployment re-examined. *ILRR* 19 (April 1966) 368-376.

Tandan, N. The decline in the female-male unemployment rate differential in Canada, 1961-1972. *Notes on Labour Statistics*. Ottawa: Statistics Canada, 1973, 5-12.

Tandan, N. A comparison of unemployment in selected industrial countries. *Notes on Labour Statistics*. Ottawa: Statistics Canada, 1972, 55-64.

Taylor, J. Hidden unemployment, hoarded labour and the Phillips curve. *SEJ* 37 (July 1970) 1-16.

Thurow, L. The changing structure of unemployment: an econometric study. *R. E. Stats.* 47 (February 1965) 137-149.

Turvey, R. Structural change and structural unemployment. *ILR* 116 (September-October 1977) 209-215.

Vanderkamp, J. The effect of out-migration on regional employment. *CJE* 3 (November 1970) 541-549.

Vanderkamp, J. An application of Lipsey's concept of structural unemployment. *R.E. Studies* 33 (July 1966) 221-225.

Vickery, C. The impact of turnover on group unemployment rates. *R. R. Stats.* 59 (November 1977) 415-426.

Vietorisz, T., R. Mier and J. Giblin. Subemployment: exclusion and inadequacy indexes. *MLR* 98 (May 1975) 3-12.

Werneke, D. Measuring economic hardship in the labor market. *AER Proceedings* 69 (May 1979) 43-47.

Winder, J. Structural unemployment. *The Canadian Labour Market*, A. Kruger and N. Meltz (eds.). Toronto: Centre for Industrial Relations, University of Toronto, 1968.

Zaidi, M. Structural unemployment, labour market efficiency and the intra-factor allocation mechanism in the United States and Canada. *SEJ* 35 (January 1969) 205-213. Comment by B. Mabry and reply 39 (October 1972) 307-310.

B. Unemployment Insurance

Barron, J. and O. Gulley. The effect of unemployment insurance on the search process. *ILRR* 32 (April 1979) 363-366.

Becker, J. *Experience Rating in Unemployment Insurance*. Baltimore: Johns Hopkins University Press, 1972.

Benjamin, D. and L. Kochin. Searching for an explanation of unemployment in interwar Britain. *JPE* 87 (June 1979) 441-478.

Brechling, F. The incentive effects of the U.S. unemployment insurance tax. *Research in Labor Economics*, R. Ehrenberg (ed.). Greenwich, Conn.: JAI Press, 1977.

Burgess, P. and J. Kingston. The impact of unemployment insurance benefits on reemployment success. *ILRR* 30 (October 1976) 25-31.

Chapin, G. Unemployment insurance, job search, and the demand for leisure. *WEJ* 9 (March 1971) 102-107. Comment by Kingston and Burgess 9 (December 1971) 447-452.

Chiswick, B. The effect of unemployment compensation on a seasonal industry: agriculture. *JPE* 84 (June 1976) 591-602.

Doherty, N. National insurance and absence from work. *EJ* 89 (March 1979) 50-65.

Edgell, L. and S. Wander. Unemployment insurance: its economic performance. *MLR* 97 (April 1974) 33-40.

Ehrenberg, R. and R. Oaxaca. Unemployment insurance, duration of unemployment and subsequent wage gain. *AER* 66 (December 1976) 754-766.

Feldstein, M. The effect of unemployment insurance on temporary layoff unemployment. *AER* 68 (December 1978) 834-846.

Feldstein, M. Unemployment compensation: adverse incentives and distributional anomalies. *National Tax Journal* 37 (June 1974) 231-244.

Feldstein, M. *Lowering the Permanent Rate of Unemployment*. Study for the Joint Economic Committee, 93 Congress, 1973.

Fields, G. Direct labor market effects of unemployment insurance. *IR* 16 (February 1971) 1-14.

Furstenberg, G. von. Stabilization characteristics of unemployment insurance. *ILRR* 29 (April 1976) 363-376.

Green, C. and J.-M. Cousineau. *Unemployment in Canada: The Impact of Unemployment Insurance*. Ottawa: Economic Council of Canada, 1976.

Grubel, H., D. Maki and S. Sax. Real and insurance induced unemployment in Canada. *CJE* 8 (May 1975) 174-191. Comments by S. Kaliski and reply 4 (November 1975) 600-605.

Haber, W. and M. Murray. *Unemployment Insurance in the American Economy*. Homewood, Ill.: Richard D. Irwin, 1966.

Halpin, T. The effect of unemployment insurance on seasonal fluctuations in employment. *ILRR* 32 (April 1979) 353-362.

Hamermesh, D. *Jobless Pay and the Economy*. Baltimore: Johns Hopkins University Press, 1977.

Hickey, J. Changes in state unemployment insurance legislation. *MLR* 97 (January 1974) 39-46.

Holen, A. and S. Horowitz. The effect of unemployment insurance and eligibility enforcement on unemployment. *Journal of Law and Economics* 17 (October 1974) 403-432.

Kaliski, S. Unemployment and unemployment insurance: testing some corollaries. *CJE* 9 (November 1976) 705-712.

Katz, A. (ed.). The economics of unemployment insurance: a symposium. *ILRR* 30 (July 1977) 431-526.

Kelly, L. Job attachment and unemployment benefits. Research Series 20. Kingston: Queen's University Industrial Relations Centre, 1972.

Lester, R. *The Economics of Unemployment Compensation*. Princeton: Princeton University Press, 1962.

Maki, D. Unemployment insurance, unemployment duration, and excess supply of labour. *RI/IR* 31 (No. 3, 1976) 368-376.

Maki, D. Regional differences in insurance-induced unemployment in Canada. *EI* 13 (September 1975) 389-400.

Marston, S. The impact of unemployment insurance on job search. *BPEA* (No. 1, 1975) 13-60.

Munts, R. Partial benefit schedules in unemployment insurance. *JHR* 5 (Spring, 1970) 160-176.

Munts, R. and I. Garfinkel. *The Work Disincentive Effects of Unemployment Insurance*. Kalamazoo, Mich.: W. E. Upjohn Institute, 1974.

Nelson, D. *Unemployment Insurance: the American Experience*. Madison: University of Wisconsin Press, 1969.

Newton, F. and H. Rosen. Unemployment insurance, income taxation, and duration of unemployment: evidence from Georgia. *SEJ* 45 (January 1979) 773-784.

Nickell, S. The effect of unemployment and related benefits on the duration of unemployment. *EJ* 89 (March 1979) 34-49.

Osberg, L. Unemployment insurance in Canada: a review of the recent amendments. *CPP* 5 (Spring 1979) 223-235.

Papier, W. Standards for improving maximum unemployment insurance benefits. *ILRR* 27 (April 1974) 376-390.

Polemarchakis, H. and L. Weiss. Fixed wages, layoffs, unemployment compensation and welfare. *AER* 68 (December 1978) 909-917.

Rea, S. Unemployment insurance and labour supply: a simulation of the 1971 Unemployment Insurance Act. *CJE* 10 (May 1977) 263-278.

Seaver, S. and J. Hall. Economic implications of unemployment insurance for agriculture. *American Journal of Agricultural Economics* 56 (December 1974) 1084-1092.

Siedule, T., N. Skoulas, and K. Newton. *The Impact of Economy-Wide Changes in the Labour Force*. Ottawa: Economic Council of Canada, 1976.

Solon, G. Labour supply effects of extended unemployment benefits. *JHR* 14 (Spring 1979) 247-55.

Swan, N. Unemployment insurance and labour force participation with application to Canada and its Maritime provinces. *Labor Law Journal* (August 1975) 511-518.

Warden, C. Jr. Unemployment Compensation: the Massachusetts experience. *Studies in the Economics of Income Maintenance*, O. Eckstein, (ed.). Washington, D.C.: Brookings Institution, 1967.

Vickery, C. Unemployment insurance: a positive reappraisal. *IR* 18 (Winter 1979) 1-17.

Part VI

Special Topics

Chapter 19

Impact of Unions

The focus in this chapter is on the wages of union members relative to non-union members. This emphasis on wages is not meant to suggest that this is the area where unions have had their most important impact. On the contrary, the most important role for unions probably has been in ensuring that their members are not subject to arbitrary treatment from management. Rather, their treatment is regulated more formally by the terms of the collective agreement which specifies such factors as work rules, seniority provisions, compensation, and grievance procedures. In essence, unionization ensures a measure of due process in the work environment, and provides for collective rather than individual bargaining.

Our emphasis on the impact of unions on wages, then, involves only one small part of the total role of unions. It is, however, the part that best can be analysed by the tools of labour economics and it is the part that most affects the subject matter of this text—the labour market. A more complete treatment of the role of unions in areas other than wage determination is given in courses and textbooks in industrial relations and collective bargaining.

Unions can have an influence on a variety of aspects of wages. They can obviously affect the wages of union members, but they can also affect the wages of non-union members, and both of these will affect the union-non-union wage differential. Unions also can affect the variety of wage structures, for example, the occupational, industrial, and regional structures, as well as structures that reflect personal characteristics, notably male-female wage differentials. In addition, as indicated earlier, unions have been discussed as affecting the aggregate wage level in the economy as a whole. While all of these dimensions of the union impact are obviously important, the focus of this chapter is on union-non-union wage differentials, involving the impact of the wages of union members as well as non-union members.

IMPACT ON WAGES OF UNION WORKERS

Unions can raise the wages of unionized workers either indirectly by restricting supply and/or directly by fixing wages. In either case they may try to alleviate any adverse employment effect by increasing the demand for union labour and/or by making the demand for union labour more inelastic. Each of these processes—restricting supply, fixing wages, increasing the demand for union labour, and making the demand for union labour more inelastic—will be discussed in turn.

Restricting Supply: Craft Unions

By restricting the supply of labour, unions can raise wages artificially relative to the situation where competition prevailed in the supply of labour. Craft unions generally have sought to raise the wages of their members by controlling entry into their craft by such devices as the apprenticeship system, discrimination, nepotism, high union dues, and such devices as the closed shop (the worker has to be a member of the union *before* being hired, i.e. the union controls the hiring hall). Because the supply of labour to the craft is reduced, wages will rise above the wage that would prevail in the absence of the craft restrictions.

Needless to say the craft union will try to control the whole trade; otherwise, the benefits of the supply restriction would also go to non-union craft workers. Hence the importance to the union of apprenticeship licensing, the closed shop, the union shop (the worker has to join the union *after* a probationary period of employment), or the agency shop (the worker must pay union dues but need not be a member of the union).

At the artificially high union wage rate, the quantity of labour supplied will exceed the quantity demanded. To the extent that the union controls entry, the scarce jobs can be rationed to the large number of workers who would like the jobs by such devices as discrimination, nepotism, or high union dues. To the extent that employers have a say in who is hired, they may ration jobs on the basis of discrimination or nepotism, but they may also ration on the basis of productivity related factors such as education or training or experience. While these productivity related factors obviously are useful requirements for employers, they may be set *artificially* high because the employer has an excess supply of applicants, given the higher unionized wage.

Restricting Supply: Professional Associations

Professional associations can also behave much like craft unions in their control over labour supply, largely through the processes of occupational licensing and certification. This setting of standards is deemed necessary, ostensibly to protect the public interest in circumstances where it is important but difficult for the consuming public to judge the quality of the professional service. The job of governing the profession has usually gone to the profession itself—hence the term self-governing professions—because only members of the profession were deemed qualified to set standards. Traditionally, this has occurred in the stereotypic professions such as medicine and law, where an uninformed clientele purchases complex services from a self-employed professional. Increasingly, however, professionals are becoming employed on a salaried basis and the rationale for self-governing powers for salaried professionals can be questioned when the employer can provide an effective mediator between the consuming public and the salaried professional.

The techniques of occupational control utilized by professional associations usually involve occupational licensing or certification. Under certification only those with the professional certificate have the right to use the professional designation or title; that is, they have a *reserve-of-title certification*. However, other practitioners are allowed to practise in the profession, albeit they cannot use the certified title. Under licensing, only those with the professional licence can practise; that is, they have the *exclusive right-to-practice licence*. Clearly the exclusive right-to-practice licence involves more control over the occupation than the reserve-of-title certification; hence, it is sought after by most professional and quasi-professional groups.

Under licensing the supply of labour to the occupation is restricted only to those with the licence. Under certification the supply restrictions are less severe in the sense that others can practise in the profession, although competition is restricted because others cannot use the professionally designated certification. Whatever the impact on the quality of the service performed, the supply of labour to the occupation is restricted and wages rise accordingly. In this sense, professional associations like craft unions raise the wages of their members.

Although they receive higher wages, members of the profession may bear costs associated with the occupational licensing requirements. Such costs could include lengthy education periods as well as practical training periods, such as internship for doctors or articling for lawyers. There is a danger, however, in that the *incumbent* professionals may try to have the brunt of the licensing costs born by *new* entrants into the profession. This could be accomplished by having increasingly stringent education or training requirements as a qualification for entry into the profession, with so-called "grandfather" clauses exempting those who are already practising. In this fashion, the new entrants bear more of the licensing costs (they will do so as long as the wage premium outweighs these costs), the existing practitioners who control the profession benefit from the restricted competition, and the consuming public gets increasingly qualified practitioners, albeit at a higher cost. Restricting grandfather clauses, or having licensing requirements set by persons other than existing practitioners, could go a long way to correct this potential abuse of occupational licensing.

Wage Bargaining: Industrial Unions

While craft unions and professional associations can raise the wages of their members indirectly by controlling labour supply, industrial unions tend to have a more direct impact by simply bargaining for a higher wage. Their ability to do so depends on the viability of their strike threat and on the ability of the employer to pay a wage that is greater than the competitive wage. The employer's ability to pay may be greater in non-competitive product markets or in sectors that are completely unionized, so that unionized employers do not have to compete with lower cost non-union employers. It is possible, then, that unions can have an impact on the wages of their members only in situations where the product market is non-competitive, or where potential competitors also are unionized. As discussed earlier, the potential impact of unions also may be greater in situations of monopsony in the labour market because union wage gains need not lead to reductions in employment.

To the extent that unions are successful in fixing wages above the competitive level, the quantity of labour supplied will exceed the quantity demanded and the scarce number of high-wage union jobs will have to be rationed. The union will try to ration in a manner that is best suited to its existing members, and this may involve discrimination and nepotism. However, with industrial unions, employers tend to control the hiring process and hence they may ration on the basis of factors to suit their own preferences (e.g. discrimination, nepotism, favoritism) or on the basis of productivity-related hiring standards with respect to such things as education, training or experience. Having a queue of applicants because of the higher unionized wage enables unionized employers to hire the most qualified applicants and this makes it difficult in empirical work to control for differences between union and non-union workers in estimating a pure union-non-union wage differential.

Alter Demand for Union Labour

To offset the adverse employment effect that would result from unions setting wages above the competitive norm, unions may also try to increase the demand for union labour and make it more inelastic. As our previous discussion of the determinants of the elasticity of demand for labour indicated, the demand for labour would be inelastic if the ratio of labour cost to total cost is small, if the demand for the product produced by labour is price inelastic, if there are few good substitute factors of production, or if the substitutes are an inelastic supply. Each of these factors will be discussed in turn, emphasizing how unions may try to affect each factor so as to make the derived demand for union labour more inelastic so as to mitigate any adverse employment effect that may emanate from union wages being set above the competitive norm.

Reduce Ratio of Union Labour Cost to Total Cost
The labour cost of unionized workers is simply the union wage times the number of union employees. Obviously the union would not want to keep these costs low by lowering union wages, but they may try to keep it low (and hence keep the demand for union labour inelastic) by keeping the number of union employees small. Craft unions and professional associations, for example, may find it in their own self-interest to try to stay small and selective

rather than merging with larger industrial units. Unions may also allow the use of probationary workers who are not union members as a way of keeping union wage costs a small portion of total cost.

Make Product Demand Inelastic

Unions also may try to make the demand for the product produced by union labour price inelastic so that wage increases can be passed on to the customer in the form of price increases without there being a substantial reduction in the demand for the product and hence in the derived demand for union labour. They could do this, for example, by supporting protective tariffs or anti-dumping laws to reduce the substitution of foreign goods, or by advertising the product by allowing the company to use the union label. They may also try to organize the whole industry so as to prevent consumers from substituting non-union for union products.

Controlling Substitute Inputs

The most important way for unions to make the demand for labour inelastic is to reduce the substitution of other inputs — such as capital or non-union labour—for union labour. They would try to prevent the substitution of non-union labour by use of the closed shop with its hiring hall, by completely organizing the plant so that it could not be run by a skeleton crew in the event of a strike, by trying to make the use of "scab" labour illegal during a strike, and by controlling the extent to which the firm can utilize part-time workers, probationary labour, or contract out for services. They may *allow* the use of non-union labour such as part-time or probationary workers to keep the union labour cost a smaller portion of total labour cost, but they will want to *control* the use of such labour to prevent its extensive substitution for union labour. Unions in particular jurisdictions may also try to prevent workers — even union workers — from other jurisdictions from competing with their own union labour. Construction trades, for example, may require licensing whereby previous work experience in the particular construction zone is a condition for the licence.

Unions may also try to prevent the substitution of capital or other inputs for union labour. Hence, their concern for technological change provisions in collective agreements and their demands to have the right to re-negotiate the collective agreement if unforeseen technological change occurs. Restrictive work practices (featherbedding rules) which require employers to employ more labour than they otherwise would employ (perhaps by fixing the ratio of union labour to other inputs) can also be viewed as devices to prevent the substitution of capital for labour. In fact, such provisions generally emerge in times of dramatic technological change (e.g. use of diesel as opposed to steam locomotives, use of automated printing presses, use of containers in shipping), when the wholesale substitution of capital for labour seems imminent.

The regulation of substitute factors of production also occurs in the professions through professional associations. Thus doctors influence the

312 *Part VI Special Topics*

extent to which paramedical personnel can be utilized, dentists seek to limit the extent to which denturists can perform dental tasks, and professors—lest we forget—may try to have control over the utilization of teaching assistants, closed-circuit television, and faculty who do not meet certain residence requirements. All of these restrictive practices on the part of professionals are instituted to meet other objectives, ostensibly to protect the consuming public from poor quality service. They do, however, have the convenient property — convenient for the incumbent professionals — of reducing the substitution of competitive inputs, and hence of allowing salaries to be higher than what they otherwise would be. One cannot help but wonder whether these restrictive practices would prevail if they resulted in lower salaries for the incumbent professionals.

Not only would unions and professional associations try to control the use of substitute inputs, they would also try to make them more expensive so as to discourage their utilization. Thus unions would support wage-fixing legislation that may raise the wages of non-union workers, for example, by minimum wage laws, or equal pay laws, or fair wage legislation that requires the payment of prevailing wages on government contracts, or extension legislation that extends the unionized wage throughout the industry.

Making Supply of Substitutes Inelastic
In addition to controlling the use of substitute inputs and trying to make them more expensive, unions may also try to make the supply of substitute inputs more inelastic. In this fashion, increases in the demand for these substitutes would raise their prices, and this may serve to choke off the use of these substitute inputs.

This could be accomplished, for example, by supporting policies that would reduce the existence of a pool of low wage labour that would be available for employers to utilize in place of union labour. Hence, unions may support restrictive immigration policies to prevent employers from having a pool of low wage labour, or they may support full employment policies and income maintenance policies that would reduce the pool of low wage labour. Obviously unions support these policies for other reasons, including their belief in the equity and fairness of such policies for unorganized labour; nevertheless, their support is made easier by the fact that such policies also tend to be beneficial for union members as well.

IMPACT ON WAGES OF NON-UNION WORKERS

Not only will unions have an impact on the wages of union members — by controlling supply, fixing wages, or altering the demand for union labour as already discussed in this chapter — but also they can have an impact on the wages of *non-union* workers. As indicated earlier, they can do so by supporting wage fixing legislation that applies mainly to non-union workers, but they can also affect the wages of non-union labour by altering the demand and supply of non-union labour, by altering traditional wage relativities, and by pressuring non-union employers to pay the union wage to avoid the threat of unionization. Each of these factors will be discussed in turn.

The demand for non-union labour would be affected in an indeterminant way by wage increases of unionized labour. To the extent that they are substitutes in demand (something that the union will try to control), the demand for non-union labour would increase as it is substituted for the higher priced union labour. However, to the extent that they are complements in demand, the demand for non-union labour would decrease as the demand for union labour decreases. This could be the case, for example, if a firm shuts down because of high union labour costs and non-union workers are also laid off, or if union and non-union labour are used in some fixed proportion and the demand for both therefore gets reduced as unions raise the wages of their members.

The supply of labour to the non-union sector will also be affected by wage increases in the union sector. To the extent that union wages reduce employment opportunities in the unionized sector, many of those who cannot get jobs in the union sector will seek employment in the non-union sector. This increase in the supply of non-union labour, other things being equal, should serve to reduce wages in the non-union sector. To a certain extent this view is implicit in dual labour market analysis; that is, labour market segmentation between the unionized and non-unionized sector may create a widening of the gap between the two sectors as the large numbers who cannot get jobs in the primary unionized sector crowd into the secondary non-unionized sector, depressing wages even further in the secondary labour market.

Contrary to this belief is the perspective, often advanced by practitioners, that non-union firms would have to raise the wages of non-union labour in order to compete with unionized firms for the work-force. In addition, firms with both union and non-union workers would have to raise the wages of non-union labour in order to preserve traditional wage differentials. While this belief has intuitive appeal, especially because comparability appears to be so important in wage determination, it ignores the market factors — in particular the supply influx from workers who cannot get jobs in the unionized sector — that would enable employers to pay lower wages to non-union labour. In essence, there is not really a need to compete with the unionized sector because there is a large pool of labour to hire that cannot get jobs in the high wage unionized sector. It is true that the unionized sector may get the top applicants because of the high wages, and it is true that the reserve of labour may dry up in periods of prosperity (hence compelling the non-union sector to pay higher wages), but it is also true that those who cannot get jobs in the union sector are a supply influx into the non-union sector, and this lowers wages in that sector.

On the other hand, employers in the non-union sector may raise wages to the extent that there is an increase in the demand for substitute non-union labour. In addition they may raise wages in order to avoid the threat of becoming unionized. This threat effect will be greater if the union wage premium is high, the non-union sector is easy to organize, the potential union is aggressive, or the employers have a strong aversion to unionization. In such circumstances, non-union employees may be paid close to the union wage (perhaps even higher if the firm has a strong aversion to unionization) and provided with similar working conditions as union workers. Such employees could receive the benefits of unionization without bearing such costs as union dues or possible strike costs. However, such benefits may be precarious in that they hinge on the willingness of employers to provide them.

Clearly the various factors can be at work simultaneously affecting the wages of non-union workers, and since they do not all work in the same direction, economic theory does not provide unambiguous predictions on the effect of unions on the wages of non-union workers. Non-union wages may increase because of wage fixing, the increased demand for substitute non-union labour, the threat effect, or as the non-union sector adjusts to restore old wage relativities. On the other hand, non-union wages may decrease because of a decrease in the demand for complementary inputs, or because of the supply influx into the non-union sector created by the reduced employment opportunities in the unionized sector. Ultimately, the impact of unions on the wages of non-union workers is an empirical proposition.

EMPIRICAL EVIDENCE ON UNION WAGE IMPACT

Empirical evidence on the impact of unions is difficult to summarize, in part because of the different data sources utilized to measure the union-non-union wage differential. The data sources can involve different industries, time periods, regions, occupations, sexes and races, as well as different units of observation, for example, the industry, the establishment, or the individual worker. In addition, in Canada there is simply a dearth of systematic empirical evidence on the union impact. In spite of these problems, some generalizations appear to emerge from the variety of studies, based mainly on U.S. data.

Empirical Generalizations

In his thorough study of the impact of unions in the U.S. prior to the 1960s, Lewis (1963, p. 194) concludes:

> In the period 1931-33, unionism may have raised the average relative wage position of union labour by more than 23 per cent and lowered that of non-union labour by more than 1 per cent. In the inflation at the end of and just following World War II, unionism had little effect on the relative wages of union and non-union labour. More recently [1950s], unionism, I estimate, has raised the average relative wage of union labour by about 7 to 11 per cent and reduced the

average relative wage of non-union labour by approximately 3 or 4 per cent.

After reviewing a variety of empirical studies Rees (1962, p. 79) also concludes: "My own best guess of the average effects of all American unions on the wages of their members in recent years would lie somewhere between 10 and 15 per cent".

Utilizing base wages (starting wages for the lowest occupational group) in establishments in Ontario, Starr (1973, 1975) finds that unionized establishments paid male workers \$.18 per hour more for males and \$.14 per hour more for females, after controlling (with multiple regression analysis) for the impact of other wage determining factors. Based on average non-union base wages of \$1.97 per hour for males and \$1.69 per hour for females, this translates into a proportionate union-non-union wage differential, $(w_u - w_n)/w_n$, of 9 per cent for males and 8 per cent for females. The extent to which these results are generalizable to the Canadian labour force as a whole remains an unanswered empirical question. Nevertheless they are comparable to the estimates proposed by Lewis and Rees.

Other empirical generalizations appear to emerge from the studies of the impact of unionization. The impact appears to be greater in the early years of union organizing and in periods of recession; in fact, in periods of inflation, the union impact may be negligible or even negative, presumably because of wage rigidities imposed by unions. The relative impact is probably greater for less-skilled workers; however, the impact of some particular craft unions has been substantial in raising the wages of their skilled members. The union impact also tends to be larger when the product market is non-competitive and when the derived demand for labour is inelastic: for example, if the ratio of union labour cost to total cost is small, or the whole industry is organized so that it is not possible to substitute the products of non-union firms.

Some Problems with Empirical Evidence

There are problems, however, associated with most of the studies that have tried to estimate the union impact on relative wages. These problems stem from three main factors: the difficulty of completely controlling for differences in the productivity of union and non-union workers; the problems of sorting out cause and effect; and the problem of estimating the union impact when one can only observe union and non-union wages. Each of these factors will be discussed in turn.

In estimating a *pure* union-non-union wage differential, it is important to control for other wage determining factors so as to be able to attribute the differential purely to unionization. If, for example, unionized establishments tend to utilize more skilled labour than non-unionized establishments, it is crucial to control for these skill differentials. Otherwise, the union-non-union wage differential will simply reflect the skill differential, not a pure union impact on wages. Controlling for skill differentials is especially important because, as indicated earlier, if unionized establishments have to pay a wage that is greater than the competitive wage, they will have a queue of applicants and will be able to hire the "cream of the crop" of workers.

To a certain extent this may be offset by the possibility that restrictive work practices in a collective agreement may reduce the productivity of union workers, or that some workers with extreme individual motivation may find their advancement opportunities greater in the non-union sector. Nevertheless, the possibility remains that union workers embody higher skill levels than non-union workers and that some of the union-non-union wage differential reflects greater skill levels. Empirical studies of the union impact try to control for these skill differences (for example, by examining a specific occupation, or by the use of multiple regression analyses). Nevertheless, it is not clear that these adjustments can *fully* control for differences in productivity-related factors.

There is also the problem of sorting out cause and effect in studies of the union impact. Usually the argument is advanced that unions cause higher wages. However, there is the possibility that cause and effect works in the opposite direction. That is, some firms may simply be high wage firms, perhaps because they are trying to reduce the turnover of workers with firm-specific human capital, or because they want to be known as a model employer, or because they want a queue of applicants from which to hire. Workers in these firms will be reluctant to leave because wages are so high. Knowing that they want to stay in the high-wage establishment, and knowing that they will probably stay there for a considerable period of time because of the high wages, they will turn to devices to try to improve the every-day work conditions of the job. One such device may be unionization with its emphasis on due process, regulating the work environment, and administered rulings that provide a degree of certainty and security for the unionized workers.

In Hirschman's (1970) terminology, the restriction of "exit" increases the use of "voice". In this case, voluntary quitting (exit) is reduced because of the high wages, and hence workers seek to have more of a say (voice) in their job by collective bargaining.

This possibility of cause and effect working in both directions suggests that some of the wage advantage of union establishments may not be due to unions, but may be attributed to other factors; in fact, unionism itself emerges because of the wage advantage. This suggests that econometric studies of the impact of unions should be based on simultaneous equation models, which consider that wages are a function of unionism as well as unionism being a function of wages. Unfortunately, the recent empirical studies based on simultaneous equation models give conflicting results.

Ashenfelter and Johnson (1972) and Schmidt and Strauss (1976) both find that unionism has a positive but statistically *insignificant* effect on wages. Schmidt (1978), on the other hand, finds that unionism has a positive, statistically significant, but quantitatively small impact on wages, and Lee (1978) and Kahn (1979) both find the union impact to be statistically significant and large. Clearly further research is needed to reconcile this conflicting evidence.

A final problem in estimating the impact of unions arises because what we tend to observe in empirical studies is the union-non-union wage differential. It is difficult to estimate the competitive wage that would prevail in the absence of unions because unionization can affect the wages of non-union workers by such things as threat effects, demand and supply spillovers, and the restoration of wage relativities. If, for example, unions raised the wages of union members by 15 per cent, and the wages of non-union workers by 5 per cent, then the measured union-non-union wage differential would be approximately 10 per cent. However, the total impact of unions would be greater; specifically, they would have raised the wages of their members by 15 per cent and the wages of non-union workers by 5 per cent above the competitive norm. Conversely, if they would have lowered non-union wages by 5 per cent then the measured union-non-union wage differential would be 20 per cent; however, they would have raised the wages of their members by 15 per cent above the competitive norm.

It is not that one measure is correct and the other incorrect. The measures indicate what the data say they indicate; that is, the union-non-union wage differential *is* the differential between union and non-union workers. However, it does not necessarily show the impact that unions have had on the wages of their members relative to what those wages would have been in the absence of unionism. Care therefore must be exercised in interpreting and comparing the results of empirical studies.

These problems with many of the empirical studies suggest that while we have gone a long way towards improving our understanding of the impact of unions, there is room for more research. Specifically what is needed are studies that can fully control for the possible skill differentials between union and non-union workers, account for the simultaneity involved to the extent that unionization may be a result as well as a cause of high wages, and estimate the separate impact of unions on union wages as well as non-union wages. In addition, more evidence is needed on the impact that unions have on a variety of factors: wage differentials between the public and private sectors, males and females, blacks and whites; the total occupational wage structure and more generally the distribution of income; and on such factors as employment, mobility and job satisfaction itself. In Canada, especially, there is a dearth of empirical evidence on virtually all aspects of union impact.

QUESTIONS

1. In focusing on the impact of unions on relative wages, economists have missed the main point of the purpose of unions. Discuss.
2. Discuss the various wage structures and wage levels that unions can affect.
3. Craft unions and professional associations will affect the wages of their members in a different manner than will industrial unions. Discuss, and indicate why this may be the case.
4. If craft unions or professional associations are able to raise the wages in their trades above the competitive norm, excess supplies of applicants would result. Discuss how the scarce jobs may be rationed.
5. Self-government is an anachronism for salaried as opposed to self-employed professionals. Discuss.
6. Distinguish between occupational licensing and certification. Give examples of each.
7. If occupational licensing is necessary, the only group that could be entrusted not to abuse the powers of licensing would be the alumni of the profession, or at least members who were about to retire. Only they have knowledge about the profession, without having a self-interest in abusing the power of licensing. Existing practitioners, while knowledgeable about the profession, have a self-interest to restrict entry by putting unnecessarily costly entry requirements on new entrants into the profession. New entrants may not find it in their self-interest to put unnecessary restrictions on their entry into the profession, but they do not yet have sufficient knowledge about the profession and what is required for proper qualifications. The general public, while having an interest in ensuring quality performance without unnecessary restrictions, may not be able to judge what requirements are necessary for professional competence. Only alumni have knowledge of the profession without having a self-interest in excessive quality restrictions; consequently, they are the persons who should be entrusted with the powers of occupational licensing, if it is necessary. Discuss.
8. Restrictions on the use of grandfather clauses would go a long way in reducing the abuses of occupational self licensing. Discuss.
9. Indicate why incumbent practitioners in a profession may want to put excessive restrictions on entry into the profession.
10. Indicate conditions under which one may expect unions to have a substantial impact on the wages of their members.
11. If you expect the wage impact of unions to differ systematically with respect to certain conditions (e.g. extent of unionization in the industry or extent of concentration in the product market), how would you capture the interaction effect in a regression equation designed to measure the impact of unions?

12. Discuss the various ways in which unions may try to alter the demand for union labour so as to minimize any adverse employment effects associated with a union wage increase? Give examples.
13. Based on the Marshallian determinants of the elasticity of demand for labour, where would you expect union wage gains to be greater, in the construction industry or in textile manufacturing, and why?
14. Discuss the various ways in which unions can affect the wages of *non-union labour*.
15. Why may one expect the skill level of union workers to be different from the skill level of non-union workers? What does this imply about union-non-union wage differentials?
16. Why may one expect high wages to cause unionism, as well as vice versa, and what does this imply about union-non-union wage differentials?
17. Why may the union-non-union wage differential not reflect the impact of unions on the wages of their members relative to what their wage would be in the absence of unionism?
18. The following union impact equation was estimated by Starr (1973, p. 56, Equation 11.3):

    $W = .361 \, CA + .00403 \, CA \cdot U + .00377 \, CA \cdot CR - .01228 \, CA \cdot RLC +$ other control variables

    where W is the male base wage rate in the establishment; CA represents the existence of a union in the establishment (coded one if the establishment has a collective agreement, zero otherwise); U represents the percentage of the industry that is unionized; CR represents industry concentration; and RLC is the ratio of wage labour cost to value added.
    (a) Theoretically justify the use of each of these explanatory variables.
    (b) What sign would you expect for each regression coefficient?
    (c) Why are the explanatory variables entered in the equation in that particular fashion: that is, multiplied by CA?
    (d) What is the effect on wages of being unionized as opposed to non-unionized?
    (e) Evaluate this affect at the following mean values of the explanatory variables: $\overline{U} = 57.6$, $\overline{CR} = 7.8$, $\overline{RLC} = 36.1$.
    (f) Compare this union impact in an establishment with the impact that would occur if the industry in which the firm operated was completely unionized, other things being equal.
    (g) Compare the union impact of part (e) with the impact that would occur if the ratio of wage labour cost to value added were only 20 per cent as opposed to the average of 36.1 per cent.

REFERENCES AND FURTHER READINGS

A. Union Impact

Ashenfelter, O. The effect of unionization on wages in the public sector: the case of fire fighters. *ILRR* 24 (January 1971) 191-202.

Ashenfelter, O. and G. Johnson. Unionism, relative wages and labor quality in U.S. manufacturing industries. *IER* 13 (October 1972) 488-507.

Ashenfelter, O. Racial discrimination and trade unionism. *JPE* 80 (May/June 1972) 435-464.

Ballentine, J. and W. Thirsk. Labour unions and income redistribution reconsidered. *CJE* 10 (February 1977) 141-148.

Block, F. and M. Kuskin. Wage determination in the union and non-union sectors. *ILRR* 31 (January 1978) 183-192.

Borjas, G. Job satisfaction, wages and unions. *JHR* 14 (Winter 1979) 21-40.

Boskin, M. Unions and relative real wages. *AER* 62 (June 1972) 466-472.

Bradley, P. (ed.). *The Public Stake in Union Power.* Charlottesville, Va.: University of Virginia Press, 1959.

Brown, C. and J. Medoff. Trade unions in the production process. *JPE* 86 (June 1978) 355-378.

Brown, W. Academic unions in higher education: impact on faculty salaries, compensation and promotion. *EI* 15 (July 1977) 385-396.

Comay, Y., A. Melnik and A. Subotnik. Bargaining, yield curves, and wage settlements. *JPE* 82 (March/April 1974) 303-313.

Ehrenberg, R. Municipal government structure: unionization and wages of fire fighters. *ILRR* 27 (October 1973) 36-48.

Diewart, W.E. The effects of unionization on wages and employment: a general equilibrium analysis. *EI* 12 (September 1974) 319-339.

Diewart, W.E. Unions in a general equilibrium model. *CJE* 7 (August 1974) 475-495.

Farber, H. Individual preferences and union wage determination: the case of the United Mine Workers. *JPE* 86 (October 1978) 923-942.

Farber, H. The United Mine Workers and the demand for coal. *Research in Labor Economics*, R. Ehrenberg (ed.). Greenwich, Conn.: JAI Press, 1978.

Foran, T. Unionism and wage differentials. *SEJ* 40 (October 1973) 269-278.

Fottler, M. The union impact on hospital wages. *ILRR* 30 (April 1977) 342-355.

Freeman, R. Individual mobility and union voice in the labor market. *AER Proceedings* 66 (May 1976) 361-368.

Freeman, R. and J. Medoff. *What Do Unions Do?* New York: Basic Books, forthcoming.

Hamermesh, D. White-collar unions, blue-collar unions and wages in manufacturing. *ILRR* 24 (January 1971) 159-170.

Hendricks, W. Labor market structure and union wage levels. *EI* 13 (September 1975) 401-416.

Hirschman, A. *Exit, Voice and Loyalty.* Cambridge, Mass.: Harvard University Press, 1970.

Johnson, G. Economic analysis of trade unionism. *AER Proceedings* 65 (May 1975) 23-28.

Johnson, G. and K. Youmans. Union relative wage effects by age and education. *ILRR* 24 (January 1971) 171-179.

Johnson, H. and P. Mieszkowski. The effect of unionization on the distribution of income. *QJE* 84 (November 1970) 539-561.

Kahn, L. Union impact: a reduced form approach. *R.E.Stats.* 59 (November 1977) 503-507.

Kahn, L. The effect of unions on the earnings of non-union workers. *ILRR* 31 (January 1978) 205-216.

Kahn, L. Unionism and relative wages: direct and indirect effects. *ILRR* 32 (July 1979) 520-532.

Kahn, L. and K. Morimune. Unions and employment stability: a segmented logit approach. *IER* 20 (February 1979) 217-235.

Kiefer, N. and S. Smith. Union impact and wage discrimination by region. *JHR* 12 (Fall 1977) 521-534.

Layard, R., D. Metcalf and S. Nickell. The effect of collective bargaining on relative and absolute wages. *BJIR* 16 (November 1978) 287-302.

Lee, L. Unionism and wage rates: a simultaneous equations model with qualititative and limited dependent variables. *IER* 19 (June 1978) 415-433.

Leigh, D. Unions and nonwage racial discrimination. *ILRR* 32 (July 1979) 439-450.

Levinson, H. M. Unionism, concentration and wage changes: toward a unified theory. *ILRR* 20 (January 1967) 198-205.

Lewis, H.G. *Unionism and Relative Wages in the United States.* Chicago: University of Chicago Press, 1963.

Lipsky, D. and J. Drotning. The influence of collective bargaining on teachers' salaries in New York State. *ILRR* 27 (October 1973) 18-35.

Mandelstamm, A. The effects of unions on efficiency in the residential construction industry. *ILRR* 18 (July 1965) 503-521.

McCormick, R. and R. Tollison. Legislatures as unions. *JPE* 86 (February 1978) 63-78.

Metcalf, D. Unions, incomes policy and relative wages in Britain. *BJIR* 15 (July 1977) 157-175.

Mitchell, D. Union wage determination. *BPEA* (No. 3, 1978) 537-592.

Mulvey, C. Collective agreements and relative earnings in U.K. manufacturing in 1973. *Economica* 43 (November 1976) 419-27.

Myers, F. Price theory and union monopoly. *ILRR* 12 (April 1959) 434-445.

Nickell, S. Trade unions and the position of women in the industrial wage structure. *BJIR* 15 (July 1977) 192-210.

Oaxaca. R. Estimation of union-non-union wage differentials within occupational regional subgroups. *JHR* 10 (Fall 1975) 529-536.

Ozanne, R. Impact of unions on wage levels and income distribution. *QJE* 73 (May 1959) 177-96.

Pencavel, J. The distributional and efficiency effects of trade unions in Britain. *BJIR* 15 (July 1977) 137-156.

Pencavel, J. Relative wages and trade unions in the U.K. *Economica* 41 (May 1974) 194-210.

Raimon, R. and V. Stockov. The effect of blue-collar unionism on white-collar earnings. *ILRR* 22 (April 1969) 358-374.

Rapping, L. Monopoly rents, wage rates and union wage effectiveness. *Quarterly Review of Economics and Business* 7 (Spring 1967) 1-47.

Reder, M. Unions and wages: the problem of measurement *JPE* 73 (April 1965) 188-196.

Rees, A. The effect of unions on resource allocation. *Journal of Law and Economics* 6 (October 1963) 69-78.

Rees. A. *The Economics of Trade Unions.* Chicago: University of Chicago Press, 1962.

Rees, A. Do unions cause inflation? *Journal of Law and Economics* 11 (October 1959) 84-94.

Rees, A. and M. Hamilton. Postwar movements of wage levels and unit labor costs. *Journal of Law and Economics* 6 (October 1963) 41-68.

Rosen, S. Unionism and the occupational wage structure in the United States. *IER* 11 (June 1970) 269-286.

Rosen, S. Trade union power, threat effects and the extent of organization. *R.E. Stats.* 36 (April 1969) 185-196.

Ryscavage, P. Measuring union nonunion earnings differences. *MLR* 97 (December 1974) 3-9.

Schlesinger, J. Market structure, union power and inflation. *SEJ* 24 (January 1958) 96-114.

Schmidt, P. Estimation of a simultaneous equations model with jointly dependent continuous and qualitative variables: the union-earnings question revisited. *IER* 19 (June 1978) 453-465.

Schmidt, P. and R. Strauss. The effect of unions on earnings and earnings on unions: a mixed logit approach. *IER* 17 (February 1976) 204-212. Comment by R. Olsen, 19 (February 1978) 259-261.

Segal, M. The relation between union wage impact and market structure. *QJE* 78 (February 1964) 296-312.

Segal, M. Unionism and wage movements. *SEJ* 28 (October 1961) 174-181.

Starr, G. *Union-Nonunion Wage Differentials.* Toronto: Ontario Ministry of Labour, 1973.

Starr, G. Union-nonunion wage differentials in Ontario. *Canadian Industrial Relations,* S. Hameed (ed.). Toronto: Butterworth, 1975, 283-294.

Swidinsky, R. Trade unions and the rate of change in money wages in Canada, 1953-1970. *ILRR* 25 (April 1972) 363-375.

Thompson, A., C. Mulvey and M. Farbman. Bargaining structure and relative earnings in Great Britain. *BJIR* 15 (July 1977) 176-191.

Throop, A. The union-nonunion wage differential and cost-push inflation. *AER* 63 (March 1968) 79-99.
Ulman, L. Marshall and Friedman on union strength. *R. E. Stats.* 37 (November 1955) 384-401.
Weiss, L. Concentration and labor earnings. *AER* 56 (March 1966) 96-117. Comment by F. Stafford and reply 58 (March 1968) 174-180.
Wright, D. (ed.). *The Impact of the Union.* New York: Harper, Brace and Co., 1951.

B. Occupational Licensing

Benham, A. and L. Benham. Regulating through the professions. *Journal of Law and Economics* 18 (October 1975) 421-428.
Blank, D. and G. Stigler. *The Demand and Supply of Scientific Personnel.* New York: National Bureau of Economic Research, 1957.
Brown, M. Some effects of physician licensing requirements on medical manpower flows in Canada. *RI/IR* 30 (No. 3, 1975) 436-451.
Dodge, D. Artificial restrictions in labour markets. *Canadian Perspectives in Economics.* Toronto: Collier-Macmillan, 1972.
Dodge, D. Occupational wage differentials, occupational licensing and returns to investment in education. *Canadian Higher Education in the Seventies,* S. Ostry (ed.). Ottawa: Economic Council of Canada, 1972.
Friedman, M. Occupational licensure, in *Capitalism and Freedom.* Chicago: University of Chicago Press, 1968, 137-160.
Friedman, M. and S. Kuznets. *Income for Independent Professional Practice.* New York: National Bureau of Economic Research, 1954.
Holen, A. Effects of professional licensing arrangements on interstate labor mobility and resource allocation. *JPE* 73 (October 1965) 492-498.
Kessel, R. Price determination in medicine. *Journal of Law and Economics* 11 (October 1958) 20-53.
Leffleur, K. Physician licensure. *Journal of Law and Economics* 21 (April 1978) 165-186.
Maurizi, A. Occupational licensing and the public interest. *JPE* 82 (March/April 1974) 399-413.
Moore, T. The purpose of licensing. *Journal of Law and Economics* 4 (October 1961) 93-117.
Pashigian, B.P. Occupational licensing and the interstate mobility of professionals. *Journal of Law and Economics* 22 (April 1979) 1-26.
Plott, C. Occupational self-regulation: a case study of the Oklahoma dry cleaners. *Journal of Law and Economics* 8 (October 1965) 195-222.
Rottenberg, S. The economics of occupational licensing. *Aspects of Labor Economics.* Princeton: Princeton University Press, 1962.
Siebert, W. Occupational licensing: the Merrison report on the regulation of the medical profession. *BJIR* 15 (March 1977) 29-38.
Shepard, L. Licensing restrictions and the cost of dental care. *Journal of Law and Economics* 21 (April 1978) 187-202.

Shimberg, B., B. Esser and D. Kruger. *Occupational Licensing.* Washington:
    Public Affair Press, 1973.
Simons, H. Some reflections on syndicalism. *JPE* 52 (March 1944) 1-25.
Thornton, R. and A.R. Weintraub. Licensing in the barbering profession.
    ILRR 32 (January 1979) 242-249.
White, W. The impact of occupational licensure of clinical laboratory
    personnel. *JHR* 13 (Winter 1978) 91-102.

C. Featherbedding (Restrictive Work Rules)

Gomberg, W. Featherbedding: an assertion of property rights. *The Annals of
    the American Academy of Political and Social Science* (January 1961).
Horowitz, M. The railroad's dual system of payment: a make work rule?
    ILRR 8 (January 1955) 177-194.
Kaufman, J. *Collective Bargaining in the Railroad Industry.* New York: King's
    Crown Press, 1954, 26-44.
Killingworth, C. The modernization of west coast longshore work rules.
    ILRR 15 (April 1962) 297-306.
Kossoris, M. Working rules in west coast longshoring. *MLR* 84 (January
    1961).
Martin, R. and R. Fryer. Management and redundancy: an analysis of
    planned organizational change. *BJIR* 8 (March 1970) 69-84.
Mathewson, S. *Restriction of Output Amongst Organized Workers.* New York:
    Viking Press, 1931.
Peitchines, S. *Labour-Management Relations in the Railway Industry.* Task
    Force on Labour Relations Study No. 20. Ottawa: Information
    Canada, 1971, 296-301.
Weinstein, P. (ed.). *Featherbedding and Technological Change.* Boston:
    D. C. Heath, 1965.

Chapter 20

Public-Private Sector
Wage Differentials

The issue of public-private sector wage differentials is a topic of inter-industry wage determination since the public sector is simply one of many industries. However, the public sector is singled out for special attention because it is a large sector, it is the subject of current policy concern mainly because of strikes and wage settlements, its impact may spill over into the private sector, and it has peculiarities that make wage determination somewhat unique.

As our earlier discussion indicated, the theoretical determinants of inter-industry wage differentials include compensating adjustments for non-pecuniary differences, short-run adjustments, and non-competitive factors. Just as these broad categories provided a convenient framework for analysing the determinants of inter-industry wage differentials, they also are convenient for categorizing the theoretical determinants of the particular inter-industry wage differential examined in this chapter — the public-private sector wage differential.

The public sector can be broadly defined to include education, health and government enterprises, as well as the more narrowly defined government employment at the federal, provincial and municipal levels. According to this broad definition, Bird (1978, p. 25) estimates Canadian public sector employment in 1975 to be approximately 2.2 million workers, or 23 per cent of the employed labour force. The breakdown of the broad public sector into its component parts as of 1975 is: federal government 18.2%, provincial government 15.8%, municipal government 11.1%, education 23.8%, hospitals 17.1%, and government enterprises 14.0%. Thus, the various levels of government—the more narrow definition of the public sector—comprise less than half of public sector employees. If one considers most hospital employees and teachers in post secondary education as provincial employees, then the provincial public sector becomes the largest element of the broad public sector. However one portions the data, the fact remains that the public sector is a large and important employer.

THEORETICAL DETERMINANTS OF
PUBLIC-PRIVATE WAGE DIFFERENTIALS

Compensating Adjustments for Non-pecuniary Differences

Inter-industry wage differentials may reflect compensating adjustments for differences in the non-pecuniary aspects of employment across industries.

With respect to the private and public sector, non-pecuniary advantages may exist with respect to such factors as job security, fringe benefits, and political visibility. To the extent that these advantages prevail in the public sector, we would expect a correspondingly lower wage to compensate for the advantages. However, to the extent that these advantages are dissipating over time, we may also expect public sector wages to rise relative to those in the private sector to compensate for the loss of these non-pecuniary advantages.

Job Security

Job security often is discussed as being more prevalent in the public than in the private sector. Theoretically this may be the case because job security could be necessary to prevent the abuses of political patronage. That is, without a modicum of job security, civil servants could be replaced each time a new political party came into power, or whenever a politician wanted to gain favour by granting patronage in the form of civil service jobs. To avoid this potential abuse, and to ensure a degree of continuity in the public sector work-force, a degree of job security may be granted.

Job security may also be more prevalent in the public sector because the costs of providing it may be less than in many elements of the private sector. Because of its size (except in some instances at the local level), the public sector has a *portfolio* of jobs in which to reallocate its work-force and it has the means of utilizing personnel policies and motivational techniques that do not require the ultimate sanction of firing a worker. If a worker is not competent at a particular job there usually are other jobs available within the public sector that would enable the worker to perform some, at least minimal, function. In addition, it may be possible within the public sector to grant job security to a *core* of workers because of the feasibility of contracting out for work or of utilizing part-time, casual employees. As well, as long as the public sector is a growth industry it is easier to grant job security.

As with many labour market phenomenon that at first glance appear to be inefficient constraints in the market, the existence of a degree of job security for civil servants *may* have elements of being a rational, low-cost, institutional response to a peculiarity of the labour market—in this case, the possible abuse of political patronage, coupled with the relatively low cost of providing job security in the large and expanding public sector.

While there is this theoretical reason to expect job security to be greater in the public sector, and while this certainly appears to be the conventional wisdom, job security appears to be waning, perhaps because of reduced growth, or increased public criticism, or because political patronage is less of a concern. Teachers, part-time and casual employees, and even the core of the civil service no longer appear to have job security.

In addition, while there may still be a degree of *employment* security, this need not imply *job* security. That is, public sector workers may be shifted to different jobs within the public sector, and these may not be the jobs for which they were hired or at which they would prefer to work. This can be the case especially because of the fluctuating nature of much government activity associated with counter-cyclical demand policies, and because many government activities can shift dramatically according to the wishes and whims of political forces. In addition, the security advantage of the public sector may be waning because of increased job security in the private sector, emanating from such factors as unionization, possible experience rating in unemployment insurance, increases in the quasi-fixed costs of employment, and legislation involving termination of employment.

In summary, while there are theoretical reasons to believe that job security would be greater in the public than private sector, in practice this security may not be as great as conventional wisdom suggests. In addition, it is probably waning relative to job security in the private sector. This has obvious implications for the existence of a public-private sector compensating wage differential and its change over time. Specifically, while the public sector at one time may have been able to pay lower wages in return for a degree of job security, this possibility may be less prevalent today. This would suggest that public sector wages may rise more rapidly than private sector wages to compensate for the relative decrease of job security over time.

Fringe Benefits
Fringe benefits provide another possible source of compensating wage differentials. Specifically, if the public sector provides more generous fringe benefits than the private sector, it should be able to recruit an adequate workforce by paying lower wages. It is total compensation, not simply wages, that is relevant.

As with job security, there are theoretical reasons to suggest that the public sector may pay more liberal fringe benefits. This occurs because in the public sector there are not adequate checks to prevent employers from saving on *current* wage costs by granting liberal retirement benefits and pension schemes, the cost of which may be born by *future* generations of taxpayers. Fringe benefits that are payable in the future, such as early retirement plans and employer-sponsored pensions, can be viewed as deferred wages in the sense that workers would willingly give up some current wages for these future benefits.

In the private sector there is a built-in check to ensure that employers are constrained in their granting of such deferred benefits: eventually they have to meet the obligation of paying for them. However, in the public sector, unless such benefits are fully funded, their costs will be born by future taxpayers. To the extent that they have little or no say in the current political process, there is no automatic mechanism to prevent public sector employers from saving on current wage costs by granting liberal deferred cost items, such as early retirement or substantial pensions or pensions indexed for future inflation.

Political Visibility and Access to Rules
Additional non-pecuniary advantages offered by the public sector could

include political visibility, access to control over political rules, and the opportunity to provide public service. For some, these factors may be valued for their own end; for others they may be valued as a means to other objectives. For example, some workers may regard a period of public sector employment as a low-wage apprenticeship period that provides them with inside knowledge, access to power sources, and contacts in the political arena. These factors may be of immense value (and hence lead to higher remuneration) in future private sector jobs as consultants, lobbyists, or simply partners in firms that do business with the government or that would benefit from inside political information.

For others, public sector employment may provide "the non-pecuniary satisfaction of doing good" — to use a phrase utilized by Reder (1975, p. 28). This could be a reason, for example, for people to do volunteer work for churches or charities, or for some to accept lower salaries in such non-profit institutions. It may be a more prevalent phenomenon throughout the public sector, especially in teaching or health care. The term "public service" means just that to many persons.

Summary of Compensating Factors

The non-pecuniary factors that we have discussed — job security, fringe benefits, and political visibility — generally are ones for which there are theoretical reasons to believe that they would be greater in the public than private sector. Certainly conventional wisdom and casual empiricism seems to suggest this to be the case. To the extent that it is true, the public sector would be expected to have lower wages to compensate for these factors.

While these non-pecuniary factors may be greater in the public than private sector, there are reasons to believe that the gap may be dissipating over time. Certainly this seems to be the case with job security and it may be the case with fringe benefits to the extent that the public sector may have reached diminishing returns with respect to fringe benefits it can provide, and the private sector is now catching up. Even with respect to the opportunity to do public service, attitudes seem to be changing so that public sector jobs are done in return for pay, like most other jobs. To the extent that these non-pecuniary factors have diminished in the public sector, one would expect the wages of public sector workers to rise relative to those of their private sector counterparts.

Short-Run Adjustments

Inter-industry wage differentials may reflect a short-run disequilibrium situation. In fact the disequilibrium wage serves as the signal for new entrants, and this supply response should restore the inter-industry wage structure to its long-run equilibrium level.

This scenario could be relevant to the public sector. In essence, the expansion of the public sector that occurred, especially in the 1950s and

1960s, would lead to increases in the demand for public sector labour and, hence, to increases in their wages. The higher wages would enable public employers to recruit the necessary work-force associated with the expansion of the public sector.

In recent years, however, there are forces at work to suggest that the rapid expansion of the public sector may have ended. Certainly political pressures are mounting as taxpayers show opposition to an ever-expanding role of the public sector. In addition, basic demographic changes may be reducing the demand for public services, especially in education as the baby boom has left the education sector, and in health as family size reduces.

Empirical evidence for Canada, in fact, indicates that the rate of expansion of the public sector had levelled off by the 1970s. According to Richard Bird (1978, p. 19): "The fastest growth in total public employment probably occurred during the 1950s. Although this growth continued through the 1960s, it did so at a relatively slower pace and by the 1970s, on most measurements, the growth of public employment levelled off and perhaps even declined". In such circumstances, we would expect public sector wages to be rising relative to private sector wages during the 1950s and 1960s, but for this pattern to stop by the 1970s.

Non-competitive Factors

Inter-industry wage differentials may also reflect non-competitive factors and it is in this area that the differences between public and private sector labour markets become most pronounced. Specific features that have important implications for public-private wage differentials and their changes over time revolve around the fact that the public sector can be characterized as subject to various peculiarities including a political constraint rather than a profit constraint, possible monopsony, an inelastic demand for labour, and a high degree of new unionization. Each of these factors will be discussed in turn, with an emphasis on their implications for public-private wage differentials and their changes over time.

Political Rather than Profit Constraint

The public sector usually is not subject to a profit constraint as traditionally exists in the private sector. Rather, the profit constraint is replaced by an ultimate political constraint and there is the belief that the political constraint is less binding. This occurs because taxpayers are diffuse, often ill-informed, and can exert pressure only infrequently and with respect to a package of issues. Public sector managers also are diffuse in the sense that lines of responsibility are not always well defined and "buck-passing" can prevail. Workers in the public sector, on the other hand, are often portrayed as a unified, distinct interest group providing direct pressure for wage increases. A more serious imperfection of the political process arises from the fact, discussed earlier, that future taxpayers have little or no representation in today's political process.

While these features of the political constraint suggest the possibility that it is less binding than the profit constraint, there still are constraining influences on wage settlements in the public sector. Taxpayer scrutiny is now extremely strong and in fact politicians may gain by appearing to be cost-conscious guardians of the public purse by reducing wage costs. Public sector workers may also be called upon to set an example of moderate wages to curb inflation. Even the alleged diffuse nature of management in the public sector may work against employees; it can be difficult to win wage gains if one doesn't know with whom one is bargaining.

Perhaps the most important feature of the political constraint that works against public sector workers is that, during a strike, tax revenues keep coming in to the public sector even though wage expenditures are reduced and public services are not provided. This is in contrast to the private sector where employers are under considerable pressure to settle because they are losing customers and sales revenues during a strike. To be sure, there can be pressure from taxpayers to have the wage savings go into general tax revenues or into tax reductions because services are not provided. Nevertheless, the fact remains that this political pressure is less stringent than the profit constraint when firms lose customers and revenues during a strike.

Monopsony

To the extent that the government sector is often the dominant employer in particular labour markets, governments may utilize their monopsony power to pay lower wage rates than if they behaved competitively. Political forces may pressure them to act as model employers and not utilize their monopsony power; nevertheless, there is also pressure to be cost conscious and this may lead them to exercise their monopsony power.

In fact the empirical evidence cited earlier in the chapter on monopsony suggested that for at least two elements of the public sector—teaching and nursing—there was some evidence of monopsony. The extent to which these results can be generalized for other elements of the public sector, or for the teaching and nursing professions as a whole, remains an unanswered empirical question.

To the extent that monopsony power exists and is exercised in the public sector, public sector wages would be lower than they would be in the absence of monopsony. However, the pressure of monopsony also means that, for a range of wage increases, unions would not have to be concerned about employment reductions. In fact as illustrated in the chapter on monopsony, wage increases may actually lead to employment increases, suggesting the possibility of a substantial union wage impact in monopsonistic labour markets.

Inelastic Demand for Public Sector Labour

The possibility of a substantial union impact on wages in the public sector is furthered by the possibility that the demand for labour in the public sector may be wage inelastic. In such circumstances unions could bargain for substantial wage increases without worrying about large reductions in the employment of their members. The inelasticity of the demand for labour may occur because non-competitive forces restrict the utilization of substitute inputs as well as substitute services.

Many of the services produced in the public sector are so-called essential services that are not provided in the private sector, and when they are so provided, they are often under government regulation. Since consumers (taxpayers) are unable to substitute other services for those provided by the public sector, their demand for these services may be relatively price (tax) inelastic, and hence the derived demand for public sector labour would be wage inelastic. In essence, wage increases can be passed on to taxpayers in the form of tax increases for the essential services without taxpayers reducing their demand for these services and hence the derived demand for labour.

This is strengthened by the fact that there are often few good inputs to substitute for public sector labour as it becomes expensive. This may reflect the nature of the public sector production function, but it may also reflect the fact that the public sector is heavily professionalized, and professional labour tends to have a degree of control over the utilization of other inputs, including non-professional labour. Often the utilization of other inputs is discouraged because it reduces the "personal touch" that professionals advocate.

While these factors suggest that the demand for public sector labour would be wage inelastic, other factors are at work in the opposite direction. Specifically, the high ratio of labour cost to total cost in many public services suggests that the demand would be elastic. In addition, substitute inputs and services certainly could be utilized, especially in the long run. Even the essentiality of the service may work against public sector employees by restricting their right to strike and reducing public sympathy during a strike. In addition, the employers may lag in the bargaining process, knowing that the essential elements of the service will be maintained and, as indicated earlier, tax revenues are still forthcoming.

Since theory does not indicate unambiguously whether the demand for public sector labour would be elastic or inelastic, we must appeal to the empirical evidence. The evidence, as given in Ehrenberg (1973) and Ashenfelter and Ehrenberg (1975), based on U.S. data, indicates that the demand for labour in the public sector is inelastic, and that the more essential the service, the greater the inelasticity.

Unionization

A final non-competitive factor — recent unionization — may also affect the wages of public sector workers relative to their private sector counterparts. This is especially the case when the unionization is coupled with the other factors discussed in this chapter — the inelastic demand for public sector labour, the possible monopsony in some public sector markets, and the absence of a profit constraint. In addition, the unionization of the public sector is a relatively recent phenomenon, and it is in the early periods of union organizing drives that the union impact on wages tends to be the greatest.

In Canada, this recent growth and high degree of unionization in the public sector is documented, for example, in Cousineau and Lacroix (1977, pp. 4-8, 44-46). Some sectors, like the federal civil service, are organized almost to their full potential. Others, like teaching and health, are now predominantly unionized.

Competitive Floor But Not Ceiling

The previously discussed factors — absence of a profit constraint, monopsony, inelastic demand, and the high degree of recent unionization — all suggested that wage determination may be different between the public and private sectors, and that non-competitive factors may give rise to an inter-industry wage differential between the public and private sectors. Most of the factors, with the exception of monopsony, would appear to favour a non-competitive wage advantage in the public sector, although a variety of subtle constraining influences are present.

However, there is a stronger reason to expect the wage advantage to be in favour of public sector workers. This is so because the forces of competition would ensure that wages in the public sector would not fall much below wages in the private sector for comparable workers. If they did, the public sector would not be in a competitive position to recruit labour, and would experience problems of recruitment, turnover and morale. That is, competition would ensure a competitive *floor* on wages in the public sector.

These same competitive forces, however, need not provide an effective *ceiling* on wages in the public sector. To be sure, if public sector wages exceeded wages of comparable workers in the private sector, there would be queues of applicants and excessive competition for public sector jobs. Nevertheless, employers in the public sector are not under a profit constraint to respond to these disequilibrium signals; they need not lower their relative wage. They *may* not pay an excessive wage if the political constraint is a binding cost constraint; nevertheless, there is no guarantee that this will be the case.

In essence, the forces of competition ensure a floor, but they need not provide an effective ceiling on wages in the public sector. Hence the potential bias, in theory, for wages in the public sector to be in excess of wages in the private sector for comparable workers. The extent to which this potential upward bias exists in practice is an empirical proposition.

EMPIRICAL EVIDENCE

Reflecting the newness of the concern over public-private sector wage differentials, it is only recently that a number of empirical studies have tried to measure such differentials. In general, the studies have tried to control for other legitimate wage determining factors by multiple regression analysis or by standardizing by sample selection: that is, by choosing groups that are similar except that one group is in the public sector and the other is in the private sector. While the empirical studies are few in number, they do provide some tentative generalizations. The extent to which these generalizations withstand further scrutiny and the test of time remains an unanswered question.

Decomposition of Public-Private Wage Differentials: Mathematical Exposition

The overall average earnings differential between public and private sector workers can be decomposed into two component parts: a portion due to differences in the endowments of wage determining factors between the two sectors, and a portion attributable to a pure inter-industry wage differential. The latter can be termed an economic rent or surplus payment because it represents payment for being in a particular industry, after controlling for the effect of the usual wage determining factors.

This decomposition technique — which will also be utilized in the subsequent chapter on male-female wage differentials — can be illustrated formally. Let y denote the dependent variable earnings, X the set of usual wage determining explanatory variables (human capital factors such as education and training, and control variables for such factors as occupation and region), and b the set of regression coefficients estimated from an earnings equation based on individuals as units of observation. In such an earnings equation, the X's can be regarded as the endowments of wage determining factors and the b's as the pay structure associated with differences in these endowments. The regression coefficient for the education variable, for example, indicates the change in earnings that results from an additional year of education — it is the monetary reward or pay structure associated with the acquisition of additional education.

Separate earnings equations can be estimated for each of the public and private sectors, respectively denoted by the subscripts g (government or public) and c (private or competitive). That is, for the public sector

$$y_g = \Sigma b_g X_g \qquad (20.1)$$

and for the private sector

$$y_c = \Sigma b_c X_c \qquad (20.2)$$

In regression analysis, the mean of the dependent variable is equal to the regression coefficients times the mean values of the explanatory variables. Therefore,

$$\bar{y}_g = \Sigma b_g \bar{X}_g \text{ and} \qquad (20.3)$$

$$\bar{y}_c = \Sigma b_c \bar{X}_c \qquad (20.4)$$

Subtracting Equation 20.4 from Equation 20.3 gives the average earnings differential between public and private sector workers: that is,

$$\bar{y}_g - \bar{y}_c = \Sigma b_g \bar{X}_g - \Sigma b_c \bar{X}_c \tag{20.5}$$

Subtracting and adding $\Sigma b_c \bar{X}_g$ to the right-hand side (and therefore not changing the equality yields

$$\bar{y}_g - \bar{y}_c = \Sigma b_g \bar{X}_g - \Sigma b_c \bar{X}_g + \Sigma b_c \bar{X}_g - \Sigma b_c \bar{X}_c \tag{20.6}$$

which, after collecting terms, yields

$$\bar{y}_g - \bar{y}_c = \Sigma(b_g - b_c)\bar{X}_g + \Sigma b_c(\bar{X}_g - \bar{X}_c) \tag{20.7}$$

The first term on the right-hand side is the differences in pay structure (b's) between public and private sector workers, evaluated for the same wage determining endowments ($\bar{X}_g$'s). This represents the pure inter-industry wage differential because it arises solely from differences in the way public and private sector workers are paid for the same wage determining characteristics. The second term on the right-hand side of Equation 20.7 is the differences in the endowments of wage determining characteristics (X's) between the public and private sector workers, evaluated according to the private sector pay structure (b_c's). Since the private sector pay structure is usually regarded as the competitive norm, it makes sense to evaluate differences in the wage-determining endowments according to that norm.

Obviously it is the first term on the right-hand-side of Equation 20.7 that is important for policy purposes since it reflects the economic rent or surplus payment associated with being in one sector as opposed to the other sector. If the public sector pays its workers more than the private sector (that is, the b_g's are greater than the b_c's) for similar levels of education, training, and other wage determining factors (that is for the $\bar{X}_g$'s), then this will result in a positive surplus payment, $\Sigma(b_g - b_c)\bar{X}_g$. The second expression, on the other hand, is not of policy concern since it represents a differential payment for different endowments of legitimate wage determining factors, such as human capital. These two components—a surplus payment, and a payment for differences in productivity-related endowments, together make up the overall average earnings differential, $\bar{y}_g - \bar{y}_c$, between public and private sector workers.

Estimates of this average earnings differential and its two component parts for full-year, full-time workers, is provided in Gunderson (1979b, p.237) based on 1971 Canadian census data. The public sector is the industry designation of public administration and the private sector is the manufacturing industry. The main results are reproduced in Table 20.1.

Clearly workers in the public sector on average have higher earnings than workers in the private sector. However, much of the differential comes about because workers in the public sector have greater endowments of wage determining factors such as education. The pure surplus payment or economic rent associated with being employed in the public as opposed to the private sector (column 2) is estimated as $492 or 6.2 per cent for males

TABLE 20.1
PUBLIC SECTOR EARNINGS ADVANTAGE AND ITS DECOMPOSITION

	Overall Differential	Amount Attributed To	
		Surplus	Endowments
Males			
Dollar Advantage	$737	$492	$245
As percent of private earnings	9.3%	6.2%	3.1%
Females			
Dollar Advantage	$989	$383	$606
As percent of private earnings	22.3%	8.6%	13.7%

Source: Gunderson (1979 b, p. 237)

and $383 or 8.6 per cent for females. Since there are over twice as many males as females in the public administration category, this would yield a pure public sector earnings advantage of approximately 7 per cent overall. These results generally are in line with those reported in Smith's (1977b) comprehensive analysis, which summarizes and updates her application of this decomposition technique in a variety of U.S. studies.

Other Empirical Evidence

These results generally are also consistent with those obtained from other Canadian data sets and employing different statistical methodology, usually standardization by sample selection. Based on calculations from taxation statistics, the Highly Qualified Manpower Survey, contract data from collective agreements, occupational wage rate surveys of municipal governments, and Pay Research Bureau data, Gunderson (1978b, p. 127) concludes: "in recent years, the wages of public sector employees in Canada appear to have exceeded those of their private sector counterparts by about five to fifteen per cent. This wage advantage appears to have been larger for females than males and for low level as opposed to high level occupations. In fact, for high level occupations evidence suggests that the public sector may not even pay the competitive wage".

This same study suggests a number of other empirical generalizations based on Canadian data. The wage advantage of public sector workers probably is a fairly recent phenomenon, emerging in the late 1960s and 1970s; during the 1950s and early 1960s public sector workers were probably paid a wage less than their private sector counterparts. This time pattern is what one would expect given the demand increases associated with the growth of the public sector in the 1950s and 1960s, and the growth of unionization over that same period. To the extent that these forces have dissipated in recent years, they would no longer be a source of wage increases in the public sector.

Wage settlements in the public sector often are quite volatile, even at the aggregate level. However, unusually high settlements in a given year tend to reflect catch-up for low settlements in previous years, or the high wage increases tend to be temporary, dissipating over time. Hence, the importance of utilizing a reasonably long time horizon in comparing wage settlements in the public and private sectors.

On the monetary value of fringe benefits between the public and private sectors, the empirical evidence is scant and difficult to compare because of different definitions utilized. However, the limited empirical evidence in Canada certainly does not indicate the public sector to be ahead of the private sector. Ostry and Zaidi (1979, p. 207), for example, indicate that in Canada during 1975-76, the value of fringe benefits as a percentage of wages were 32.6% in municipalities, 31.4% in education, 28.5% in government, and 27.1% in hospitals — compared to 32.1% in the manufacturing sector. Based on 1976 Canadian data from the Pay Research Bureau, Gunderson (1978b, p. 152) also concluded: "all that can really be determined on the basis of the available data is that the value of fringe benefits has increased rapidly in the private sector, and that currently they appear to be roughly comparable to those in the public sector". In the United States, however, Smith (1977, pp. 26-31) finds that fringe benefits are a slightly higher proportion of wage costs in the public than the private sector and that they have increased more rapidly in the public than the private sector. Clearly this is an area where more empirical evidence is needed on a consistent, comparable basis so as to make viable comparisons on a total compensation basis.

Many of the previous empirical generalizations based on Canadian data also are generally true for the United Kingdom and the United States. This latter evidence — reviewed in Gunderson (1978c) — indicates that currently there appears to be a public sector wage advantage in both the United Kingdom and the United States. As is the case with Canada, this advantage is fairly recent, emerging in the 1970s in the United Kingdom and in the 1960s in the United States. There are differences in the patterns of the wage advantage, however, being larger for public corporations in the United Kingdom, larger at the federal level in the United States, and larger for provincial and municipal employees in Canada. These differences are to be expected, given the ultimate importance of political factors in the wage determination process in the public sector, and the fact that political pressures may differ across countries, over time, and with respect to different elements of the public sector.

SOME POLICY IMPLICATIONS

A variety of policy issues follow from the previous theoretical and empirical analysis. The key question becomes: should the apparent public sector wage advantage be curbed? There are feasible ways of doing so, largely by altering the institutional environment in which public sector bargaining and wage determination occurs.

Certainly a period of moderation in public sector wage increases would be in order, given the apparent advantage of five to fifteen per cent, probably centring on seven per cent. To the extent that this is a pure public sector wage advantage, the moderation should not result in problems of recruitment, turnover or morale. However, there are reasons to suggest that a wholesale restrictionist policy on public sector settlements may be premature.

While the evidence does indicate a current pure wage advantage in favour of workers in the public sector, there is not a wealth of empirical work in this area. In essence, there is a danger in making policy changes based on the results of a limited number of empirical studies, no matter how carefully conducted. In addition the public sector advantage is not tremendously large, probably in the neighbourhood of seven per cent, and much of this advantage may be attributable to the higher degree of unionization in the public sector. The wage advantage may be temporary, arising because of the earlier growth of the public sector and because of the new unionization in that sector. This is buttressed by the fact that new forces are emerging that would suggest some built-in checks on wages in the public sector: i.e., the rapid growth is probably over (in part because of political pressure and in part because of demographic changes); the possibilities for new unionization are largely exhausted; political pressures are leaning in the direction of restraint on public expenditures; and the period of wage controls may already have reduced the public sector wage advantage to the extent that these controls were more effective in curbing wage settlements in the public sector.

A final reason for exercising caution in the wholesale application of pressures to reduce public sector settlements arises because the incidence of such a restrictionist policy probably would fall disproportionately on the group experiencing the largest public sector wage advantage — females and lower wage workers in general. To the extent that these groups are already in a disadvantaged position in the labour market, curbing any public sector wage advantage would probably worsen their position. For these various reasons — the wage advantage is small, probably temporary, and already being brought under check, and it favours relatively disadvantaged groups— caution should be exercised in suggesting policies to curb wage settlements in the public sector.

QUESTIONS

1. Since the public sector is simply one of many industries, public-private sector wage differentials are really a special topic of inter-industry wage differentials. Discuss.
2. Discuss various possible definitions of the public sector.
3. Are there any *theoretical* reasons to believe that job security and fringe benefits may be different in the public and the private sector?
4. Indicate how the various determinants of the public-private sector wage differential may have *changed* during the 1950s and 1960s in Canada,

338   *Part VI   Special Topics*

and how this may have affected the wage differential over that period.

5. Cousineau and Lacroix (1977, p. 113) indicate: "because of its particular characteristics as an employer, the public sector is particularly 'vulnerable' to the unionization of its employees and to union pressure". Discuss.

6. The fact that wage determination in the public sector ultimately depends on political factors may well work against workers in the public sector, even though we traditionally think that this puts them in a better position than when wages are under the ultimate profit constraint in the private sector. Discuss.

7. Criticisms of public sector wages as being too high often implicitly assume that private sector wages are the correct norm. What is so virtuous about private sector wages given that they can reflect market imperfections, unequal bargaining power, and a variety of non-economic constraints? Discuss.

8. The potential upward bias for wages in the public sector relative to the private sector occurs because the market provides a reasonably effective floor on wages in the public sector but it does not necessarily provide an effective ceiling. Discuss.

9. Based on your knowledge of the determinants of the elasticity of demand for labour, would you expect the demand for public sector labour to be inelastic or elastic and why? Why might one expect the elasticity to differ across different elements of the public sector?

10. Differences in the elasticity of demand for labour between the public and the private sector, by themselves, are not sufficient conditions for a wage differential between the two sectors. Discuss.

11. Ehrenberg (1973) provides empirical estimates of the wage elasticity of demand for public sector labour in the U.S., ranging from -1.00 in public welfare to $-.28$ in health, fire and protection services. What does this imply about the expected employment impact of a wage change in each of these sectors?

12. In Canada by the mid-1970s about two-thirds of employees in public administration were unionized compared to about one-third for workers in other industries. Discuss the implication of this phenomenon for public-private sector wage differentials.

13. (a) What variables would you utilize as determinants of wages in a micro wage equation (individual worker is the unit of observation) to be estimated separately for public and private sector workers?

    (b) Why would you want to estimate *separate* wage equations for public and private sector workers rather than a single wage equation for both, with a dummy variable for public as opposed to private sector workers?

    (c) How would you test to see if the underlying wage determination process is different in the two sectors?

    (d) Based on this regression analysis, illustrate formally how one could decompose the overall average earnings differential between the public and the private sector into two components: a portion due to an economic rent or pure surplus payment, and a portion attributable to different endowments of productivity related factors.

(e) Which is the portion that public policy is concerned with and why?

(f) Discuss some possible pitfalls in employing this methodology to estimate a pure public-private sector wage differential.

14. Decompose the overall average public-private sector wage differential by adding and subtracting $\Sigma b_g \bar{X}_c$ to the right-hand side of Equation 20.5. Is this also a reasonable decomposition technique?

15. Just as with measuring a pure impact of unions on relative wages, it is difficult to measure a pure public-private sector wage differential. It is extremely important, but difficult, to control for differences in the quality of labour, and to consider wage spillover effects between the two sectors. Discuss.

16. In estimating a pure public-private sector wage differential, one could try to control for the influences of various legitimate wage determining factors by multiple regression analysis or by standardizing via sample selection. In the latter technique one simply chooses two samples of workers that are similar except that one group is in the public sector and the other in the private sector. Discuss the strengths and weaknesses of these alternative approaches.

17. Why might it not be surprising to find the public-private sector wage differential to differ across components of the public sector, or to differ across various levels of government, or to differ in different countries?

18. In Canada in the year 1975, the rate of increase in base wages in collective agreements was 20.0 per cent in the provincial public sector and 21.3 per cent in the health-education-welfare sector, compared to 14.4 per cent in the private sector. These large increases in particular elements of the public sector apparently triggered public reaction. Why might it be a bit hazardous to react to specific public sector increases in a particular year; that is, why might one expect public sector wage settlements to be more volatile than private sector wages?

19. What current forces are at work to suggest that public sector wage settlements are under pressure to be more moderate now and in the near future?

20. Even if there is a pure public sector wage advantage of 7 per cent based on 1971 Canadian Census data, perhaps the appropriate policy response is one of benign neglect. Do you agree or disagree and why?

21. In many instances in the public sector, wages are set by wage arbitration. Discuss the various criteria that you think would be appropriate to utilize in deciding upon the appropriate wage. Indicate any theoretical and practical problems associated with the criteria that you have discussed.

REFERENCES AND FURTHER READINGS

Annable, J. Jr. A theory of wage determination in public employment. *Quarterly Review of Economics and Business* 14 (Winter 1974) 53-58.

Arthurs, H. *Collective Bargaining by Public Employees in Canada: Five Models.* Ann Arbor, Mich.: Institute of Labor and Industrial Relations, 1971.

Ashenfelter, O. The effects of unionization of wages in the public sector: the case of fire fighters. *ILRR* 24 (January 1971) 191-202.

Ashenfelter, O. and R. Ehrenberg. The demand for labor in the public sector. *Labor in the Public and Nonprofit Sectors,* D. Hamermesh (eds.). Princeton, N.J.: Princeton University Press, 1975.

Bessette, L. Détermination des salaires dans la fonction publique fédérale américaine: applicabilité au Quebec. *RI/IR* 32 (No. 2, 1977) 161-171.

Bird, R. The growth of the public service in Canada. *Public Employment and Compensation in Canada,* D. Foot (ed.). Toronto: Butterworths, 1978.

Burton, J. Local government bargaining and management structure. *IR* 11 (May 1972) 123-139.

Carlson, R. and J. Robinson. Toward a public employment theory. *ILRR* 22 (January 1969) 243-248. Comments by J. Craft and reply 23 (October 1969) 89-100.

Cousineau, J.-M. and R. Lacroix. *Wage Determination in Major Collective Agreements in the Private and Public Sectors.* Ottawa: Economic Council of Canada, 1977.

Craft, J. Fire fighter strategy in wage negotiations. *Quarterly Review of Economics and Business* 11 (Autumn 1971) 65-76.

Dean, A. Earnings in the public and private sectors, 1950-1975. *National Institute Economic Review* (November 1975) 60-70.

Derber, M. and others. Bargaining and budget making in Illinois public institutions. *ILRR* 27 (October 1973) 59-62.

Donoian, H. A new approach to setting the pay of federal blue collar workers. *MLR* 92 (April 1969) 30-34.

Doston, A. A general theory of public employment. *Public Administration Review* 16 (Summer 1956) 197-211.

Doyle, P. Municipal pension plans. *MLR* 100 (November 1977) 24-31.

Ehrenberg, R. *The Demand for State and Local Government Employees: An Economic Analysis.* Lexington, Mass.: D.C. Heath, 1972.

Ehrenberg, R. The demand for state and local government employees. *AER* 63 (June 1973) 366-379.

Ehrenberg, R. Municipal government structure, unionization and wages of fire fighters. *ILRR* 27 (October 1973) 36-48.

Ehrenberg, R. Heterogeneous labor, minimum hiring standards, and job vacancies in public employment. *JPE* 81 (November/December 1973) 1442-1459.

Ehrenberg, R. and G. Goldstein. A model of public sector wage determination. *Journal of Urban Economics* 2 (1975) 223-245.

Field, C. and R. Keller. How salaries of large cities compare with industry and federal pay. *MLR* (November 1976) 23-28.

Fogel, W. and D. Lewin. Wage determination in the public sector. *ILRR* 27 (April 1974) 410-431.

Freeman, R. Demand for labor in a nonprofit market: university faculty. *Labor in the Public and Nonprofit Sectors,* D. Hamermesh (ed.). Princeton, N.J.: Princeton University Press, 1975.

Freund, J. Market and union influence on municipal employee wages. *ILRR* 27 (April 1974) 391-404.

Frey, D. Wage determination in public schools and the effects of unionization. *Labor in the Public and Nonprofit Sectors.* D. Hamermesh (ed.). Princeton, N.J.: Princeton University Press, 1975.

Gavett, T. Comparability wage programs. *MLR* 94 (September 1971) 38-43.

Gerwin, D. Compensation decisions in public organizations. *IR* 8 (February 1969) 174-184.

Goldenberg, S. Collective bargaining in the provincial public services. *Collective Bargaining in the Public Service.* Toronto: Institute of Public Administration of Canada, 1973.

Gunderson, M. Data on public sector wages in Canada. *Public Employment and Compensation in Canada,* D. Foot (ed.). Toronto: Butterworths, 1978a, 107-126.

Gunderson, M. Public-private wage and nonwage differentials in Canada: some calculations from published tabulations. *Public Employment and Compensation in Canada,* D. Foot (ed.). Toronto: Butterworths, 1978b, 127-166.

Gunderson, M. Public sector wage determination: a review of the literature. *Public Employment and Compensation in Canada,* D. Foot (ed.). Toronto: Butterworths, 1978c, 167-188.

Gunderson, M. Wage determination in the public sector: Canada and the U.S. *Labour and Society* 4 (January 1979a) 49-70.

Gunderson, M. Earnings differentials between the public and private sectors. *CJE* 12 (May 1979b) 228-242.

Harel, G. Job evaluation and wage setting in the public sector of Israel. *RL/IR* 31 (No. 2) 284-299.

Hawkesworth, R. Private and public sector pay. *BJIR* (July 1976) 206-213.

Hirsch, W. A model of municipal labour markets. *Journal of Urban Economics* 2 (1975) 333-348.

Holley, H. Jr. Unique complexities of public sector labor relations. *Personnel Journal* 55 (February 1976) 72-75.

Kasper, H. The impact of collective bargaining on public school teachers. *ILRR* 24 (October 1970) 57-72. Comment by R. Baird and J. Landon and reply 25 (April 1972) 410-423.

Katz, H. Municipal pay determination: the case of San Francisco. *IR* 18 (Winter 1979) 44-58.

King, S. Wage differences narrow between government and private hospitals. *MLR* 97 (April 1974) 56-57.

Koczak, S. Collective bargaining and comparability in the federal sector. *IRRA* (December 1975) 197-204.

Lewin, D. Aspects of wage determination in local government employment. *Public Administration Review* 34 (March/April 1974) 149-155.

Lewin, D. Wage parity and the supply of police and firemen. *IR* 12 (February 1973) 77-85.

Lewin, D. Public employment relations: confronting the issues. *IR* (October 1973) 309-321.

Lewin, D. The prevailing wage principle and public wage decisions. *Public Personnel Management* 3 (November/December 1974) 473-485.

Lewis, L. Federal pay comparability procedures. *MLR* 92 (February 1969) 10-13.

Lipsky, D. and J. Droting. The influence of collective bargaining on teachers' salaries in New York State. *ILRR* 27 (October 1973) 18-35.

Love, T. and G. Sulzner. Political implications of public employee bargaining. *IR* 11 (February 1972) 18-33.

Ostry, S. and M. Zaidi. *Labour Economics in Canada*. 3rd ed. Toronto: Macmillan, 1979.

Owen, J. Toward a public employment wage theory: some econometric evidence on teacher quality. *ILRR* 25 (January 1972) 213-222.

Perloff, S. Comparing municipal industry and federal pay. *MLR* 94 (October 1971) 46-50.

Phillips, P. Collective bargaining dynamics and the public interest sector: the market and politics. *Collective Bargaining in the Essential and Public Service Sector,* M. Gunderson (ed.). Toronto: University of Toronto Press, 1975.

Plunket, T. Municipal collective bargaining. *Collective Bargaining in the Public Service.* Toronto: Institute of Public Administration of Canada, 1973.

Quinn, J. Wage differentials among older workers in the public and private sectors. *JHR* 14 (Winter 1979) 41-62.

Quinn, J. Postal sector wages. *IR* 18 (Winter 1979) 92-96.

Reder, M. The theory of employment and wages in the public sector. *Labor in the Public and Nonprofit Sectors,* D. Hammermesh (ed.). Princeton, N.J.: Princeton University Press, 1975.

Rufolo, A. Local government wages and services. *Federal Reserve Bank of Philadelphia Business Review* (January/February 1977) 13-20.

Seiling, M. Private hospitals closing wage gap. *MLR* 100 (May 1977) 46-47.

Schmenner, R. The determination of municipal employee wages. *R.E. Stats.* 55 (February 1973) 83-90.

Shaw, L. and R.T. Clark Jr. The practical differences between public and private sector collective bargaining. *U.C.L.A. Law Review* 19 (August 1972) 867-886.

Smith, S. Pay differentials between federal government and private sector workers. *ILRR* 29 (January 1976) 179-197. Also comment by W. Bailey and reply 31 (October 1977) 78-87.

Smith, S. Government wage differentials by sex. *JHR* 11 (Spring 1976) 185-199.

Smith, S. Are postal workers over- or under-paid? *IR* 15 (May 1976) 168-176.

Smith, S. Government wage differentials. *Journal of Urban Economics* 4 (July 1977) 248-277.

Smith, S. *Equal Pay in the Public Sector: Fact or Fantasy.* Princeton, N.J.: Industrial Relations Section, 1977.

Subbaro, A. Impasse choice and wages in the Canadian federal service. *IR* 18 (Spring 1979) 233-236.

Thompson, M. and J. Cairnie. Compulsory arbitration: the case of British Columbia teachers. *ILRR* 29 (October 1973) 3-17.

Thornton, R. The effects of collective negotiations on relative teachers salaries. *Quarterly Review of Economics and Business* 11 (Winter 1971) 37-47.

Wellington, H. and R. Winter. The limits of collective bargaining in public employment. *Yale Law Journal* 78 (June 1969) 115-130.

Wellington, H. and R. Winter. Structuring collective bargaining in public employment. *Yale Law Journal* 79 (April 1970) 805-870.

Wellington, H. and R. Winter. *The Unions and the Cities.* Washington: Brookings Institute, 1971.

Williams, C. Collective bargaining in the public sector: a re-examination. *RI/IR* 28 (No. 1, 1973) 17-33.

Williams, C. and G. Swimmer. The relationship between public and private sector wages in Alberta. *RI/IR* 30 (No. 2, 1975) 217-226.

Wilkins, J. Wage and benefit determination in the public service in Canada. *Collective Bargaining in the Public Service.* Toronto: Institute of Public Administration of Canada, 1973.

Wilkins, J. Senior salary levels in government. *Canadian Business Review* 1 (Spring 1974) 41-44.

Wiseman, S. Wage criteria for collective bargaining. *ILRR* 9 (January 1956) 252-267.

Chapter 21

Discrimination and Male-Female Earnings Differentials

The economic analysis of discrimination provides a good application for many of the basic principles of labour market economics. In addition it indicates the limitations of some of these tools in an area where non-economic factors may play a crucial role. In fact, many would argue that discrimination is not really an economic phenomena, but rather is sociological or psychological in nature. While recognizing the importance of these factors in any analysis of discrimination, the basic position taken here is that economics does have a great deal to say about discrimination. More specifically, it can indicate the labour market impact of the sociological or psychological constraints and preferences. More important, economics may shed light on the expected impact of alternative policies designed to combat discrimination in the labour market.

Although the focus of this analysis is on sex discrimination in the labour market, it is important to realize that discrimination can occur against various groups and in different markets. Discrimination can occur in the housing market, product market, capital market and human capital market (e.g. education and training), as well as in the labour market. It can be based on a variety of factors including race, age, language, national origin, or political affiliation, as well as on sex.

In order to better understand the economics of sex discrimination, the reasons, sources and forms of sex discrimination are first discussed. Various theories of discrimination are then presented and empirical evidence is given to document the existence of sex discrimination in the labour market. The chapter concludes with a discussion of alternative policies to combat discrimination in the labour market.

DISCRIMINATION: REASONS AND SOURCES

Reasons for Discrimination

Labour market discrimination against females may result because males have a preference for working with or buying from fellow males. This prejudice would be especially strong against females in supervisory positions or in jobs of responsibility. STAT DISGR.

Discrimination may also occur because of erroneous information on the labour market worth of females. Such erroneous information could

344

come from females who consistently underestimate their own capacity in labour market or it could come from employers who consistently underestimate the productivity of females. Erroneous information on the part of employers may come from the subjective reports of co-workers or supervisors, or it may be based on sex-biased test scores.

Because information on individual workers is extremely costly to acquire, employers may judge individual females on the basis of the average performance of all females. Although, from the employers' viewpoint, such statistical judgment may be efficient, it could be inequitable for many individual females. As Weisskoff (1972, p. 164) points out: "Discrimination is the process of forming stereotyped views that all members of a particular group are assumed to possess the characteristics of the group. Thus, the case of an individual female applicant is not considered on the basis of her particular job history or aspirations. Such treatment may reduce the cost of screening applicants, but it cannot be considered equitable".

Males may also discriminate for reasons of job security. To protect their high wage jobs from low wage female competition, males would use the forces of governments, unions and business cartels to ensure that power remains in their hands and is used to further their own ends.

Obviously, discrimination can occur for any, or all, of the previously mentioned reasons of preference, erroneous information, statistical judgment, or job security. As we shall see later, the effectiveness of policies designed to combat discrimination often depends on the reasons for the discrimination. *OPEN SENTENCE FOR Policies.*

Sources of Discrimination

Labour market discrimination can come from a variety of sources. *Employers may discriminate* in their hiring and promotion policies as well as their wage policies. To a certain extent the forces of competition would deter employers' discriminating since they would forgo profits by not hiring and promoting females who are as productive as their male counterparts. However, profit-maximizing firms do have to respond to pressure from their customers and male employees. For this reason they may be reluctant to hire and promote females, or they may pay females a lower wage than equally productive males. In addition, firms in the large not-for-profit sector (e.g. government, education, hospitals) may be able to discriminate without having to worry about losing profits by not hiring and promoting females.

In addition to discrimination on the part of employers, *male co-workers* may also discriminate for reasons of prejudice, misinformation or job security. Representing the wishes of a male majority, craft unions may discriminate through the hiring hall or apprenticeship system and industrial unions may discriminate by bargaining for male wages that exceed female wages for the same work. Another potential source of discrimination is *customers* who may be reluctant to purchase the services of females or who may not patronize establishments that employ females, especially in positions of responsibility.

THEORIES OF LABOUR MARKET DISCRIMINATION

Alternative theories of sex discrimination in the labour market can be classified according to whether they focus on the demand or supply side of the labour market, or on non-competitive aspects of labour markets.

Demand Theories of Discrimination

Demand theories of discrimination have the common result that the demand for female labour is reduced relative to the demand for equally productive male labour. The decreased demand for female labour would reduce the employment of females and, unless the supply of female labour is perfectly elastic, the decreased demand would reduce the wages of females relative to the wages of equally productive males. How does discrimination lead to a reduction in the demand for female labour?

According to Becker (1971, p. 14), employers act as if $W_f(1 + d_f)$ were the net wage paid to females, male co-workers act as if $W_m(1 - d_m)$ were the net wage they receive when working with females, and consumers act as if $p_c(1 + d_c)$ were the price paid for a product sold by a female. In all cases, the discrimination coefficient, "d", represents the cost, in per cent, associated with hiring, working with, or buying from females. For example, a firm that has a discrimination coefficient of .10 and that can hire all the female labour it wants at $2.00 per hour, would act as if it paid $2.00(1 + .10) = \$2.20$ each time it hired a female. Clearly such discrimination reduces the demand for females relative to equally productive males.

Arrow (1973) gives a neoclassical theory of discrimination based on the firm's desired demand for labour when the firm maximizes utility (rather than simply profits) and the firm's utility is increased by employing fewer workers from minority groups. Again, this results in a reduced demand for female labour and lower female wages.[1]

The reduced demand for female labour in the discriminatory sector

---

[1] Arrow's (1973) neoclassical theory of discrimination can be presented formally as follows. Assume that the firm maximizes utility, U, which is a positive function of its profits, Π, and a negative function of the number of females, F, it employs (discrimination). That is $U = \mu(\Pi,F)$ where the partial derivatives are denoted by $U_\Pi > 0$ and $U_F < 0$ and where $\Pi = P \cdot Q(M + F) - W_m M - W_f F$. For simplicity we have assumed that output, Q, is produced by perfectly substitutable male and female labour of equal productivity so that the output is denoted by the production function $Q(M+F)$. Utility maximizing firms will hire females until $U_F=0$ which, from the utility function, implies $U_\Pi \Pi_F + U_F = 0$. Since $\Pi_F = PQ_F - W_F$, utility maximization implies $U_\Pi(PQ_F - W_F) + U_F = 0$, which upon rearrangement yields $W_F = PQ_F + U_F/U_\Pi$. Thus female wages will be less than their marginal revenue product, PQ_F, since $U_F < 0$ and $U_\Pi > 0$. In addition, female wages will be less than male wages if males are paid a wage equal to their marginal revenue product.

would create excess supply and low female wages in the non-discriminatory sector. As Zellner (1972, p. 157) points out:

> Assuming that discrimination takes the form of a preference for males over comparable females in masculine occupations, it results in a demand curve for women to the left of that which would prevail in this sector in a non-discriminatory situation, thereby lowering female employment in masculine occupations. This reduced demand for women in the masculine sector increases their supply to those occupations in which males are not preferred to females, thus creating a "feminine" sector. Discrimination therefore directly lowers the female wage in masculine occupations by reducing demand for women in this sector, and indirectly lowers the female wage in feminine occupations by increasing their supply to this sector.

The demand for female labour relative to male labour also depends on information concerning their relative productivity. To the extent that employers consistently underestimate the productivity of females, they would correspondingly reduce their demand for female labour. This misinformation on the part of employers may be due to their own ingrained prejudices as well as to erroneous information fostered by male customers and co-workers.

Supply Theories of Discrimination

Supply theories of discrimination have the common result that the supply of female labour is increased by discrimination or, conversely, that the female asking wage is reduced by discrimination.

The crowding hypothesis, as put forth by Fawcett (1918) and Edgeworth (1922), and formalized by Bergmann (1971), implies that females tend to be segregated into "female-type" jobs. The resulting abundance of supply lowers their marginal productivity and hence their wage. Thus, even if females are paid a wage equal to their marginal productivity, their wage will be less than male wages that are not depressed by an excess supply.

In a similar vein, dual labour market theory posits two separate and distinct labour markets. The primary or core labour market (unionized, monopolistic, expanding) provides secure employment at high wages. The secondary or peripheral labour market (non-unionized, highly competitive, declining) is characterized by unstable employment at low wages. Men tend to be employed in the primary labour market, women in the secondary labour market. Prejudice on the part of the dominant group and its desire to exclude female competition will prevent the entry of women into the primary labour market. Unions, occupational licensing, discriminatory employment tests, and barriers to education and training, can all work against the entry of females into the core labour market. Female immobility may also result because of women's stronger ties to the household and their tendency to move to the places of their husbands' employment. For these various reasons, females tend to be crowded into jobs in the secondary labour market with its concomitant unstable employment and low wages. Their low wages and undesirable working conditions in turn create high absenteeism and turnover which further depress wages in the secondary labour market.

Females' attitudes on their own labour market worth also may induce them to lower their asking wage when seeking employment. Because of conditioning in a male-dominated labour market, females may erroneously underestimate their own labour market worth. This would tend to lower female asking (reservation) wages; that is, the female labour supply schedule would be shifted vertically downwards. Employers would naturally foster these attitudes because they lead to lower labour costs.

Non-Competitive Theories of Discrimination

In theory, male-female wage differentials for equally productive workers are inconsistent with competitive equilibrium. As long as females could be paid a wage lower than that of equally productive males, firms that do not have an aversion to hiring females would increase their profits by hiring females. The resultant increased demand for females would bid up their wages, and the process would continue until the male-female wage differential is eliminated. Firms that do not have an aversion to hiring females would be maximizing profits by employing large numbers of females; firms that have an aversion to hiring females would be forgoing profits by employing only males. According to competitive theory, discrimination leads to a segregation of males and females, not wage differentials. It also implies that discrimination should be reduced over time since firms that discriminate will go out of business as they forgo profits to discriminate.

Some would argue that these predictions of competitive economic theory are at variance with the facts. Male-female wage differentials seem to persist, and discrimination does not appear to be declining over time. What then are some of the factors that may explain this persistence in the face of competitive forces?

Arrow (1973, pp. 20-23) attributes the persistence of male-female wage differentials to costs of adjustment and imperfect information. Even if they do acquire the information that profits can be increased by hiring low wage females to do certain jobs performed by higher wage males, firms cannot immediately replace their male workers by an all-female work-force. There are fixed costs associated with recruiting and hiring; consequently, firms want to spread these fixed costs as much as possible by retaining their existing work-force. Firms may replace male turnover by new female recruits, but they would be reluctant to immediately replace their male work-force. In essence, Arrow implies that the long run may be a very long time.

Stiglitz (1973) provides a queuing theory to explain the persistence of male-female wage differentials for equally productive workers. He argues that some firms pay wages greater than competitive market wages in order to reduce turnover, improve morale, or secure the advantages of always having a queue from which to hire workers. Other firms pay greater than competitive wages because of union or minimum wage pressure, or because of a necessity to share monopoly or oligopoly profits with their workers. The resultant higher-than-competitive wage enables these high wage firms to hire from a queue of available workers. Rationing of the scarce jobs may be carried out on the basis of nepotism or discrimination. Thus, discriminatory wage differentials may exist in a long-run competitive equilibrium when profit-maximizing firms minimize labour costs by paying high wages in order to reduce turnover or improve morale, or because they face institutional constraints such as unions or minimum wage legislation.

As an alternative explanation for the persistence of discrimination, Freeman (1973) argues that discrimination comes mainly from non-competitive sectors, mainly the government and trade unions. Reflecting majority wishes, governments discriminate both in their own hiring practices and in the provision of education and training. In the case of sex discrimination, this would reduce the skill endowment of minorities and reduce the number of professional-managerial females who would hire fellow females. Also reflecting the wishes of a male majority, unions could discriminate against females, especially in apprenticeship and training programs. Freeman also emphasizes the importance of social pressure in sanctioning instances of non-discrimination, especially when profits can be made through discrimination.

In the same vein, Thurow (1969) emphasizes that majority groups use the power inherent in governments, unions and business monopolies to further their own ends through discrimination and segregation. He implies that an alteration in the power structure would do most to improve the economic position of minorities.

Monopsony is another non-competitive factor that can affect female wages relative to male wages, mainly in two ways. First, if females tend to be employed by monopsonists, their wages will be reduced correspondingly. Because of their immobility (tied to household and to husbands' places of employment), females may not have the effective threat of mobility necessary to receive a competitive wage. Second, monopsonists may try to differentiate their work-force so as to pay the higher wage rate only to some employees. One obvious way of differentiating workers is by sex. Thus, the company may pay higher wages to male employees and yet not have to pay these higher wages to its female employees who do the same work, simply because the female employees do not consider themselves direct competitors with male employees doing the same job. Employers find it in their interest to foster this attitude, since it enables them to maintain the wage differentials based on sex. The formal monopsony model of sex discrimination with separate male-female labour supply schedules was discussed earlier in Chapter 11.

Productivity Differences: Choice or Discrimination?

Female wages may differ from male wages because of productivity differences that arise because of differences in the human capital endowments and differences in the absenteeism and turnover of males and females. The human capital endowments could include *acquired* attributes such as education, training, labour market information, mobility and labour market experience, as well as more *innate* characteristics such as intelligence, strength, perseverance or dexterity. In general there is little reason to believe the *net* endowment of these *innate* characteristics to differ substantially between the sexes, and in an increasingly mechanized society the innate characteristic for which there may be the greatest difference — physical strength — takes on reduced importance. It is in the area of acquired human capital endowments that productivity differences may arise.

Human capital formation will occur until the present value of the benefits (usually in the form of increased earnings) equals the present value of the cost (both direct cost and the opportunity cost of the earnings forgone while acquiring human capital). Because of their dual role in the household and in the labour market, women traditionally have a shorter expected length of stay in the labour market. Consequently, they have a reduced benefit period from which to recoup the costs of human capital formation. In addition, their time in the labour market tends to be intermittent and subject to a considerable degree of uncertainty, thus creating rapid depreciation of their human capital and preventing them from acquiring continuous labour market experience. For this reason it may be economically rational for females (or firms) to be reluctant to invest in female human capital formation that is labour market oriented.

The human capital decision therefore may reflect rational choice, but it may also reflect discrimination as well as rational choice subject to discriminatory constraints. Females may be discriminated against in the returns they receive for acquiring human capital as well as in borrowing to finance the cost of human capital formation. In addition, family and peer group pressures may close off certain avenues of human capital formation. Most important, female responsibility for household tasks may reflect discrimination more than choice. Whatever the reason, females tend to acquire less labour-market-oriented human capital than males, and consequently their wages and employment opportunities are reduced in the labour market. This occurs even if in the labour market there is no discrimination on the part of firms, co-workers or customers. Differences in wage and employment opportunities may reflect productivity differences, which in turn may come about because of rational economic choice as well as discrimination prior to entering the labour market.

Productivity and hence wage differences may also occur because of differences in the absenteeism and turnover of females. This is especially the case if female turnover occurs primarily as a result of leaving the labour force (which would reduce earnings as explained earlier), and male turnover occurs primarily to move to a higher paying job. Higher absenteeism for females would also occur, in large part, because of their household responsibilities, especially care of children. In addition to causing lower wages, higher absenteeism and turnover may be the result of low wages: cause and effect work in both directions to reinforce each other.

As with the case of the acquisition of human capital, so with absenteeism and turnover, it is difficult to know how much of the differences in behaviour between the sexes is a matter of economic choice as opposed to discrimination. The fact that the household responsibility of females is so important in these aspects of productivity makes it more understandable that there will be increased pressure for a more equitable division of labour in the household as well as more day care facilities for children. In addition, in empirical work that attempts to control for productivity differences between males and females, we should be careful in interpreting the productivity adjusted wage and employment pattern as ones that are free of discrimination. The discrimination may simply be occurring outside of the labour market.

EVIDENCE ON MALE-FEMALE EARNINGS DIFFERENTIALS

Empirical studies have employed a variety of techniques to estimate the male-female earnings differential and to see how much of the differential reflects discrimination. The results are quite varied, in part because of different data sources and methodology, but also in part because of an emphasis on different aspects of discrimination. Some studies focus on wage discrimination within the same establishment and occupation; others involve measures of sex discrimination that also reflect the crowding of females into low wage establishments, occupations and industries;[2] and other studies utilize measures of earnings differentials that could reflect discrimination outside of the labour market, perhaps in educational institutions or in households.

As with many differences in empirical research, it is not that one method is correct and the other incorrect. They simply show different things. Hence, it is important to know exactly what the study is attempting to measure, especially in making comparisons across studies or in utilizing the results for policy purposes.

With these qualifications in mind, some generalizations can be made on the empirical evidence, based largely on the Canadian studies referred to in the bibliography. On average, females tend to earn 50 to 60 per cent of what males earn in a year.[3] This unadjusted ratio may reflect wage discrimi-

---

2 Evidence of the disproportionate number of females in low wage occupations and industries in Canada is given in Gunderson (1976, pp. 111-118).

3 Holmes (1976) also indicates that when one considers the lower potential working years of females, their present value of expected lifetime earnings is only about 40 per cent of that of males.

nation, the segregation of females into low wage firms, occupations and industries, as well as differences in productivity-related factors such as education, training, experience, and absenteeism and turnover. Differences in these productivity-related factors may reflect unconstrained choices and they may reflect pre-labour market discrimination, perhaps in educational institutions or in the household.

Unfortunately the evidence does not enable one to state precisely the relative contributions of each and all of these factors to the overall earnings differential. Studies that make some *rough* adjustments find that females who work full-time, and with levels of education, training and experience, and with occupational and industrial distributions similar to those of males, tend to earn approximately 80 per cent of what males earn. This is the case, for example, in Ostry (1968), where adjustments were made by examining males and females with similar characteristics, and it is the case in Robb (1978) and Gunderson (1979), where differences in these characteristics were controlled for by multiple regression analysis.[4]

Because of the lack of data, the adjustment factors involved in arriving at the adjusted ratio of .80 are quite crude. In particular, they do not reflect differences in such factors as absenteeism or turnover, nor do they reflect differences in the extent to which the education or training is labour market oriented, or the extent to which experience is continuous. The possibility that the earnings gap of .20, implied by an adjusted female/male earnings ratio of .80, cannot be fully attributed to wage discrimination (but may reflect other discrimination) is reinforced by studies that utilize data on male-female wage differentials within the same narrowly-defined occupations within the same establishments.

Gunderson (1975), for example, finds the earnings ratio to be approximately .82 in such circumstances.[5] In addition, within incentive pay jobs where pay would be more directly linked with productivity, the earnings ratio averaged .88. To the extent that the incentive pay system reflects productiv-

---

[4] The methodology—first utilized with U.S. data by Oaxaca (1973), Blinder (1973), and Malkiel and Malkiel (1973)—is identical to that which was formally presented in the previous chapter to decompose the public-private sector wage differential. Separate earnings equations are estimated for males and females. Subtracting the female from the male earnings equations, evaluated at the mean of the explanatory variables, yields

$$\bar{y}_m - \bar{y}_f = \Sigma b_m \bar{X}_m - \Sigma b_f \bar{X}_f$$

Subtracting and adding $\Sigma b_f \bar{X}_m$ from the right-hand side, and collecting terms, yields

$$\bar{y}_m - \bar{y}_f = \Sigma b_m (\bar{X}_m - \bar{X}_f) + \Sigma (b_m - b_f) \bar{X}_f$$

That is, the average male-female earnings differential can be decomposed into two parts: a portion attributable to differences in endowments of wage determining characteristics (some of which may reflect pre-labour market discrimination), and a portion attributable to different wage payments for the same characteristics (i.e. wage discrimination).

[5] The actual measure of the wage differential estimated was the proportionate male-female wage differential $(w_m - w_f)/w_f$ of .22, which implies a female to male wage ratio w_f/w_m of .82.

ity, this suggests that the marginal productivity of females averages 88 per cent of males. Much of this difference, of course, may reflect pre-labour market discrimination as well as occupational segregation. (Recall that occupational segregation would result in a lower marginal productivity of females as they were crowded into female-type jobs). If the marginal physical product of females is 88 per cent of males, but their wage averaged only 82 per cent of males, the adjusted ratio of female to male earnings for equally productive workers is .93.[6] That is, in the particular data set analysed, females tended to earn 93 per cent of what equally productive males earned in the same establishment.

Clearly this adjusted ratio is much higher than the adjusted ratio of approximately .80 implied by regression analysis. The different ratios, however, indicate different things. In particular, the adjusted ratio of .93 suggests that wage discrimination (narrowly defined as unequal pay for equally productive work) within the same narrowly-defined occupations within the same establishments is small — but it does exist. The small magnitude of wage discrimination may be expected because such discrimination is most blatant, and is subject to equal pay laws.

This suggests that discrimination within the labour market probably occurs more in the form of the segregation of females into low wage occupations, industries and establishments rather than in the form of wage discrimination within the same establishment. In addition, discrimination outside the labour market, in particular within educational institutions and households, may be partly responsible for differences in such factors as the labour market orientation of education and training, or in differences in absenteeism and turnover or continuous work experience. The extent to which each and all of these factors, however, contribute to the fact that on average females earn only 50 to 60 per cent of what males earn, remains an unanswered question.

The numbers utilized throughout this discussion are meant to be illustrative more than definitive, since they are based on a limited number of empirical studies. Nevertheless the evidence does seem to suggest the existence of sex discrimination in a variety of forms — wage discrimination within the same establishment; segregation into low wage establishments, occupations and industries; and possibly discrimination outside of the labour market. Hence, the importance of various policies designed to combat sex discrimination in its various forms.

POLICIES TO COMBAT SEX DISCRIMINATION

Because of the variety of sources and forms of discrimination, policies to combat discrimination have also tended to take on a variety of forms. The main thrusts of public policy have been in the areas of equal pay legislation,

---

[6] If w_f/w_m is .82 and $MPP_f/MPP_m = .88$, then $(w_f/w_m)/(MPP_f/MPP_m) = .82/.88 = .93$. Therefore, $w_f/w_m = .93$ when $MPP_f = MPP_m$.

equal employment opportunity legislation, affirmative action, policies designed to facilitate female employment, and policies designed to alter attitudes and preferences. Each of these will be discussed in turn.

Equal Pay Legislation

The history, coverage, extent, and enforcement of equal pay in Canada is reviewed in Cook and Eberts (1976), and Agarwal and Jain (1978). As indicated in Agarwal and Jain (1978, p. 172), as of 1977, "all jurisdictions in Canada have laws which require equal pay for equal work without discrimination on the basis of sex". Although there are important differences in the laws of each jurisdiction, they basically require equal pay for substantially similar work within the same establishment. The scope of the law is limited by the fact that it deals with only one aspect of discrimination — wage discrimination within an establishment—and as our earlier discussion of the empirical evidence indicated, this is probably a quantitatively small aspect of discrimination. In addition, the enforcement of the law can be difficult because it often relies upon individuals to complain and because there are problems of interpreting what is meant by equal work, although the courts have interpreted this rather broadly. The limited empirical evidence in Gunderson (1975, 1976) also finds no impact of equal pay legislation in narrowing male-female wage differentials, although confirmation of this result would require further evidence over a longer period of time so that all adjustments could occur.

A more serious problem associated with equal pay laws is the possibility, associated with all forms of wage fixing, that they could reduce employment opportunities for females. Faced with having to pay females a higher wage, firms may substitute other factors of production (capital or male labour) for female labour. Or firms may cut back their output or even go out of business because of the higher female wage costs. These are the familiar substitution and scale effects, respectively, predicted by economic theory to result from any wage fixing legislation.

This potential adverse employment effect of equal pay legislation has long been recognized. At the turn of the century, Rathbone (1917, p. 57) writes that equal pay for equal work has been adopted "by the more astute and enlightened of the trade unionists, who see in it an effective way of maintaining the exclusion of women while appearing as the champions of equality between the sexes". In the same vein, Brady (1947, p. 53) writes: "When an extraordinary number of women are added to the labour force in a short period, they are seen as a serious threat to wage levels, and official action on equal pay is the result. . . . The timing, phrasing and interpretation of the orders and laws have made clear . . . that they are designed to protect men, and to prevent the degradation of the wage structure".

Equal pay laws have also been condemned on the grounds that they prevent women from accepting lower wages to obtain on-the-job training which would improve their future wages and employability. To cite Sawhill (1973, p. 394),

> Equal pay laws are not very helpful. Although they may guarantee equal wages to women working side by side with men and although they have obvious moral and symbolic value, they tend to reduce the training alternatives available to women, which is a major source of the sex differential. Much more emphasis needs to be placed on opening up employment opportunities.

Equal employment opportunity legislation has been suggested as one device for expanding employment opportunities for females.

Equal Employment Opportunity Legislation

Equal employment opportunity legislation — also termed fair employment practices legislation — is designed to prevent discrimination in recruiting, hiring and promotion. The history, coverage, extent, enforcement and legal issues involved with equal employment laws in Canada are thoroughly reviewed in Cook and Eberts (1976).

In general, provincial equal employment opportunity legislation is part of the Human Rights Code of each province. Usually, complaints concerning discrimination in employment are made by the individual party to the Human Rights Commission. An officer of the Commission tries to reach a settlement by conciliation. If this is unsuccessful, a board of inquiry investigates and makes a final decision. Most provinces have appeal procedures to regular courts. Although the Commissions generally act only on complaints, on a more informal basis they can and do persuade employers to increase their quotas of female employees.

In spite of the fact that this procedure is time consuming and cumbersome, equal employment opportunity legislation does have the virtue of increasing the demand for female labour at the recruiting, hiring and promotion stages. This in turn should increase female wages *and* employment. Unlike equal pay laws which increase female wages at the expense of their employment, equal employment opportunity legislation would work through the market to increase both the wages and employment of females.

Some have argued that equal pay and equal employment legislation are complementary, in that one is useless without the other. The argument is that without equal employment opportunity legislation, equal pay would result in employers refusing to recruit, hire and promote females. Similarly, without equal pay, equal employment opportunity legislation would result in employers hiring females but paying them lower wages than equally productive males. However, this ignores the economic argument that the increased demand for females resulting from equal employment opportunity legislation would work through the market to increase female wages. Equal pay may be a natural by-product of equal employment opportunities.

Affirmative Action

Affirmative action programs are related to equal employment opportunity legislation in the sense that they are designed to increase the employment opportunities for women. In the Canadian context, affirmative action policies are discussed in Cook and Eberts (1976). As they indicate, affirmative action programs may be voluntary, as when government agencies assist employers with advice and information. Or they may be more coercive, as is often the case in the United States when courts have ordered employers to move towards employing a larger quota of women, or when governments have required affirmative action before they provided funding or a government contract (i.e. contract compliance).

As indicated in Cook and Eberts (1976, p. 184), "one of the main advantages of affirmative action is that it shifts the costs of securing compliance with generally accepted social goals from the individual to the broader group". In essence, the pressure is on the employer to prove that discrimination does not exist, rather than for the individual worker to prove that discrimination does exist. This distinction is important since it may uncover pockets of discrimination that would otherwise go unnoticed or unchallenged, and it may shift the cost of reducing discrimination onto those who discriminate. To the extent that affirmative action is successful, like equal employment opportunities legislation, it should increase *both* the employment opportunities for women *and*, because of this increased demand for their services, the wages of women.

Policies to Facilitate Female Employment

In addition to the various direct policies such as equal pay and equal employment opportunity legislation, and affirmative action, there are a variety of policies that can indirectly affect the employment opportunities and wages of women. These could be labelled *facilitating* policies, in that they are generally designed to expand the range of choices open to women and hence to facilitate their participation in labour market activities in a non-discriminatory fashion.

Currently, women tend to have the primary responsibility for household tasks, especially the bearing and raising of children. This may reflect historical tradition, comparative advantage (which itself may be historically determined), or discrimination within the household. Whatever the origin, this responsibility can create tensions over the equitable division of labour within the household when both parties engage in labour market work. Women can be confronted with an unpleasant "choice": to retain primary responsibility for household work with all of the burden that this implies, including the difficulty of performing well in both the household and labour market; or to insist upon sharing household responsibilities and risk social and possibly family disapproval. For many the choice is evident; for others it is a difficult one.

To minimize some of the conflict inherent in such a choice, and to expand the employment opportunities available to women, facilitating policies have been suggested. Improved availability of day care, flexible working hours, part-time jobs, and childbirth leaves are examples of such facilitating policies. In the interests of equality they would apply to males as well as females, so as to maximize the opportunities of households to allocate their labour amongst various market and non-market alternatives.

Certainly such policies are not without their costs, which could be substantial in some areas such as subsidized day care. Consequently there is legitimate debate over the efficiency of such policies. What is less contentious, from the perspective of economics at least, is that at a minimum such facilitating policies be allowed to emerge in response to market demands. This may require, for example, that day-care expenses be tax deductible or that quality regulations do not restrict excessively the availability of day care. Or it may require that government policies do not discourage flexible working arrangements by increasing quasi-fixed costs of employment which may encourage employers to utilize only a core of male workers.

To a large extent these institutional features—flexible hours, part-time jobs, child-care leaves and day-care arrangements—are emerging as endogenous responses to the increased labour market role of women. Their emergence, however, may be subject to impediments reflecting discrimination, government policies designed to achieve other objectives, or simply the slow operation of market forces subject to inertia and fixed costs.

Considerable debate emerges over the appropriate role of public policy in this area. Some would argue that such facilitating policies should be discouraged in order to preserve the traditional sex division of labour. Others argue that public policies should be neutral by simply removing impediments to the emergence of these facilitating policies. Others argue for a more active role — subsidized day care, extended child-care leave — to compensate for discrimination elsewhere in the system, including past discrimination.

The role of protectionist policies takes on an interesting light in the context of policies designed to facilitate the labour market work of women. Such protectionist policies could include special provisions requiring employers to provide free transportation for women on night shifts, or prohibiting the employment of women in some specific occupations. Some may argue that such protective devices would enable women to take on some jobs they would otherwise be reluctant to do. Most would argue that such protective devices simply protect male jobs by reducing the employment opportunities of females and by perpetuating the stereotype of women as in need of outside protection. If such protection is desirable, it should be provided to all workers, male and female, through labour standards laws or collective agreements.

This suggests another institutional arrangement for facilitating the labour market work of females — unionization. The rationale for increasing the role of women in unions is really two-fold. The first is to have women share in the wage and job security gains that unions obtain for their members. In order to obtain these gains, it is not only necessary for women to unionize; they must aspire to powerful positions within the union or at least ensure that their minority rights are guaranteed. The second rationale for increasing the role of women in unions is to ensure effective monitoring of equal pay, equal employment opportunities, and affirmative action. As Brady (1947, p. 57) earlier stated:

> Through increasing participation of women in unions, the women workers, acting in their own interest, can narrow the difference between women's rates and men's rates. The continued study of the character of the work process and of comparative occupational wage rates will define the meaning of "equivalence", "comparability" and "equity" so that the existence of discrimination is proved and its magnitude measured.

Females may be more willing and able to press for equal pay and employment opportunities through the union both because the apparatus is available (shop steward, grievance procedure) and because reprisal by the company is less likely when the worker is protected by a union.

Alter Tastes and Attitudes

Economics traditionally regards tastes and preferences as exogenously given, and then inquires into what happens to the demand for something when such factors as relative prices and income change. In the area of sex discrimination, this is a legitimate inquiry. Equal pay and equal employment opportunity legislation can be viewed as policies designed to raise the "price" of discrimination to those who discriminate. The price in this case is the legal costs which include court costs and the expected fine. The contention is that raising the price of discrimination will reduce the quantity demanded.

In the area of discrimination, however, some have suggested the utilization of public policies designed to alter the basic tastes and preferences that give rise to discrimination, since tastes and preferences of employers, co-workers and customers are an important source of discrimination. The dominant group, for example, may find it important to foster uniform preferences for discrimination and to punish non-discriminators. Preferences are also shaped by the media, the education system, and the socio-economic system in general. Preferences are not immutable over time, nor are they likely to be the same for all firms, employees or customers. For this reason, many anti-discrimination policies are designed to alter basic tastes, preferences and attitudes.

In practice, of course, changing basic tastes and attitudes is a difficult task. Specific policies have been instituted and include: removal of sex stereotyping in schoolbooks, guidance programs and television; provision of information in the labour market performance and attachment of females; and politicization of women to raise their own group awareness. The process will be slow, but many argue that the results at least will be long lasting.

QUESTIONS

1. "If females are paid a wage equal to their marginal productivity, then sex discrimination in the labour market does not exist". Discuss.
2. "Male-female wage differentials for equally productive workers will not persist in the long run because the forces of competition would remove these differentials". Discuss.
3. If the proportionate male-female wage differential, $(W_m - W_f)/W_f$, is .25, what is the ratio of female to male wages, W_f/W_m ?
4. What impact would you expect unions to have on male-female wage differentials and why?
5. How would we expect male-female wage differentials to change over time in response to both short-run cyclical and long-run trend forces?
6. If we adjusted the gross male-female wage differential for all of the productivity related factors that influence wages (e.g. education, experience, absenteeism, turnover, etc.) and found that the wage gap would be zero if males and females had the same productivity related characteristics, would this indicate the absence of sex discrimination?
7. What impact would equal pay laws have on the wages and employment of female workers? What impact would equal employment opportunity laws (fair employment laws) have on the wages and employment of female workers?
8. Would you expect sex discrimination to be more prevalent in capitalist or socialist-communist economies and why?
9. For policy purposes does it matter if the reason for discrimination is prejudice, erroneous information, or job security? Does it matter if the main source of discrimination is employers, co-workers, or customers?
10. Does the occupational distribution of women yield any insight into the possible employment effect of policies to raise women's wages via equal pay, minimum wages, or unions? More specifically, are women employed in occupations where the demand for female labour is elastic or inelastic? Are women employed in monopsonistic labour markets?
11. Based on the utility maximization theory given in footnote 1, show that male wages will exceed their marginal revenue product when nepotism exists whereby, other things being equal, the firm's utility is increased when it employs more males.
12. How would one explain the large variation in the male-female earnings gap found in the various Canadian empirical studies? That is, why do some studies find a much larger differential than others?
13. Based on the decomposition technique discussed in footnote 3, indicate how an alternative decomposition could be utilized by subtracting

$\Sigma b_m \bar{X}_f$ rather than $\Sigma b_f \bar{X}_m$ from the right-hand side. Which decomposition is correct?

14. Roberta Robb (1978) estimated separate earnings equations for males as well as single females thirty years of age and over and finds wage discrimination to be considerably less than in the case when males are compared to all females. Why might one expect this to be the case?
15. Holmes (1976) finds a substantially higher ratio of female to male earnings in Canada at higher levels of education than at lower levels. Why might this be the case?

REFERENCES AND FURTHER READINGS

Adams, A. Black-white occupational differentials in Southern metropolitan employment. *JHR* 7 (Fall 1972) 500-518.

Adams, A., J. Krishan and D. Larison. Plantwide seniority, black employment, and employer affirmative action. *ILRR* 26 (October 1972) 686-690.

Agarwal, N. and Harish Jain. Pay discrimination against women in Canada. *ILR* 117 (March-April 1978) 169-178.

Aigner, D. and G. Cain. Statistical theories of discrimination in labour markets. *ILRR* 30 (January 1972) 175-189.

Alexis, M. A theory of labour market discrimination with interdependent utilities. *AER* 63 (May 1972) 296-302.

Allison, E. Sex linked earning differentials in the beauty industry. *JHR* 11 (Summer 1976) 383-390.

Allison, E. Male-female professionals: a model of career choice. *IR* 17 (October 1978) 333-337.

American Economic Review. Findings of the AEA committee on the status of women in the economics profession. 58 (December 1973) 1049-1061.

Antos, J. and S. Rosen. Discrimination in the market for public school teachers. *Journal of Econometrics* 3 (January 1975) 123-150.

Archibald, K. *Sex and the Public Service.* A Report to the Public Service Commission of Canada. Ottawa: Queen's Printer, 1970.

Arrow, K. The theory of discrimination. *Discrimination in the Labour Market,* O. Ashenfelter and A. Rees (eds.). Princeton, N.J.: Princeton University Press, 1973.

Arrow, K. Models of job discrimination. *Racial Discrimination in Economic Life,* A. Pascal (ed.). Lexington, Mass.: Lexington Books, 1972.

Arrow, K. Simple mathematical models of race in the labor market. *Racial Discrimination in Economic Life,* A. Pascal (ed.). Lexington, Mass.: Lexington Books, 1972.

Ashenfelter, O. Racial discrimination and trade unions. *JPE* 80 (May/June 1972) 435-464.

Ashenfelter, O. Some evidence on the effect of unionism on the average wage of black workers relative to white workers, 1900-1967. *IRRA*

(December 1971) 217-225.

Ashenfelter, O. Changes in labor market discrimination over time. *JHR* 5 (Fall 1970) 403-430. Comment by H. Terrill 6 (Summer 1971) 384-390.

Ashenfelter, O. and J. Heckman. Measuring the effect of an antidiscrimination program. *Evaluating the Labor-Market Effects of Social Programs,* O. Ashenfelter and J. Blum (eds.). Princeton, N.J.: Princeton University Press, 1976.

Barnes, W. and E. Jones. Differences in male and female quitting. *JHR* 9 (Fall 1974) 439-451.

Barrett, N. and R. Morgenstern. Why do blacks and women have high unemployment rates? *JHR* 9 (Fall 1974) 439-451.

Bartal, K. and R. Bartal. Women in managerial and professional positions: the United States and the Soviet Union. *ILRR* 28 (July 1975) 524-534.

Batchelder, A. The decline in the relative income of negro men. *QJE* 78 (November/December 1964) 525-548.

Bayer, A. and H. Astin. Sex differences in academic rank and salary among science doctorates in teaching. *JHR* 3 (Spring 1968) 191-200.

Becker, G. *The Economics of Discrimination.* Chicago: University of Chicago Press, 1971.

Bell, D. Occupational discrimination as a source of income differences: lessons of the 1960's. *AER* 62 (May 1972) 363-372.

Bell, D. Bonuses, quotas, and the employment of black workers. *JHR* 6 (Summer 1971) 309-320.

Beller, A. The economics of enforcement of an antidiscrimination law: title VII of the Civil Rights Act of 1964. *Journal of Law and Economics* 21 (October 1978) 359-380.

Bergmann, B. Occupation segregation, wages, and profits when employers discriminate by race or sex. *Eastern Economic Journal* 1 (April/July 1974) 103-110.

Bergmann, B. and W. Krause. Evaluating and forecasting progress in racial integration of employment. *ILRR* 25 (April 1972) 399-409.

Bergmann, B. and J. Lyle. The occupational standing of negroes by areas and industries. *JHR* 6 (Fall 1971) 411-433.

Bergmann, B. The effect on white incomes of discrimination in employment. *JPE* 79 (March/April 1971) 294-313.

Bergquest, V.A. Women's participation in labor organizations. *MLR* 97 (October 1974) 3-9.

Blandy, R. Equal pay in Australia. *Journal of Industrial Relations* 5 (April 1963) 13-28.

Blinder, A. Wage discrimination: reduced form and structural estimates. *JHR* 8 (Fall 1973) 436-455.

Blitz, R. Women in the professions, 1870-1970. *MLR* 97 (May 1974) 34-39.

Blitz, R. and C. Ow. A cross-sectional analysis of women's participation in the professions. *JPE* 81 (January/February 1973) 131-144.

Borjas, G. Biased screening and discrimination in the labor market. *AER* 68 (December 1978) 918-922.

Borjas, G. Discrimination in HEW. *Journal of Law and Economics* 21 (April 1978) 97-110.

Boskin, M. The effects of government expenditures and taxes on female labor. *AER* 64 (May 1974) 251-256.

Brady, D. Equal pay for women workers. *Annals of the American Academy of Political and Social Science* (May 1947) 53-60.

Brown, G. How type of employment affects earnings differences by sex. *MLR* 99 (July 1976) 25-30.

Buckley, J. Equal pay: progress and problems (America). *International Journal of Social Economics* 1 (January 1974) 4-95.

Buckley, J. Pay differences between men and women in the same job. *MLR* 94 (November 1971) 36-40.

Canada Department of Labour, Women's Bureau. *Facts and Figures about Women in the Labour Force.* Ottawa: Queen's Printer, annual.

Canada Department of Labour, Women's Bureau. *Women at Work in Canada.* Ottawa: Queen's Printer, 1965.

Chiplin, B. and P. Sloan. *Sex Discrimination in the Labour Market.* London: Macmillan, 1976.

Chiplin, B. and P. Sloan. Personal characteristics and sex differentials in professional employment. *EJ* 86 (December 1976) 729-745.

Chiplin, B. and P. Sloan. Male-female earnings differences: a further analysis. *BJIR* 14 (March 1976) 77-81.

Chiplin, B. and P. Sloan. Equal employment opportunities for women. *IRJ* 6 (Autumn 1975) 20-28.

Chiplin, B. and P. Sloan. Sexual discrimination in the labour market. *BJIR* 12 (November 1974) 371-402.

Chiplin, B. and P. Sloan. Economic consequences of the Equal Pay Act. *IRJ* 1 (December 1970).

Chiswick, B. Racial discrimination in the labor market: a test of alternative hypothesis. *JPE* 81 (November/December 1973) 1330-52.

Cohen, M. Sex differences in compensation. *JHR* 6 (Fall 1971) 434-447.

Cook, A. *The Working Mother: A Survey of Problems and Programs in Nine Countries.* Ithaca, N.Y.: New York State School of Industrial and Labor Relations, Cornell University, 1975.

Cook, A. Equal pay: where is it? *IR* 14 (May 1975) 158-176.

Cook, G. and M. Eberts. Policies affecting work. *Opportunity for Choice: A Goal for Women in Canada.* Ottawa: Statistics Canada, 1976, 143-202.

Cooney, R. A comparative study of work opportunities for women. *IR* 17 (February 1978) 64-74.

Corazzine, A. Equality of employment opportunity in the Federal Civil Service. *JHR* 7 (Fall 1972) 424-445.

Corcoran, M. and G. Duncan. Work history, labour force attachment, and earnings differences between races and sexes. *JHR* 14 (Winter 1979) 3-20.

Cussel, F., S. Director and S. Doctors. Discrimination within internal labor markets. *IR* 14 (October 1975) 337-344.

De Tray, D. and D. Greenberg. On estimating differences in earnings. *SEJ* 44 (October 1977) 348-353.

Dewey, L. Women in labor unions. *MLR* 94 (February 1971) 42-48.

Edgeworth, F. Equal pay to men and women for equal work. *EJ* 32 (December 1922) 431-457.

Epstein, C. *Women's Place: Options and Limits in Professional Careers.* California: University of California Press, 1971.

Fawcett, M. Equal pay for equal work. *EJ* 28 (March 1918) 1-6.

Ferber, M. and H. Lowry. The sex differential in earnings. *ILRR* 29 (April 1976) 377-387. Also comment by D. Snyder and P. Hudis and reply 32 (April 1979) 378-386.

Ferber, M. and A. Westmiller. Sex and race differentials in nonacademic wages on a university campus. *JHR* 11 (Summer 1976) 366-373.

Ferriss, A. *Indicators of Trends in the Status of American Women.* New York: Russell Sage Foundation, 1971.

Flanagan, R. Discrimination theory, labor turnover, and racial unemployment differentials. *JHR* 13 (Spring 1978) 187-207.

Flanagan, R. Labor force experience, job turnover, and racial wage differentials. *R.E. Stats.* 56 (November 1974) 521-529.

Flanagan, R. Segmented market theories and racial discrimination. *IR* 12 (October 1973) 253-273.

Flanagan, R. Racial wage discrimination and employment segregation. *JHR* 8 (Fall 1973) 456-471.

Flanders, D. and P. Anderson. Sex discrimination in employment: theory and practice. *ILRR* 26 (April 1973) 938-955.

Formley, J. The extent of wage and salary discrimination against non-white labor. *SEJ* 35 (October 1968) 140-150.

Frank, R. Family location constraints and the geographic distribution of female professionals. *JPE* 86 (February 1978) 117-130.

Franklin, A. A framework for the analysis of inter-urban negro-white economic differentials. *ILRR* 7 (April 1968) 367-374.

Freeman, R. Labor market discrimination: analysis, findings and problems. *Frontiers of Quantitative Economics,* M. Intriligator and D. Kendrick (eds.). Amsterdam: North Holland, 1974, 501-555.

Freeman, R. Decline of labor market discrimination and economic analysis. *AER* 63 (May 1973) 280-287.

Freeman, R. Changes in the labor market for Black Americans, 1948-72. *BPEA* (No. 1, 1973) 67-132.

Fuchs, V. Recent trends and long-run prospects for female earnings. *AER Proceedings* 64 (May 1974) 236-242.

Fuchs, V. Differences in hourly earnings between men and women. *MLR* 94 (May 1971) 9-15.

Galenson, M. *Women and Work: An International Comparison.* Ithaca, N.Y.: New York State School of Industrial Relations, Cornell University, 1973.

Garfinkle, S. Occupation of women and black workers, 1962-74. *MLR* (November 1975) 25-35.

Gaumer, G. Sex discrimination and job tenure. *IR* 14 (February 1975) 121-129.

Geoffrey, R. and R. Sainte-Marie. *Attitude of Union Workers to Women in Industry.* Studies of the Royal Commission on the Status of Women in Canada. Ottawa: Information Canada, 1970.

Ginzburg, E. Paycheck and apron-revolution in womenpower. *IR* 7 (May 1968) 193-203.

Godazzi, A. Problems of equal pay for men and women workers. *Employment of Women: Regional Trade Union Seminar 1968.* Paris: Organizations for Economic Cooperation and Development, 1970.

Goldberg, M. The economic exploitation of women. *Review of Radical Political Economy* 2 (Spring 1970) 35-47.

Goldfarb, R. and J. Hosek. Explaining male-female differentials for the same job. *JHR* 11 (Winter 1976) 98-108.

Gordon, N. and T. Morton. The staff salary structure of a large urban university. *JHR* 11 (Summer 1976) 374-382.

Gordon, N. and T. Morton. A low mobility model of wage discrimination — with special reference to sex differentials. *Journal of Economic Theory* 7 (March 1974) 241-253.

Gordon, M. Introduction: women in the labor force. *IR* 7 (May 1968) 187-192.

Gordon, N., T. Morton and I. Brader. Faculty salaries: is there discrimination by sex, race, and discipline? *AER* 64 (June 1974) 419-427.

Gramm, W.L. Household utility maximization and the working wife. *AER* 65 (March 1975) 90-100.

Gramm, W.L. The demand for the wife's nonmarket time. *SEJ* 41 (July 1974) 124-133.

Grossman, A. Women in the labor force: the early years. *MLR* (November 1975) 3-9.

Gunderson, M. Male female wage differentials and the impact of equal pay legislation. *R.E. Stats.* 57 (November 1975) 426-470.

Gunderson, M. Sex discrimination in wage payments. *Canadian Industrial Relations,* S. M. Hameed (ed.). Toronto: Butterworths, 1975, 309-319.

Gunderson, M. Equal pay in Canada. *Equal Pay for Women: Progress and Problems in Seven Countries,* B.O. Pettman (ed.). London: MCB Books, 1976, 129-146.

Gunderson, M. Time pattern of male-female wage differentials. *RI/IR* 31 (No. 1, 1976) 57-71.

Gunderson, M. Work patterns. *Opportunity for Choice: A Goal for Women in Canada,* G. Cook (ed.). Ottawa: Statistics Canada, 1976, 93-142.

Gunderson, M. The influence of the status and sex composition of occupations on the male-female earnings gap. *ILRR* 31 (January 1978) 217-226.

Gunderson, M. Decomposition of male-female earnings differential: Canada 1970, *CJE* 12 (August 1979) 479-484.

Guthrie, H. The prospect of equality of incomes between white and black families under varying rates of unemployment. *JHR* 5 (Fall 1970) 431-446. Comment by H. Terrell 6 (Summer 1971) 384-390 and by L. Atkinson and B. Bergmann 7 (Fall 1972) 545-547.

Gwartney, J. Discrimination and income differentials. *AER* 60 (June 1970). Also comment by O. Ashenfelter and M. Tausig and reply by J. Gwartney 61 (September 1971) 746-755. Also B. Kiker and W.P. Liles 64 (June 1974) 492-501.

Gwartney, J. Discrimination, achievement, and pay-offs of a college degree. *JHR* 7 (Winter 1972) 66-70.

Gwartney, J., and K. McCaffree. Variance in discrimination among occupations. *SEJ* 38 (October 1971) 141-155.

Gwartney, J. Changes in the non-white/white income ratio—1939-67. *AER* 60 (December 1970) 872-883.

Gwartney, J. and C. Hawarth. Employer costs and discrimination: the case of baseball. *JPE* 82 (July/August 1974) 873-881.

Gwartney, J. and J. Long. The relative earnings of blacks and other minorities. *ILRR* 31 (August 1978) 336-346.

Gwartney, J. and R. Stroup. Measurement of employer discrimination according to sex. *SEJ* 39 (August 1973) 575-587.

Haessel, W. and J. Palmer. Market power and employment discrimination. *JHR* 13 (Fall 1978) 545-560.

Hamilton, M. Sex and income inequality among the employed. *Annals of the American Academy of Political and Social Science* 409 (Spring 1973) 42-52.

Harrison, B. Human capital, black poverty and radical economics. *IR* 10 (October 1971) 277-286.

Harrison, E. The working woman: barriers in employment. *Public Administration Review* 24 (June 1964) 78.

Haworth, J., J. Gwartney and C. Haworth. Earnings, productivity, and changes in employment discrimination during the 1960's. *AER* 65 (March 1975) 158-168. Also additional evidence by S. Long 67 (March 1977) 225-227.

Hedges, J. Women workers and manpower demands in the 1970's. *MLR* 93 (June 1970) 19-29.

Hedges, J. and S. Bemis. Sex stereotyping: its decline in skilled trades. *MLR* 97 (May 1974) 14-22.

Hoffman, E. Faculty salaries: is there discrimination by sex, race, and discipline? *AER* 66 (March 1976) 196-198.

Holter, H. Women's occupational situation in Scandinavia. *ILR* 93 (August 1966).

Holmes, R. Male-female earnings differentials in Canada. *JHR* 11 (Winter 1976) 109-112.

Ignatin, G. The economics of discrimination: theory and practice. *IRRA* (December 1971) 70-79.

Industrial and Labor Relations Review. Symposium on Evaluating the Impact of Affirmative Action. 29 (July 1976) 485-584.

Izraeli, D. and K. Gaier. Sex and interoccupational wage differences in Israel. *IR* 18 (Spring 1979) 227-232.

Johnson, G. and F. Stafford. The earnings and promotion of women faculty. *AER* 69 (December 1974) 888-903.

Johnson, W. Racial wage discrimination and industrial structure. *Bell Journal of Economics* 9 (Spring 1978) 70-81.

Judek, S. *Women in the Public Service.* Ottawa: Economics and Research Branch, Canada Department of Labour, 1968.

Kahne, H. Economic perspectives on the role of women in the American economy. *Journal of Economic Literature* 13 (December 1975) 1249-1292.

Kiker, B. and W. Liles. Earnings, employment and racial discrimination: additional evidence. *AER* 64 (June 1974) 492-501.

King, A. Is occupational segregation the cause of the flatter experience-earnings profile of women? *JHR* 12 (Fall 1977) 541-549.

Koch, J. and J. Chiemar. Sex discrimination and affirmative action in faculty salaries. *EI* 14 (March 1976) 16-24.

Kreps, J. *Sex in the Market Place: American Women and Work.* Baltimore: Johns Hopkins Press, 1971.

Kruger, A. The economics of discrimination *JPE* 71 (October 1963) 481-486.

Landes, E. Sex differences in wages and employment: a test of the specific capital hypothesis. *EI* 15 (October 1977) 523-538.

Landes, W. The economics of fair employment laws. *JPE* 76 (July/August 1968) 507-552.

Landes, W. The effect of state fair employment laws on the economic position of nonwhites. *AER* 62 (May 1967) 578-590.

Laroque, P. Women's rights and widows pensions. *ILRR* 106 (July 1972) 1-10.

Larson, C. Equal pay for women in the United Kingdom. *ILR* 103 (January 1971) 1-11.

Leigh, D. and V.L. Rawlins. Racial differences in male unemployment rates: evidence from low-income areas. *R.E. Stats.* 56 (May 1974) 150-158.

Lianos, T. A note on discrimination in the labour market. *SEJ* 43 (October 1976) 1177-1180.

Lloyd, C. (ed.). *Sex, Discrimination, and the Division of Labor.* New York: Columbia University Press, 1975.

Long, J. Employment discrimination in the federal sector. *JHR* 11 (Winter 1976) 86-97.

Long, J. Public-private sectoral differences in employment discrimination. *SEJ* 42 (July 1975) 89-96.

Lyle, J. and J. Ross. *Women in Industry.* Lexington, Mass.: Lexington Books, 1973.

Madden, J. Economic rationale for sex differences in education. *SEJ* 44 (April 1978) 778-797.

Madden, J. The development of economic thought on the "women problem". *Review of Radical Political Economy* 4 (July 1972) 21-39.

Madden, J. *The Economics of Sex Discrimination.* Lexington, Mass.: Lexington Books, 1972.

Malkiel, B. and J. Malkiel. Male-female pay differentials in professional employment. *AER* 63 (September 1973) 693-705.

Mancke, R. Lower pay for women: a case of economic discrimination? *IR* 10 (October 1971) 316-326. Comment by M. Straber and reply 11 (May 1972) 279-288.

Mantell, E. Discrimination based on education in the labor market for engineers. *R.E. Stats.* 56 (May 1974) 158-166.

Marshall, R. The economics of racial discrimination; a survey. *JEL* 12 (September 1974) 849-871.

Masters, S. The effect of educational differences and labor-market discrimination in the relative earnings of black males. *JHR* (Summer 1974) 342-360. Comment by J. Boulet and J. Rowley and reply *CJE* 10 (February 1977) 149-155.

Masters, S. *Black-White Income Differentials.* New York: Academic Press, 1975.

MacLeod, N. Female earnings in manufacturing: a comparison with male earnings. *Notes on Labour Statistics,* Statistics Canada No. 72-207, 1971, 41-48.

McNally, G. Patterns of female labour force activity. *IR* 7 (May 1968) 204-218.

McNulty, D. Differences in pay between men and women workers. *MLR* 12 (December 1967) 40-43.

Miles, R. Discrimination in employment: a complementary collection: introduction. *IR* 10 (October 1971) 272-276.

Mincer, J. and S. Polechek. Family investment in human capital: earnings of women. *JPE* 82 (March/April 1974) 576-S108. Also comment by S. Sandell and D. Shapiro and reply *JHR* 13 (Winter 1978) 103-134.

Moore, W. and R. Newman. An analysis of the quality differentials in male-female academic placements. *EI* 15 (July 1977) 413-433.

Myrdal, G. *An American Dilemma,* 2 volumes. New York: Harper and Brothers, 1944, republished 1962.

Nieuwenbuysen, J. Equal pay for women in Australia. *International Journal of Social Economics* 1 (January 1974) 96-110.

Oaxaca, R. Male-female wage differentials in urban labour markets. *IER* 14 (October 1973) 693-709.

Oaxaca, R. Sex discrimination in wages. *Discrimination in Labor Markets,* O. Ashenfelter and A. Rees (eds.). Princeton, N.J.: Princeton University Press, 1974.

O'Neill, D. The effect of discrimination on earnings: evidence from military test score results. *JHR* 5 (Fall 1970) 475-486.

Oppenhaimer, V. The sex-labelling of jobs. *IR* 7 (May 1968) 219-234.

Oster, S. Industry differences in discrimination against women. *QJE* 89 (May 1975) 215-229.

Osterman, P. Sex discrimination in professional employment: a case study. *ILRR* 32 (July 1979) 451-464.

Ostry, S. *The Female Worker in Canada.* Ottawa: Queen's Printer, 1968.

Organization for Economic Co-operation and Development. *Employment of Women.* Paris: Organization for Economic Co-operation and Development, 1970.

Organization for Economic Co-operation and Development. *Re-entry of Women to the Labour Market after an Interruption in Employment.* Paris: Organization for Economic Co-operation and Development, 1971.

Pascal, H. (ed.). *Racial Discrimination in Economic Life.* Lexington, Mass.: D. C. Heath, 1972.

Phelps, E. The statistical theory of racism and sexism. *AER* 62 (September 1972) 659-661.

Polachek, S. Sex differences in college major. *ILRR* (July 1974) 498-508.

Polachek, S. Potential biases in measuring male-female discrimination. *JHR* 10 (Spring 1975) 205-229.

Raphael, E. Working women and their membership in labour unions. *MLR* 97 (May 1974) 27-33.

Rapping, L. Union-induced racial entry barriers. *JHR* 5 (Fall 1970) 447-474.

Rasmussen, D. A note on the relative income of non white men, 1948-64. *QJE* 84 (February 1970) 168-172.

Rasmussen, D. Discrimination and the incomes of non-white males. *American Journal of Economics and Sociology* 30 (October 1971) 377-382.

Rathbone, E. The remuneration of women's services. *EJ* 27 (March 1917) 55-68.

Reagan, B. Two supply curves for economists: implications of mobility and career attachment of women. *AER* 65 (May 1974) 100-107.

Reich, M. Who benefits from racism? *JHR* 13 (Fall 1978) 524-544.

Review of Radical Political Economy. The Political Economy of Women. 4 (July 1972) 1-154.

Robb, R.E. Earnings differentials between males and females in Ontario. *CJE* 11 (May 1978) 350-359.

Robson, R. and M. Lapointe. *A Comparison of Men's and Women's Salaries and Employment Fringe Benefits in the Academic Profession.* Study No. 2 for the Royal Commission on the Status of Women in Canada. Ottawa: Information Canada, 1971.

Sanborn, H. Pay differences between men and women. *ILRR* 17 (July 1964) 534-550.

Sawhill, E. The economics of discrimination against women: some new findings. *JHR* 8 (Summer 1973) 383-395.

Scheller, B. Class discrimination vs. racial discrimination. *R.E. Stats.* 53 (August 1971) 263-269.

Schrank, W. Sex discrimination in faculty salaries. *CJE* 10 (August 1977) 411-433.

Shea, J. and others. *Dual Careers.* Center for Human Research. Columbus, O.: Ohio State University, 1970.

Simchak, M. Equal pay in the United States. *ILR* 103 (June 1971) 541-557.

Simiral, M. The impact of the public employment program on sex-related wage differentials. *ILRR* (July 1978) 509-519.

Simon, J. The effect of fixed-wage rises on discriminated against minorities. *ILRR* 21 (October 1967) 96-97. Also comment by S. Baldwin 21 (July 1968) 581-582.

Smith, J. and F. Welch. Black-white male wage rates: 1960-70. *AER* 67 (June 1977) 323-338.

Smith, S. Government wage differentials by sex. *JHR* 11 (Spring 1976) 185-199.

Smuts, R. *Women and Work in America.* New York: Columbia University, 1959.

Somers, D. Occupational rankings for men and women by earnings. *MLR* 97 (August 1974) 34-51.

Sorkin, A. Occupational status of women, 1870-1970. *American Journal of Economics and Sociology* 32 (July 1973) 235-244.

Staines, G., R. Quinn, and L. Shepherd. Trends in occupational sex discrimination: 1969-73. *IR* 14 (February 1976) 88-98.

Stiglitz, J. Approaches to the economics of discrimination. *AER Proceedings* 63 (May 1973) 287-296.

Stiglitz, J. Themes of discrimination and economic policy. *Patterns of Racial Discrimination*, G. Von Furstenburg et al. (eds.). Lexington, Mass.: D. C. Heath, 1974.

Strasser, A. Differentials and overlaps in earnings of blacks and whites. *MLR* 94 (December 1971) 16-26.

Strauss, R. Industrial patterns of male negro employment. *JHR* 7 (Winter 1972) 116-118.

Struyk, R. Explaining variation in hourly wage rates of urban minority females. *JHR* 8 (Summer 1973) 349-364.

Sturdinant, F. and W. Hanselman. Discrimination in the market place: another dimension. *Social Science Quarterly* 52 (December 1971) 625-630.

Suter, L. and H. Miller. Income differences between men and career
    women. *American Journal of Sociology* 78 (January 1973) 962-974.
Sweet, J. Labor force reentry by mothers of young children. *Social Science
    Research* 1 (June 1972) 189-210.
Sweet, J. *Women in the Labor Force.* New York: Seminar Press, 1973.
Takahashi, N. Women's wages in Japan and the question of equal pay.
    ILR 111 (January 1975) 51-68.
Taylor, D. Discrimination and occupational wage differences in the market
    for unskilled labor. *ILRR* 7 (April 1968) 375-390.
Thalmann-Antenen, H. Equal pay: the position in Switzerland. *ILR* 104
    (October 1971) 275-288.
Thurow, L. *Poverty and Discrimination.* Washington: Brookings Institute,
    1969.
Tsuchigane, R. and N. Dodge. *Economic Discrimination Against Women in the
    United States.* Lexington, Mass.: D. C. Heath, 1974.
Vangsnes, K. Equal pay in Norway. *ILR* 103 (April 1971) 379-392.
Weiss, L. and J. Williamson. Black education, earnings and interregional
    migration. *AER* 62 (June 1972) 372-383. Also comment by C. Link and
    reply 65 (March 1975) 236-244.
Weiss, R. The effect of education on the earnings of blacks and whites.
    R.E. Stats. 52 (May 1970) 150-159.
Weiskoff, F. Women's place in the labor market. *AER* 62 (May 1972) 161-166.
Welch, F. Labor market discrimination: an interpretation of income
    differences in the rural South. *JPE* (June 1967) 225-240.
Wilensky, H. Women's work: economic growth, ideology, structure. *IR* 7
    (May 1968) 235-248.
Wolff, E. Occupational earnings behaviour and the inequality of earnings by
    sex and race in the U.S. *Review of Income and Wealth* 2 (1976) 152-166.
Zellner, H. Discrimination against women, occupational segregation, and
    the relative wage. *AER Proceedings* 62 (May 1972) 157-160.
Zincone, L. and F. Close. Sex discrimination in a paramedical profession.
    ILRR 32 (October 1978) 74-85.

Index